-FAKE-

VOLUME TWO

BY SANAMI MATOH

FAKE

-FAKE-

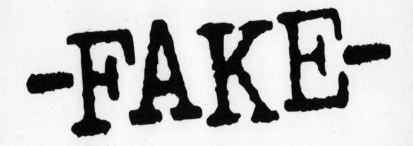

TABLE OF CONTENTS

Translator - Nan Rymer
English Adaption - Stuart Hazleton
Editor - Julie Taylor
Contributing Editor - Jodi Bryson
Retouch and Lettering - Rob Steen
Cover Artist - Raymond Makowski

Managing Editor - Jill Freshney
Production Coordinator - Antonio DePietro
Production Managers - Jennifer Miller, Mutsumi Miyazaki
Art Director - Matt Alford
Editorial Director - Jeremy Ross
VP of Production - Ron Klamert
President & C.O.O. - John Parker
Publisher & C.E.O. - Stuart Levy

Email: editor@TOKYOPOP.com
Come visit us online at www.TOKYOPOP.com

A  Manga

TOKYOPOP Inc.
5900 Wilshire Blvd. Suite 2000
Los Angeles, CA 90036

Fake Vol. 2

ISBN: 1-59182-327-7

First TOKYOPOP printing: July 2003

10 9 8 7 6 5 4 3

Printed in the USA

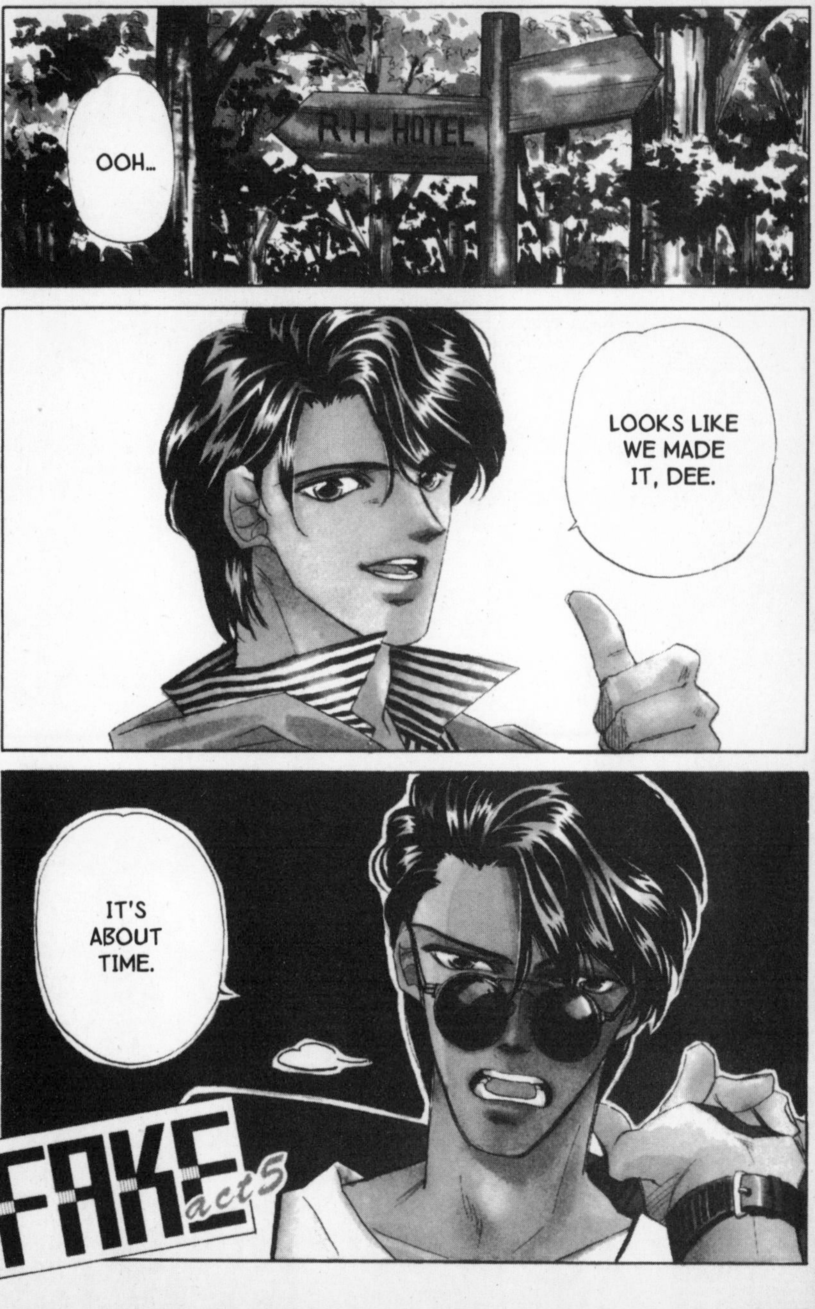
R·H HOTEL
OOH...
LOOKS LIKE WE MADE IT, DEE.
IT'S ABOUT TIME.
FAKE act 5

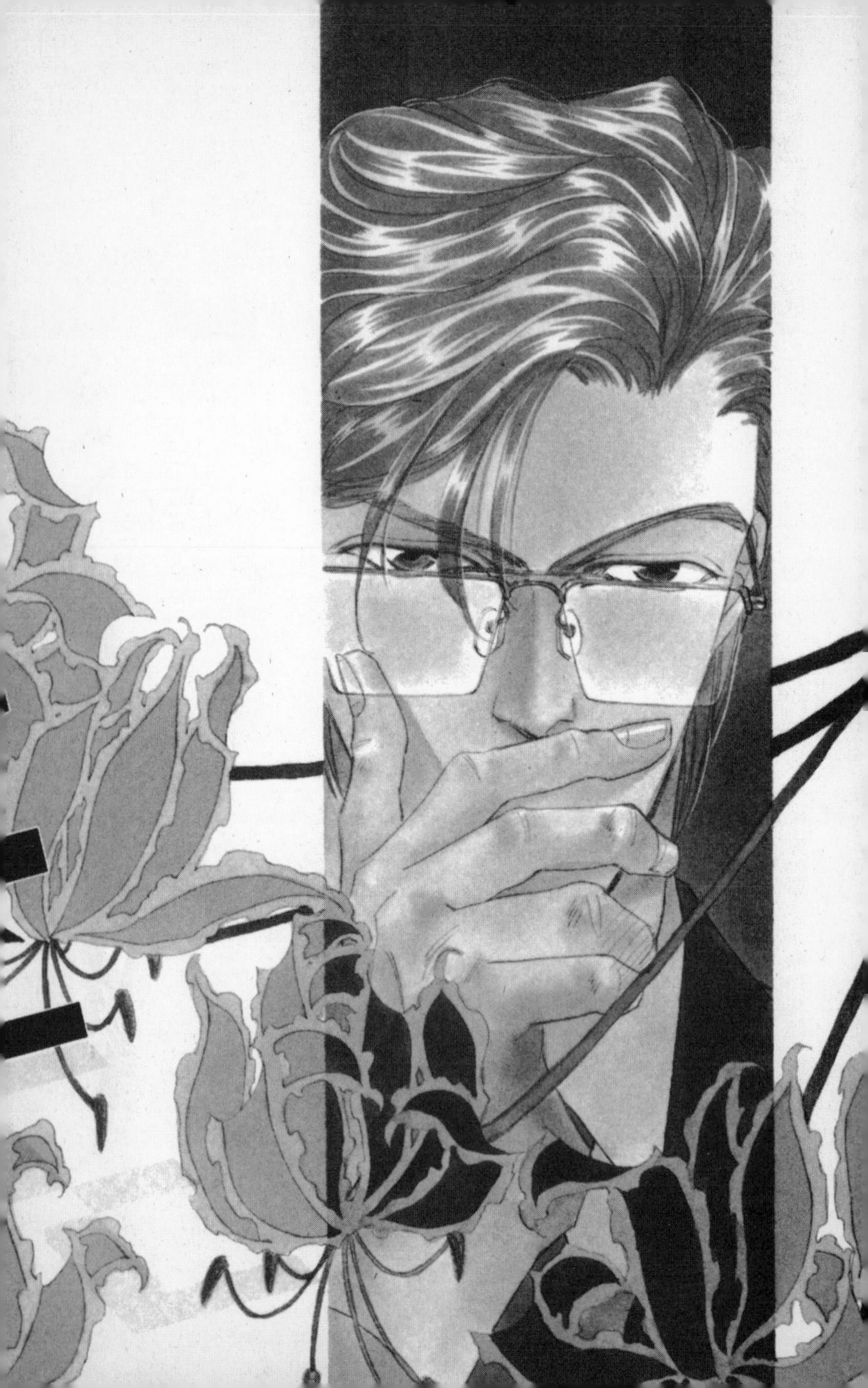

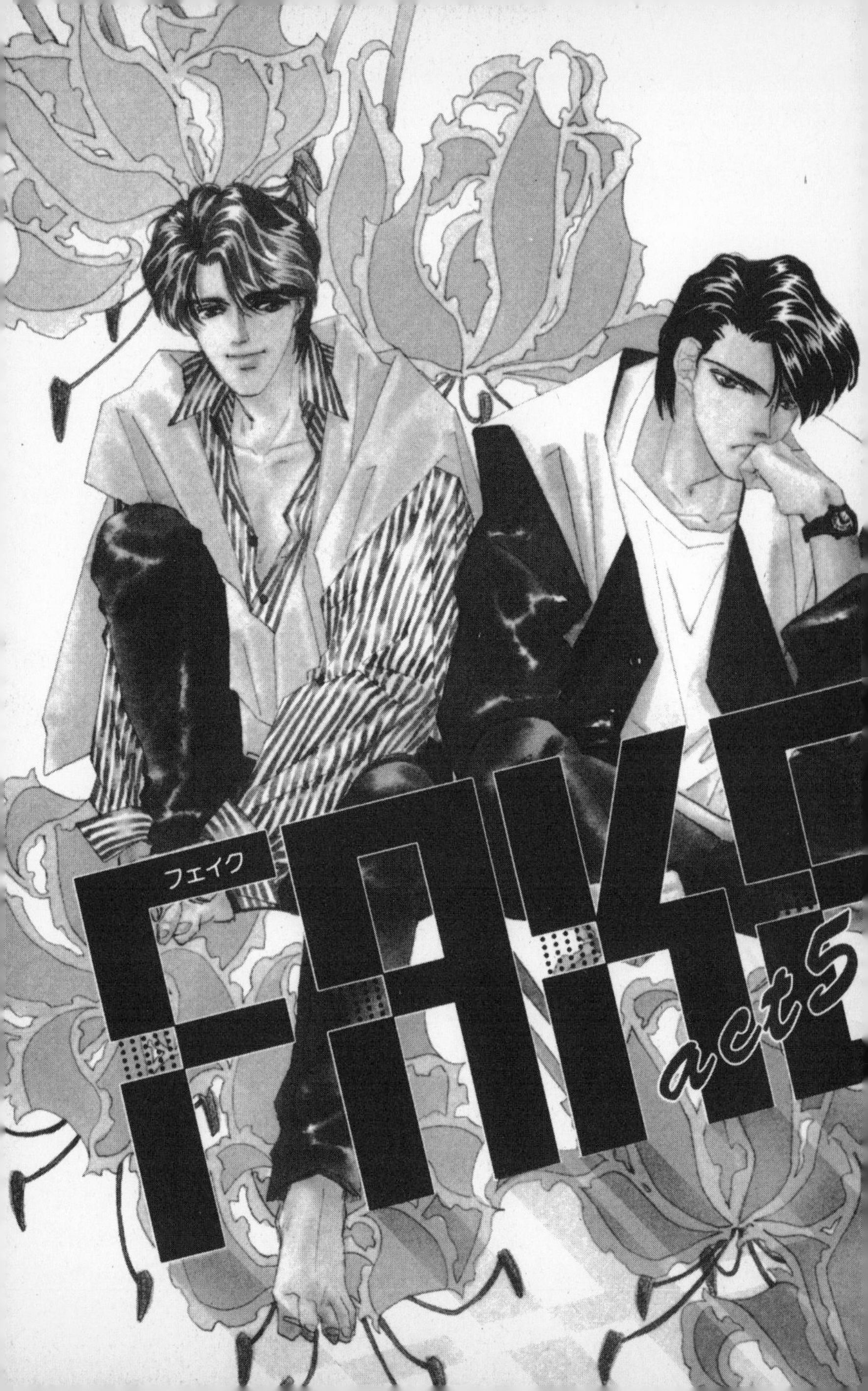
フェイク
FAKE
act5

FAKE

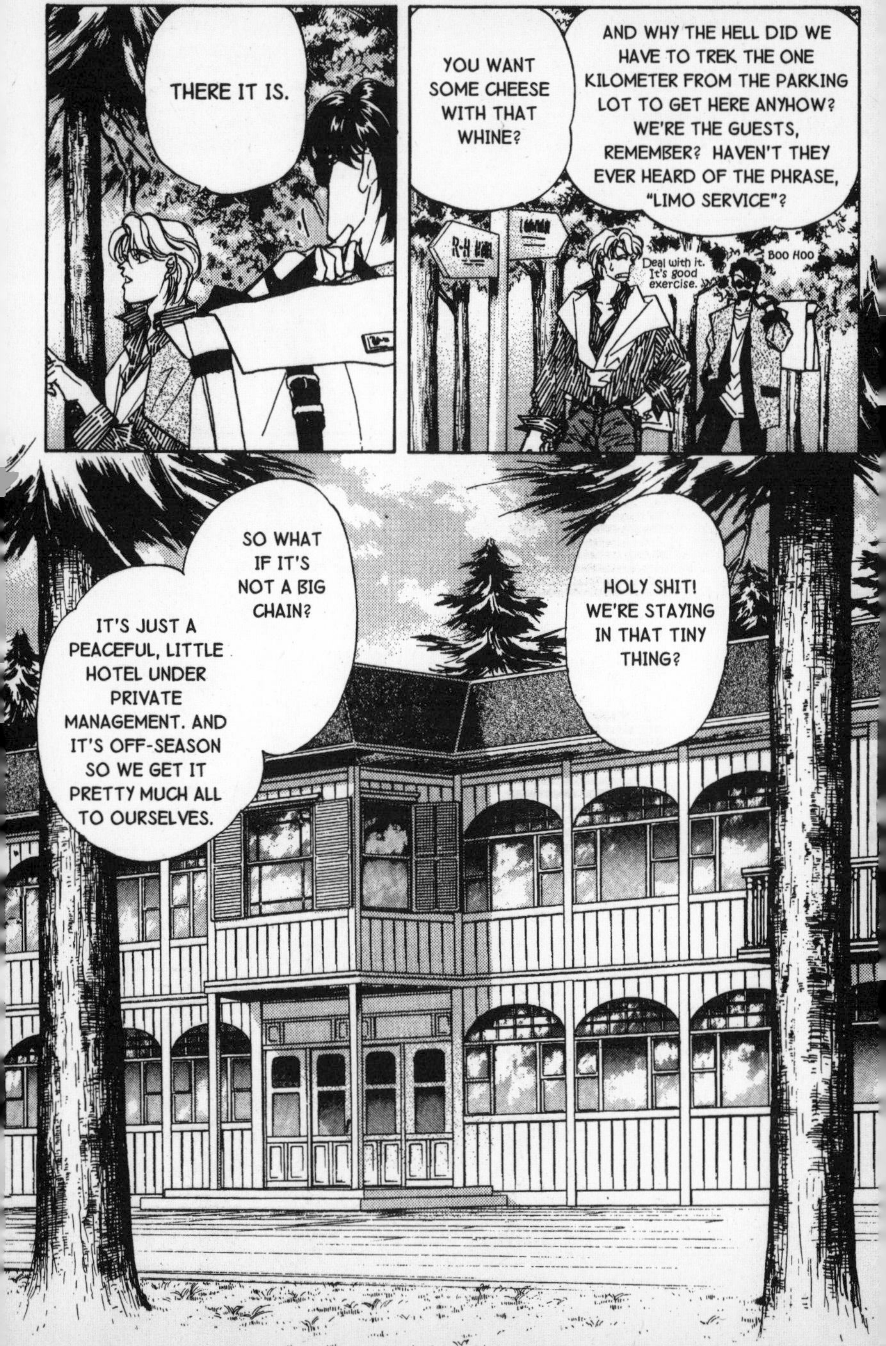
AND WHY THE HELL DID WE HAVE TO TREK THE ONE KILOMETER FROM THE PARKING LOT TO GET HERE ANYHOW? WE'RE THE GUESTS, REMEMBER? HAVEN'T THEY EVER HEARD OF THE PHRASE, "LIMO SERVICE"?
YOU WANT SOME CHEESE WITH THAT WHINE?
BOO HOO
Deal with it. It's good exercise.
THERE IT IS.
HOLY SHIT! WE'RE STAYING IN THAT TINY THING?
SO WHAT IF IT'S NOT A BIG CHAIN?
IT'S JUST A PEACEFUL, LITTLE HOTEL UNDER PRIVATE MANAGEMENT. AND IT'S OFF-SEASON SO WE GET IT PRETTY MUCH ALL TO OURSELVES.

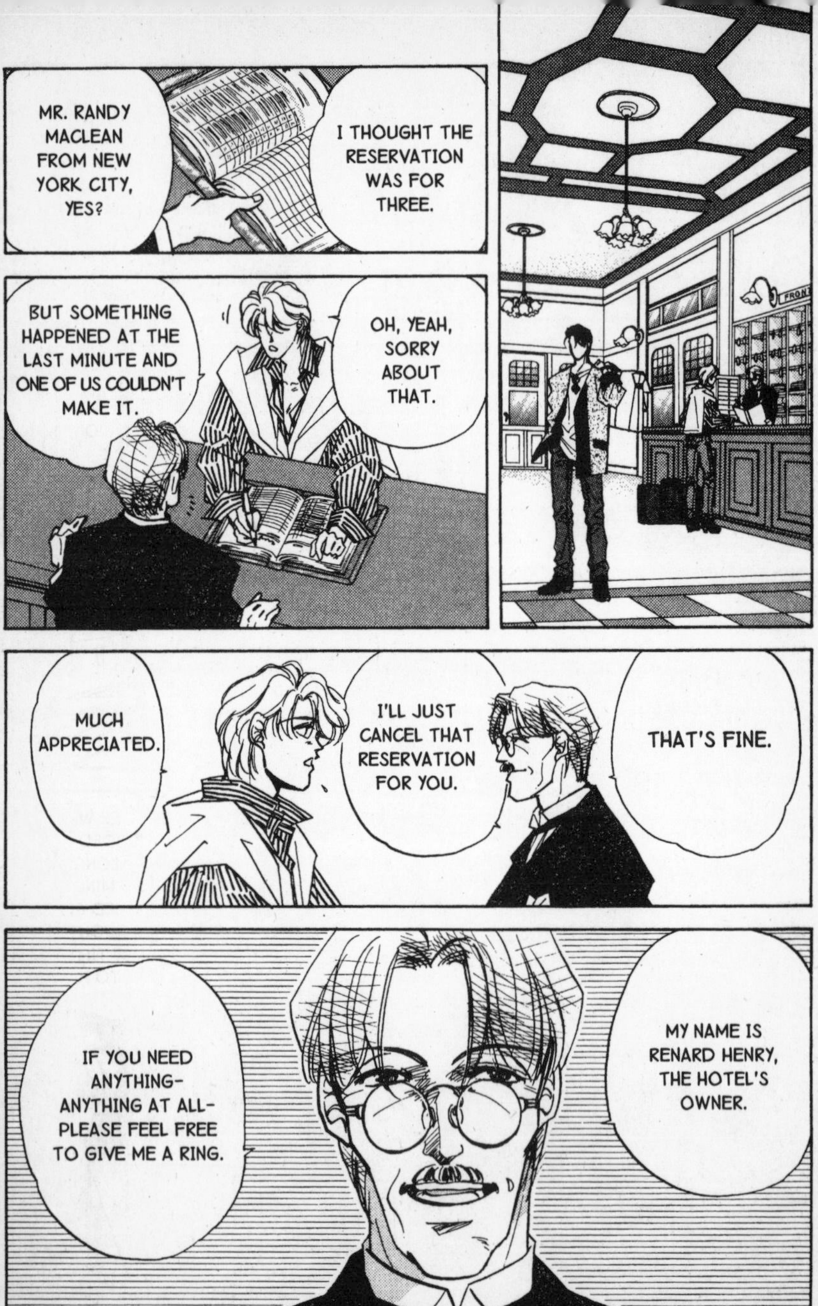
I THOUGHT THE RESERVATION WAS FOR THREE.
MR. RANDY MACLEAN FROM NEW YORK CITY, YES?
OH, YEAH, SORRY ABOUT THAT.
BUT SOMETHING HAPPENED AT THE LAST MINUTE AND ONE OF US COULDN'T MAKE IT.
FRONT
THAT'S FINE.
I'LL JUST CANCEL THAT RESERVATION FOR YOU.
MUCH APPRECIATED.
MY NAME IS RENARD HENRY, THE HOTEL'S OWNER.
IF YOU NEED ANYTHING- ANYTHING AT ALL- PLEASE FEEL FREE TO GIVE ME A RING.

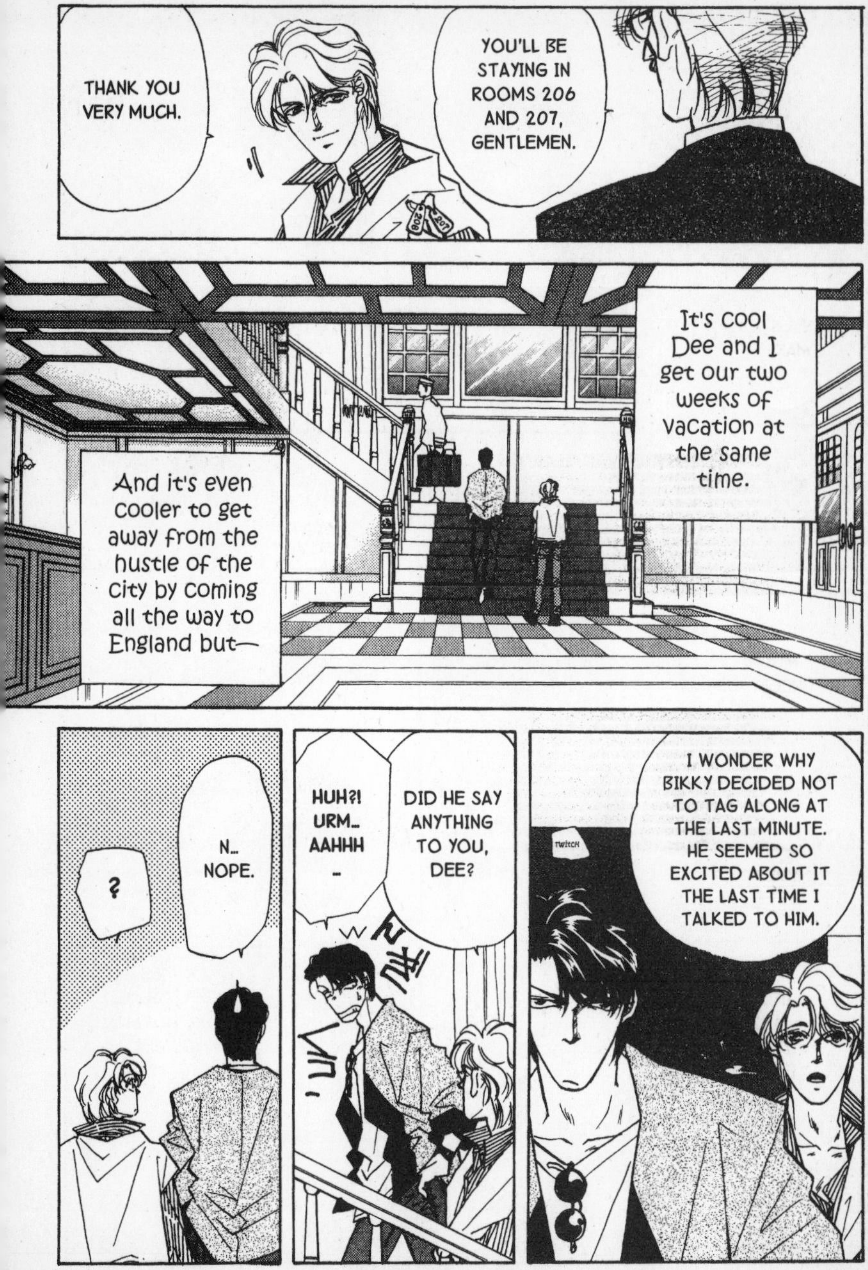
YOU'LL BE STAYING IN ROOMS 206 AND 207, GENTLEMEN.
THANK YOU VERY MUCH.
206
207
It's cool Dee and I get our two weeks of vacation at the same time.
And it's even cooler to get away from the hustle of the city by coming all the way to England but—
I WONDER WHY BIKKY DECIDED NOT TO TAG ALONG AT THE LAST MINUTE. HE SEEMED SO EXCITED ABOUT IT THE LAST TIME I TALKED TO HIM.
TWITCH
DID HE SAY ANYTHING TO YOU, DEE?
HUH?! URM... AAHHH...
N... NOPE.
?

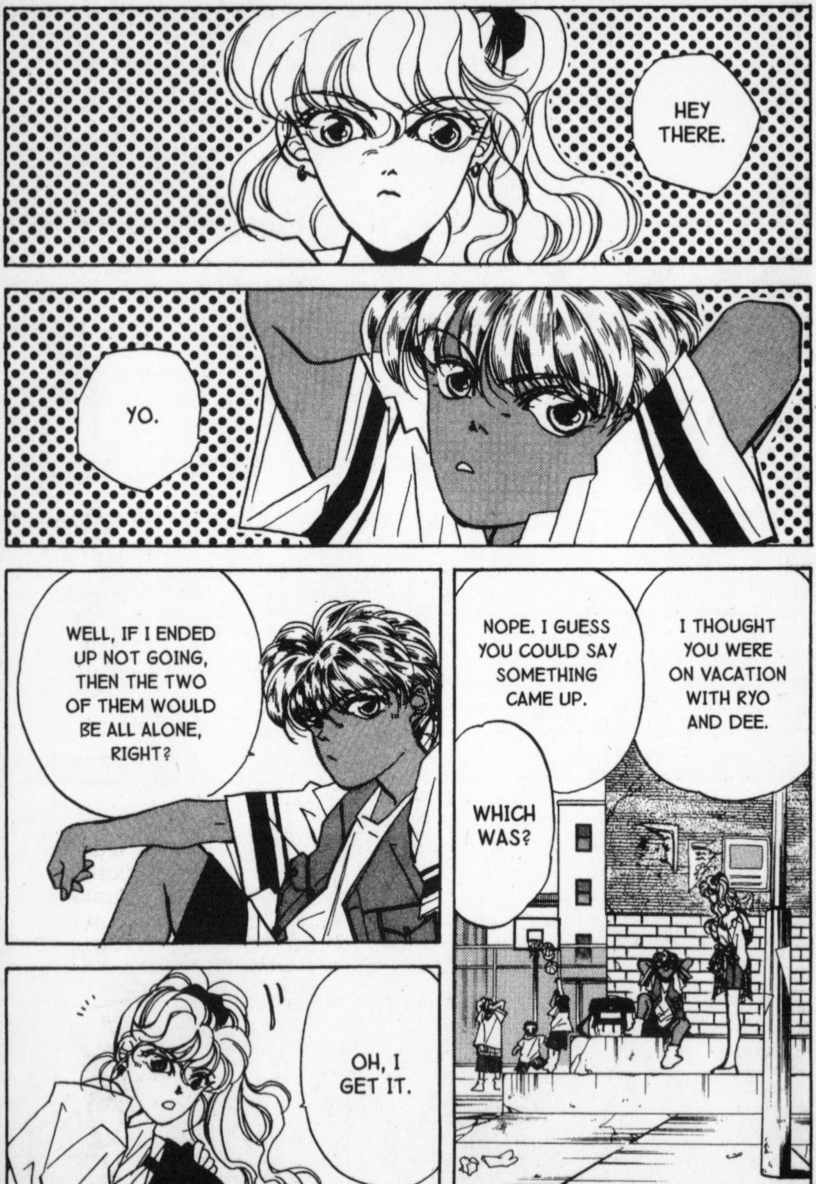
HEY THERE.
YO.
I THOUGHT YOU WERE ON VACATION WITH RYO AND DEE.
NOPE. I GUESS YOU COULD SAY SOMETHING CAME UP.
WHICH WAS?
WELL, IF I ENDED UP NOT GOING, THEN THE TWO OF THEM WOULD BE ALL ALONE, RIGHT?
OH, I GET IT.

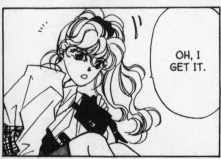

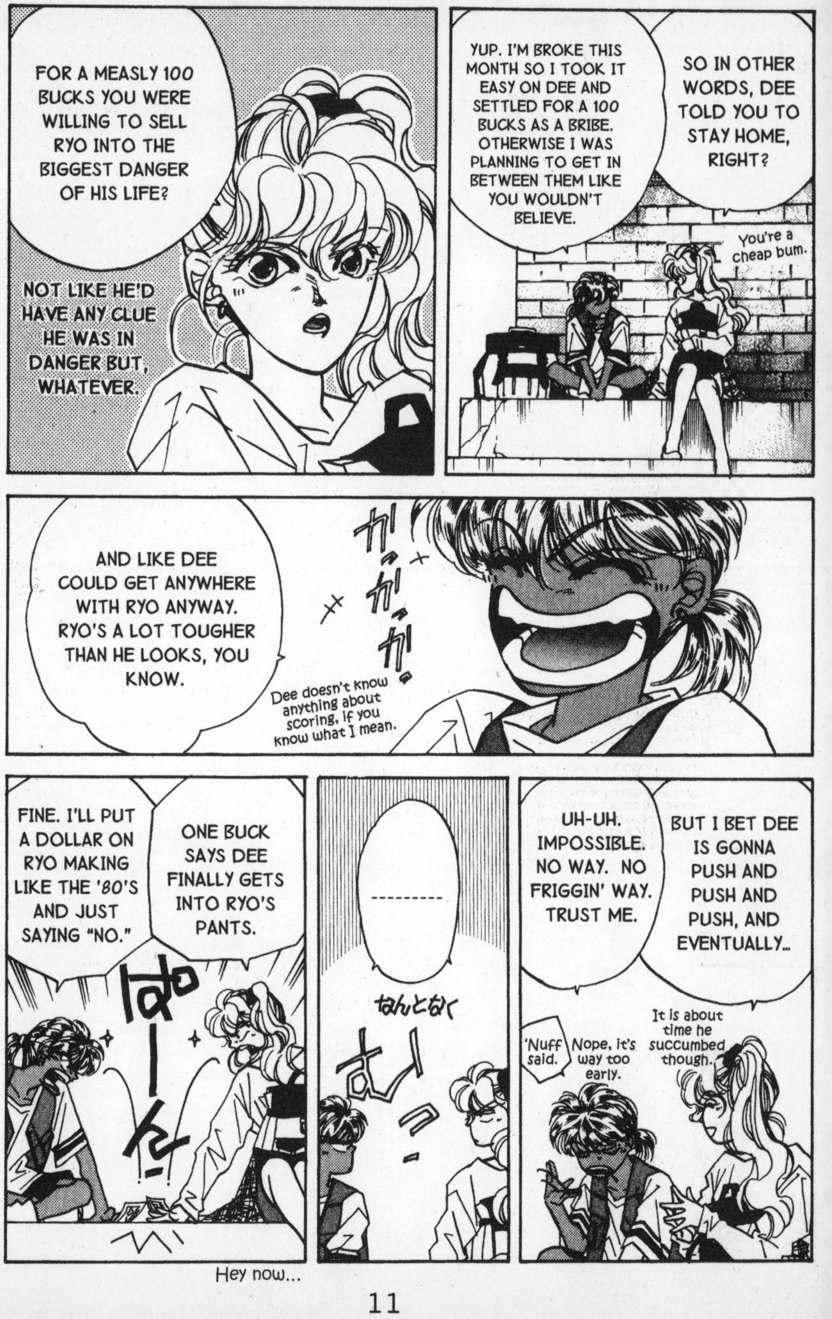
SO IN OTHER WORDS, DEE TOLD YOU TO STAY HOME, RIGHT?
YUP. I'M BROKE THIS MONTH SO I TOOK IT EASY ON DEE AND SETTLED FOR A 100 BUCKS AS A BRIBE. OTHERWISE I WAS PLANNING TO GET IN BETWEEN THEM LIKE YOU WOULDN'T BELIEVE.
You're a cheap bum.
FOR A MEASLY 100 BUCKS YOU WERE WILLING TO SELL RYO INTO THE BIGGEST DANGER OF HIS LIFE?
NOT LIKE HE'D HAVE ANY CLUE HE WAS IN DANGER BUT, WHATEVER.
AND LIKE DEE COULD GET ANYWHERE WITH RYO ANYWAY. RYO'S A LOT TOUGHER THAN HE LOOKS, YOU KNOW.
Dee doesn't know anything about scoring, if you know what I mean.
BUT I BET DEE IS GONNA PUSH AND PUSH AND PUSH, AND EVENTUALLY...
UH-UH. IMPOSSIBLE. NO WAY. NO FRIGGIN' WAY. TRUST ME.
It is about time he succumbed though.
Nope, it's way too early.
'Nuff said.

なんとなく
ONE BUCK SAYS DEE FINALLY GETS INTO RYO'S PANTS.
FINE. I'LL PUT A DOLLAR ON RYO MAKING LIKE THE '80'S AND JUST SAYING "NO."

Hey now...

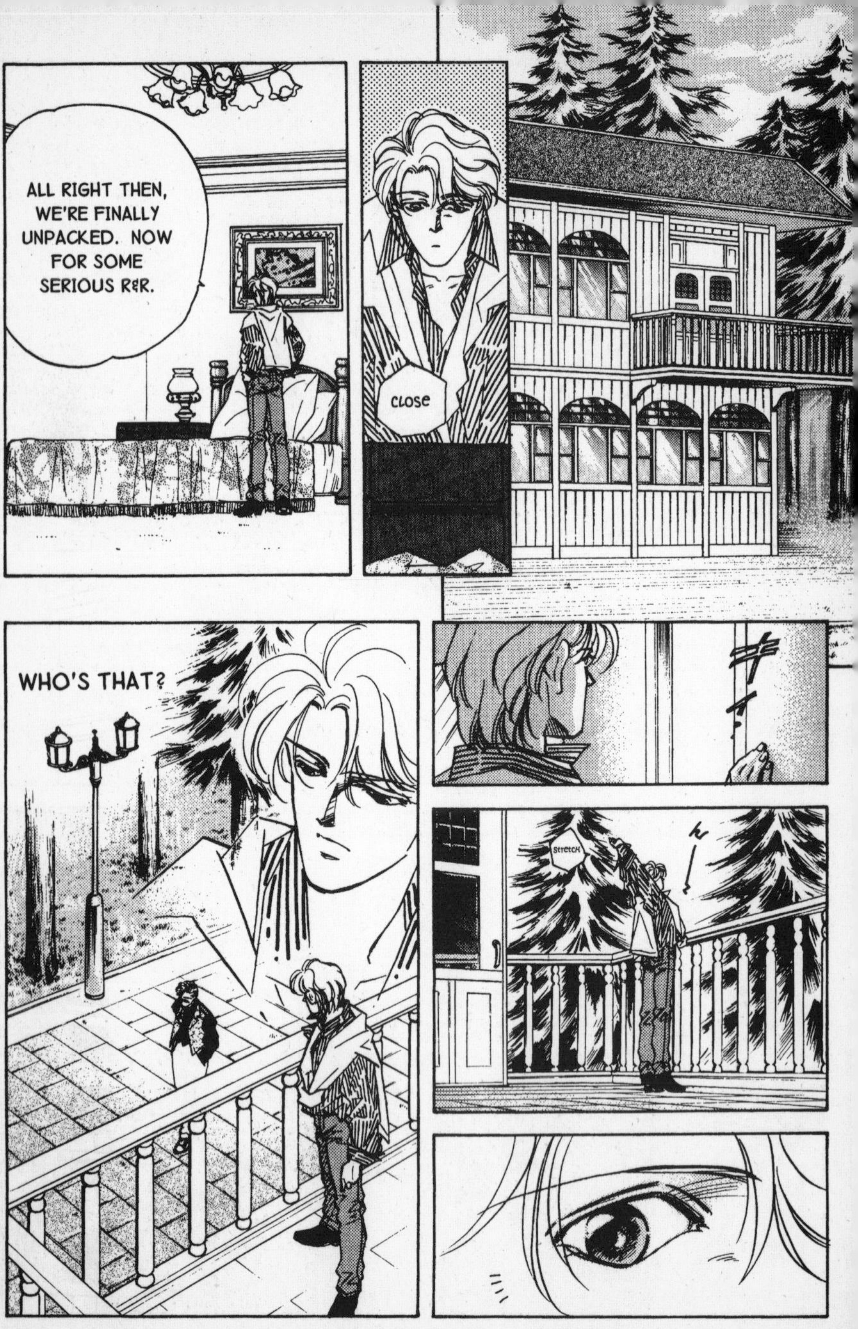
CLOSE
ALL RIGHT THEN, WE'RE FINALLY UNPACKED. NOW FOR SOME SERIOUS R&R.
STRETCH
WHO'S THAT?

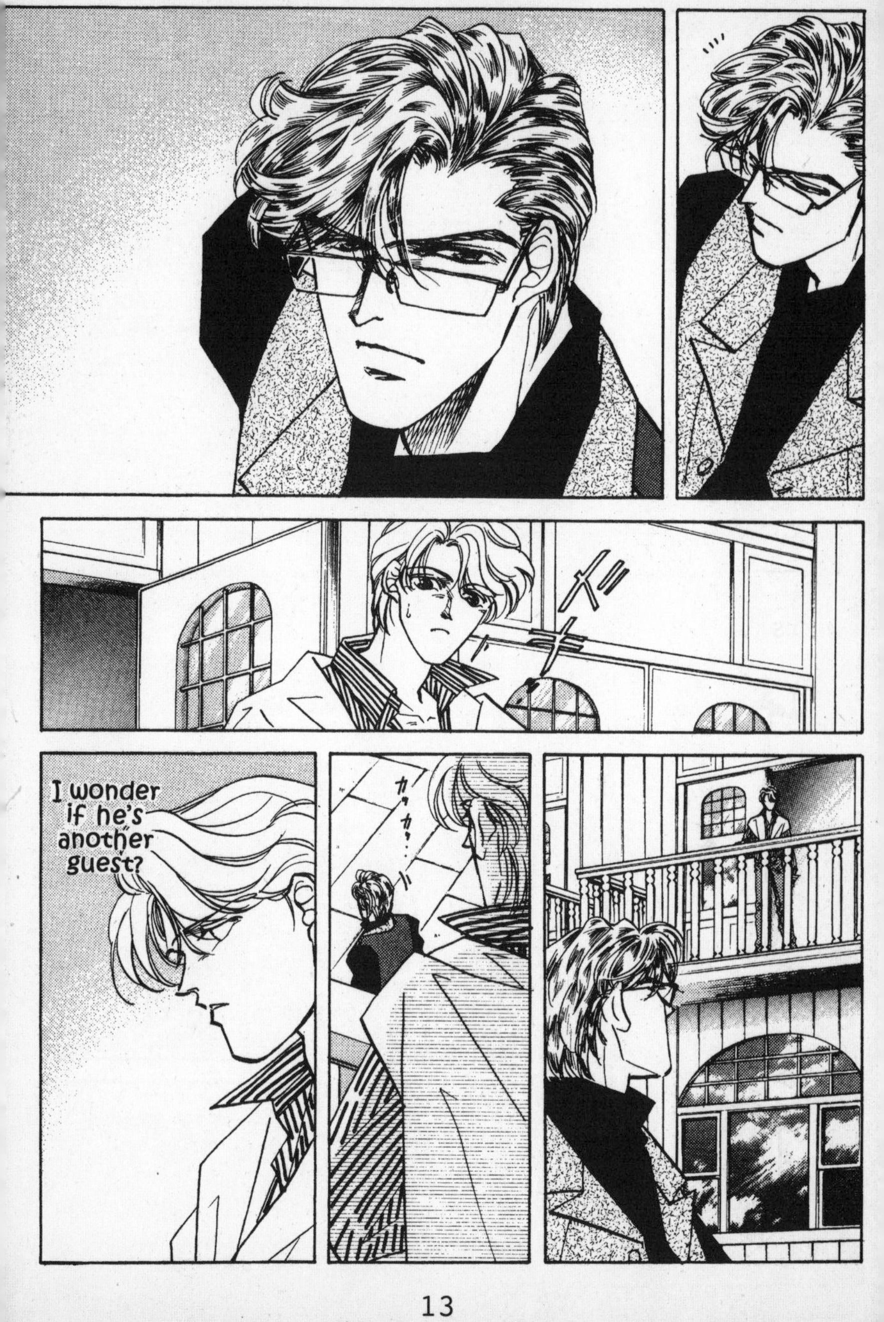
I wonder if he's another guest?

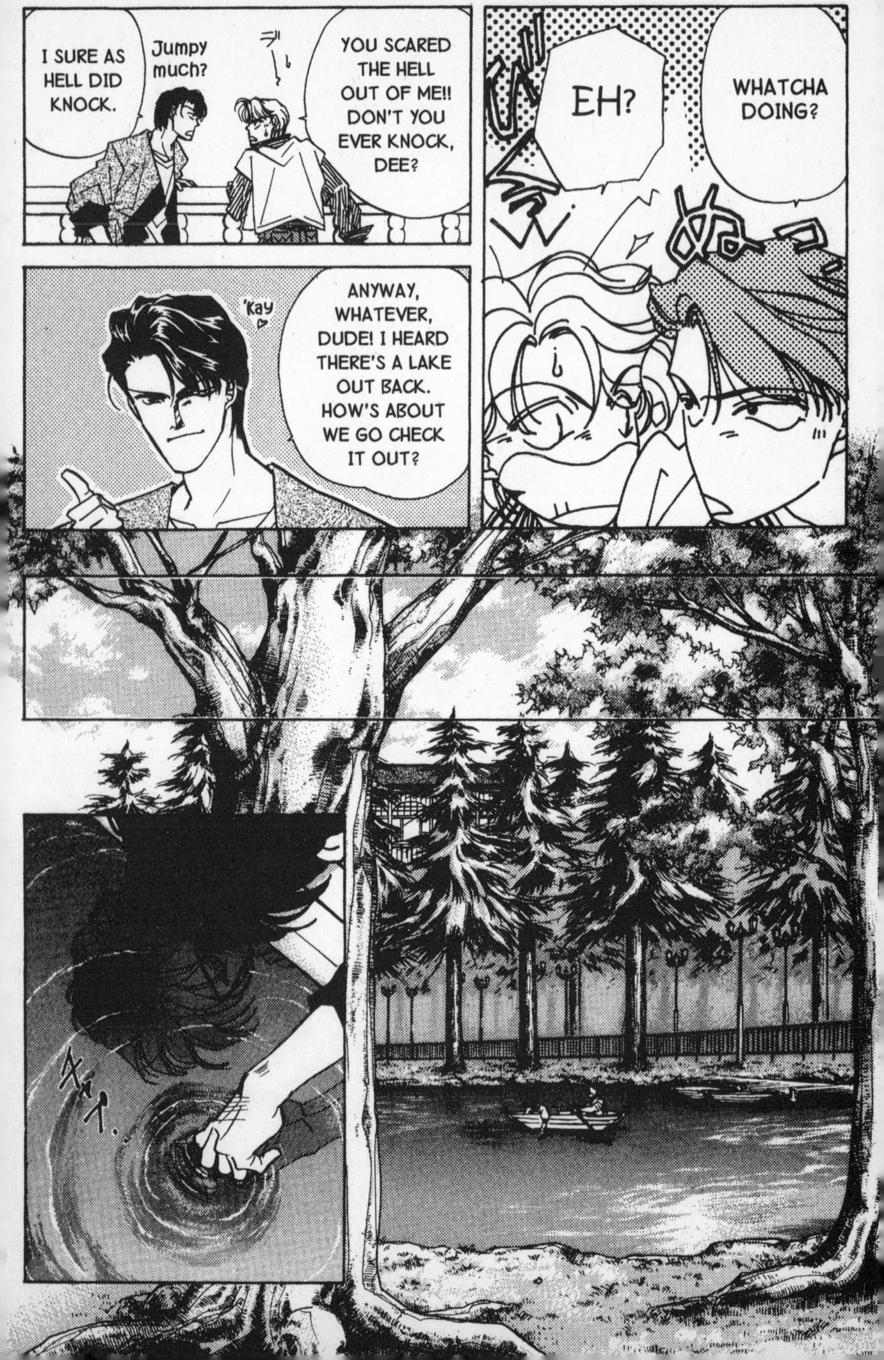
WHATCHA DOING?
EH?
YOU SCARED THE HELL OUT OF ME!! DON'T YOU EVER KNOCK, DEE?
Jumpy much?
I SURE AS HELL DID KNOCK.
ANYWAY, WHATEVER, DUDE! I HEARD THERE'S A LAKE OUT BACK. HOW'S ABOUT WE GO CHECK IT OUT?
'Kay ♡

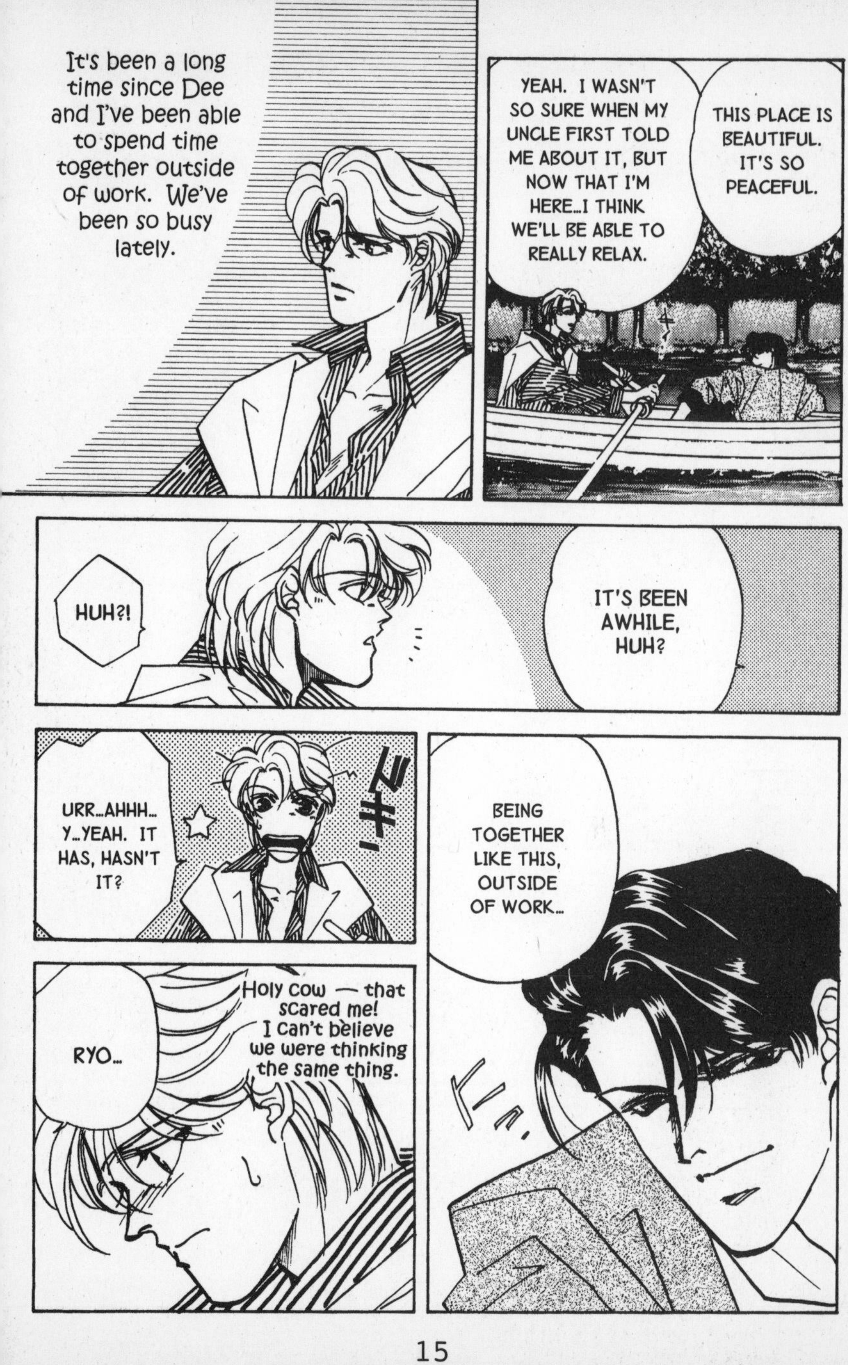
THIS PLACE IS BEAUTIFUL. IT'S SO PEACEFUL.
YEAH. I WASN'T SO SURE WHEN MY UNCLE FIRST TOLD ME ABOUT IT, BUT NOW THAT I'M HERE...I THINK WE'LL BE ABLE TO REALLY RELAX.
It's been a long time since Dee and I've been able to spend time together outside of work. We've been so busy lately.
IT'S BEEN AWHILE, HUH?
HUH?!
BEING TOGETHER LIKE THIS, OUTSIDE OF WORK...
URR...AHHH... Y...YEAH. IT HAS, HASN'T IT?
Holy cow — that scared me! I can't believe we were thinking the same thing.
RYO...

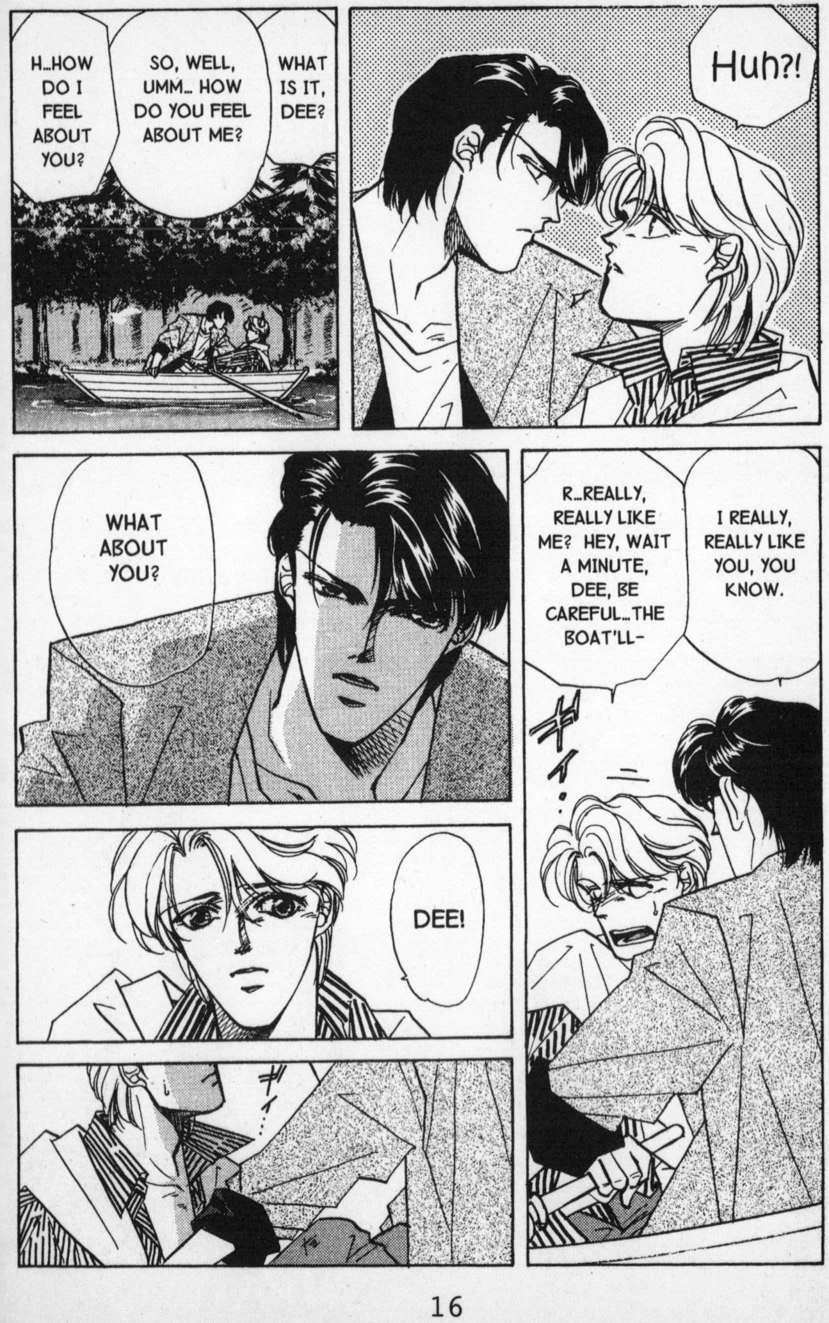
Huh?!
WHAT IS IT, DEE?
SO, WELL, UMM... HOW DO YOU FEEL ABOUT ME?
H...HOW DO I FEEL ABOUT YOU?
I REALLY, REALLY LIKE YOU, YOU KNOW.
R...REALLY, REALLY LIKE ME? HEY, WAIT A MINUTE, DEE, BE CAREFUL...THE BOAT'LL-
WHAT ABOUT YOU?
DEE!

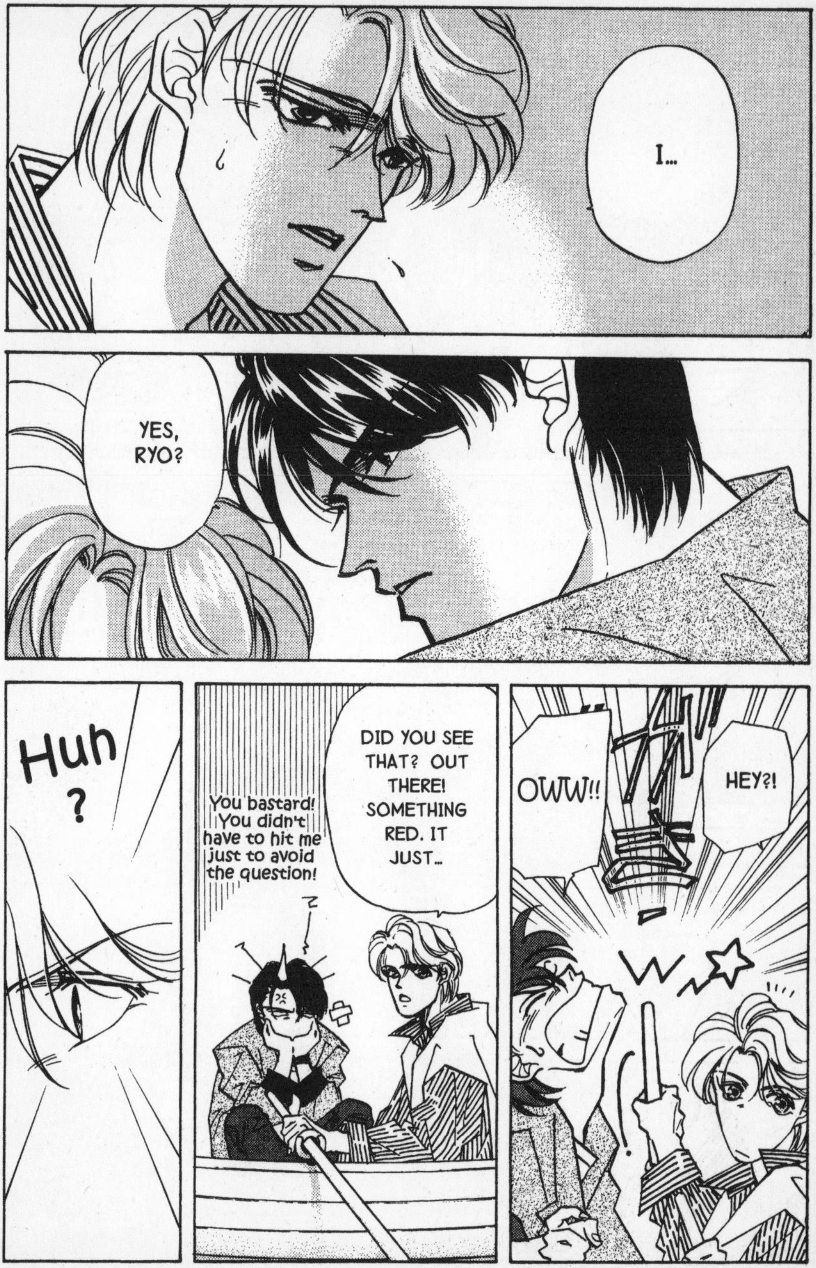
I...
YES, RYO?
HEY?!
OWW!!
DID YOU SEE THAT? OUT THERE! SOMETHING RED. IT JUST...
You bastard! You didn't have to hit me just to avoid the question!
Huh ?

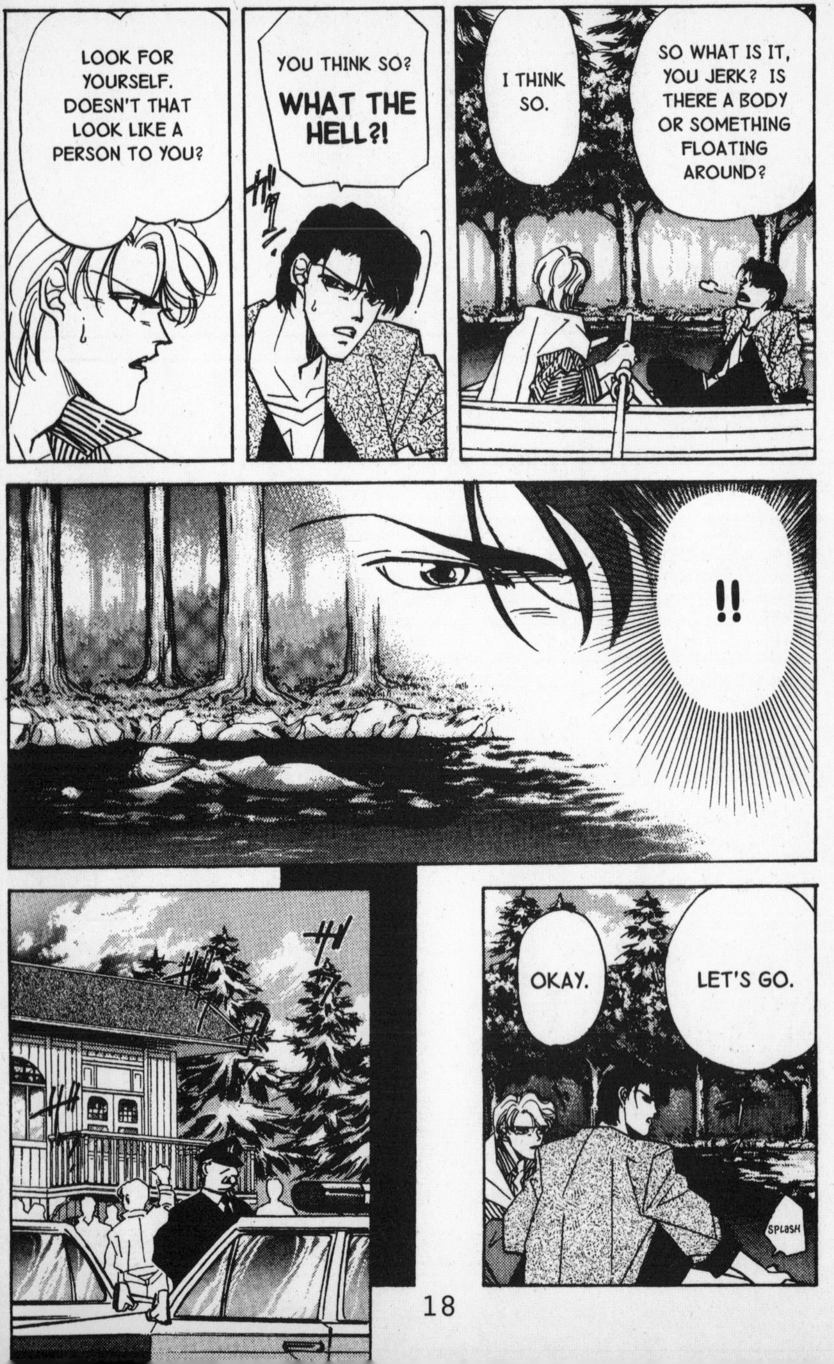
SO WHAT IS IT, YOU JERK? IS THERE A BODY OR SOMETHING FLOATING AROUND?
I THINK SO.
YOU THINK SO? **WHAT THE HELL?!**
LOOK FOR YOURSELF. DOESN'T THAT LOOK LIKE A PERSON TO YOU?
!!
LET'S GO.
OKAY.
SPLASH

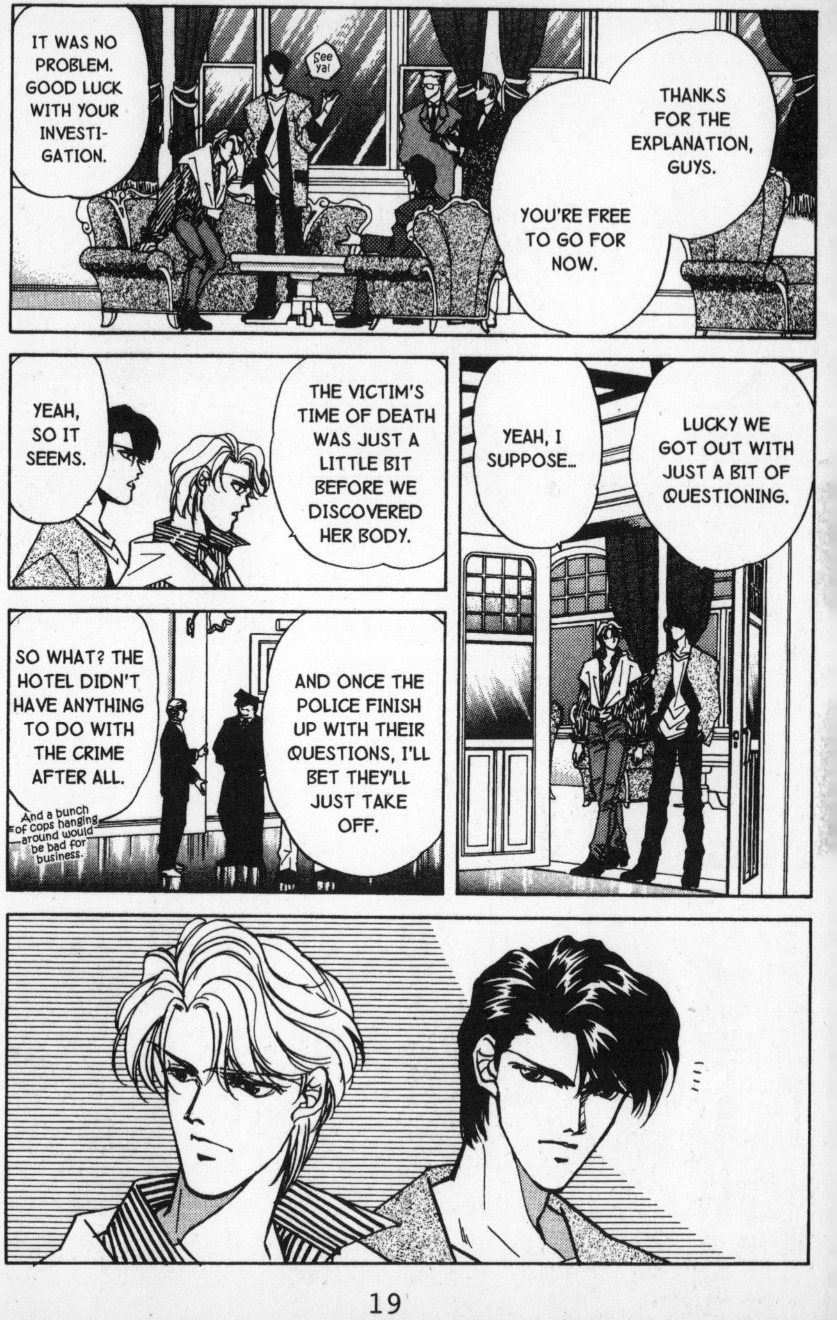
THANKS FOR THE EXPLANATION, GUYS.
YOU'RE FREE TO GO FOR NOW.
See ya!
IT WAS NO PROBLEM. GOOD LUCK WITH YOUR INVESTI-GATION.
LUCKY WE GOT OUT WITH JUST A BIT OF QUESTIONING.
YEAH, I SUPPOSE...
THE VICTIM'S TIME OF DEATH WAS JUST A LITTLE BIT BEFORE WE DISCOVERED HER BODY.
YEAH, SO IT SEEMS.
AND ONCE THE POLICE FINISH UP WITH THEIR QUESTIONS, I'LL BET THEY'LL JUST TAKE OFF.
SO WHAT? THE HOTEL DIDN'T HAVE ANYTHING TO DO WITH THE CRIME AFTER ALL.
And a bunch of cops hanging around would be bad for business.

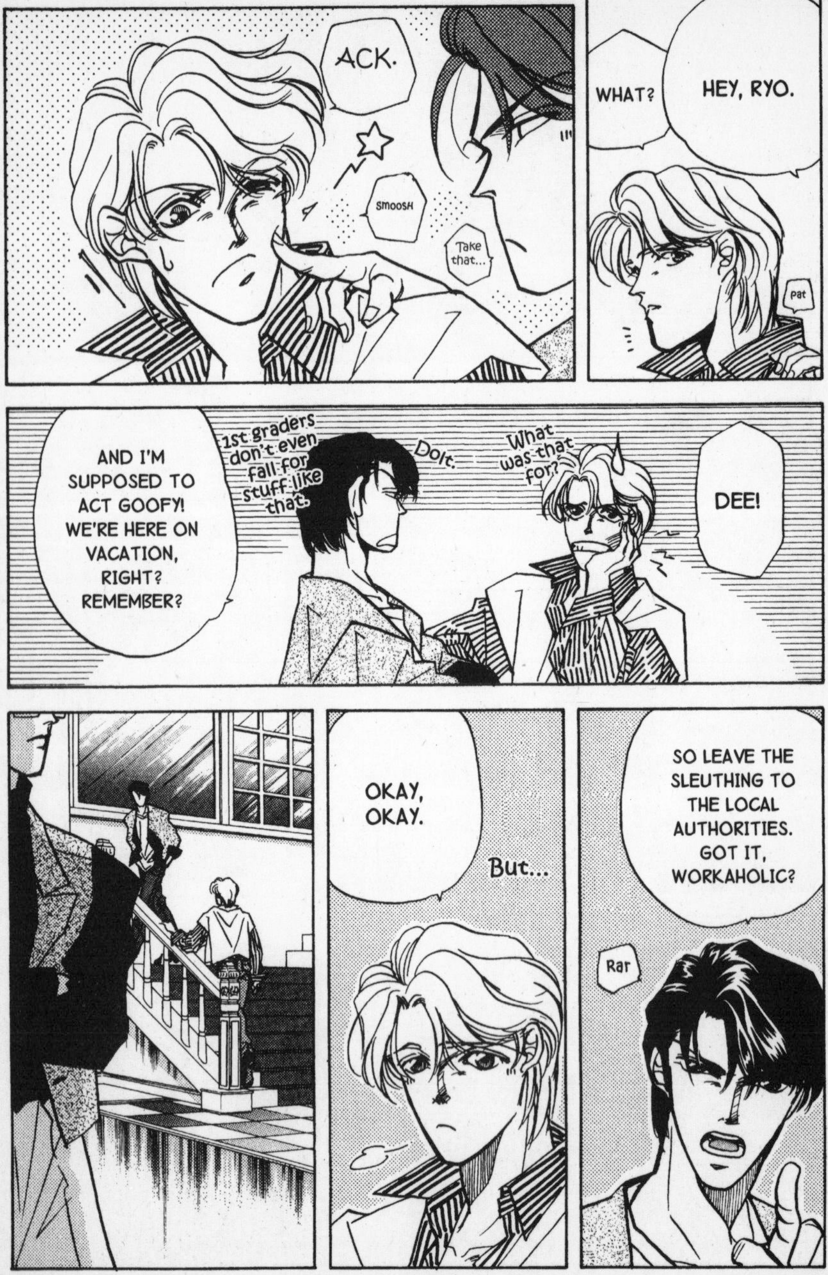
HEY, RYO.
WHAT?
pat
Take that...
SMOOSH
ACK.
DEE!
What was that for?
Dolt.
1st graders don't even fall for stuff like that.
AND I'M SUPPOSED TO ACT GOOFY! WE'RE HERE ON VACATION, RIGHT? REMEMBER?
SO LEAVE THE SLEUTHING TO THE LOCAL AUTHORITIES. GOT IT, WORKAHOLIC?
Rar
OKAY, OKAY.
But...

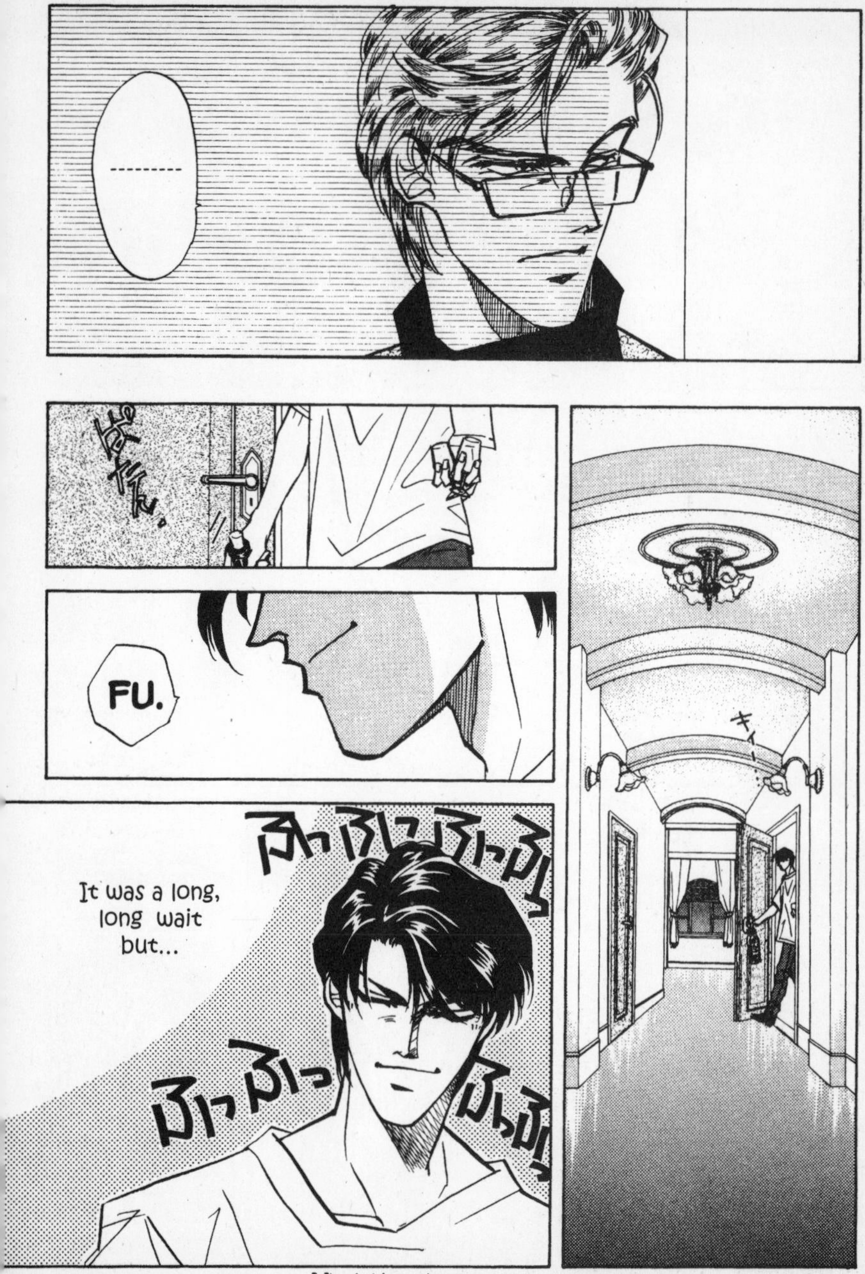

ぱたん。
FU.
It was a long, long wait but...
ふっふっふっふっ
ふっふっふっふっ
キィー
What's his problem anyway?!

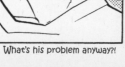

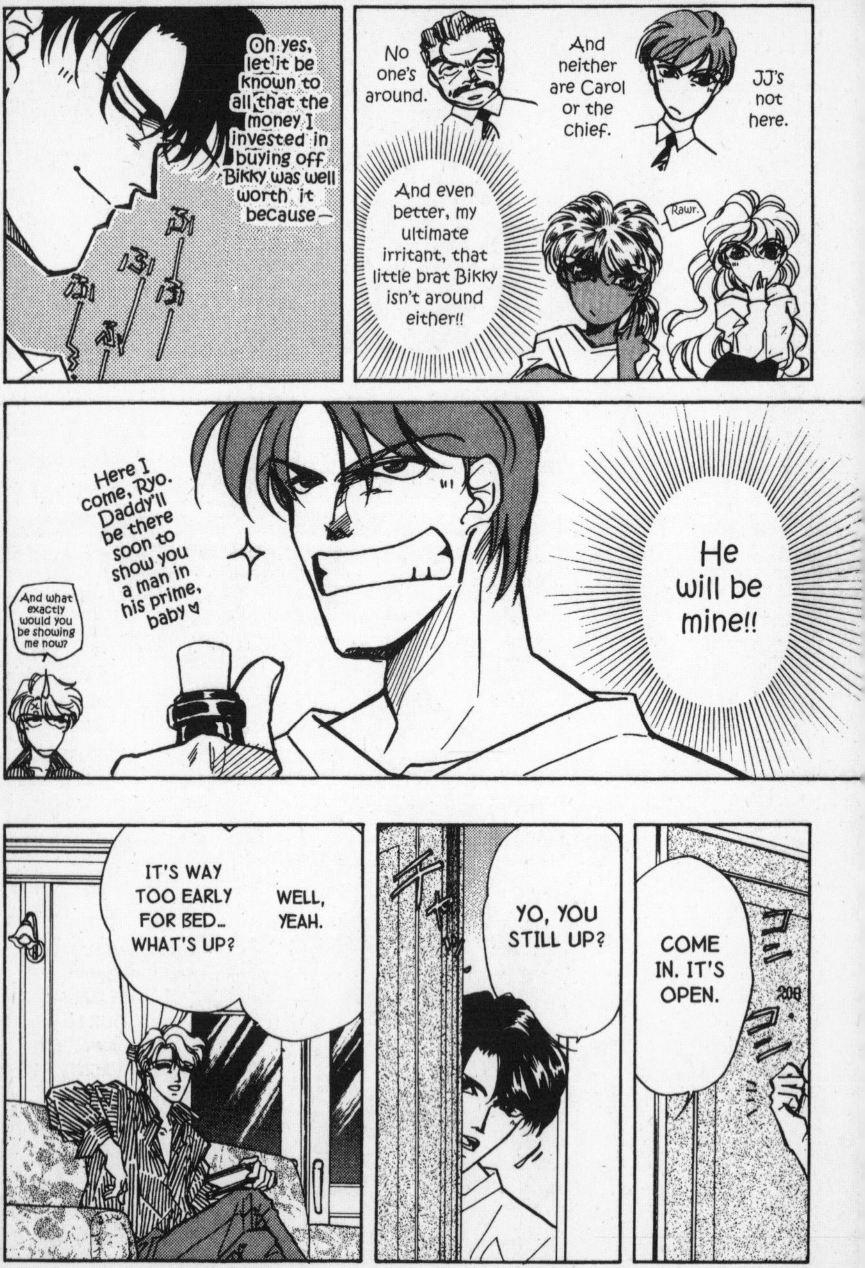
JJ's not here.
And neither are Carol or the chief.
No one's around.
Rawr.
And even better, my ultimate irritant, that little brat Bikky isn't around either!!
Oh yes, let it be known to all that the money I invested in buying off Bikky was well worth it because—
He will be mine!!
Here I come, Ryo. Daddy'll be there soon to show you a man in his prime, baby♡
And what exactly would you be showing me now?
COME IN. IT'S OPEN.
YO, YOU STILL UP?
WELL, YEAH.
IT'S WAY TOO EARLY FOR BED... WHAT'S UP?

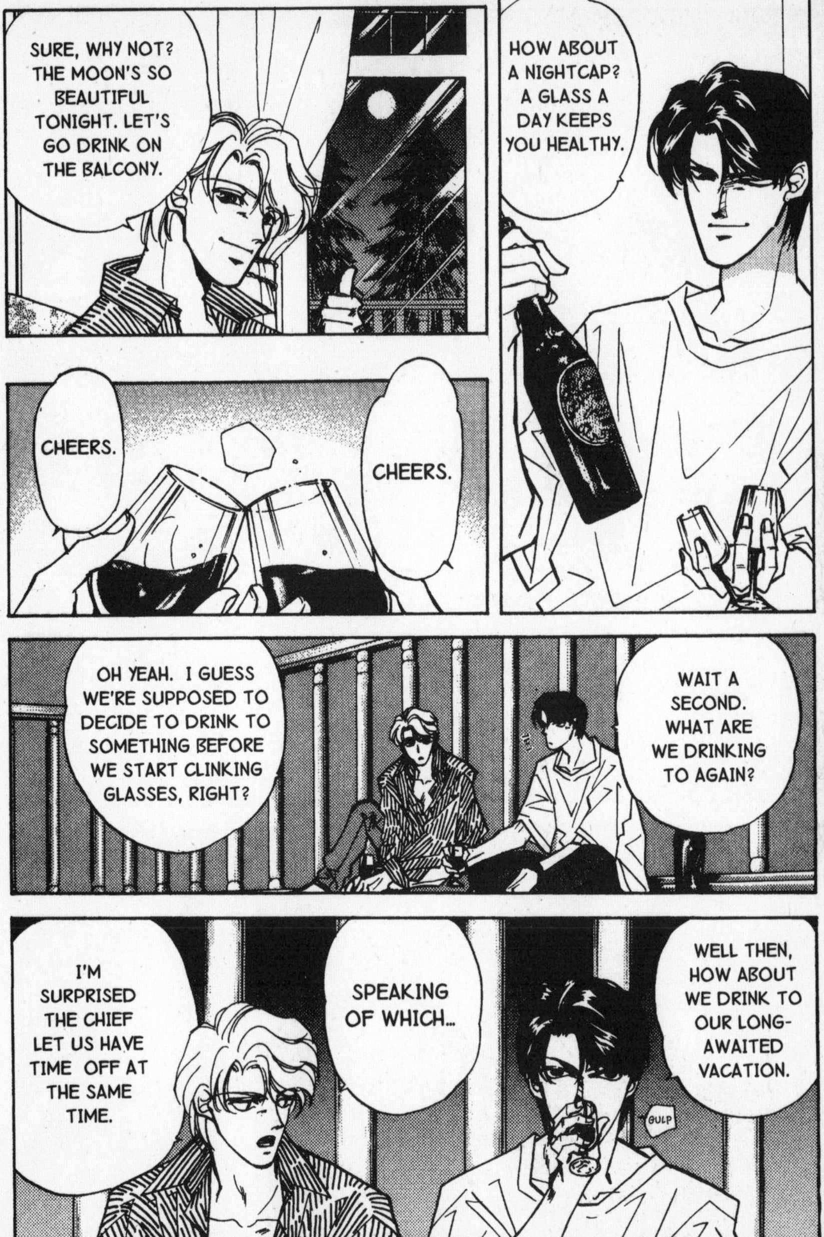
HOW ABOUT A NIGHTCAP? A GLASS A DAY KEEPS YOU HEALTHY.
SURE, WHY NOT? THE MOON'S SO BEAUTIFUL TONIGHT. LET'S GO DRINK ON THE BALCONY.
CHEERS.
CHEERS.
WAIT A SECOND. WHAT ARE WE DRINKING TO AGAIN?
OH YEAH. I GUESS WE'RE SUPPOSED TO DECIDE TO DRINK TO SOMETHING BEFORE WE START CLINKING GLASSES, RIGHT?
WELL THEN, HOW ABOUT WE DRINK TO OUR LONG-AWAITED VACATION.
GULP
SPEAKING OF WHICH...
I'M SURPRISED THE CHIEF LET US HAVE TIME OFF AT THE SAME TIME.

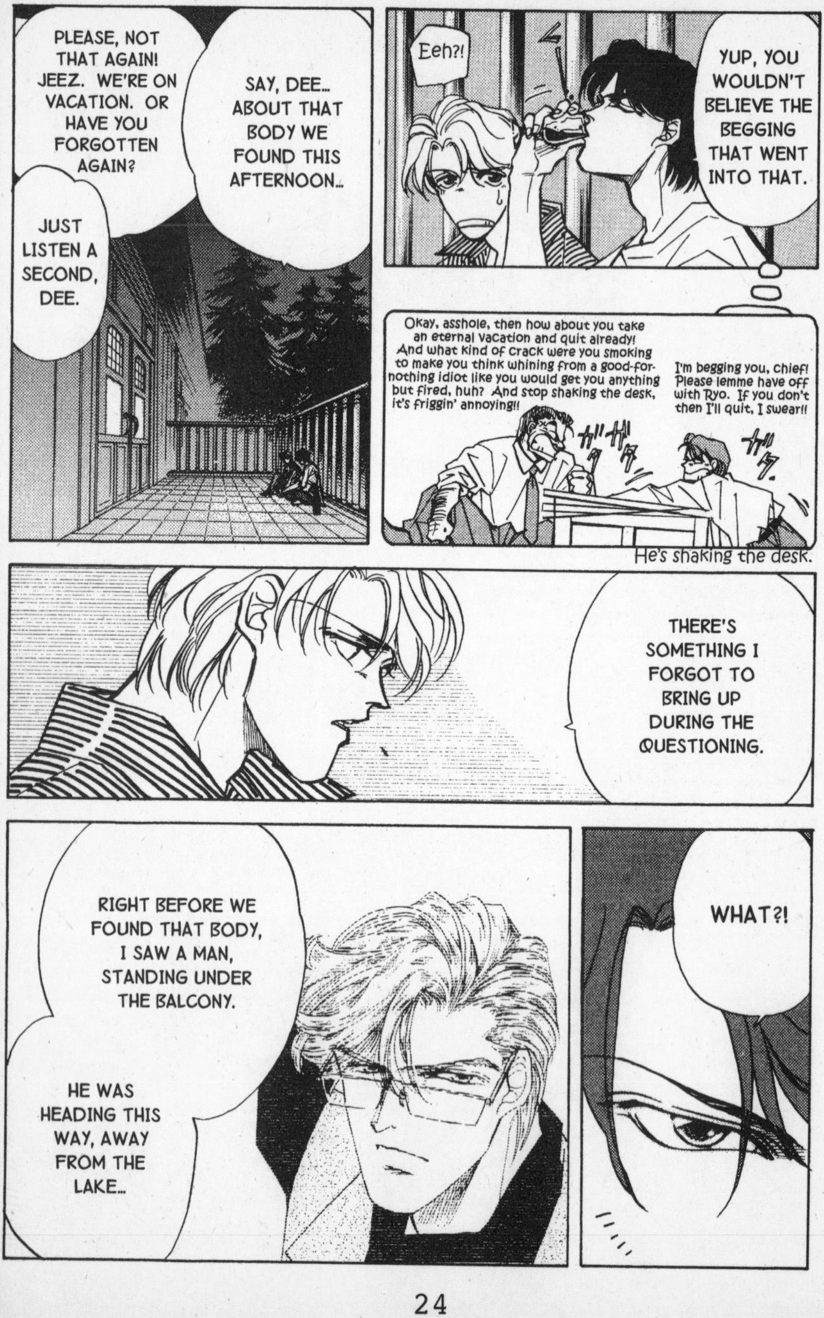
SAY, DEE... ABOUT THAT BODY WE FOUND THIS AFTERNOON...
PLEASE, NOT THAT AGAIN! JEEZ. WE'RE ON VACATION. OR HAVE YOU FORGOTTEN AGAIN?
JUST LISTEN A SECOND, DEE.
YUP, YOU WOULDN'T BELIEVE THE BEGGING THAT WENT INTO THAT.
Eeh?!
I'm begging you, chief! Please lemme have off with Ryo. If you don't then I'll quit, I swear!!
Okay, asshole, then how about you take an eternal vacation and quit already! And what kind of crack were you smoking to make you think whining from a good-for-nothing idiot like you would get you anything but fired, huh? And stop shaking the desk, it's friggin' annoying!!
He's shaking the desk.
THERE'S SOMETHING I FORGOT TO BRING UP DURING THE QUESTIONING.
RIGHT BEFORE WE FOUND THAT BODY, I SAW A MAN, STANDING UNDER THE BALCONY.
HE WAS HEADING THIS WAY, AWAY FROM THE LAKE...
WHAT?!

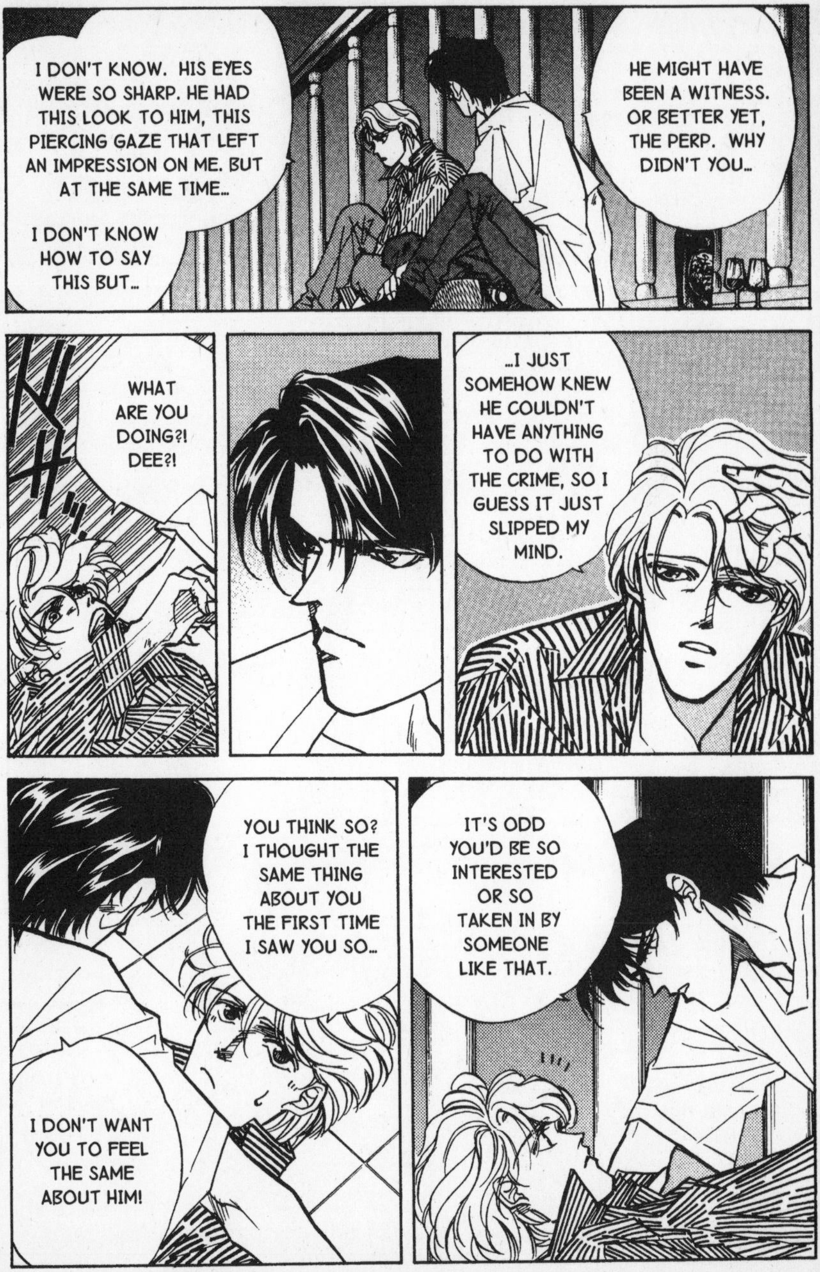
HE MIGHT HAVE BEEN A WITNESS. OR BETTER YET, THE PERP. WHY DIDN'T YOU...
I DON'T KNOW. HIS EYES WERE SO SHARP. HE HAD THIS LOOK TO HIM, THIS PIERCING GAZE THAT LEFT AN IMPRESSION ON ME. BUT AT THE SAME TIME...
I DON'T KNOW HOW TO SAY THIS BUT...
...I JUST SOMEHOW KNEW HE COULDN'T HAVE ANYTHING TO DO WITH THE CRIME, SO I GUESS IT JUST SLIPPED MY MIND.
WHAT ARE YOU DOING?! DEE?!
IT'S ODD YOU'D BE SO INTERESTED OR SO TAKEN IN BY SOMEONE LIKE THAT.
YOU THINK SO? I THOUGHT THE SAME THING ABOUT YOU THE FIRST TIME I SAW YOU SO...
I DON'T WANT YOU TO FEEL THE SAME ABOUT HIM!

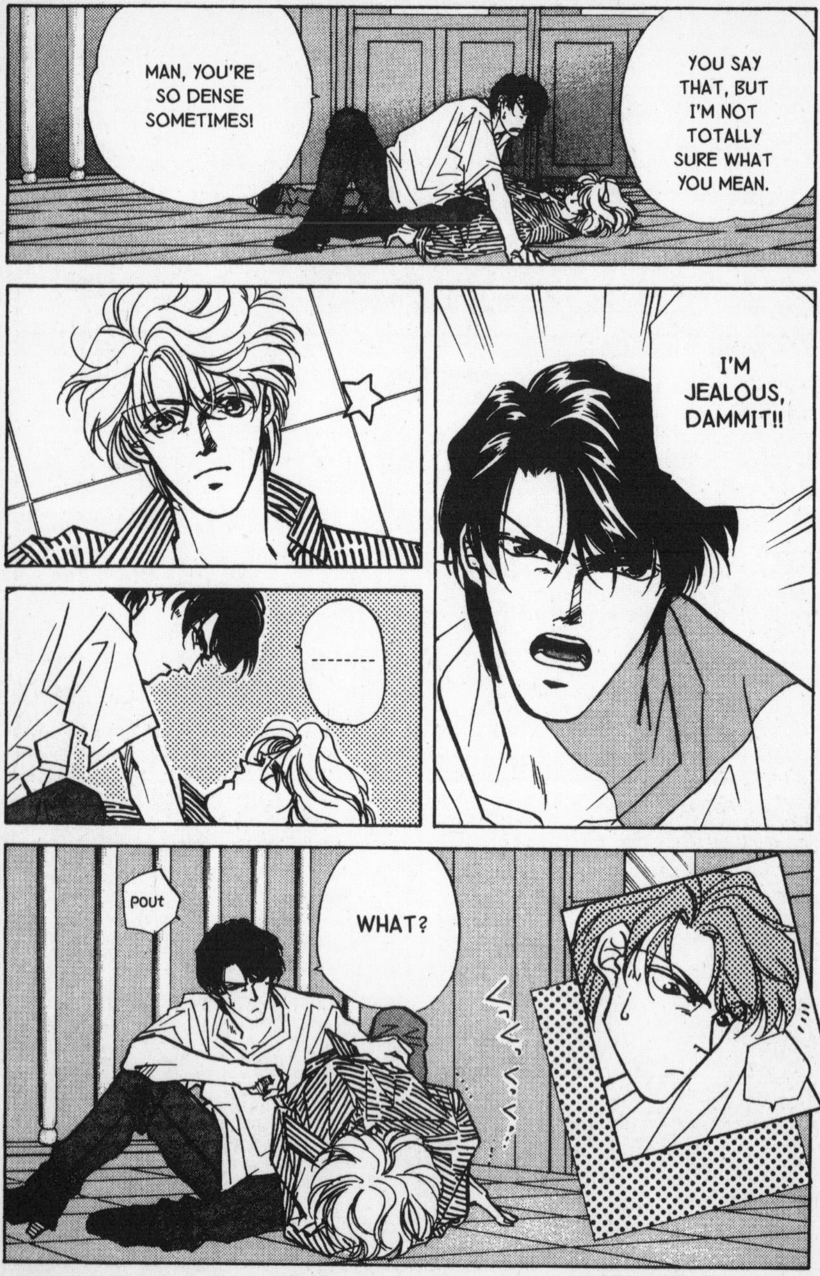
MAN, YOU'RE SO DENSE SOMETIMES!
YOU SAY THAT, BUT I'M NOT TOTALLY SURE WHAT YOU MEAN.

I'M JEALOUS, DAMMIT!!
pout
WHAT?
vrvrvrvr...

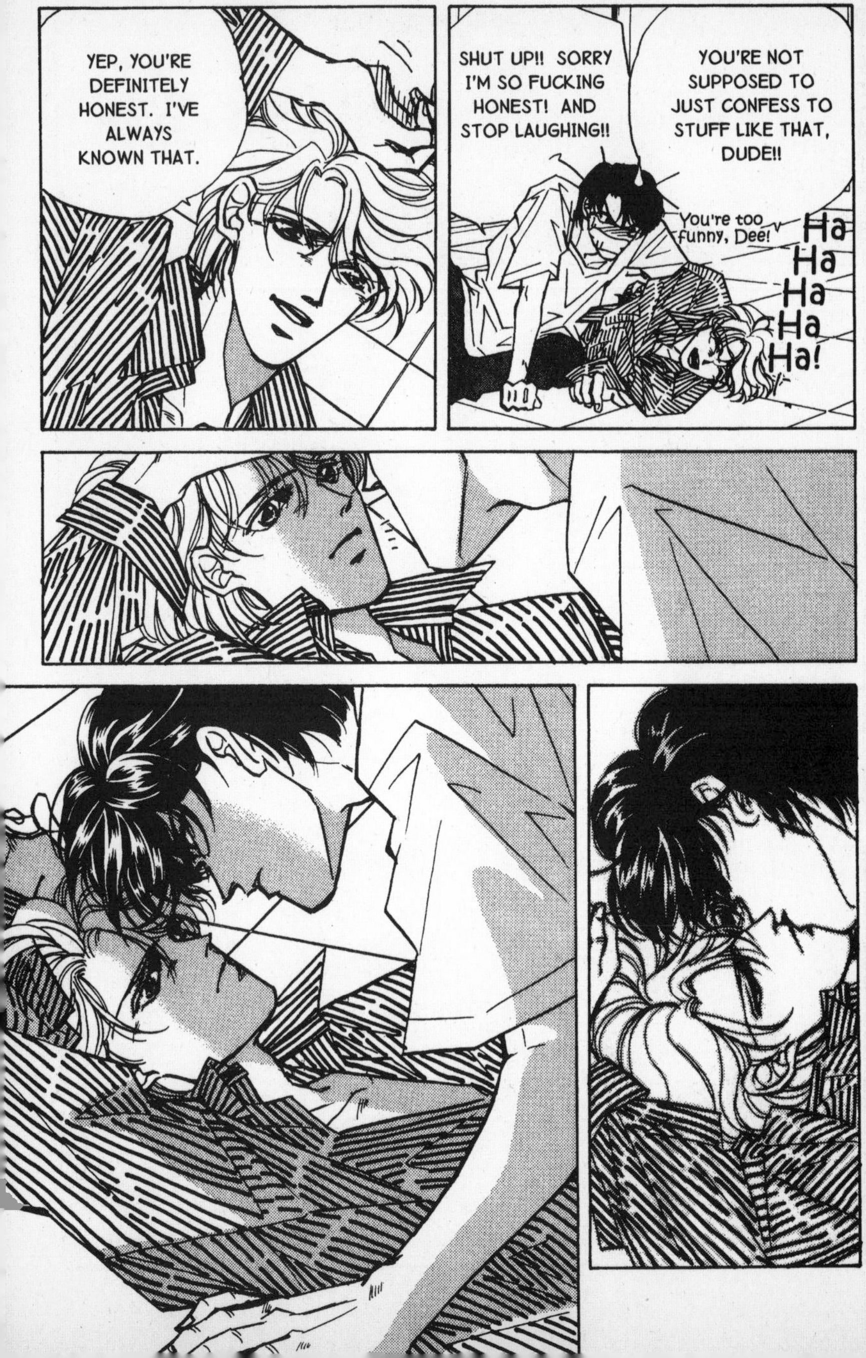
YOU'RE NOT SUPPOSED TO JUST CONFESS TO STUFF LIKE THAT, DUDE!!
You're too funny, Dee!
Ha Ha Ha Ha Ha!
SHUT UP!! SORRY I'M SO FUCKING HONEST! AND STOP LAUGHING!!
YEP, YOU'RE DEFINITELY HONEST. I'VE ALWAYS KNOWN THAT.

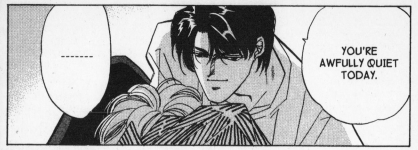

YOU'RE AWFULLY QUIET TODAY.

I'M JUST THINKING...
ABOUT WHAT?
ABOUT YOU. ABOUT WHAT YOU WANT.
HUH?!
YOU TOLD ME BEFORE TO NEVER "DISMISS" YOU AS A JOKE AGAIN.
SO I WAS THINKING ABOUT IT, ABOUT WHAT YOU MEANT...
IS THAT WHY YOU AREN'T TRYING TO GET OUT OF ME KISSING YOU?
IT'S NOT LIKE THAT. IT'S HARD TO EXPLAIN. IT'S JUST...

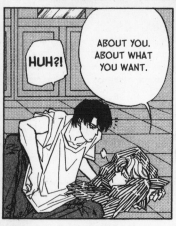

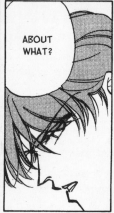

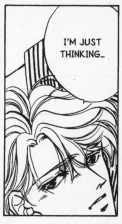

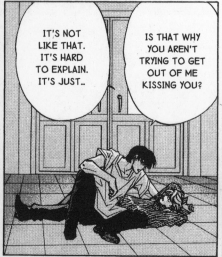

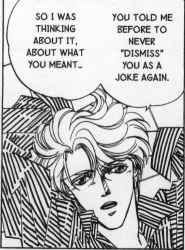

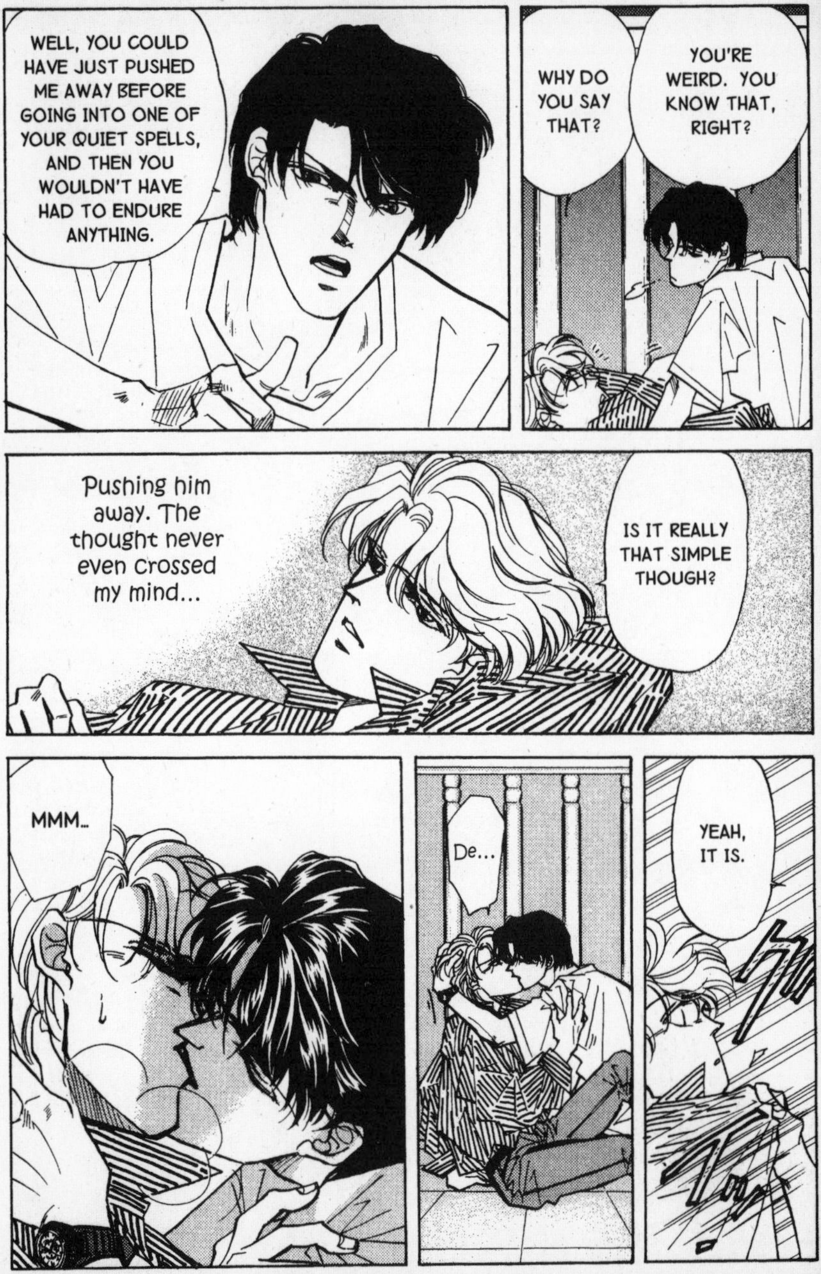
YOU'RE WEIRD. YOU KNOW THAT, RIGHT?
WHY DO YOU SAY THAT?
WELL, YOU COULD HAVE JUST PUSHED ME AWAY BEFORE GOING INTO ONE OF YOUR QUIET SPELLS, AND THEN YOU WOULDN'T HAVE HAD TO ENDURE ANYTHING.
IS IT REALLY THAT SIMPLE THOUGH?
Pushing him away. The thought never even crossed my mind...
YEAH, IT IS.
De...
MMM...

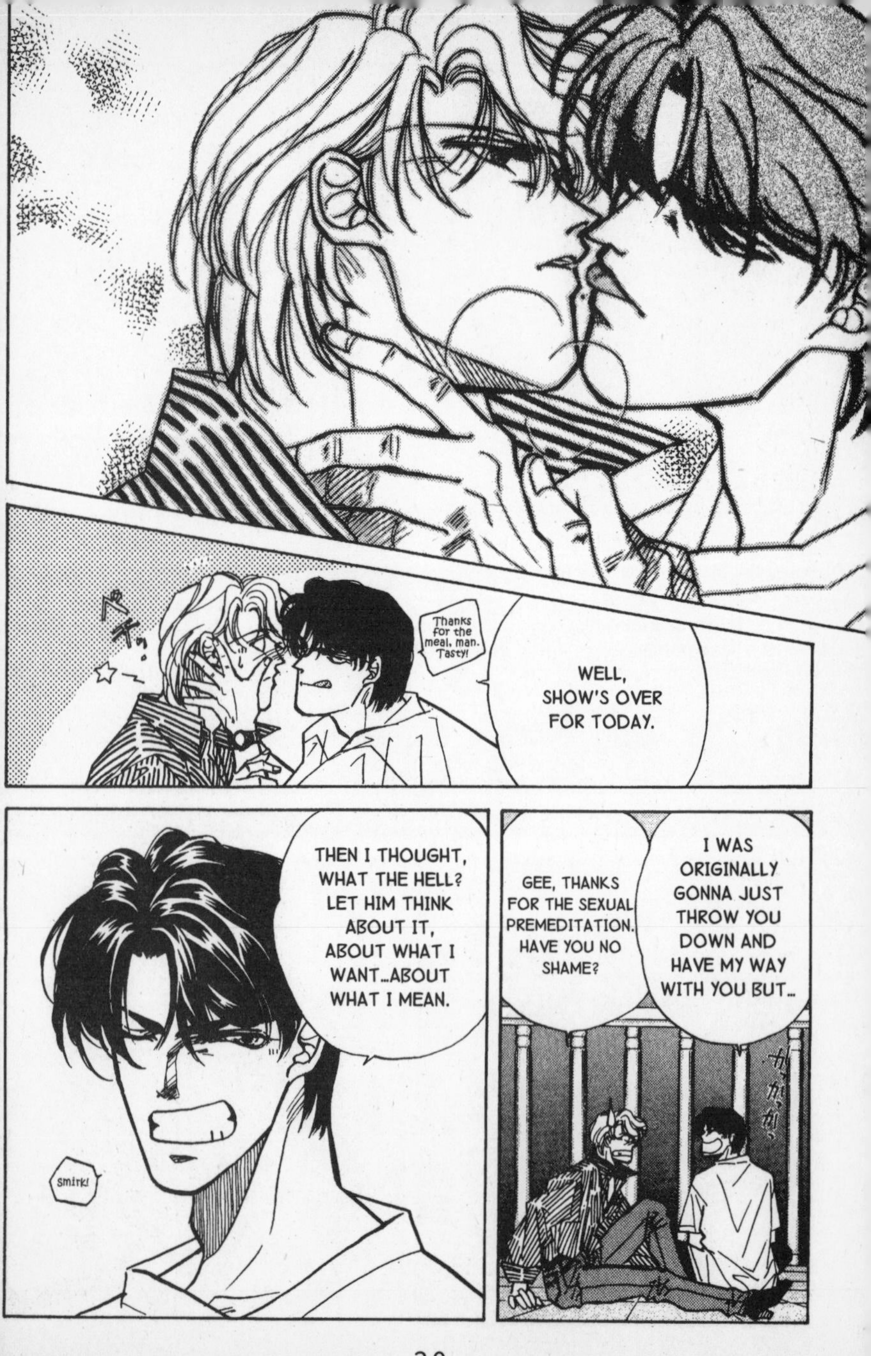
WELL, SHOW'S OVER FOR TODAY.
Thanks for the meal, man. Tasty!
I WAS ORIGINALLY GONNA JUST THROW YOU DOWN AND HAVE MY WAY WITH YOU BUT...
GEE, THANKS FOR THE SEXUAL PREMEDITATION. HAVE YOU NO SHAME?
THEN I THOUGHT, WHAT THE HELL? LET HIM THINK ABOUT IT, ABOUT WHAT I WANT...ABOUT WHAT I MEAN.
smirk!

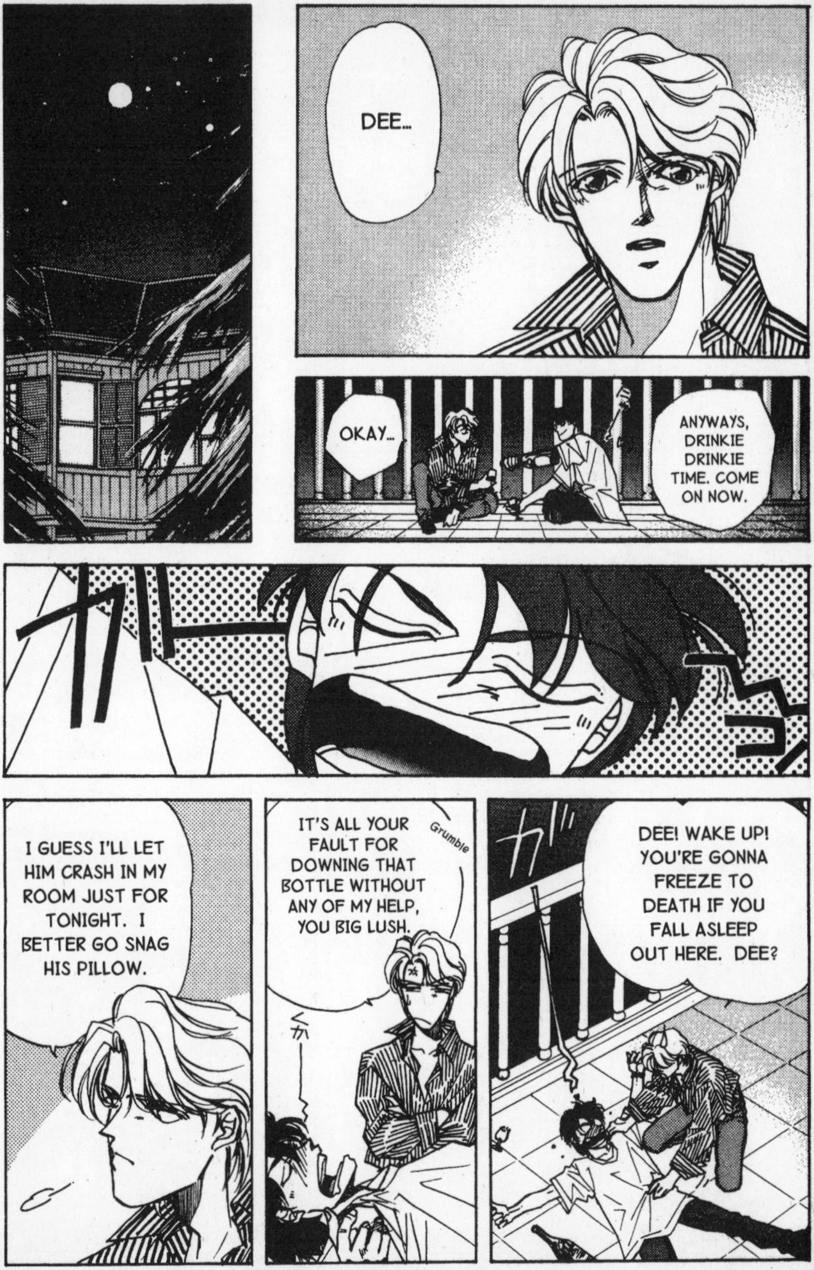
DEE...
ANYWAYS, DRINKIE DRINKIE TIME. COME ON NOW.
OKAY...
DEE! WAKE UP! YOU'RE GONNA FREEZE TO DEATH IF YOU FALL ASLEEP OUT HERE. DEE?
Grumble
IT'S ALL YOUR FAULT FOR DOWNING THAT BOTTLE WITHOUT ANY OF MY HELP, YOU BIG LUSH.
I GUESS I'LL LET HIM CRASH IN MY ROOM JUST FOR TONIGHT. I BETTER GO SNAG HIS PILLOW.

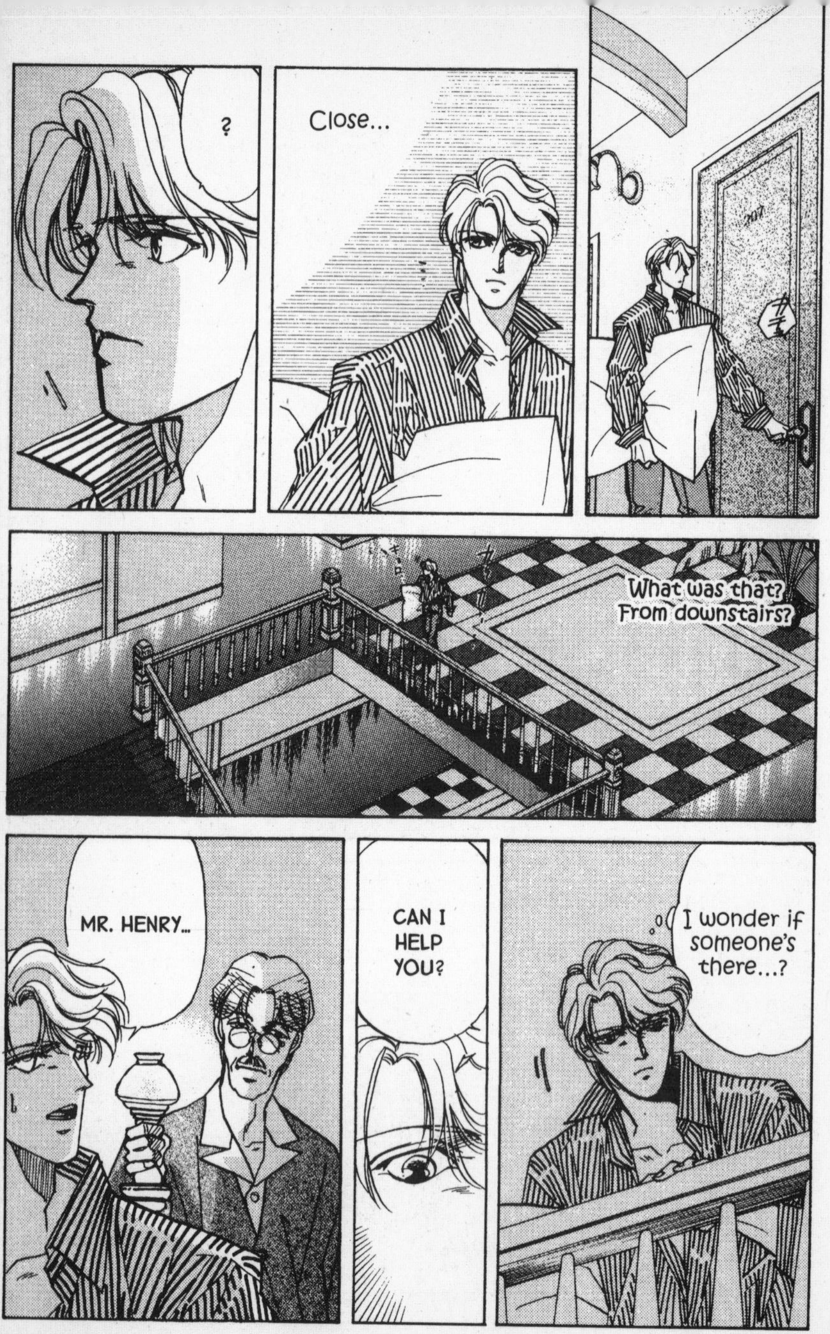
Close...
?
What was that? From downstairs?
I wonder if someone's there...?
CAN I HELP YOU?
MR. HENRY...

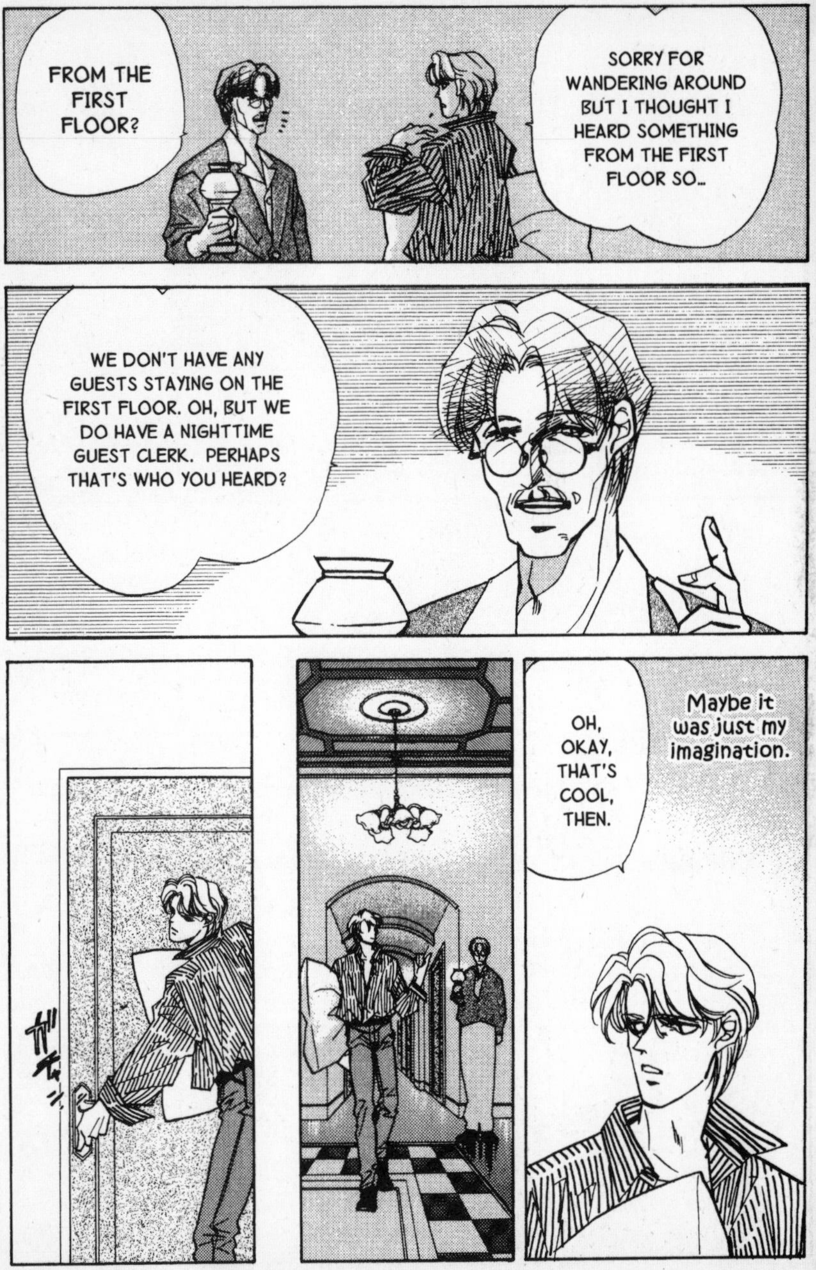
SORRY FOR WANDERING AROUND BUT I THOUGHT I HEARD SOMETHING FROM THE FIRST FLOOR SO...
FROM THE FIRST FLOOR?
WE DON'T HAVE ANY GUESTS STAYING ON THE FIRST FLOOR. OH, BUT WE DO HAVE A NIGHTTIME GUEST CLERK. PERHAPS THAT'S WHO YOU HEARD?
OH, OKAY, THAT'S COOL, THEN.
Maybe it was just my imagination.

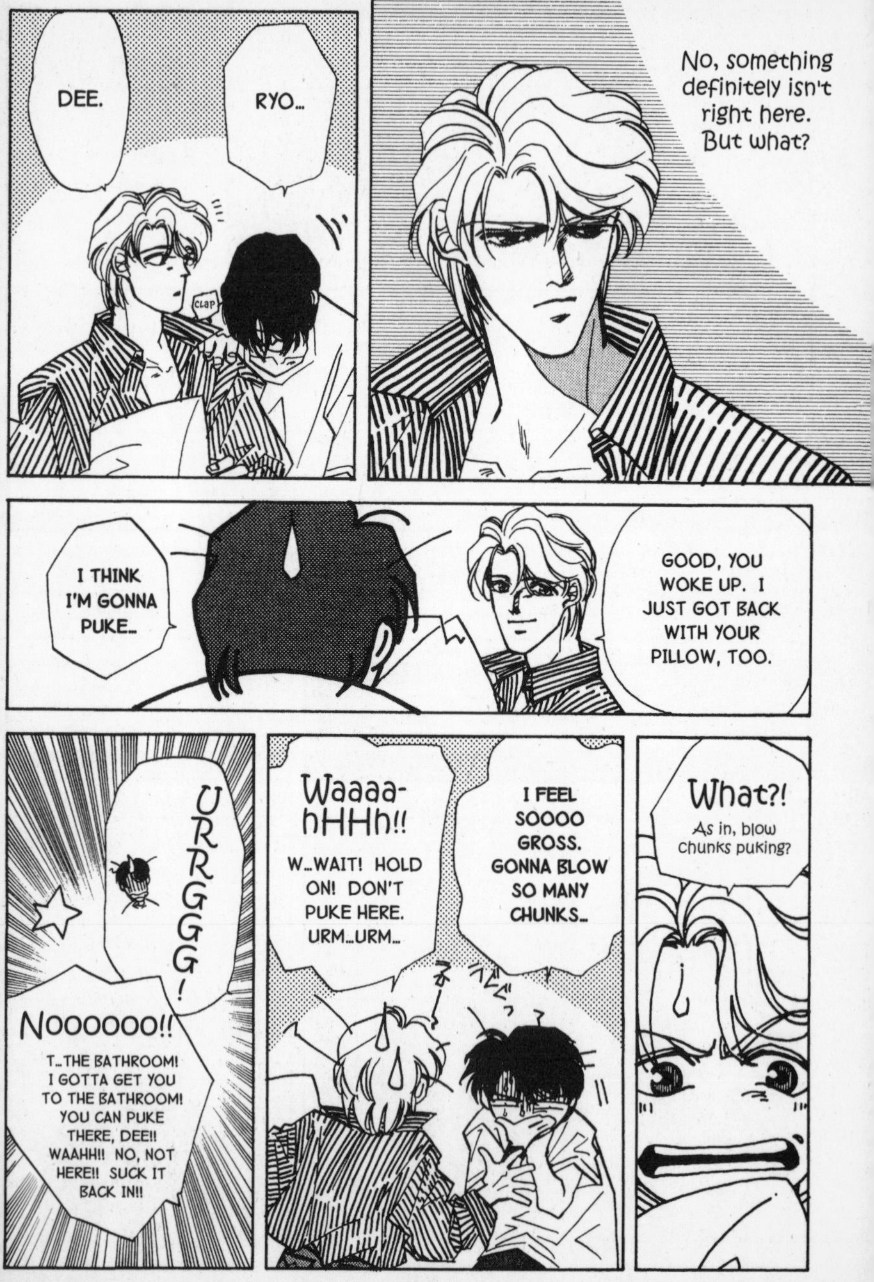
No, something definitely isn't right here. But what?
RYO...
DEE.
CLAP
GOOD, YOU WOKE UP. I JUST GOT BACK WITH YOUR PILLOW, TOO.
I THINK I'M GONNA PUKE..
What?! As in, blow chunks puking?
I FEEL SOOOO GROSS. GONNA BLOW SO MANY CHUNKS..
Waaaa-hHHh!! W...WAIT! HOLD ON! DON'T PUKE HERE. URM...URM...
URRGGG!
Noooooo!! T..THE BATHROOM! I GOTTA GET YOU TO THE BATHROOM! YOU CAN PUKE THERE, DEE!! WAAHH!! NO, NOT HERE!! SUCK IT BACK IN!!

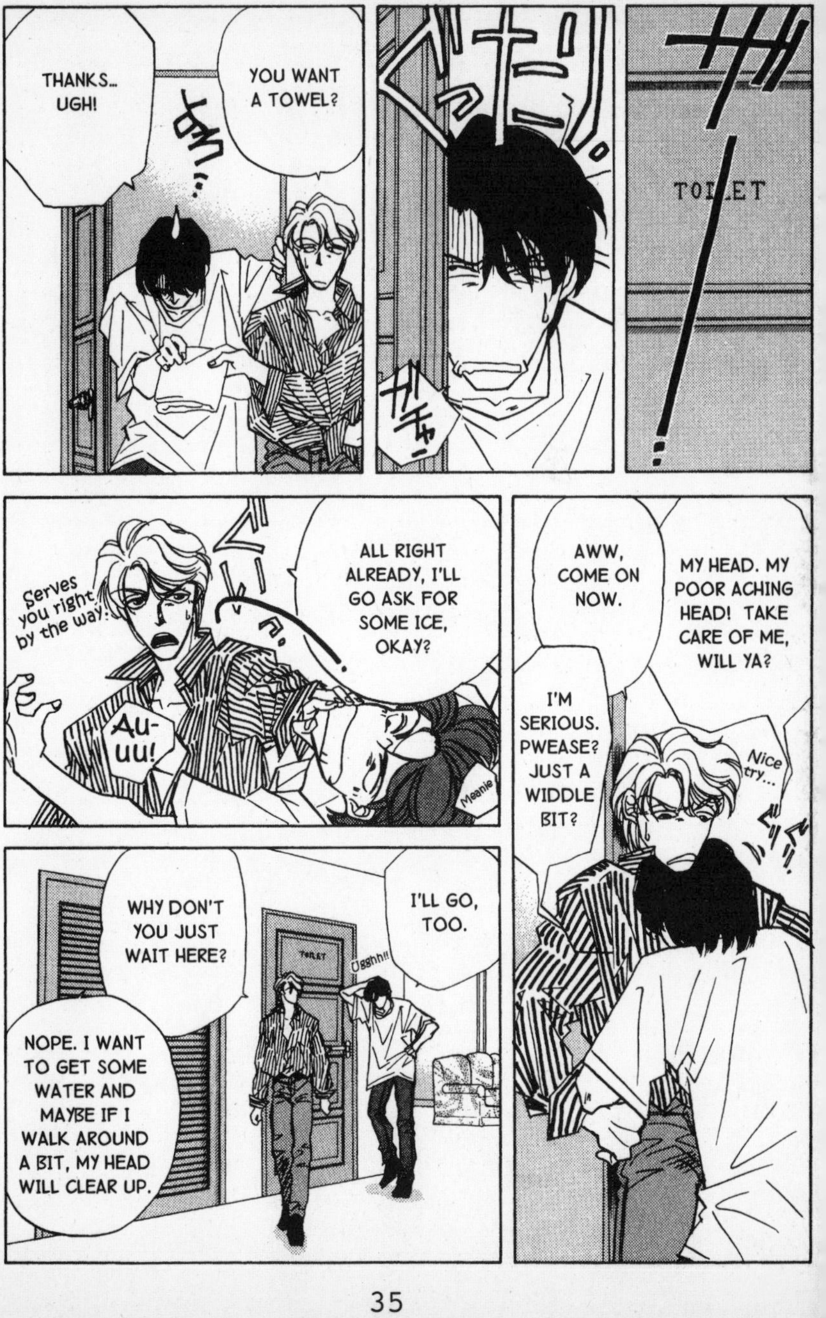
TOILET
YOU WANT A TOWEL?
THANKS... UGH!
MY HEAD. MY POOR ACHING HEAD! TAKE CARE OF ME, WILL YA?
AWW, COME ON NOW.
I'M SERIOUS. PWEASE? JUST A WIDDLE BIT?
Nice try...
ALL RIGHT ALREADY, I'LL GO ASK FOR SOME ICE, OKAY?
Serves you right by the way.
Au-uu!
Meanie
I'LL GO, TOO.
WHY DON'T YOU JUST WAIT HERE?
TOILET
Ugghh!!
NOPE. I WANT TO GET SOME WATER AND MAYBE IF I WALK AROUND A BIT, MY HEAD WILL CLEAR UP.

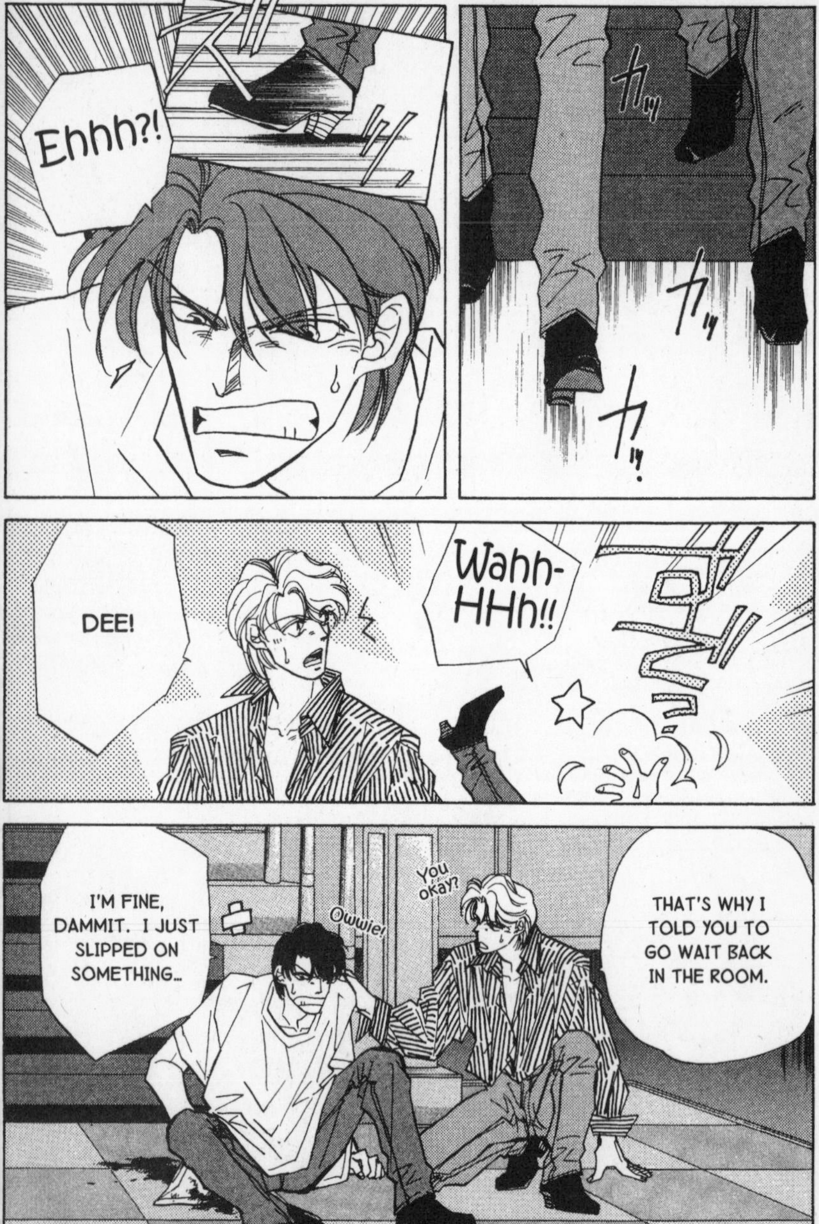
Ehhh?!
Wahh-HHh!!
DEE!
THAT'S WHY I TOLD YOU TO GO WAIT BACK IN THE ROOM.
You okay?
Owwie!
I'M FINE, DAMMIT. I JUST SLIPPED ON SOMETHING...

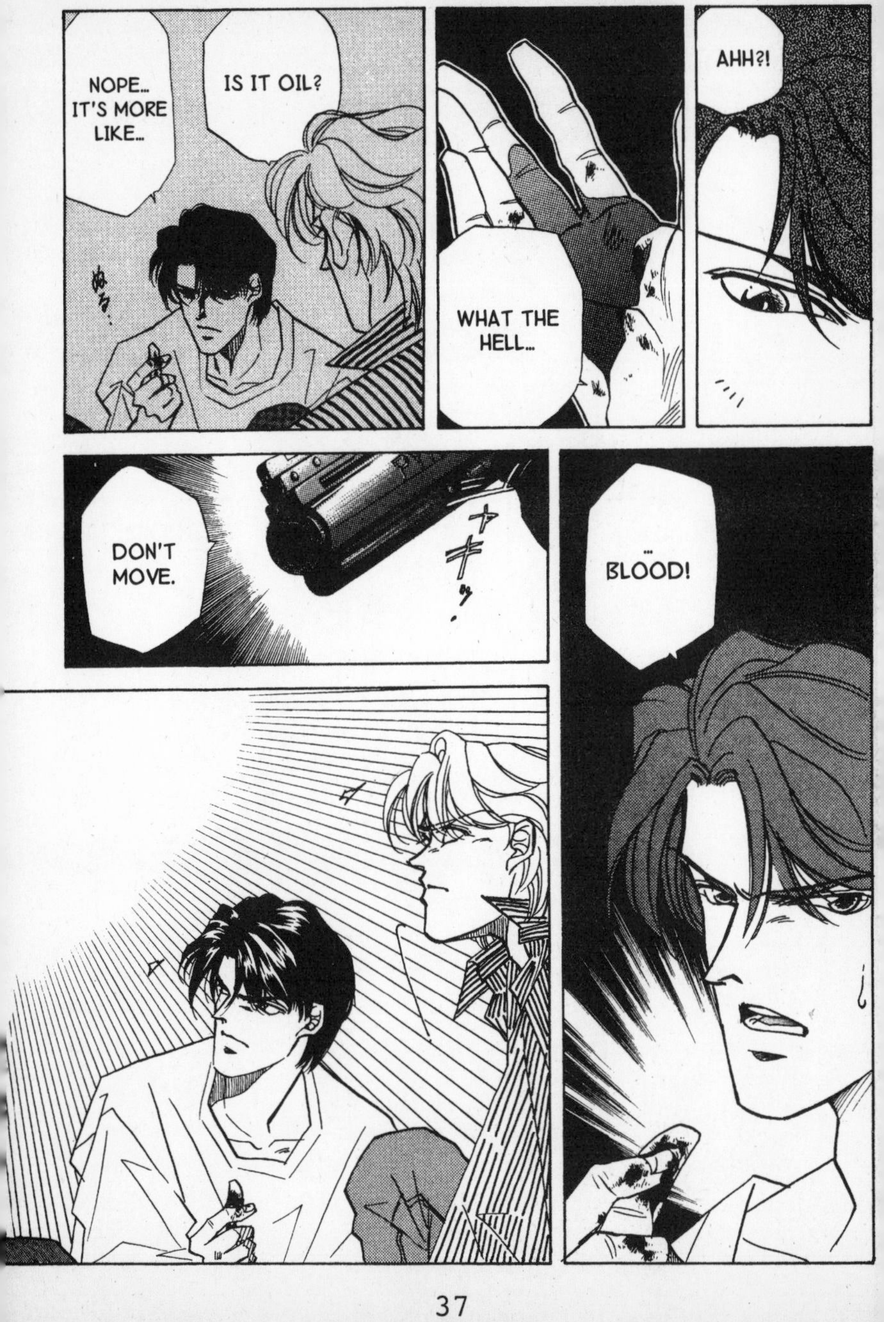
AHH?!
WHAT THE HELL...
IS IT OIL?
NOPE... IT'S MORE LIKE...
...BLOOD!
DON'T MOVE.

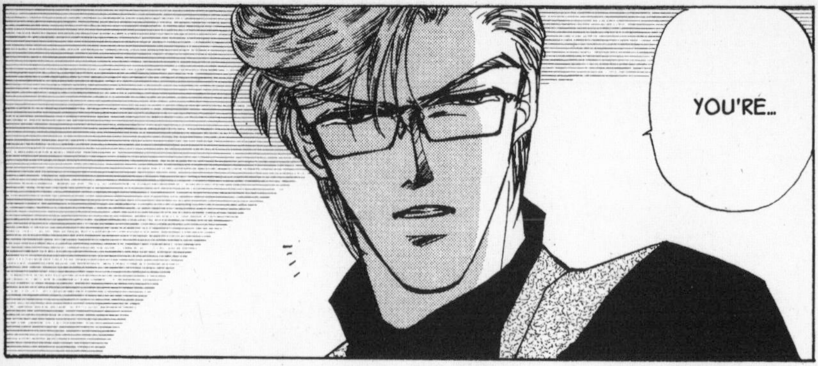
YOU'RE...
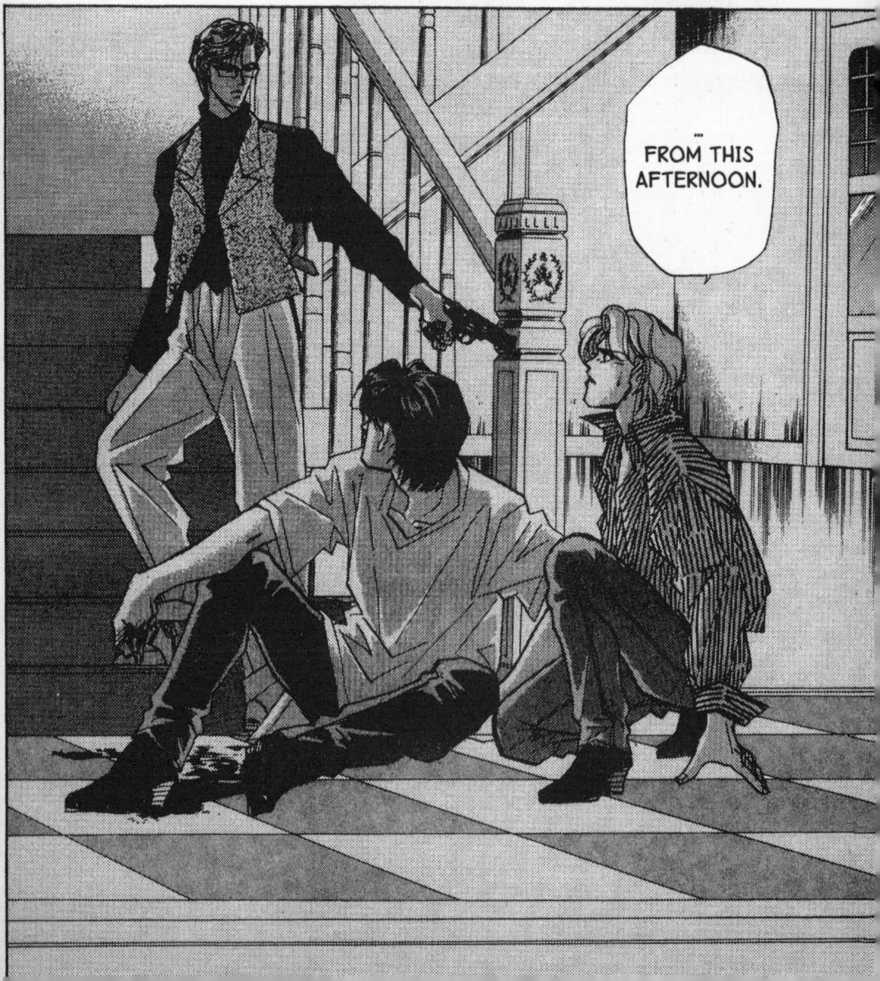
...FROM THIS AFTERNOON.

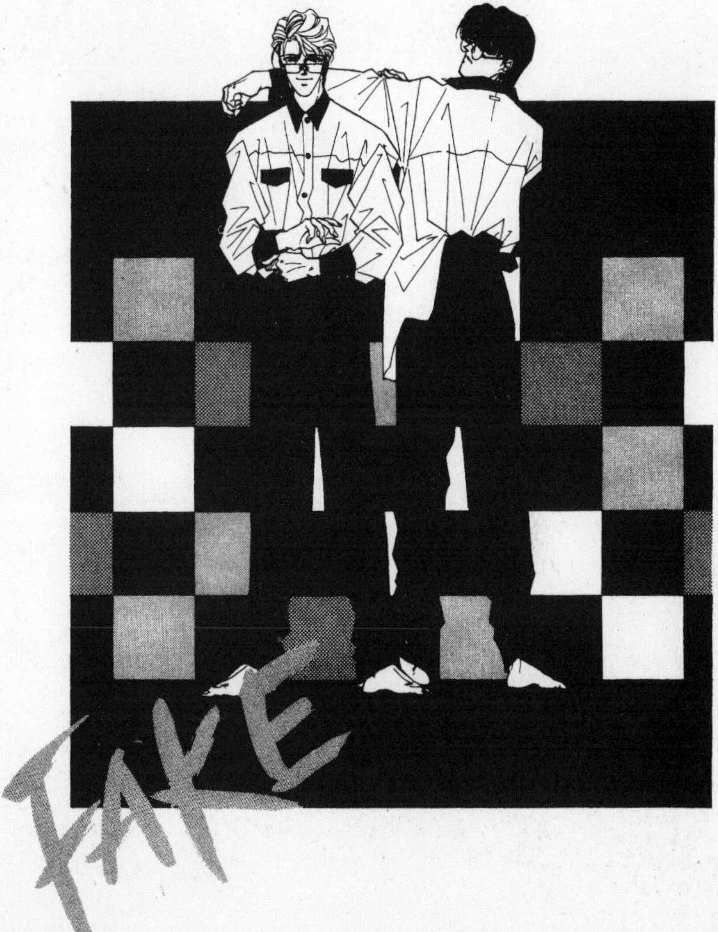
FAKE

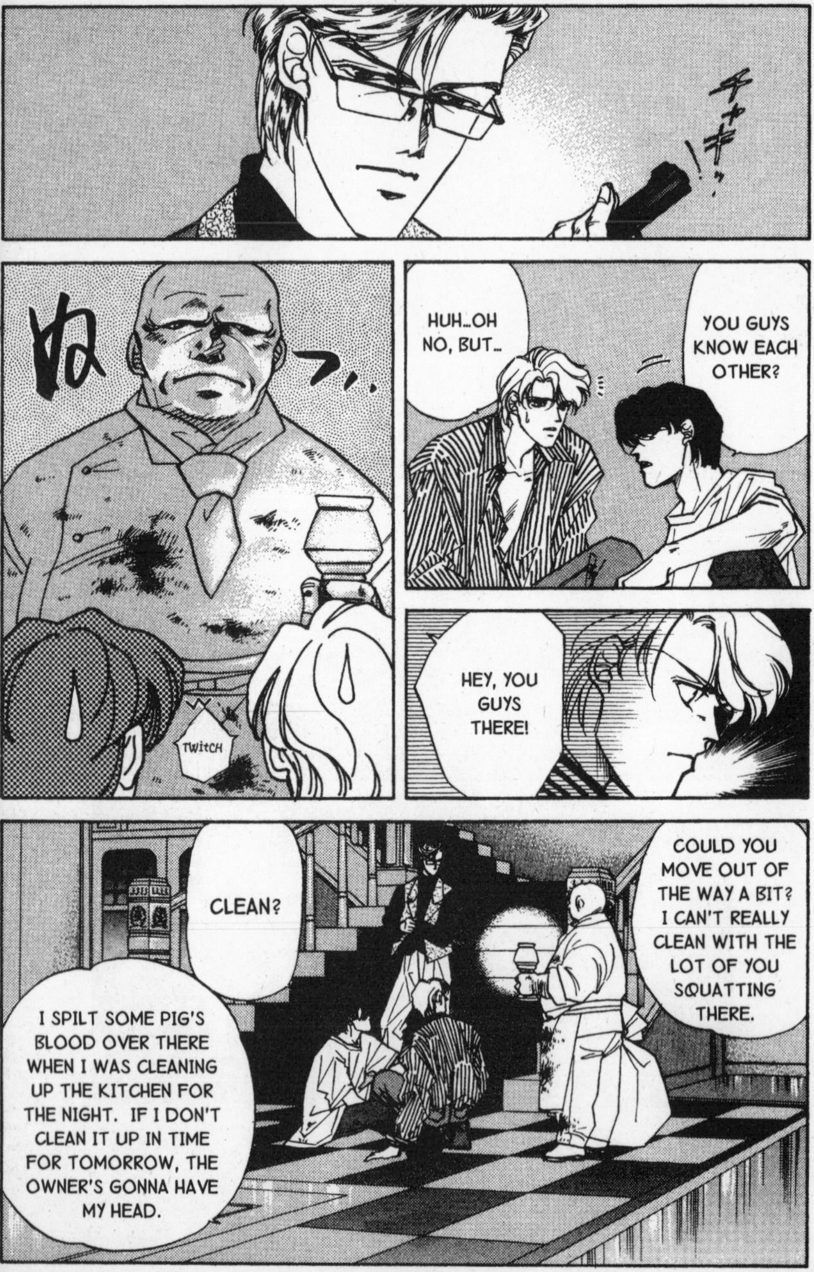
YOU GUYS KNOW EACH OTHER?
HUH...OH NO, BUT...
HEY, YOU GUYS THERE!
ぬっ...
TWITCH
COULD YOU MOVE OUT OF THE WAY A BIT? I CAN'T REALLY CLEAN WITH THE LOT OF YOU SQUATTING THERE.
CLEAN?
I SPILT SOME PIG'S BLOOD OVER THERE WHEN I WAS CLEANING UP THE KITCHEN FOR THE NIGHT. IF I DON'T CLEAN IT UP IN TIME FOR TOMORROW, THE OWNER'S GONNA HAVE MY HEAD.

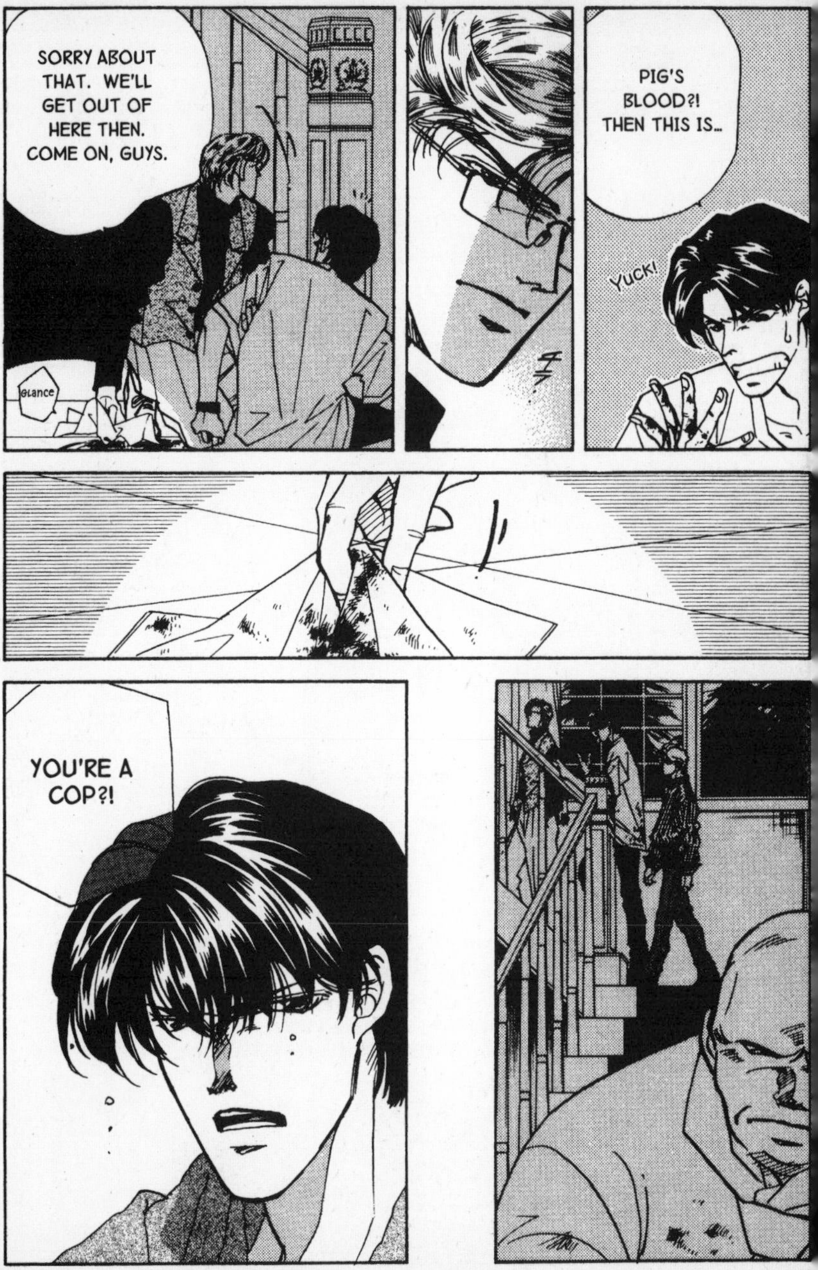
PIG'S BLOOD?! THEN THIS IS...
YUCK!
SORRY ABOUT THAT. WE'LL GET OUT OF HERE THEN. COME ON, GUYS.
GLANCE
YOU'RE A COP?!

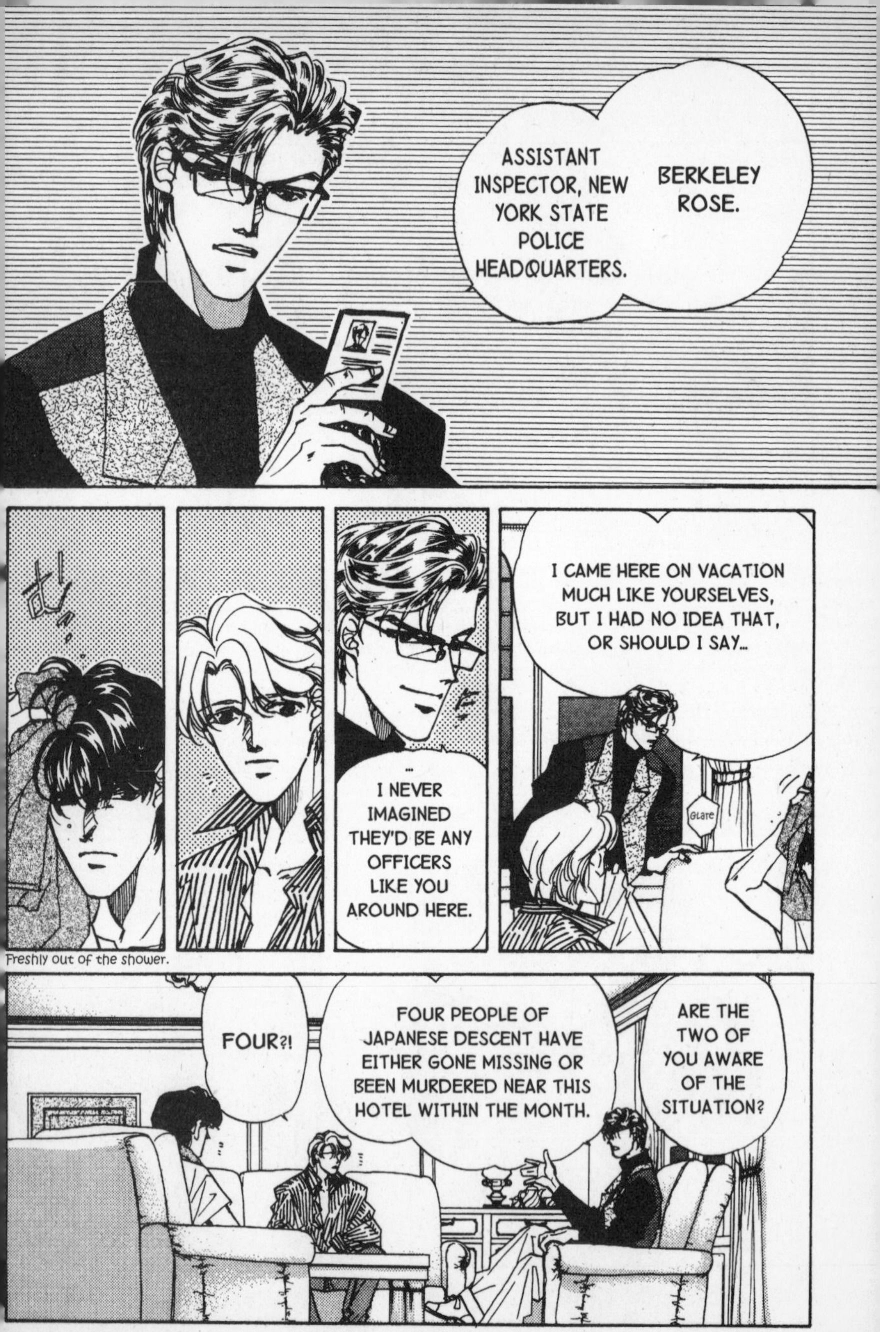
BERKELEY ROSE.
ASSISTANT INSPECTOR, NEW YORK STATE POLICE HEADQUARTERS.
I CAME HERE ON VACATION MUCH LIKE YOURSELVES, BUT I HAD NO IDEA THAT, OR SHOULD I SAY...
Glare
... I NEVER IMAGINED THEY'D BE ANY OFFICERS LIKE YOU AROUND HERE.
Freshly out of the shower.
ARE THE TWO OF YOU AWARE OF THE SITUATION?
FOUR PEOPLE OF JAPANESE DESCENT HAVE EITHER GONE MISSING OR BEEN MURDERED NEAR THIS HOTEL WITHIN THE MONTH.
FOUR?!

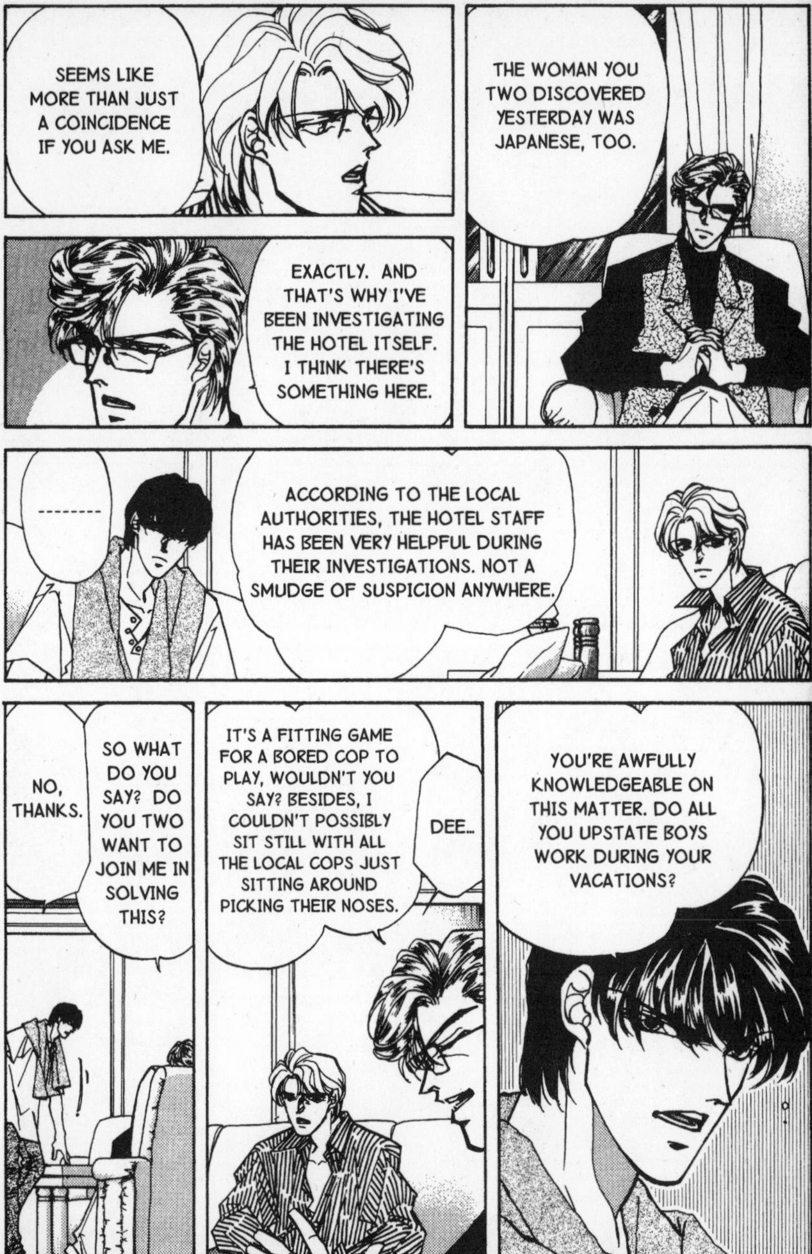
THE WOMAN YOU TWO DISCOVERED YESTERDAY WAS JAPANESE, TOO.
SEEMS LIKE MORE THAN JUST A COINCIDENCE IF YOU ASK ME.
EXACTLY. AND THAT'S WHY I'VE BEEN INVESTIGATING THE HOTEL ITSELF. I THINK THERE'S SOMETHING HERE.
ACCORDING TO THE LOCAL AUTHORITIES, THE HOTEL STAFF HAS BEEN VERY HELPFUL DURING THEIR INVESTIGATIONS. NOT A SMUDGE OF SUSPICION ANYWHERE.

YOU'RE AWFULLY KNOWLEDGEABLE ON THIS MATTER. DO ALL YOU UPSTATE BOYS WORK DURING YOUR VACATIONS?
DEE...
IT'S A FITTING GAME FOR A BORED COP TO PLAY, WOULDN'T YOU SAY? BESIDES, I COULDN'T POSSIBLY SIT STILL WITH ALL THE LOCAL COPS JUST SITTING AROUND PICKING THEIR NOSES.
SO WHAT DO YOU SAY? DO YOU TWO WANT TO JOIN ME IN SOLVING THIS?
NO, THANKS.

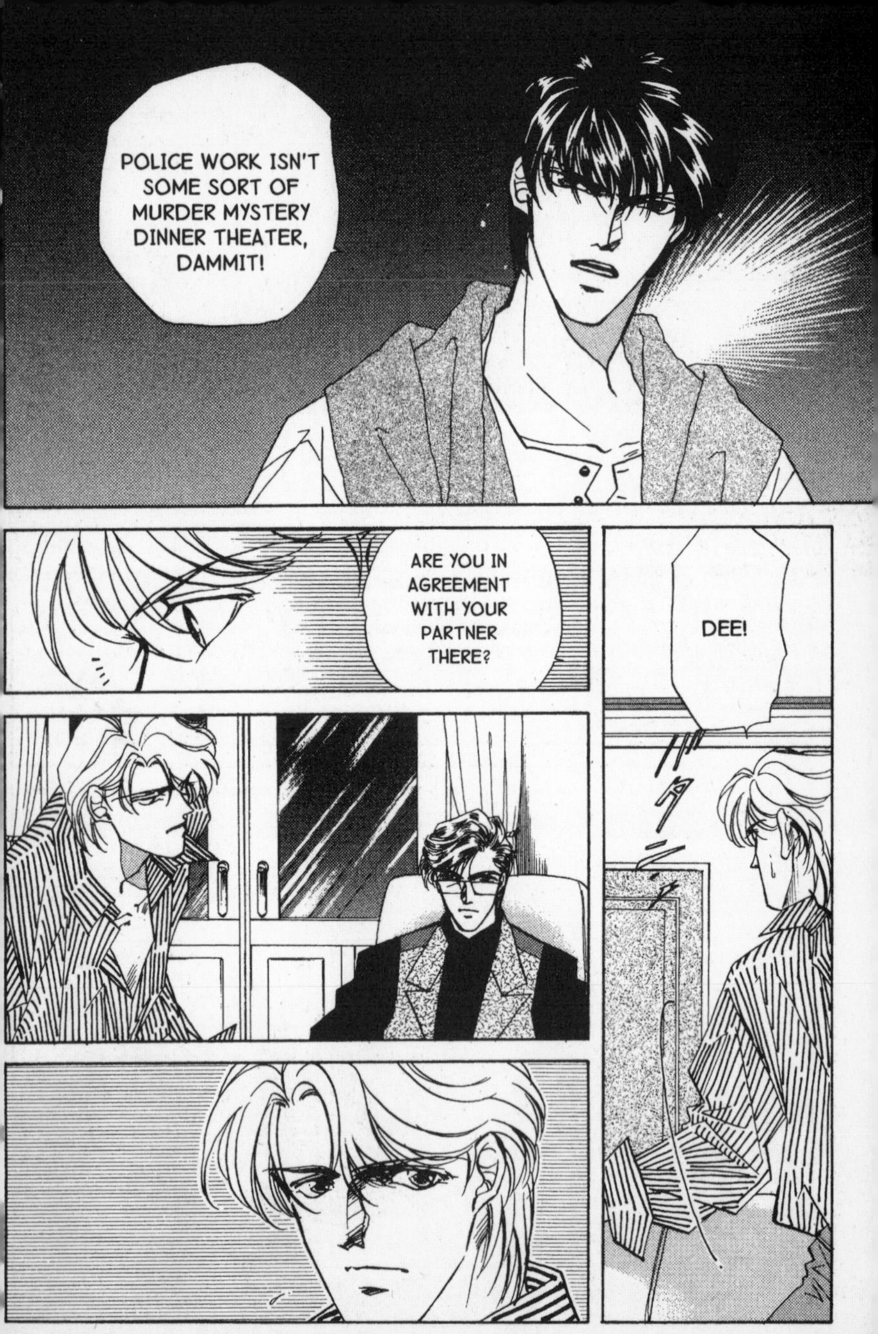
POLICE WORK ISN'T SOME SORT OF MURDER MYSTERY DINNER THEATER, DAMMIT!
DEE!
ARE YOU IN AGREEMENT WITH YOUR PARTNER THERE?

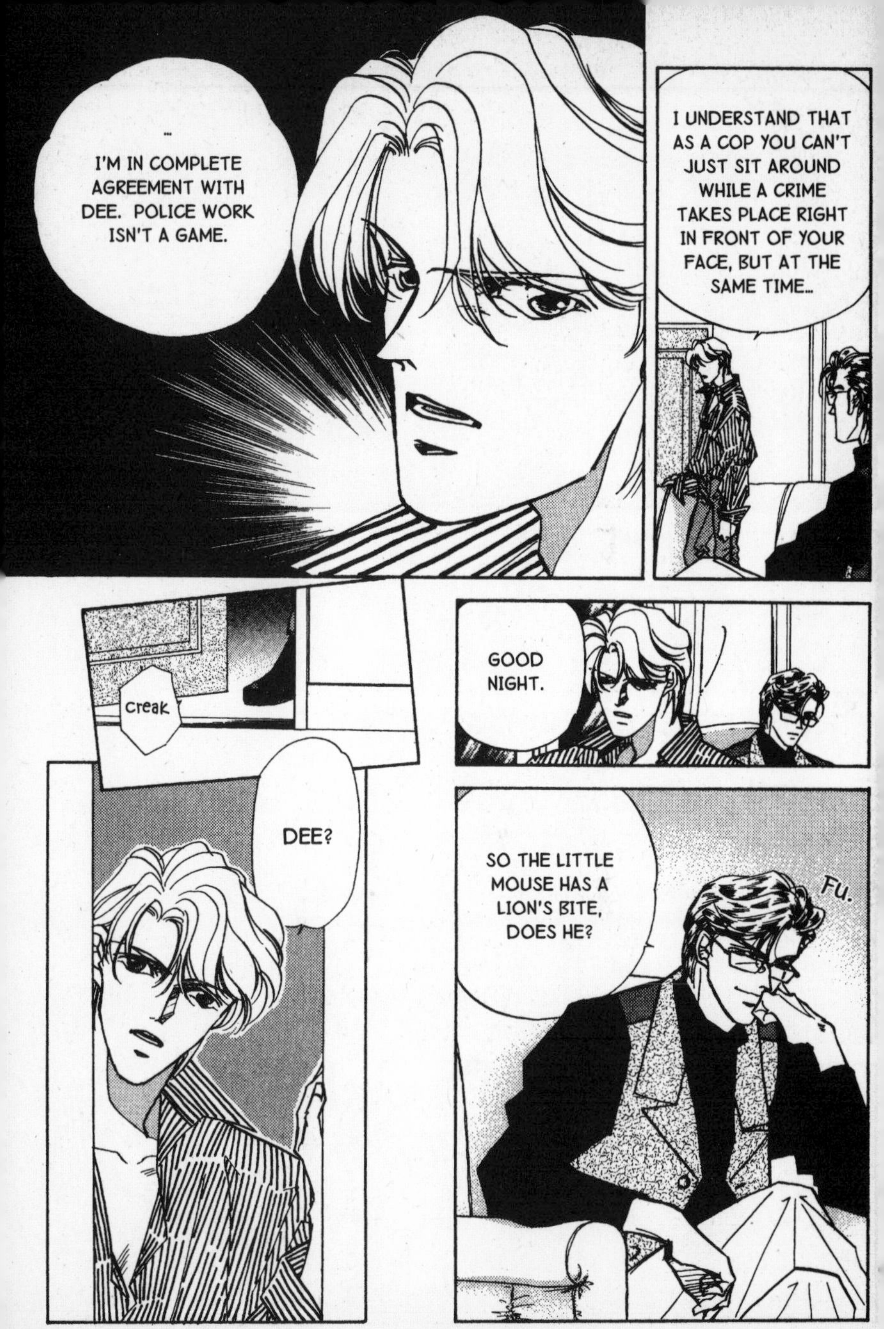
I UNDERSTAND THAT AS A COP YOU CAN'T JUST SIT AROUND WHILE A CRIME TAKES PLACE RIGHT IN FRONT OF YOUR FACE, BUT AT THE SAME TIME...
... I'M IN COMPLETE AGREEMENT WITH DEE. POLICE WORK ISN'T A GAME.
GOOD NIGHT.
creak
SO THE LITTLE MOUSE HAS A LION'S BITE, DOES HE?
Fu.
DEE?

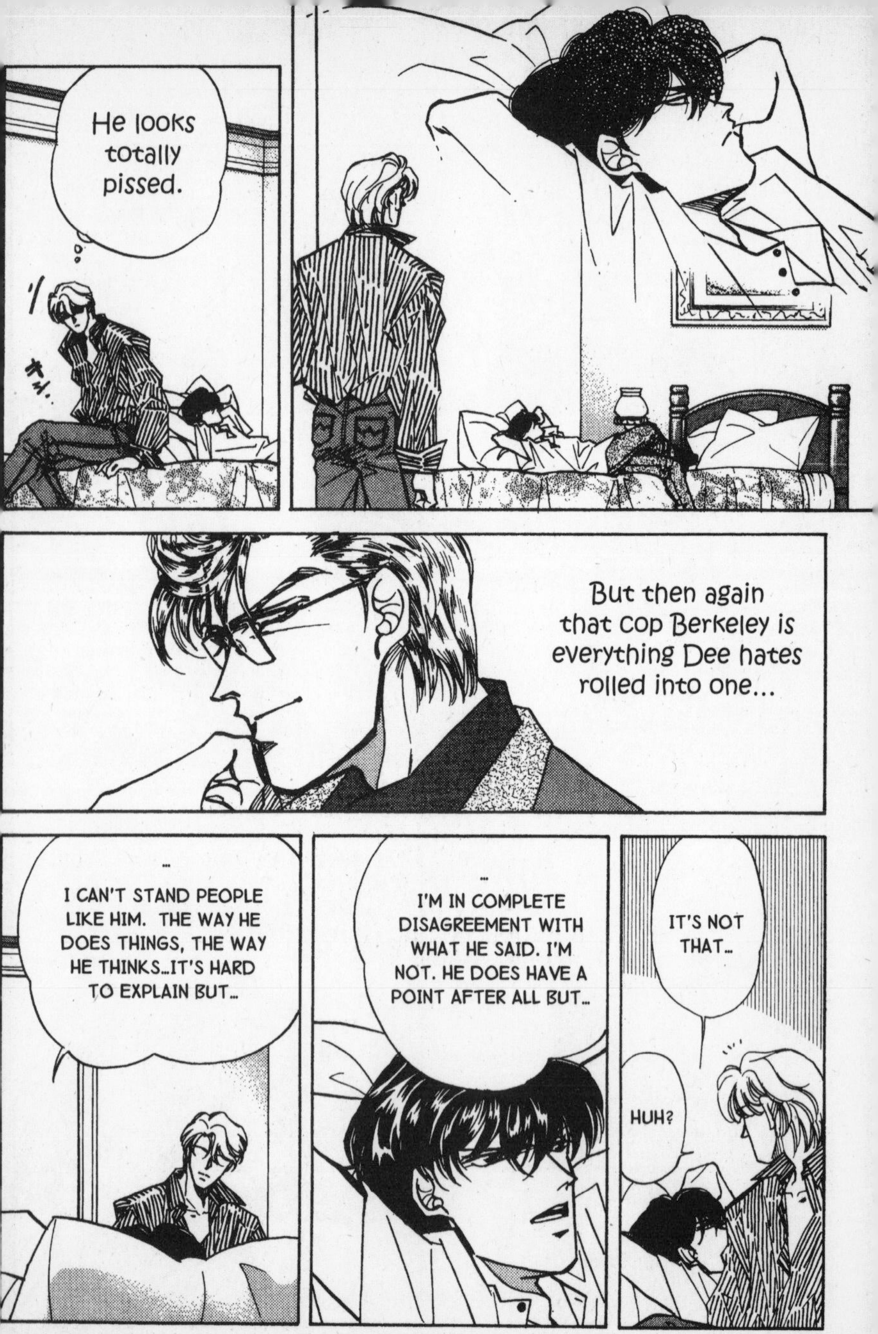
He looks totally pissed.
キシ…
But then again that cop Berkeley is everything Dee hates rolled into one...
IT'S NOT THAT...
HUH?
... I'M IN COMPLETE DISAGREEMENT WITH WHAT HE SAID. I'M NOT. HE DOES HAVE A POINT AFTER ALL BUT...
... I CAN'T STAND PEOPLE LIKE HIM. THE WAY HE DOES THINGS, THE WAY HE THINKS...IT'S HARD TO EXPLAIN BUT...

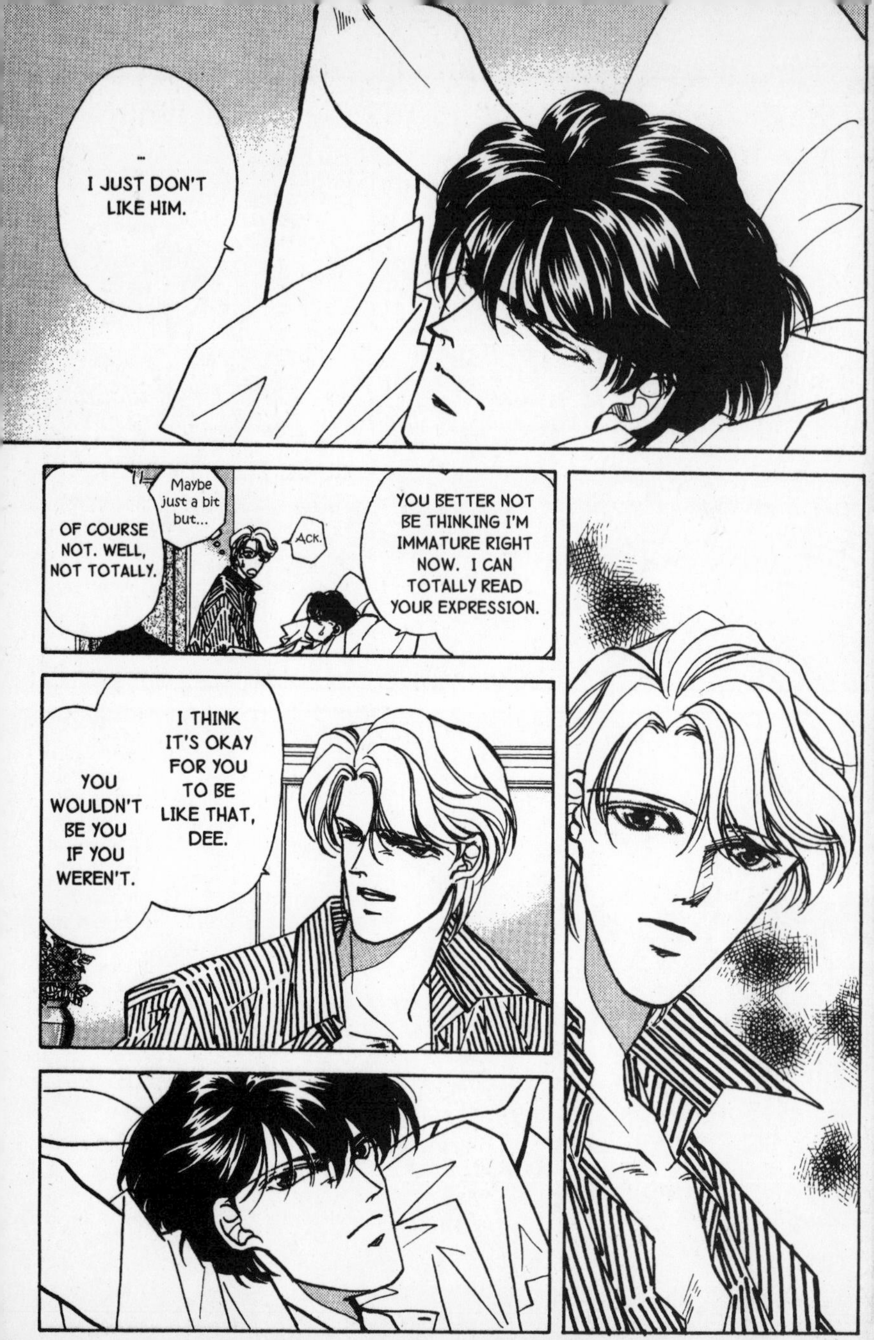
... I JUST DON'T LIKE HIM.
YOU BETTER NOT BE THINKING I'M IMMATURE RIGHT NOW. I CAN TOTALLY READ YOUR EXPRESSION.
Ack.
OF COURSE NOT. WELL, NOT TOTALLY.
Maybe just a bit but...
I THINK IT'S OKAY FOR YOU TO BE LIKE THAT, DEE.
YOU WOULDN'T BE YOU IF YOU WEREN'T.

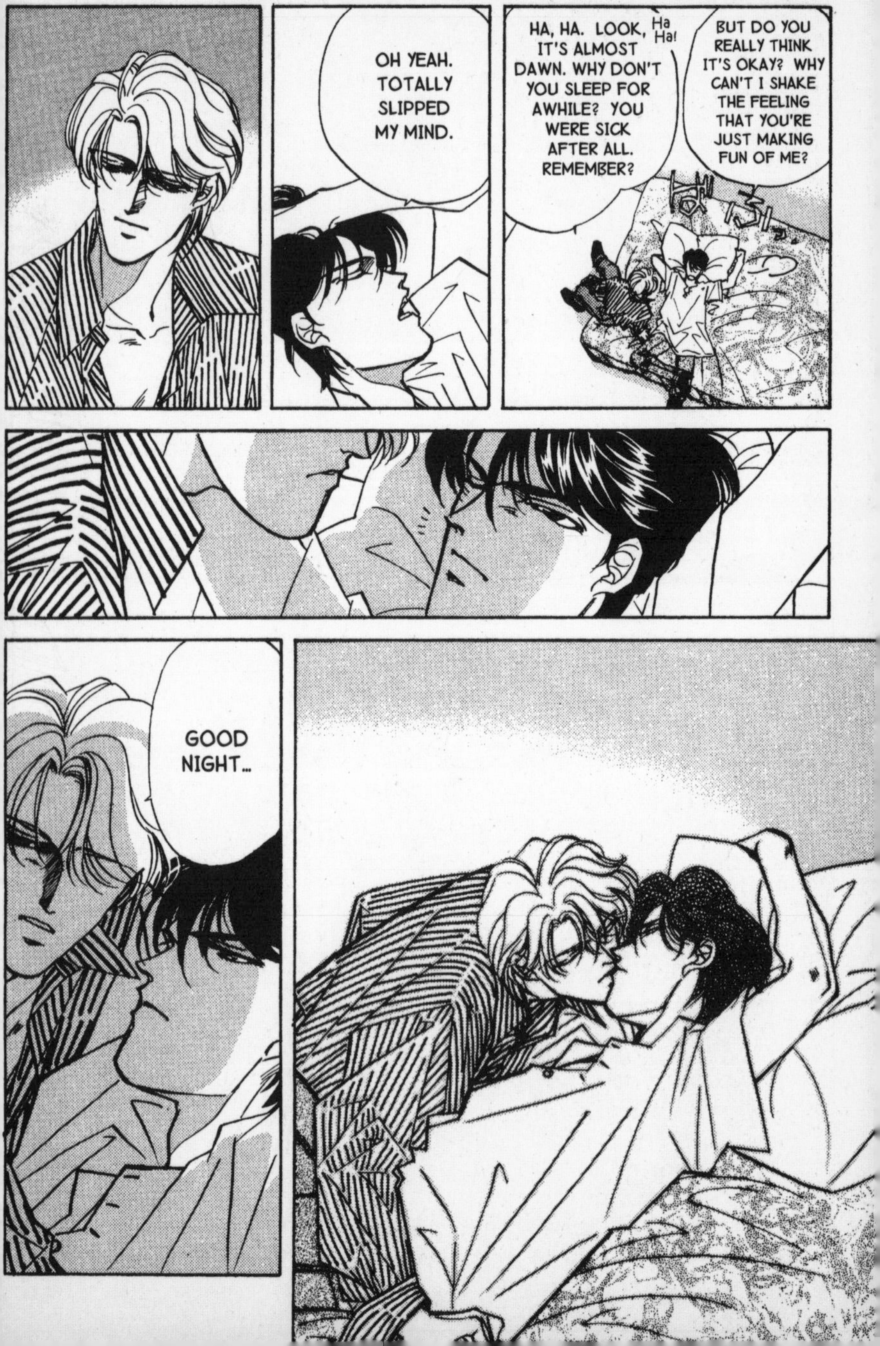
BUT DO YOU REALLY THINK IT'S OKAY? WHY CAN'T I SHAKE THE FEELING THAT YOU'RE JUST MAKING FUN OF ME?
HA, HA. LOOK, IT'S ALMOST DAWN. WHY DON'T YOU SLEEP FOR AWHILE? YOU WERE SICK AFTER ALL. REMEMBER?
Ha Ha!
OH YEAH. TOTALLY SLIPPED MY MIND.
GOOD NIGHT...

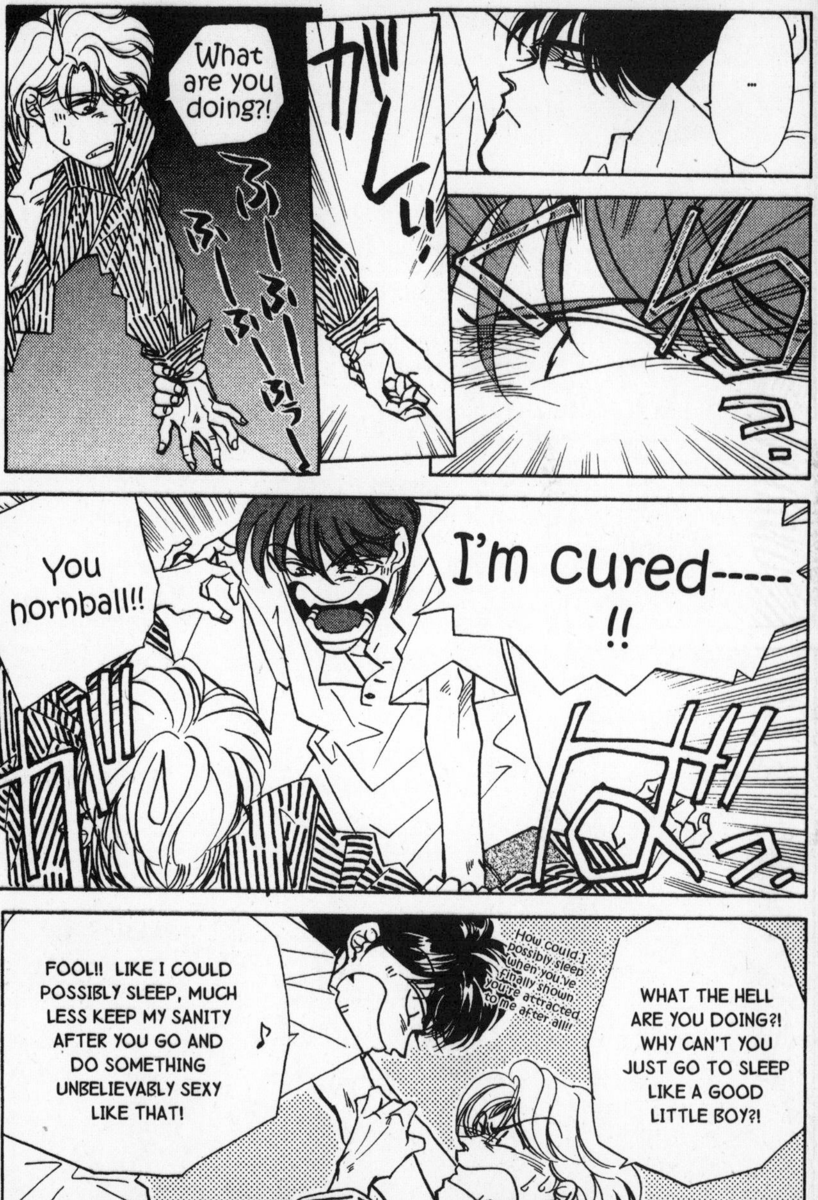
...
What are you doing?!
I'm cured-----!!
You hornball!!
WHAT THE HELL ARE YOU DOING?! WHY CAN'T YOU JUST GO TO SLEEP LIKE A GOOD LITTLE BOY?!
How could I possibly sleep when you've finally shown you're attracted to me after all!!
FOOL!! LIKE I COULD POSSIBLY SLEEP, MUCH LESS KEEP MY SANITY AFTER YOU GO AND DO SOMETHING UNBELIEVABLY SEXY LIKE THAT! ♪

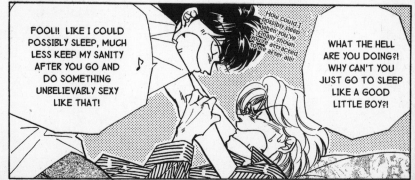

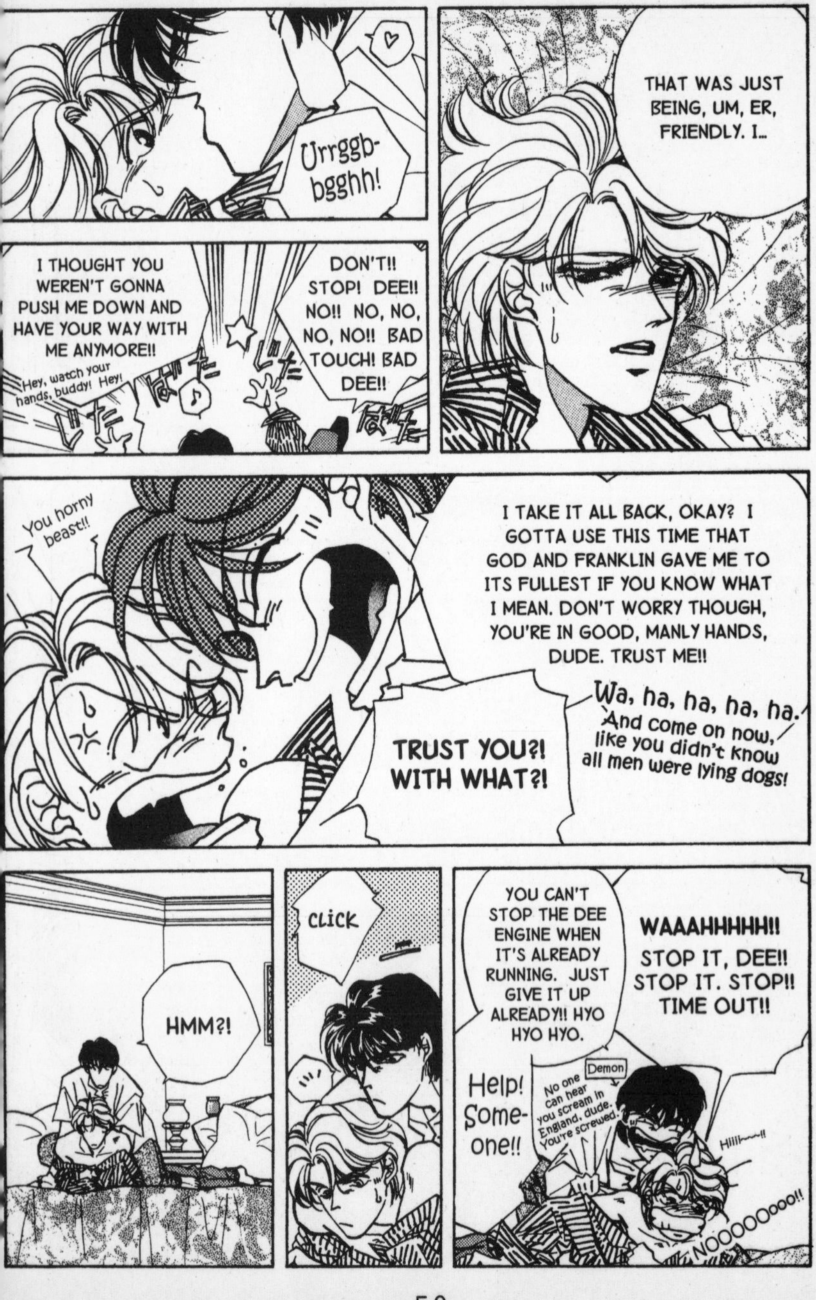
THAT WAS JUST BEING, UM, ER, FRIENDLY. I...
Urrggb-bgghh!
DON'T!! STOP! DEE!! NO!! NO, NO, NO, NO!! BAD TOUCH! BAD DEE!!
I THOUGHT YOU WEREN'T GONNA PUSH ME DOWN AND HAVE YOUR WAY WITH ME ANYMORE!!
Hey, watch your hands, buddy! Hey!
I TAKE IT ALL BACK, OKAY? I GOTTA USE THIS TIME THAT GOD AND FRANKLIN GAVE ME TO ITS FULLEST IF YOU KNOW WHAT I MEAN. DON'T WORRY THOUGH, YOU'RE IN GOOD, MANLY HANDS, DUDE. TRUST ME!!
Wa, ha, ha, ha, ha.
And come on now, like you didn't know all men were lying dogs!
TRUST YOU?! WITH WHAT?!
You horny beast!!
WAAAHHHHH!! STOP IT, DEE!! STOP IT. STOP!! TIME OUT!!
YOU CAN'T STOP THE DEE ENGINE WHEN IT'S ALREADY RUNNING. JUST GIVE IT UP ALREADY!! HYO HYO HYO.
Demon
No one can hear you scream in England, dude. You're screwed.
Help! Some-one!!
Hiiii~~!!
NOOOOOooo!!
CLICK
HMM?!

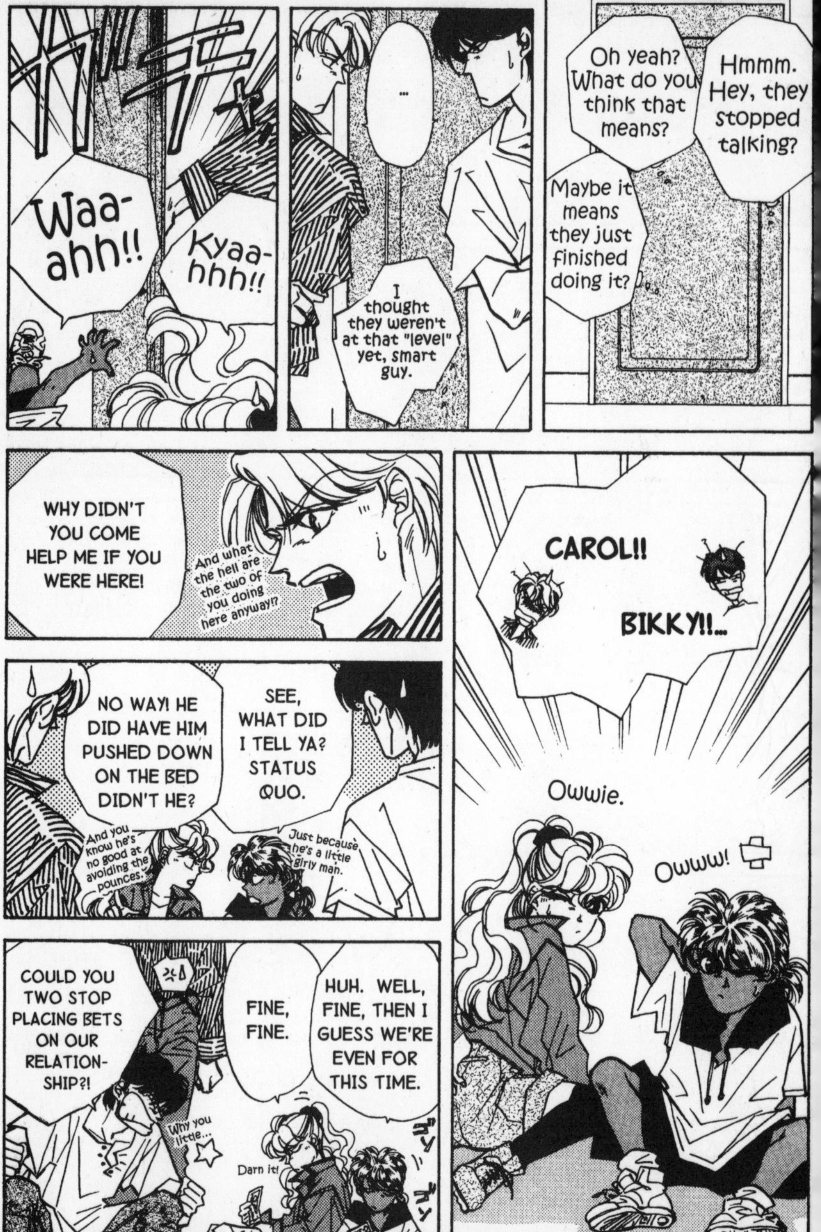
Hmmm. Hey, they stopped talking?
Oh yeah? What do you think that means?
Maybe it means they just finished doing it?
...
I thought they weren't at that "level" yet, smart guy.
Kyaa-hhh!!
Waa-ahh!!
CAROL!!
BIKKY!!...
Owwww!
Owwie.
And what the hell are the two of you doing here anyway!?
WHY DIDN'T YOU COME HELP ME IF YOU WERE HERE!
SEE, WHAT DID I TELL YA? STATUS QUO.
NO WAY! HE DID HAVE HIM PUSHED DOWN ON THE BED DIDN'T HE?
Just because he's a little girly man.
And you know he's no good at avoiding the pounces.
HUH. WELL, FINE, THEN I GUESS WE'RE EVEN FOR THIS TIME.
FINE, FINE.
COULD YOU TWO STOP PLACING BETS ON OUR RELATION-SHIP?!
Darn it!
Why you little...

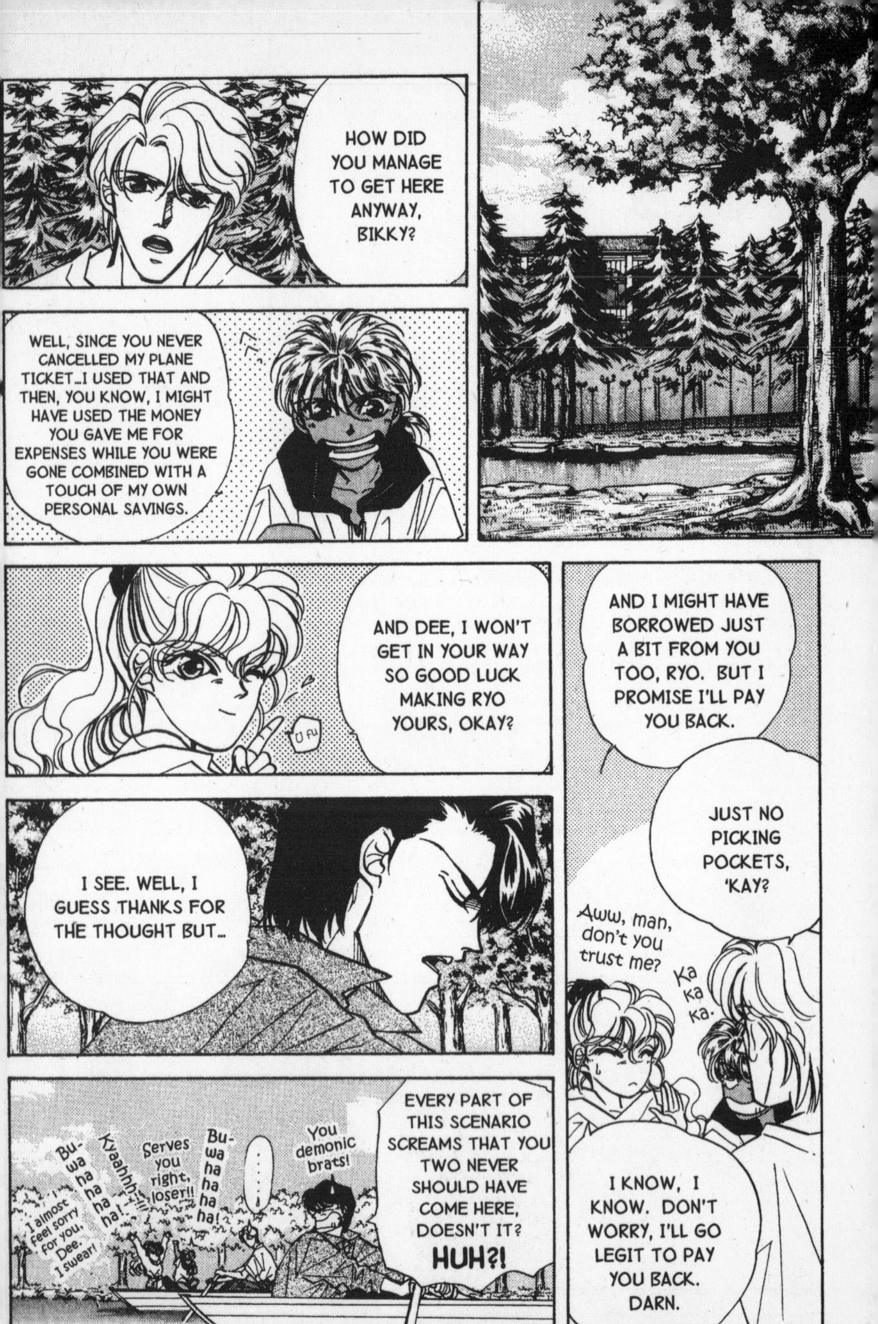
HOW DID YOU MANAGE TO GET HERE ANYWAY, BIKKY?
WELL, SINCE YOU NEVER CANCELLED MY PLANE TICKET...I USED THAT AND THEN, YOU KNOW, I MIGHT HAVE USED THE MONEY YOU GAVE ME FOR EXPENSES WHILE YOU WERE GONE COMBINED WITH A TOUCH OF MY OWN PERSONAL SAVINGS.
AND I MIGHT HAVE BORROWED JUST A BIT FROM YOU TOO, RYO. BUT I PROMISE I'LL PAY YOU BACK.
JUST NO PICKING POCKETS, 'KAY?
Aww, man, don't you trust me?
Ka ka ka.
I KNOW, I KNOW. DON'T WORRY, I'LL GO LEGIT TO PAY YOU BACK. DARN.
AND DEE, I WON'T GET IN YOUR WAY SO GOOD LUCK MAKING RYO YOURS, OKAY?
U fu
I SEE. WELL, I GUESS THANKS FOR THE THOUGHT BUT...
EVERY PART OF THIS SCENARIO SCREAMS THAT YOU TWO NEVER SHOULD HAVE COME HERE, DOESN'T IT? HUH?!
You demonic brats!
Bu-wa ha ha ha ha ha!
Serves you right, loser!!
Kyaahhh!!
Bu-wa ha ha ha ha!
I almost feel sorry for you, Dee. I swear!

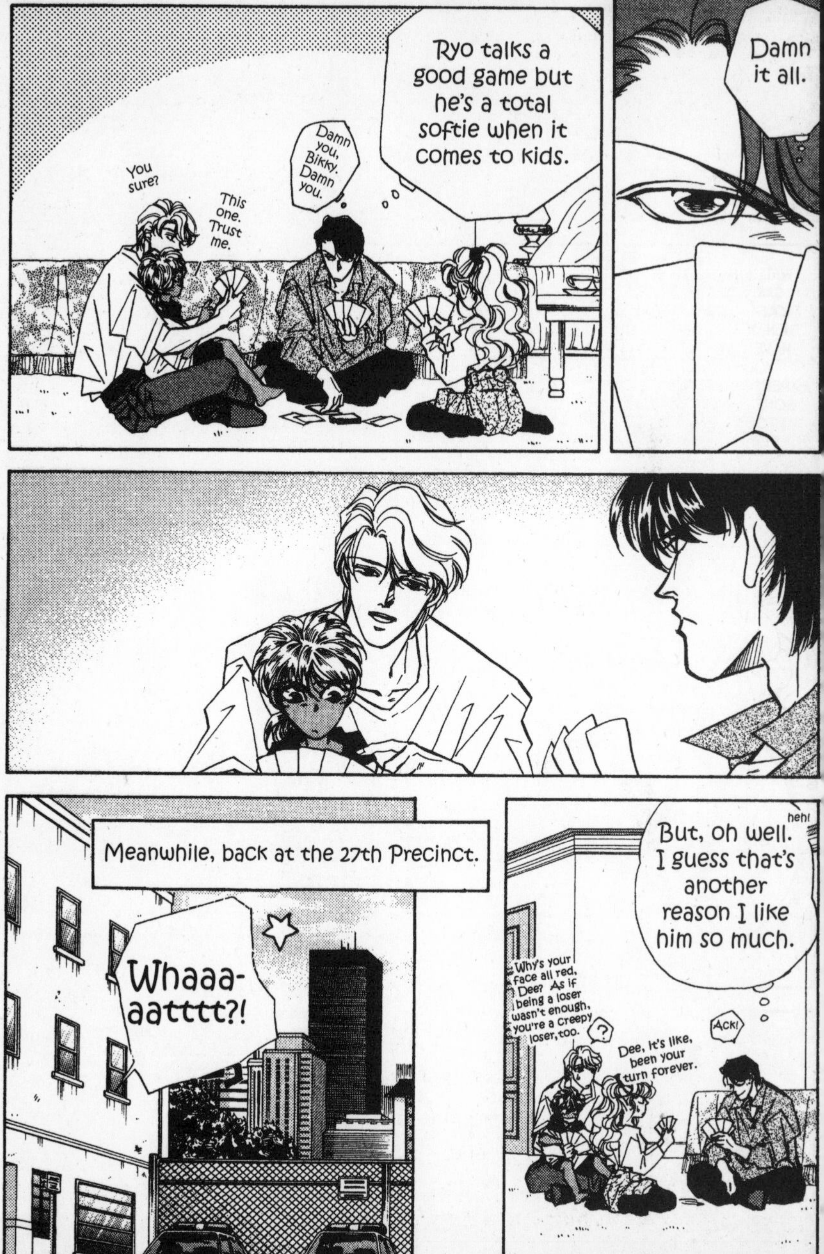
Damn it all.
Ryo talks a good game but he's a total softie when it comes to kids.
Damn you, Bikky. Damn you.
This one. Trust me.
You sure?
heh!
But, oh well. I guess that's another reason I like him so much.
Ack!
Dee, it's like, been your turn forever.
?
Why's your face all red, Dee? As if being a loser wasn't enough, you're a creepy loser, too.
Meanwhile, back at the 27th Precinct.
Whaaa-aatttt?!

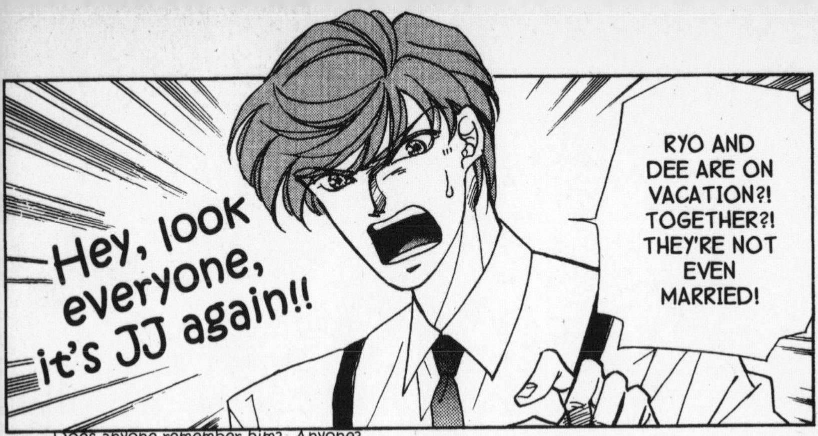
RYO AND DEE ARE ON VACATION?! TOGETHER?! THEY'RE NOT EVEN MARRIED!
Hey, look everyone, it's JJ again!!

Does anyone remember him? Anyone?

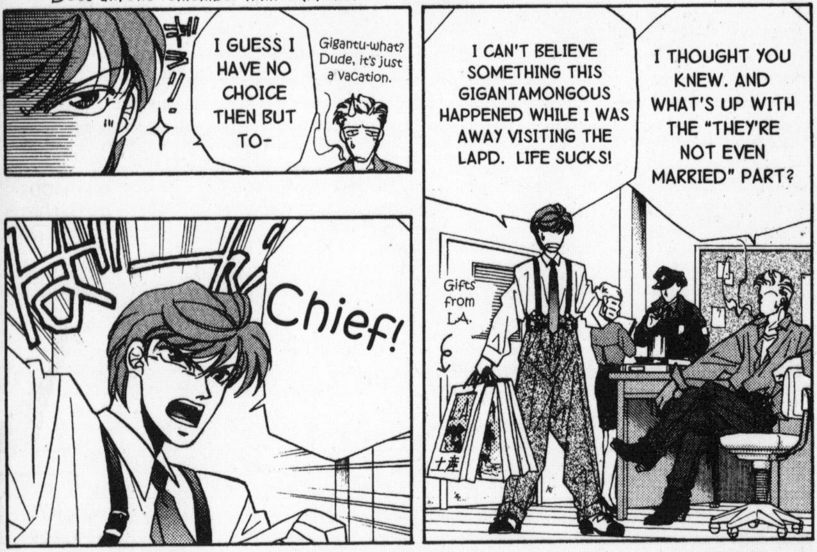
I CAN'T BELIEVE SOMETHING THIS GIGANTAMONGOUS HAPPENED WHILE I WAS AWAY VISITING THE LAPD. LIFE SUCKS!
I THOUGHT YOU KNEW. AND WHAT'S UP WITH THE "THEY'RE NOT EVEN MARRIED" PART?
Gifts from L.A.
I GUESS I HAVE NO CHOICE THEN BUT TO-
Gigantu-what? Dude, it's just a vacation.
Chief!

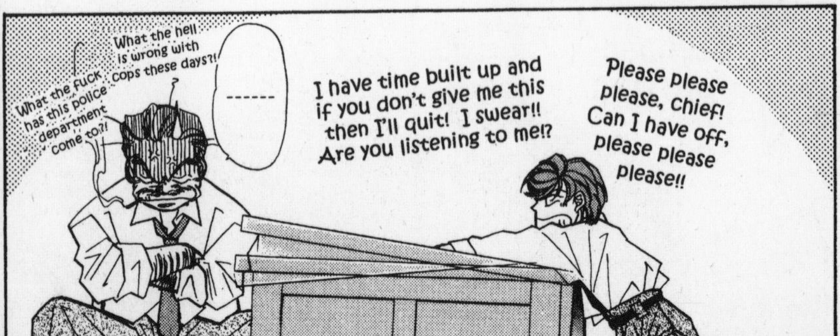
Please please please, Chief! Can I have off, please please please!!
I have time built up and if you don't give me this then I'll quit! I swear!! Are you listening to me!?

What the hell is wrong with cops these days?!
What the fuck has this police department come to?!

Especially like his good old buddy when it comes down to the little things.

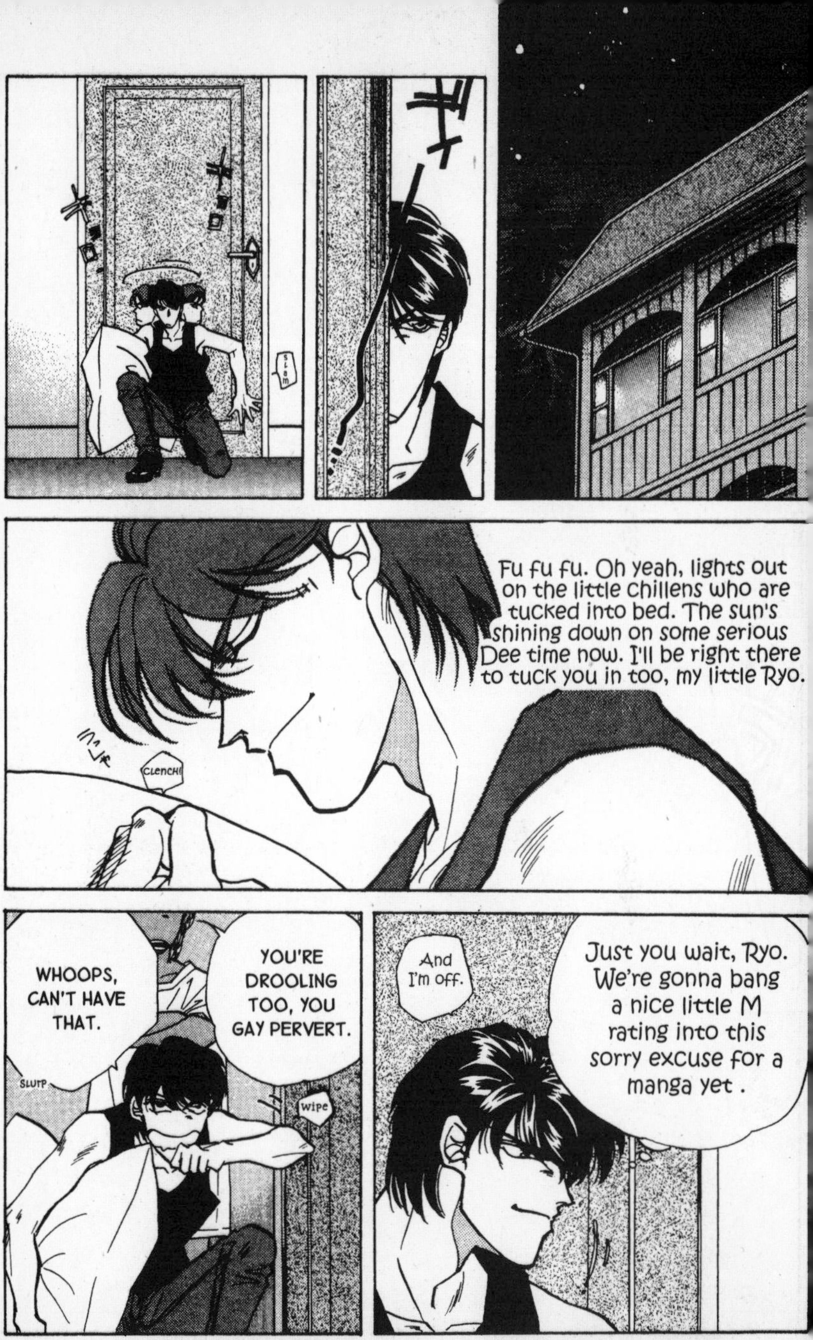

slam
Fu fu fu. Oh yeah, lights out on the little chillens who are tucked into bed. The sun's shining down on some serious Dee time now. I'll be right there to tuck you in too, my little Ryo.
CLENCH!
And I'm off.
Just you wait, Ryo. We're gonna bang a nice little M rating into this sorry excuse for a manga yet .
YOU'RE DROOLING TOO, YOU GAY PERVERT.
WHOOPS, CAN'T HAVE THAT.
wipe
SLURP

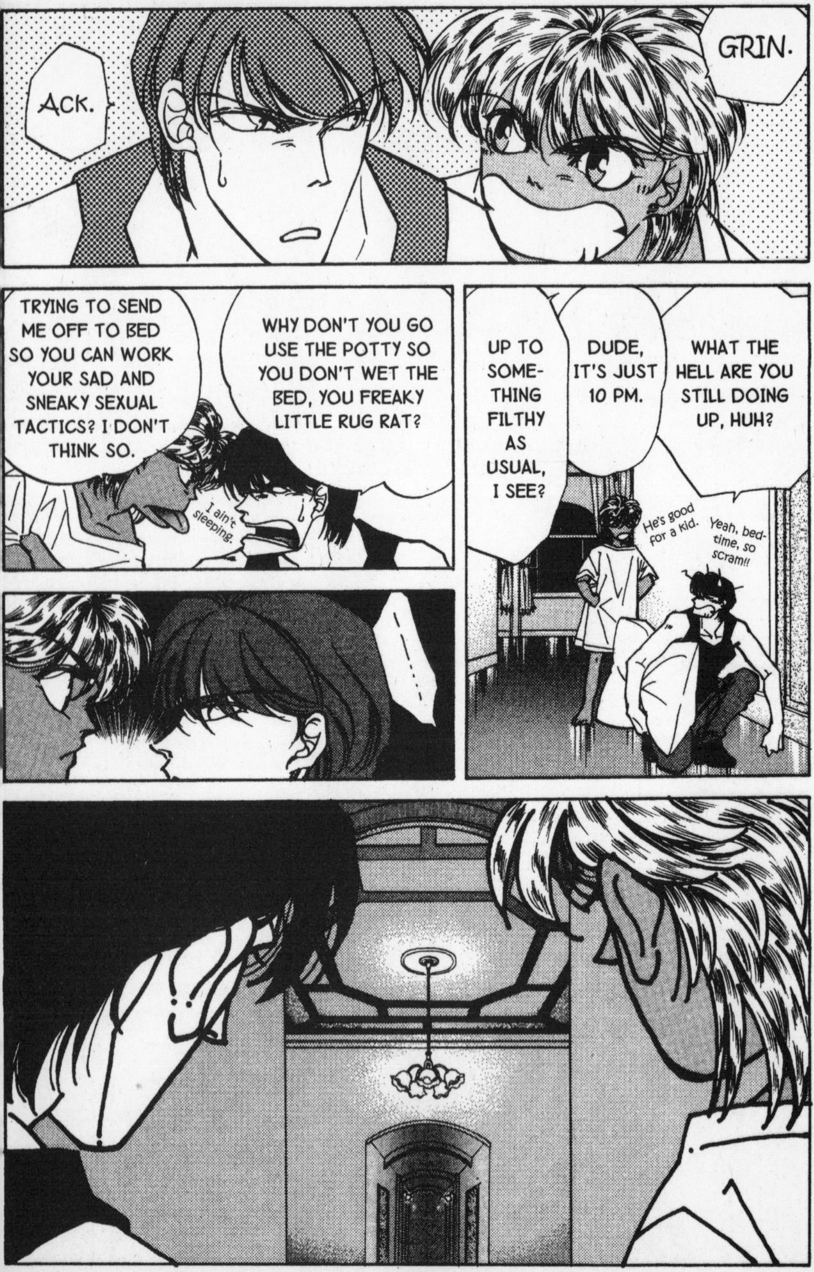
GRIN.
ACK.
WHAT THE HELL ARE YOU STILL DOING UP, HUH?
DUDE, IT'S JUST 10 PM.
UP TO SOMETHING FILTHY AS USUAL, I SEE?
Yeah, bed-time, so scram!!
He's good for a kid.
WHY DON'T YOU GO USE THE POTTY SO YOU DON'T WET THE BED, YOU FREAKY LITTLE RUG RAT?
TRYING TO SEND ME OFF TO BED SO YOU CAN WORK YOUR SAD AND SNEAKY SEXUAL TACTICS? I DON'T THINK SO.
I ain't sleeping.

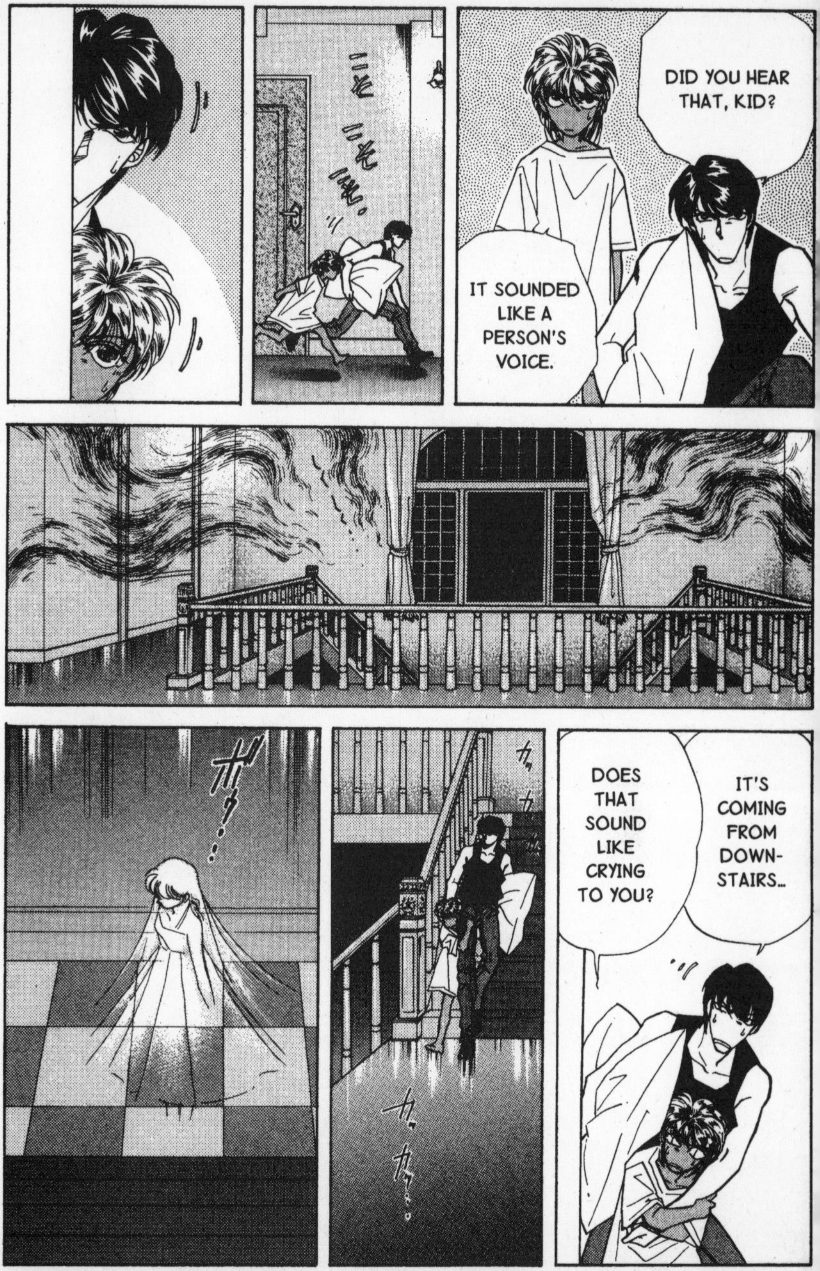
DID YOU HEAR THAT, KID?
IT SOUNDED LIKE A PERSON'S VOICE.
IT'S COMING FROM DOWN-STAIRS...
DOES THAT SOUND LIKE CRYING TO YOU?

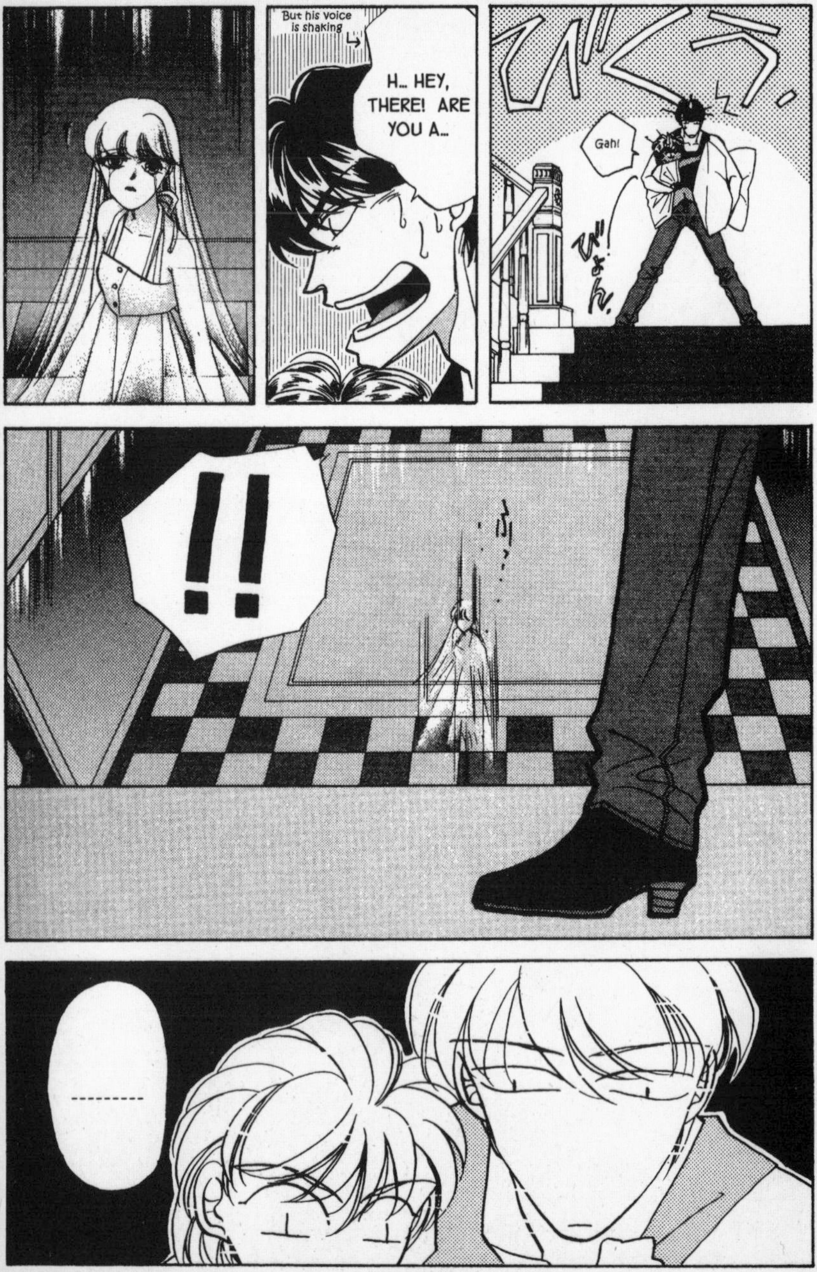
Gah!
But his voice is shaking
H... HEY, THERE! ARE YOU A...
!!

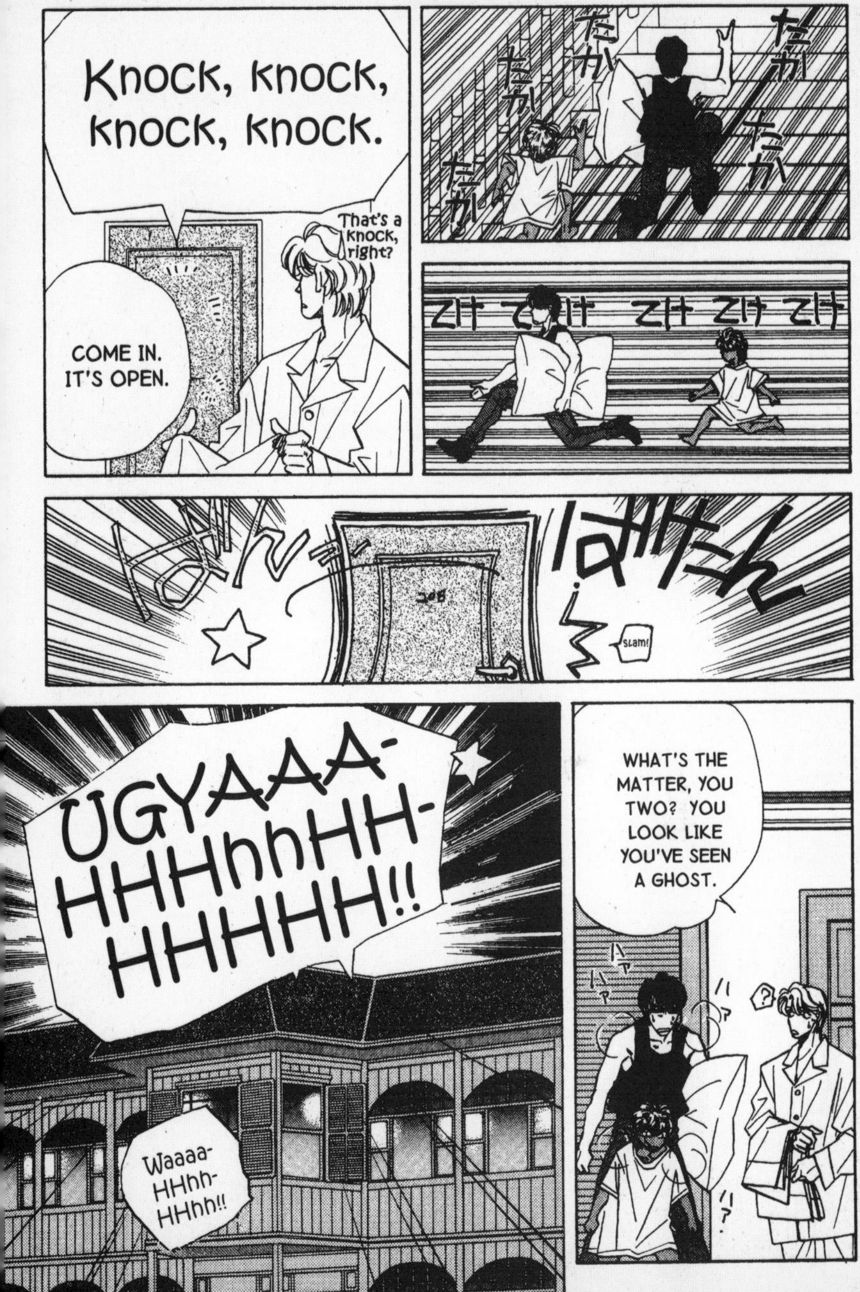
たか たか
たか たか
てけ てけ てけ てけ てけ
Knock, knock, knock, knock.
That's a knock, right?
COME IN. IT'S OPEN.
Slam!
WHAT'S THE MATTER, YOU TWO? YOU LOOK LIKE YOU'VE SEEN A GHOST.
UGYAAA-HHHhhHH-HHHHHH!!
Waaaa-HHhh-HHhh!!

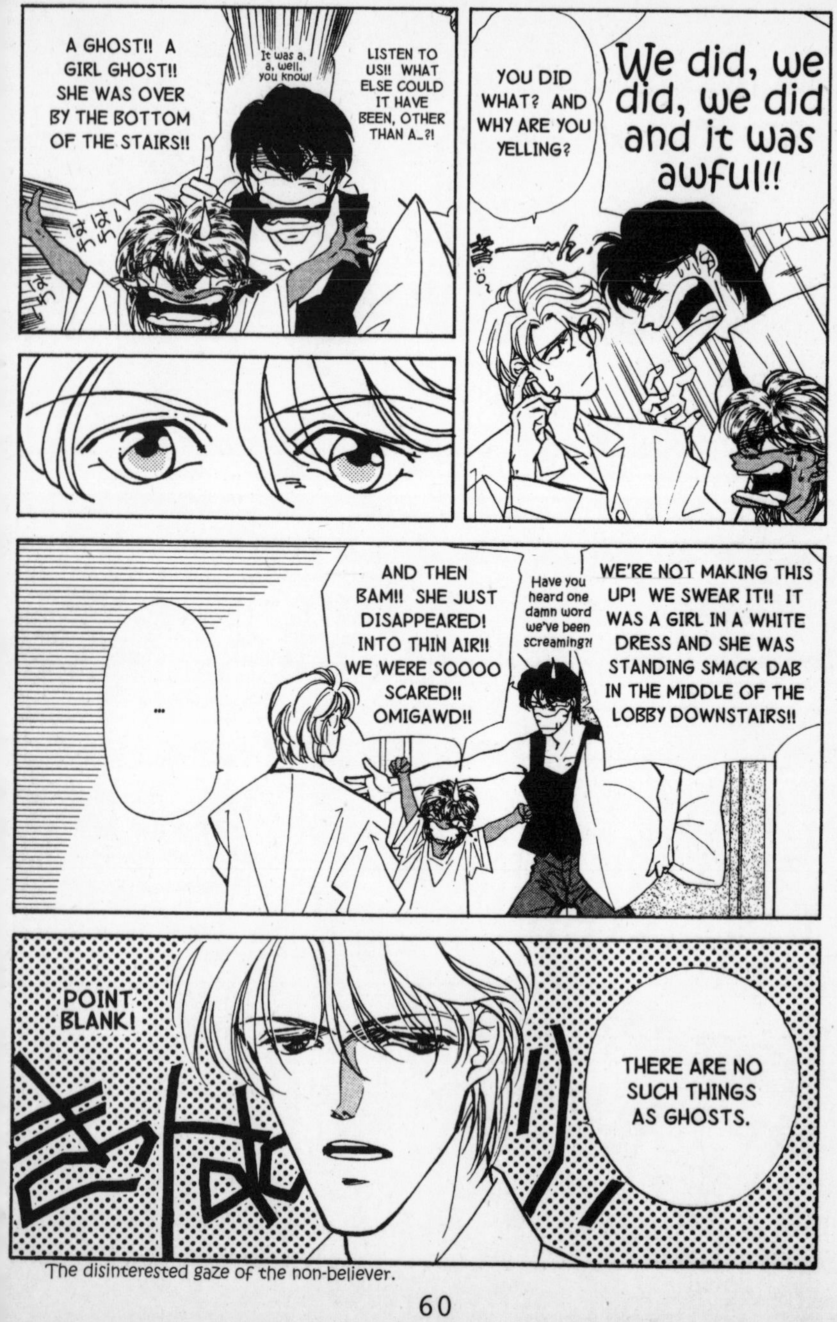
A GHOST!! A GIRL GHOST!! SHE WAS OVER BY THE BOTTOM OF THE STAIRS!!
It was a, a, well, you know!
LISTEN TO US!! WHAT ELSE COULD IT HAVE BEEN, OTHER THAN A...?!
YOU DID WHAT? AND WHY ARE YOU YELLING?
We did, we did, we did and it was awful!!
AND THEN BAM!! SHE JUST DISAPPEARED! INTO THIN AIR!! WE WERE SOOOO SCARED!! OMIGAWD!!
Have you heard one damn word we've been screaming?!
WE'RE NOT MAKING THIS UP! WE SWEAR IT!! IT WAS A GIRL IN A WHITE DRESS AND SHE WAS STANDING SMACK DAB IN THE MIDDLE OF THE LOBBY DOWNSTAIRS!!
...
POINT BLANK!
THERE ARE NO SUCH THINGS AS GHOSTS.
The disinterested gaze of the non-believer.

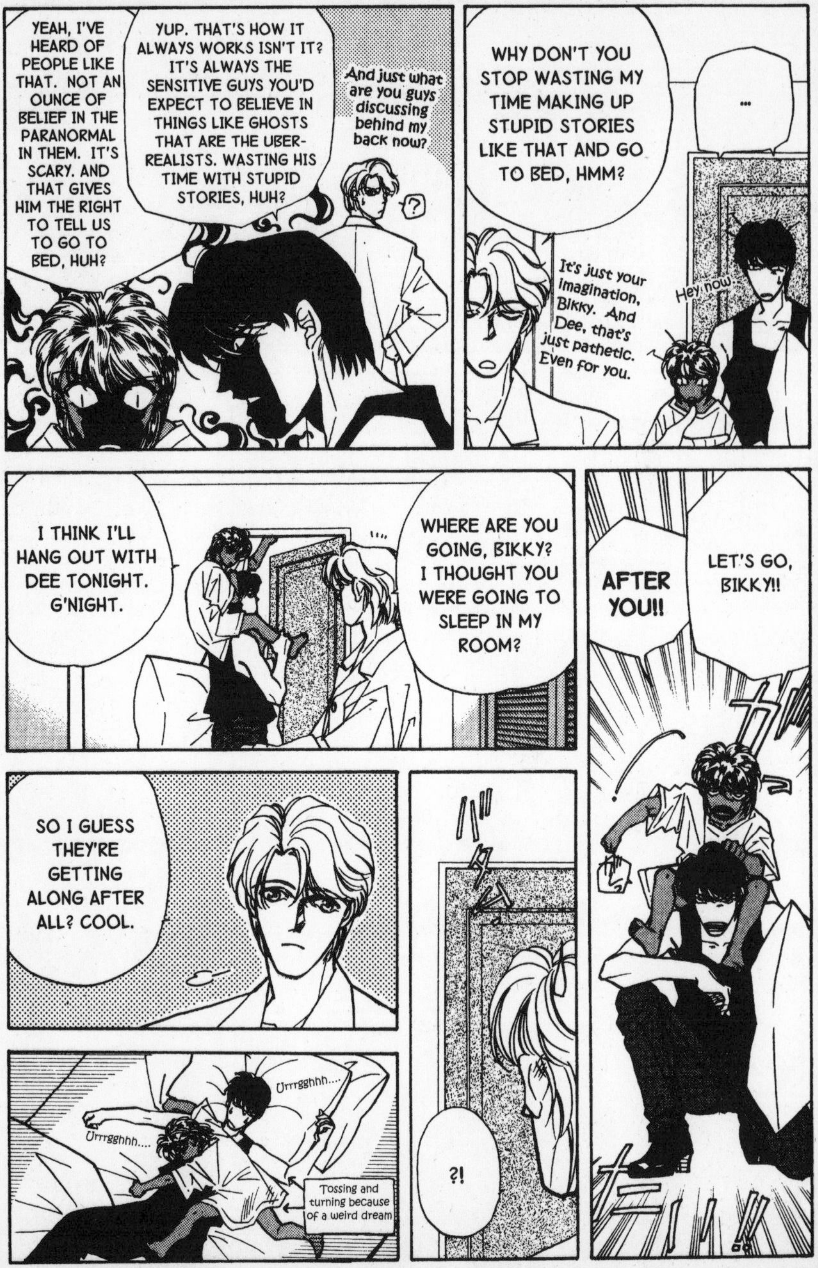
YEAH, I'VE HEARD OF PEOPLE LIKE THAT. NOT AN OUNCE OF BELIEF IN THE PARANORMAL IN THEM. IT'S SCARY. AND THAT GIVES HIM THE RIGHT TO TELL US TO GO TO BED, HUH?
YUP. THAT'S HOW IT ALWAYS WORKS ISN'T IT? IT'S ALWAYS THE SENSITIVE GUYS YOU'D EXPECT TO BELIEVE IN THINGS LIKE GHOSTS THAT ARE THE UBER-REALISTS. WASTING HIS TIME WITH STUPID STORIES, HUH?
And just what are you guys discussing behind my back now?
?
WHY DON'T YOU STOP WASTING MY TIME MAKING UP STUPID STORIES LIKE THAT AND GO TO BED, HMM?
...
It's just your imagination, Bikky. And Dee, that's just pathetic. Even for you.
Hey now...
I THINK I'LL HANG OUT WITH DEE TONIGHT. G'NIGHT.
WHERE ARE YOU GOING, BIKKY? I THOUGHT YOU WERE GOING TO SLEEP IN MY ROOM?
LET'S GO, BIKKY!!
AFTER YOU!!
?!
SO I GUESS THEY'RE GETTING ALONG AFTER ALL? COOL.
Urrrgghhh....
Urrrgghhh....
Tossing and turning because of a weird dream

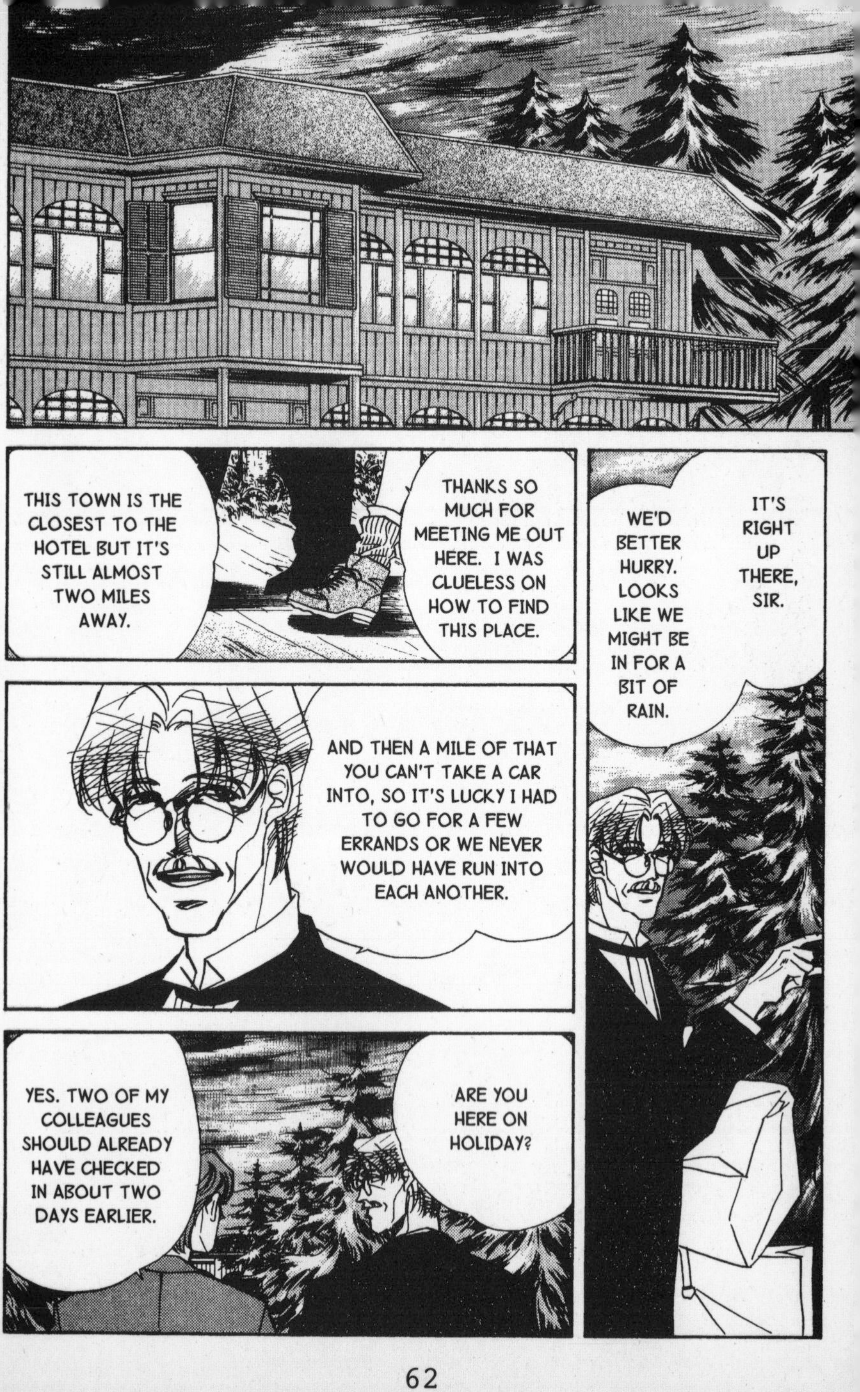
IT'S RIGHT UP THERE, SIR.
WE'D BETTER HURRY. LOOKS LIKE WE MIGHT BE IN FOR A BIT OF RAIN.
THANKS SO MUCH FOR MEETING ME OUT HERE. I WAS CLUELESS ON HOW TO FIND THIS PLACE.
THIS TOWN IS THE CLOSEST TO THE HOTEL BUT IT'S STILL ALMOST TWO MILES AWAY.
AND THEN A MILE OF THAT YOU CAN'T TAKE A CAR INTO, SO IT'S LUCKY I HAD TO GO FOR A FEW ERRANDS OR WE NEVER WOULD HAVE RUN INTO EACH ANOTHER.
ARE YOU HERE ON HOLIDAY?
YES. TWO OF MY COLLEAGUES SHOULD ALREADY HAVE CHECKED IN ABOUT TWO DAYS EARLIER.

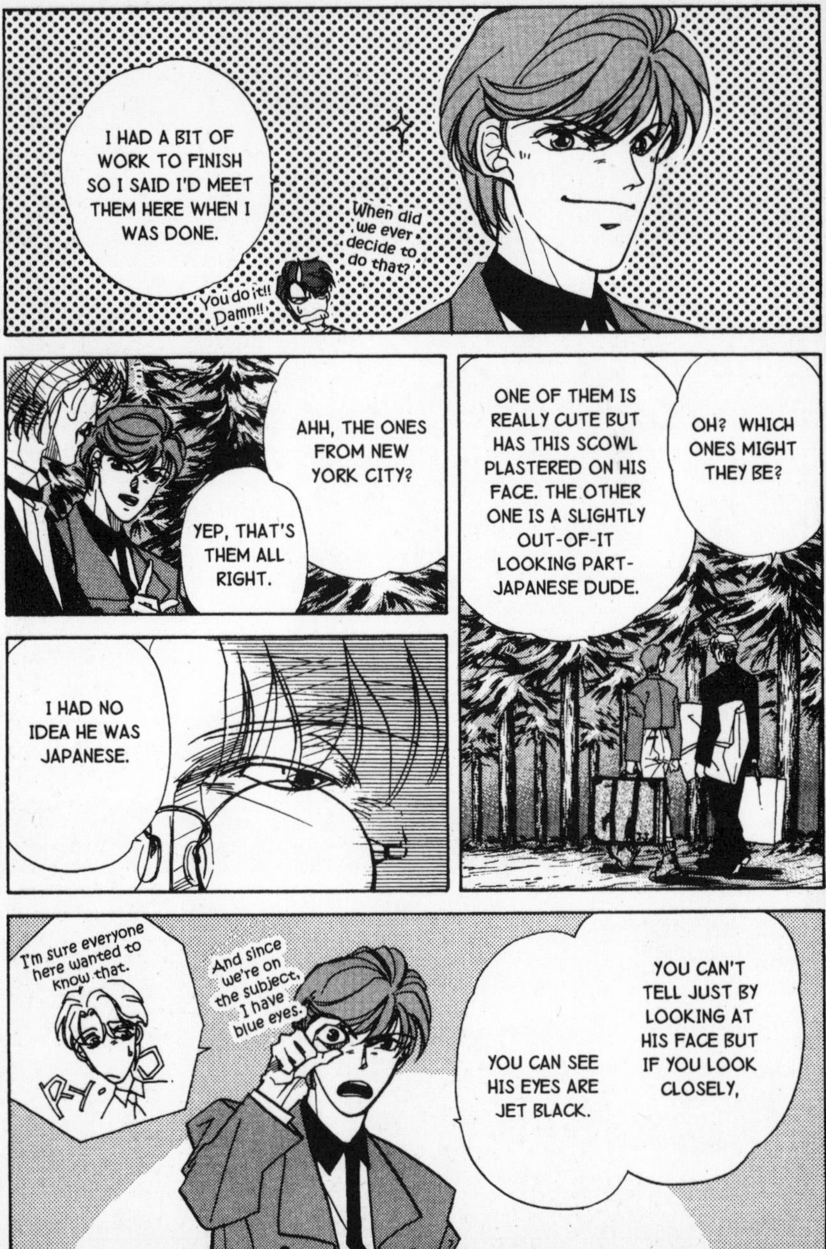
I HAD A BIT OF WORK TO FINISH SO I SAID I'D MEET THEM HERE WHEN I WAS DONE.
When did we ever decide to do that?
You do it!! Damn!!
OH? WHICH ONES MIGHT THEY BE?
ONE OF THEM IS REALLY CUTE BUT HAS THIS SCOWL PLASTERED ON HIS FACE. THE OTHER ONE IS A SLIGHTLY OUT-OF-IT LOOKING PART-JAPANESE DUDE.
AHH, THE ONES FROM NEW YORK CITY?
YEP, THAT'S THEM ALL RIGHT.
I HAD NO IDEA HE WAS JAPANESE.
YOU CAN'T TELL JUST BY LOOKING AT HIS FACE BUT IF YOU LOOK CLOSELY,
YOU CAN SEE HIS EYES ARE JET BLACK.
And since we're on the subject, I have blue eyes.
I'm sure everyone here wanted to know that.

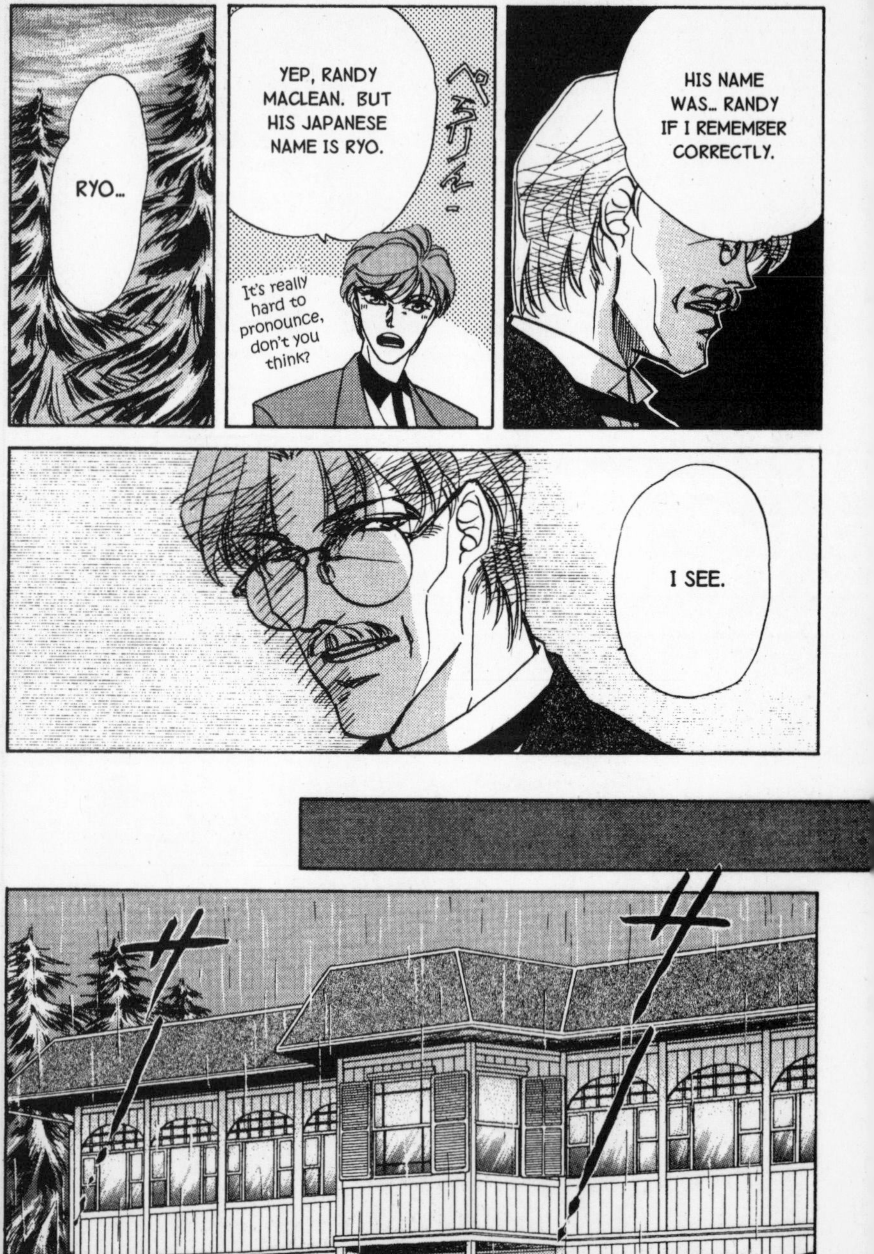
HIS NAME WAS... RANDY IF I REMEMBER CORRECTLY.
YEP, RANDY MACLEAN. BUT HIS JAPANESE NAME IS RYO.
It's really hard to pronounce, don't you think?
RYO...
I SEE.

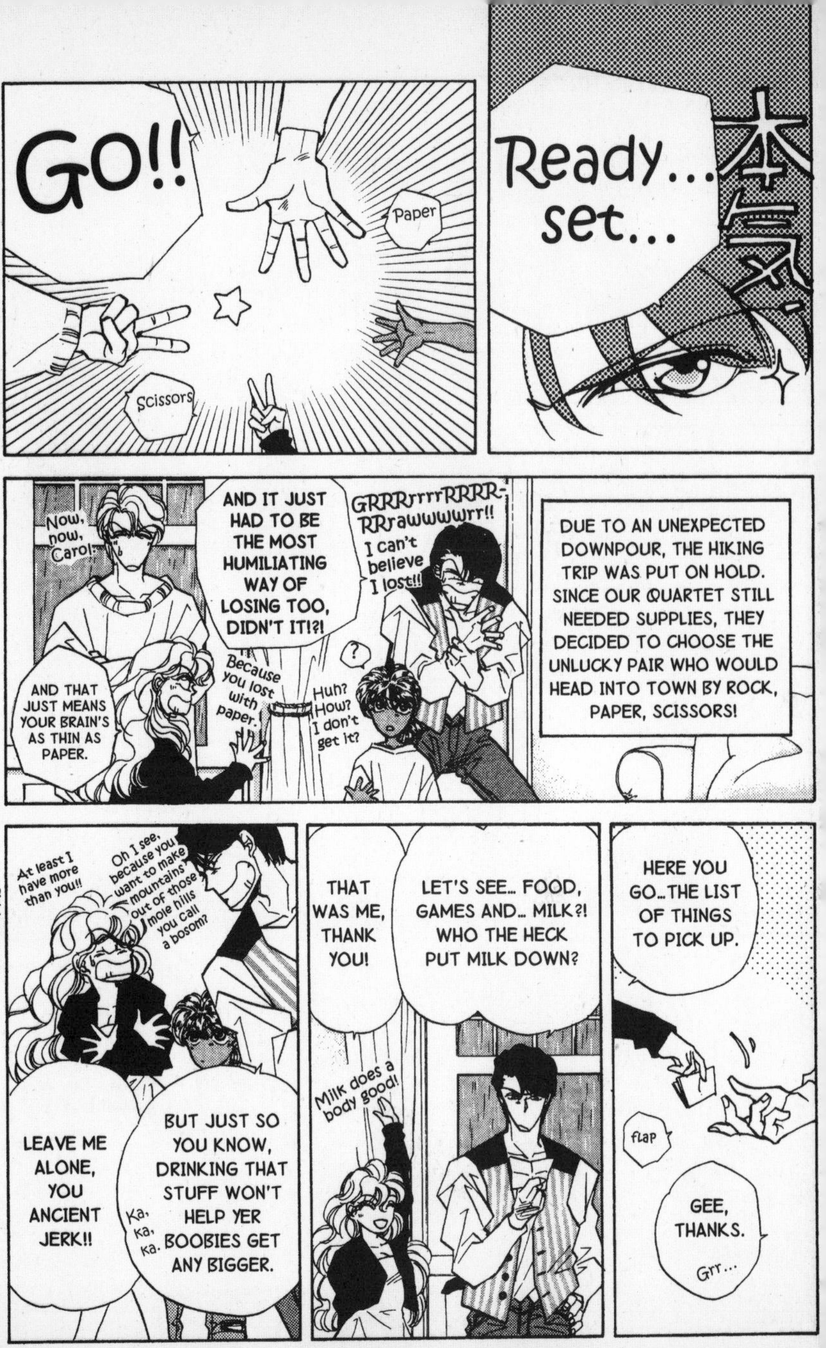
本気
Ready... set...
GO!!
Paper
Scissors
DUE TO AN UNEXPECTED DOWNPOUR, THE HIKING TRIP WAS PUT ON HOLD. SINCE OUR QUARTET STILL NEEDED SUPPLIES, THEY DECIDED TO CHOOSE THE UNLUCKY PAIR WHO WOULD HEAD INTO TOWN BY ROCK, PAPER, SCISSORS!
GRRRrrrrRRRR-RRrawwwwrr!! I can't believe I lost!!
AND IT JUST HAD TO BE THE MOST HUMILIATING WAY OF LOSING TOO, DIDN'T IT!?!
Now, now, Carol.
?
Because you lost with paper.
Huh? How? I don't get it?
AND THAT JUST MEANS YOUR BRAIN'S AS THIN AS PAPER.
HERE YOU GO... THE LIST OF THINGS TO PICK UP.
flap
GEE, THANKS.
Grr...
LET'S SEE... FOOD, GAMES AND... MILK?! WHO THE HECK PUT MILK DOWN?
THAT WAS ME, THANK YOU!
Milk does a body good!
Oh I see, because you want to make mountains out of those mole hills you call a bosom?
At least I have more than you!!
BUT JUST SO YOU KNOW, DRINKING THAT STUFF WON'T HELP YER BOOBIES GET ANY BIGGER.
Ka, ka, ka.
LEAVE ME ALONE, YOU ANCIENT JERK!!

I'd hope so...

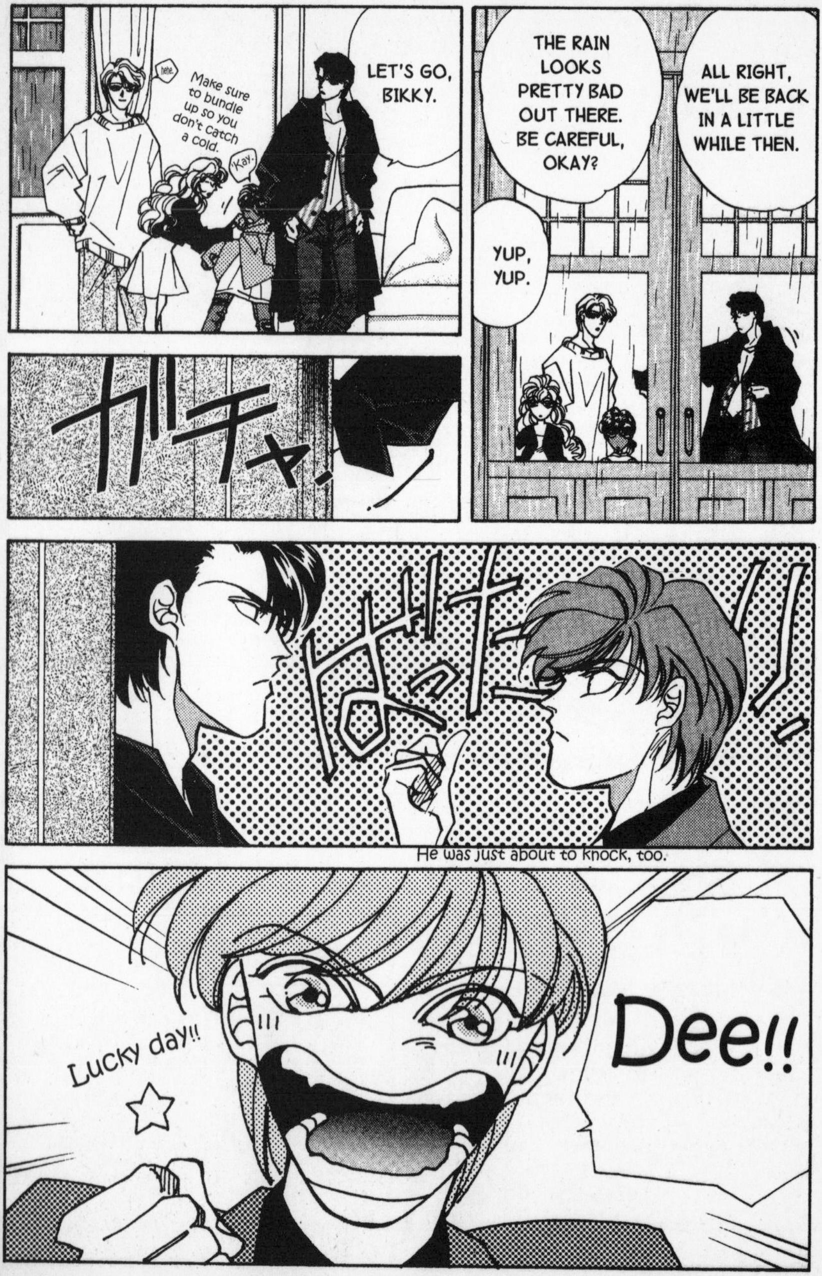
hehe.
Make sure to bundle up so you don't catch a cold.
'Kay.
LET'S GO, BIKKY.
THE RAIN LOOKS PRETTY BAD OUT THERE. BE CAREFUL, OKAY?
ALL RIGHT, WE'LL BE BACK IN A LITTLE WHILE THEN.
YUP, YUP.
ガチャ
He was just about to knock, too.
Lucky day!!
Dee!!

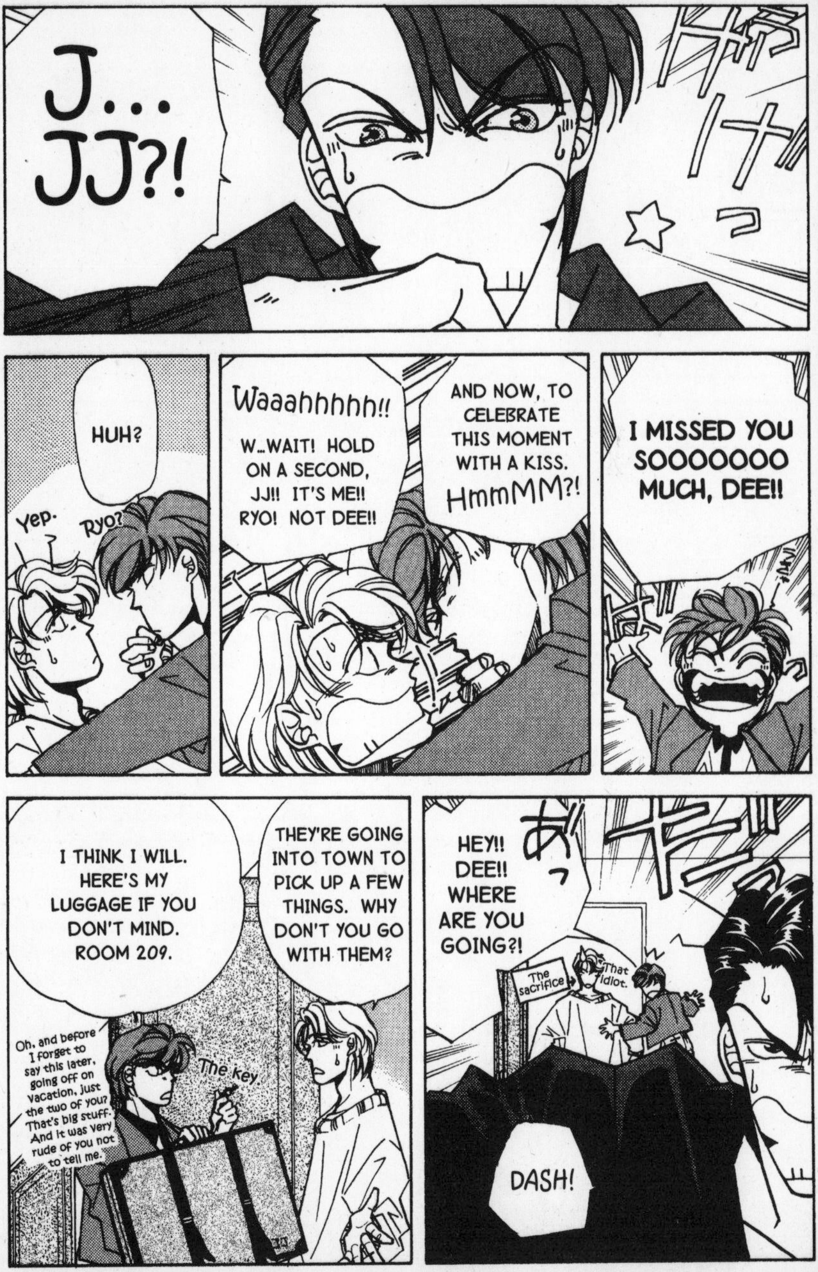
J... JJ?!
I MISSED YOU SOOOOOOO MUCH, DEE!!
AND NOW, TO CELEBRATE THIS MOMENT WITH A KISS. HmmMM?!
Waaahhhhh!!
W...WAIT! HOLD ON A SECOND, JJ!! IT'S ME!! RYO! NOT DEE!!
HUH?
Ryo?
Yep.
HEY!! DEE!! WHERE ARE YOU GOING?!
The sacrifice
That idiot.
DASH!
THEY'RE GOING INTO TOWN TO PICK UP A FEW THINGS. WHY DON'T YOU GO WITH THEM?
I THINK I WILL. HERE'S MY LUGGAGE IF YOU DON'T MIND. ROOM 209.
The key.
Oh, and before I forget to say this later, going off on vacation, just the two of you? That's big stuff. And it was very rude of you not to tell me.

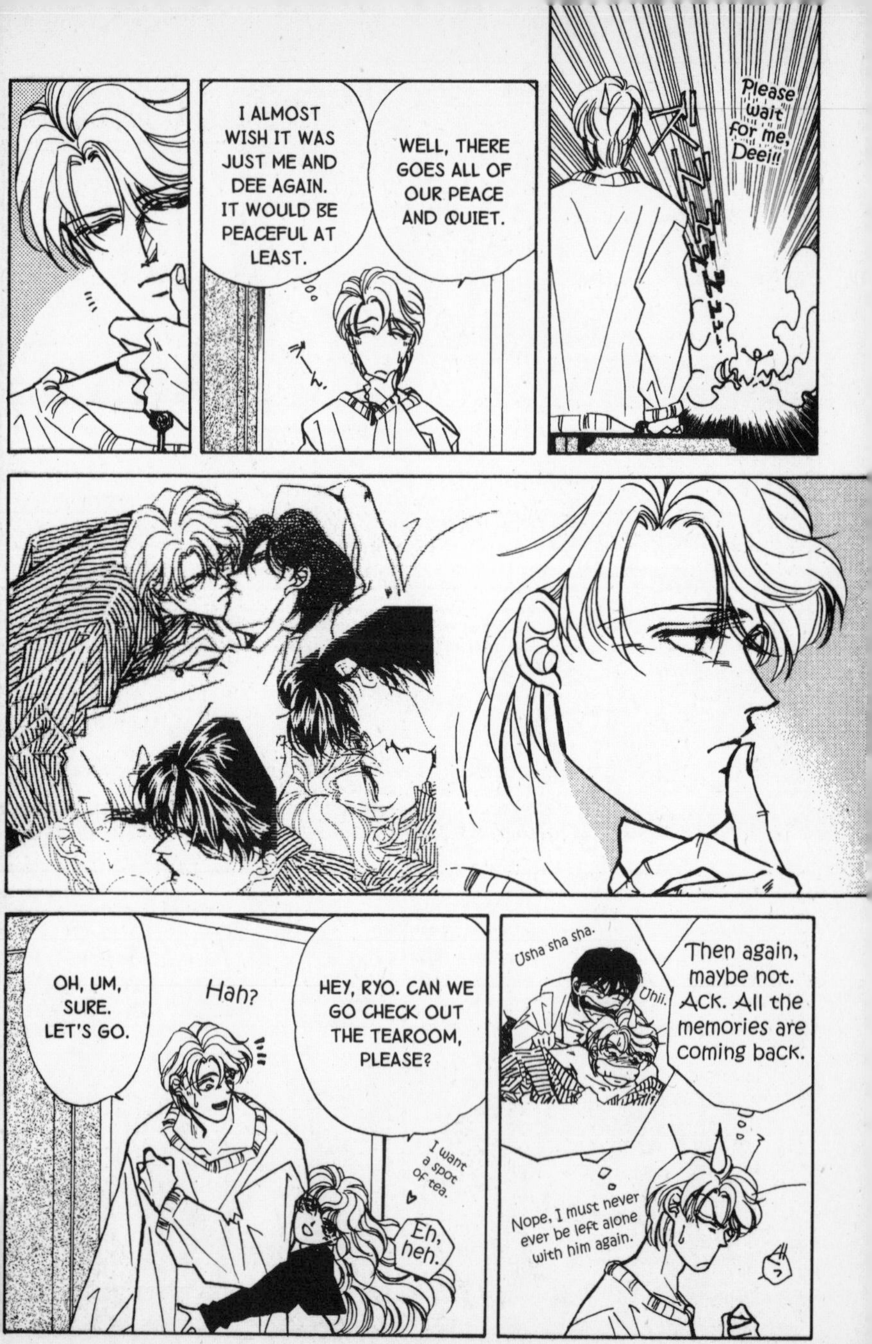
Please wait for me, Deei!!
WELL, THERE GOES ALL OF OUR PEACE AND QUIET.
I ALMOST WISH IT WAS JUST ME AND DEE AGAIN. IT WOULD BE PEACEFUL AT LEAST.
Then again, maybe not. Ack. All the memories are coming back.
Usha sha sha.
Uhii.
Nope, I must never ever be left alone with him again.
HEY, RYO. CAN WE GO CHECK OUT THE TEAROOM, PLEASE?
I want a spot of tea.
Eh, heh.
Hah?
OH, UM, SURE. LET'S GO.

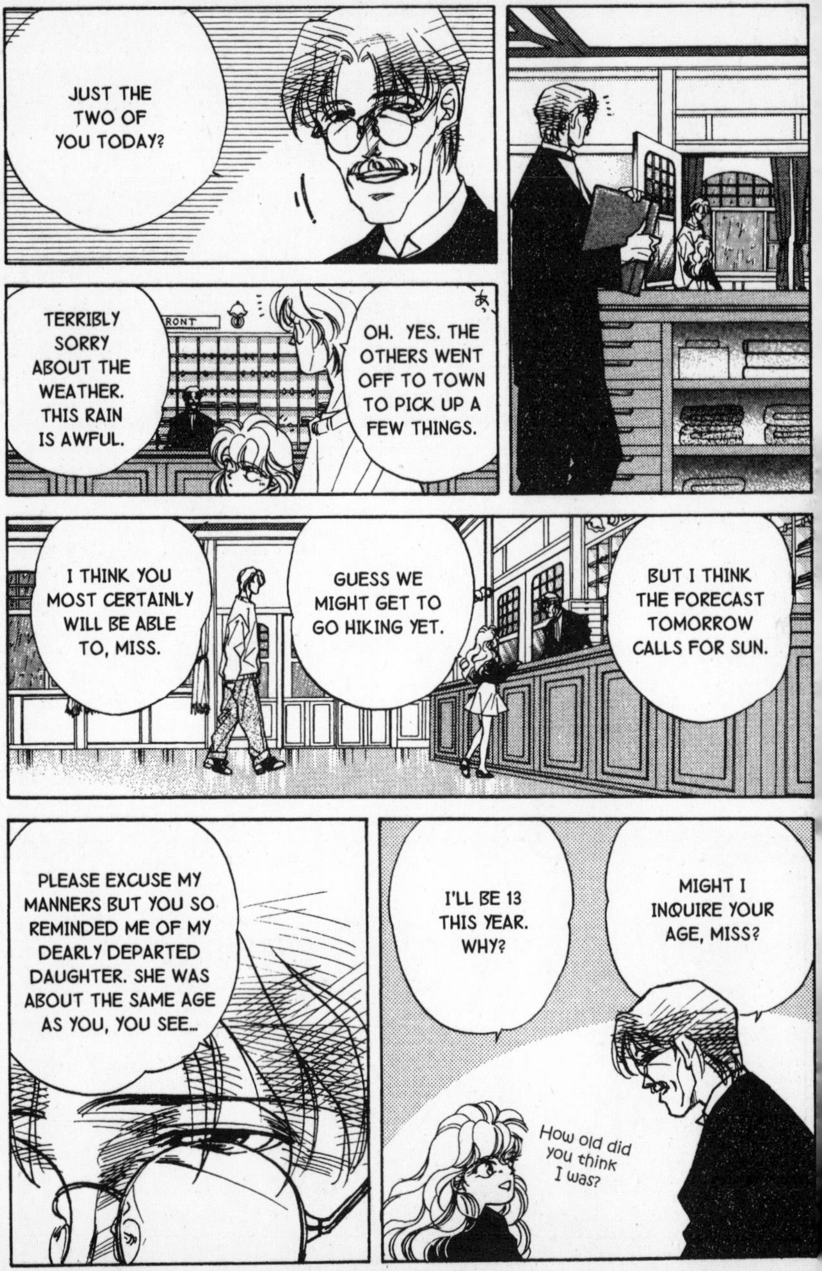
JUST THE TWO OF YOU TODAY?
あ、
OH. YES. THE OTHERS WENT OFF TO TOWN TO PICK UP A FEW THINGS.
TERRIBLY SORRY ABOUT THE WEATHER. THIS RAIN IS AWFUL.
BUT I THINK THE FORECAST TOMORROW CALLS FOR SUN.
GUESS WE MIGHT GET TO GO HIKING YET.
I THINK YOU MOST CERTAINLY WILL BE ABLE TO, MISS.
MIGHT I INQUIRE YOUR AGE, MISS?
I'LL BE 13 THIS YEAR. WHY?
How old did you think I was?
PLEASE EXCUSE MY MANNERS BUT YOU SO REMINDED ME OF MY DEARLY DEPARTED DAUGHTER. SHE WAS ABOUT THE SAME AGE AS YOU, YOU SEE...

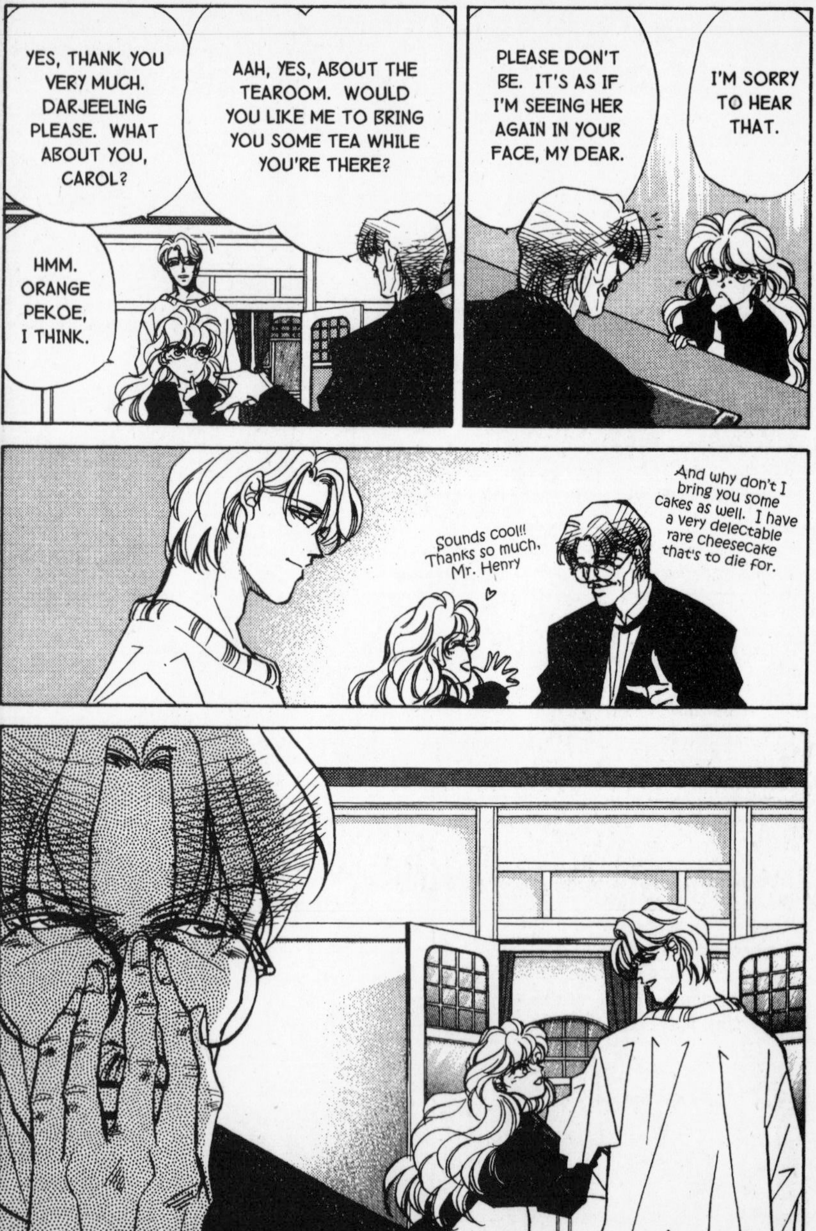
I'M SORRY TO HEAR THAT.
PLEASE DON'T BE. IT'S AS IF I'M SEEING HER AGAIN IN YOUR FACE, MY DEAR.
AAH, YES, ABOUT THE TEAROOM. WOULD YOU LIKE ME TO BRING YOU SOME TEA WHILE YOU'RE THERE?
YES, THANK YOU VERY MUCH. DARJEELING PLEASE. WHAT ABOUT YOU, CAROL?
HMM. ORANGE PEKOE, I THINK.
And why don't I bring you some cakes as well. I have a very delectable rare cheesecake that's to die for.
Sounds cool!! Thanks so much, Mr. Henry

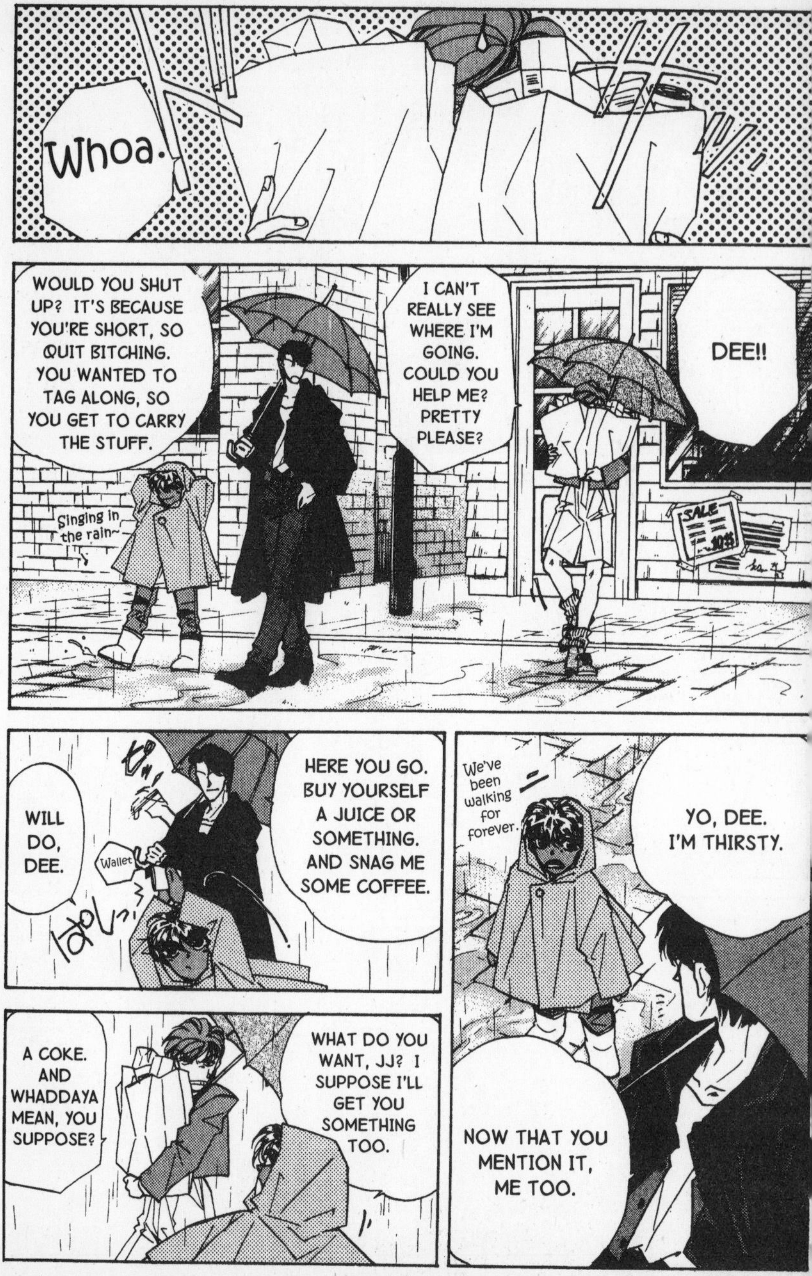
Whoa.
DEE!!
I CAN'T REALLY SEE WHERE I'M GOING. COULD YOU HELP ME? PRETTY PLEASE?
WOULD YOU SHUT UP? IT'S BECAUSE YOU'RE SHORT, SO QUIT BITCHING. YOU WANTED TO TAG ALONG, SO YOU GET TO CARRY THE STUFF.
Singing in the rain~
YO, DEE. I'M THIRSTY.
We've been walking for forever.
NOW THAT YOU MENTION IT, ME TOO.
HERE YOU GO. BUY YOURSELF A JUICE OR SOMETHING. AND SNAG ME SOME COFFEE.
Wallet
WILL DO, DEE.
WHAT DO YOU WANT, JJ? I SUPPOSE I'LL GET YOU SOMETHING TOO.
A COKE. AND WHADDAYA MEAN, YOU SUPPOSE?

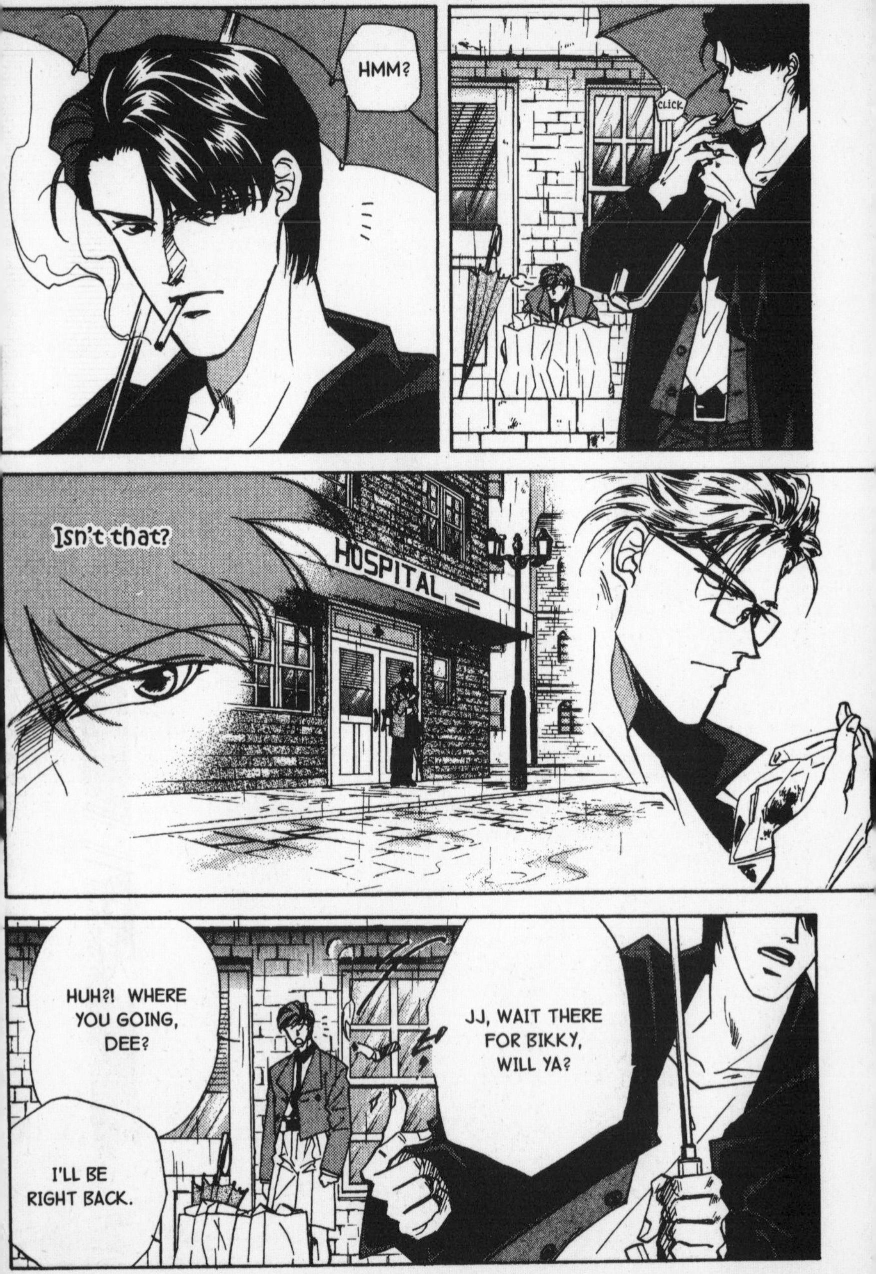
CLICK
HMM?
Isn't that?
JJ, WAIT THERE FOR BIKKY, WILL YA?
HUH?! WHERE YOU GOING, DEE?
I'LL BE RIGHT BACK.
HOSPITAL

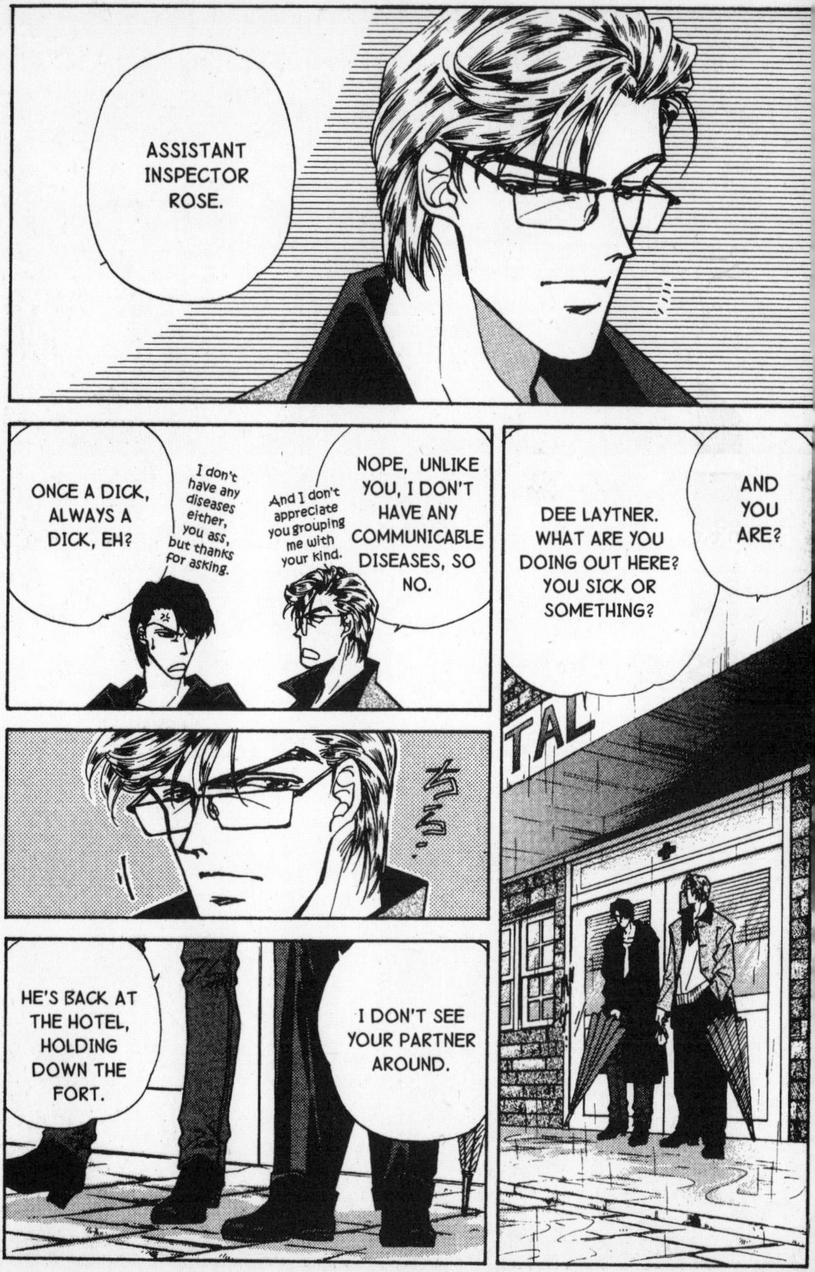
ASSISTANT INSPECTOR ROSE.
AND YOU ARE?
DEE LAYTNER. WHAT ARE YOU DOING OUT HERE? YOU SICK OR SOMETHING?
TAL
NOPE, UNLIKE YOU, I DON'T HAVE ANY COMMUNICABLE DISEASES, SO NO.
And I don't appreciate you grouping me with your kind.
I don't have any diseases either, you ass, but thanks for asking.
ONCE A DICK, ALWAYS A DICK, EH?
I DON'T SEE YOUR PARTNER AROUND.
HE'S BACK AT THE HOTEL, HOLDING DOWN THE FORT.

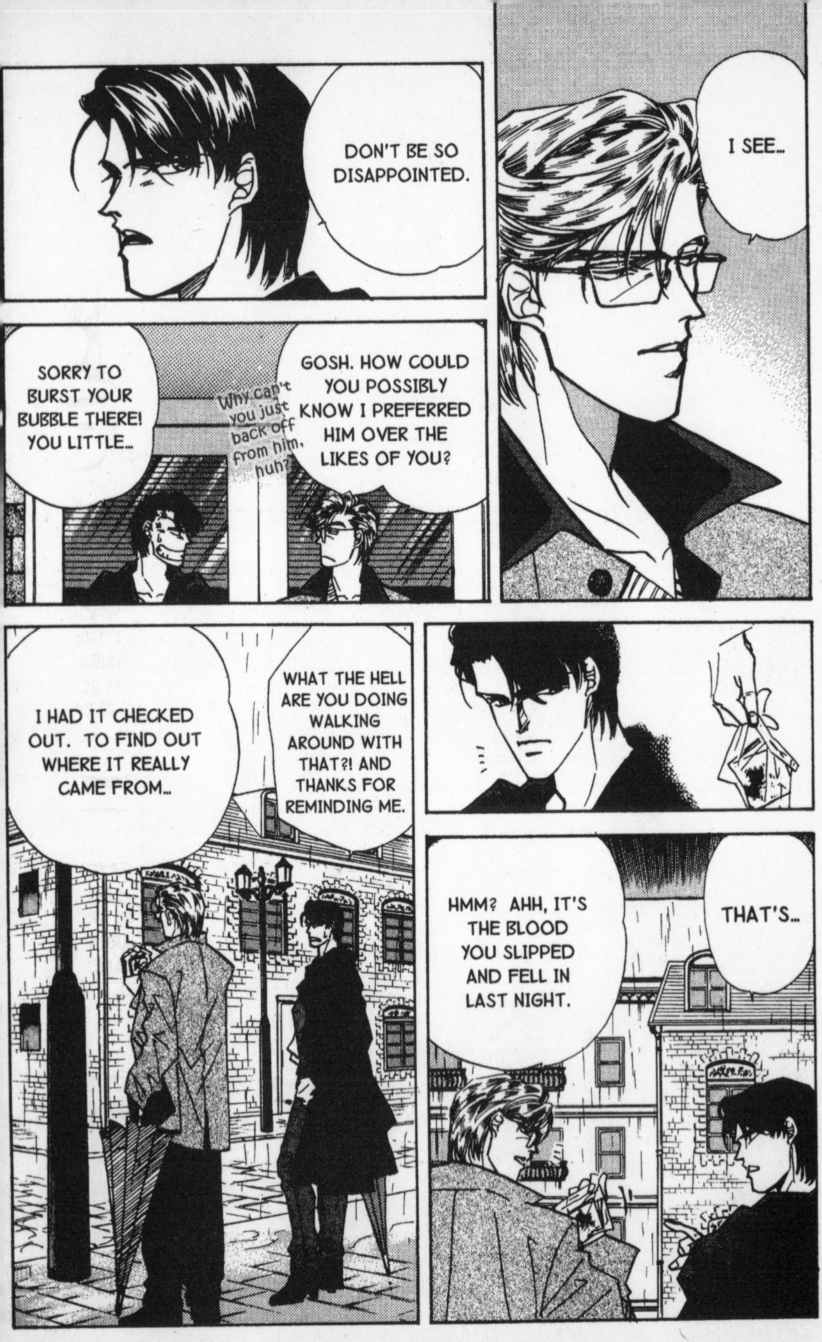
I SEE...
DON'T BE SO DISAPPOINTED.
GOSH. HOW COULD YOU POSSIBLY KNOW I PREFERRED HIM OVER THE LIKES OF YOU?
Why can't you just back off from him, huh?
SORRY TO BURST YOUR BUBBLE THERE! YOU LITTLE...
THAT'S...
HMM? AHH, IT'S THE BLOOD YOU SLIPPED AND FELL IN LAST NIGHT.
WHAT THE HELL ARE YOU DOING WALKING AROUND WITH THAT?! AND THANKS FOR REMINDING ME.
I HAD IT CHECKED OUT. TO FIND OUT WHERE IT REALLY CAME FROM...

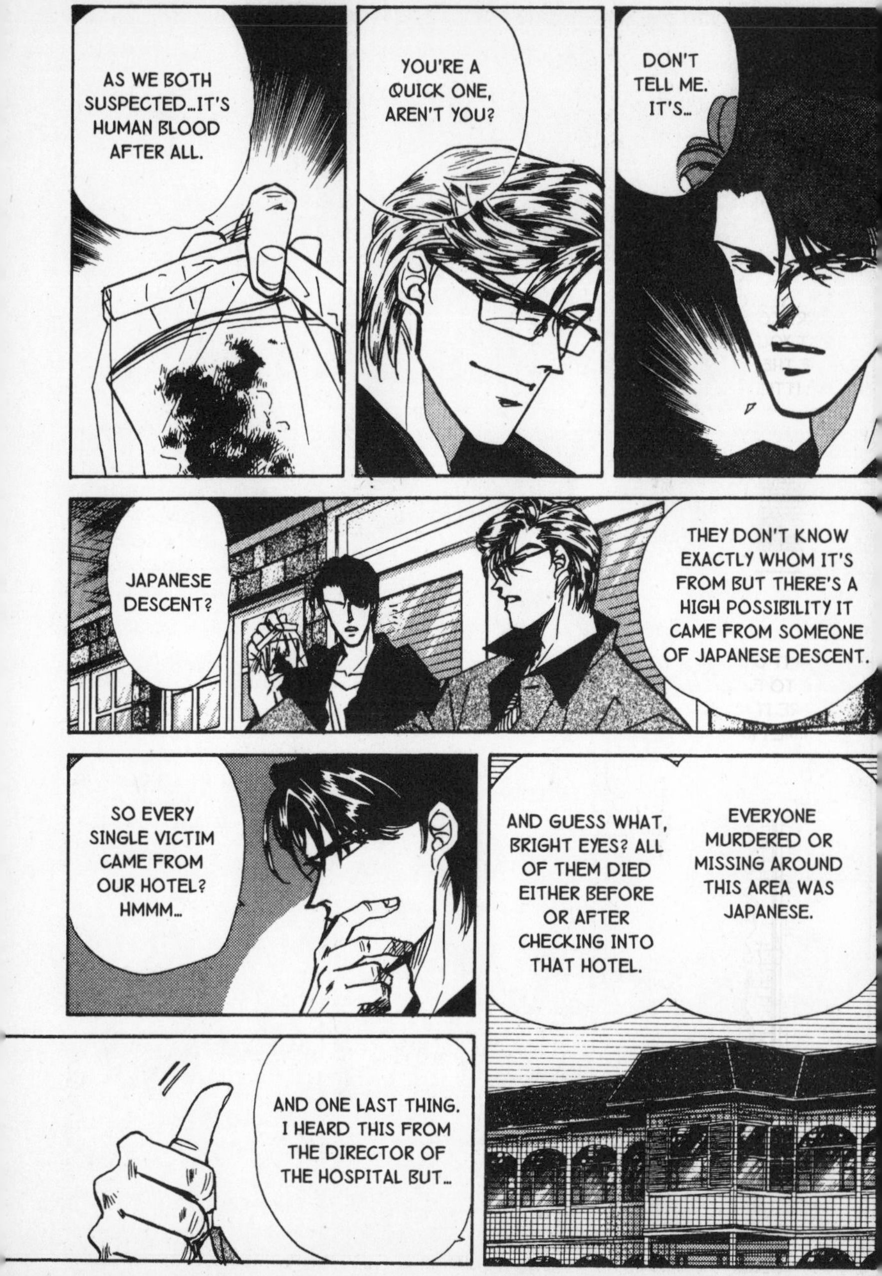
DON'T TELL ME. IT'S...
YOU'RE A QUICK ONE, AREN'T YOU?
AS WE BOTH SUSPECTED...IT'S HUMAN BLOOD AFTER ALL.
THEY DON'T KNOW EXACTLY WHOM IT'S FROM BUT THERE'S A HIGH POSSIBILITY IT CAME FROM SOMEONE OF JAPANESE DESCENT.
JAPANESE DESCENT?
EVERYONE MURDERED OR MISSING AROUND THIS AREA WAS JAPANESE.
AND GUESS WHAT, BRIGHT EYES? ALL OF THEM DIED EITHER BEFORE OR AFTER CHECKING INTO THAT HOTEL.
SO EVERY SINGLE VICTIM CAME FROM OUR HOTEL? HMMM...
AND ONE LAST THING. I HEARD THIS FROM THE DIRECTOR OF THE HOSPITAL BUT...

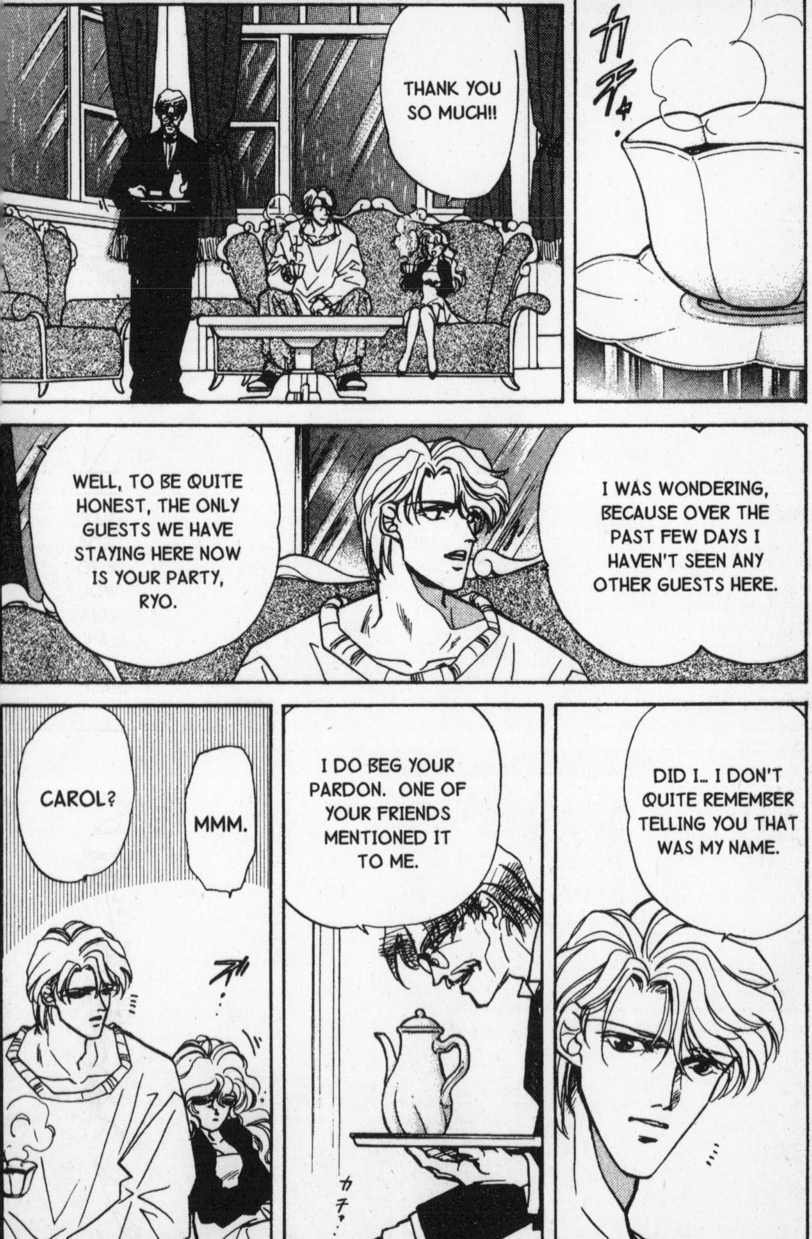
THANK YOU SO MUCH!!
I WAS WONDERING, BECAUSE OVER THE PAST FEW DAYS I HAVEN'T SEEN ANY OTHER GUESTS HERE.
WELL, TO BE QUITE HONEST, THE ONLY GUESTS WE HAVE STAYING HERE NOW IS YOUR PARTY, RYO.
DID I... I DON'T QUITE REMEMBER TELLING YOU THAT WAS MY NAME.
I DO BEG YOUR PARDON. ONE OF YOUR FRIENDS MENTIONED IT TO ME.
CAROL?
MMM.

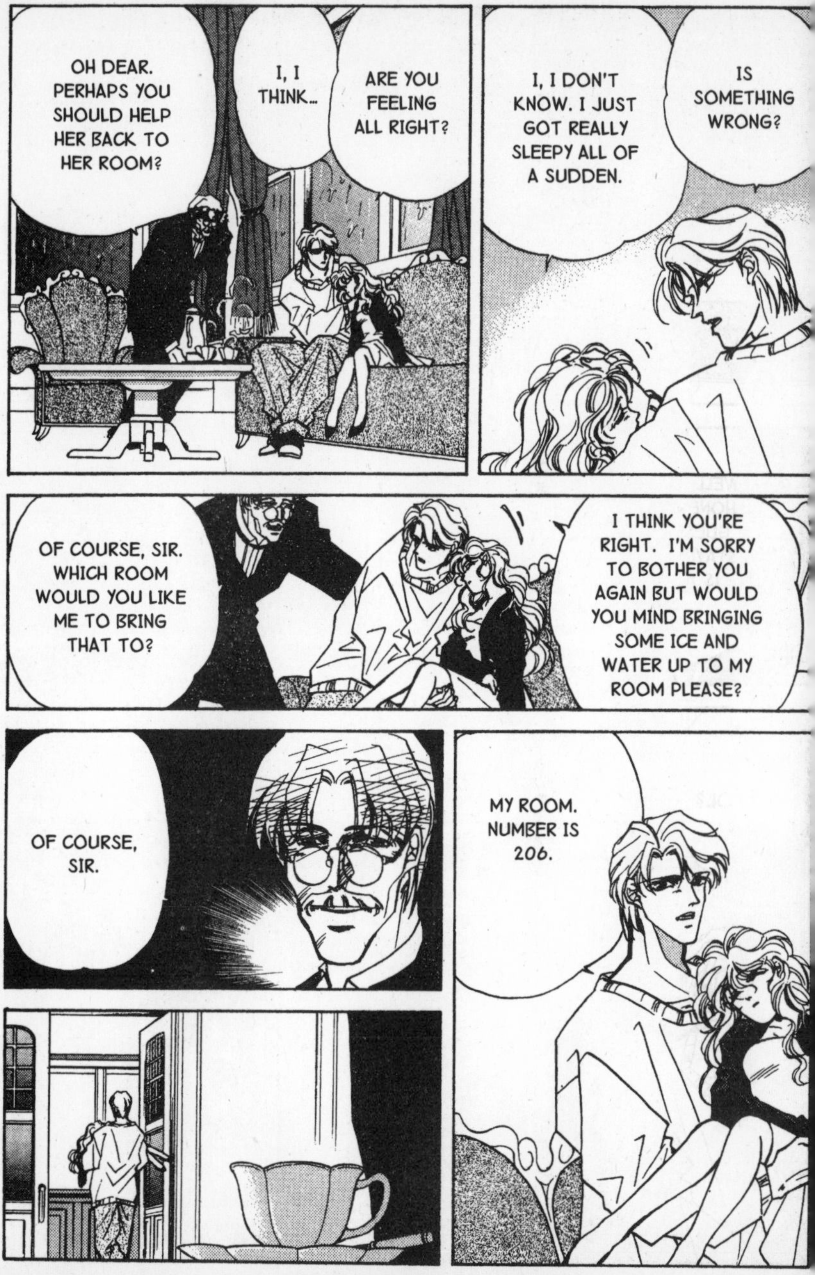
IS SOMETHING WRONG?
I, I DON'T KNOW. I JUST GOT REALLY SLEEPY ALL OF A SUDDEN.
ARE YOU FEELING ALL RIGHT?
I, I THINK...
OH DEAR. PERHAPS YOU SHOULD HELP HER BACK TO HER ROOM?
I THINK YOU'RE RIGHT. I'M SORRY TO BOTHER YOU AGAIN BUT WOULD YOU MIND BRINGING SOME ICE AND WATER UP TO MY ROOM PLEASE?
OF COURSE, SIR. WHICH ROOM WOULD YOU LIKE ME TO BRING THAT TO?
MY ROOM. NUMBER IS 206.
OF COURSE, SIR.

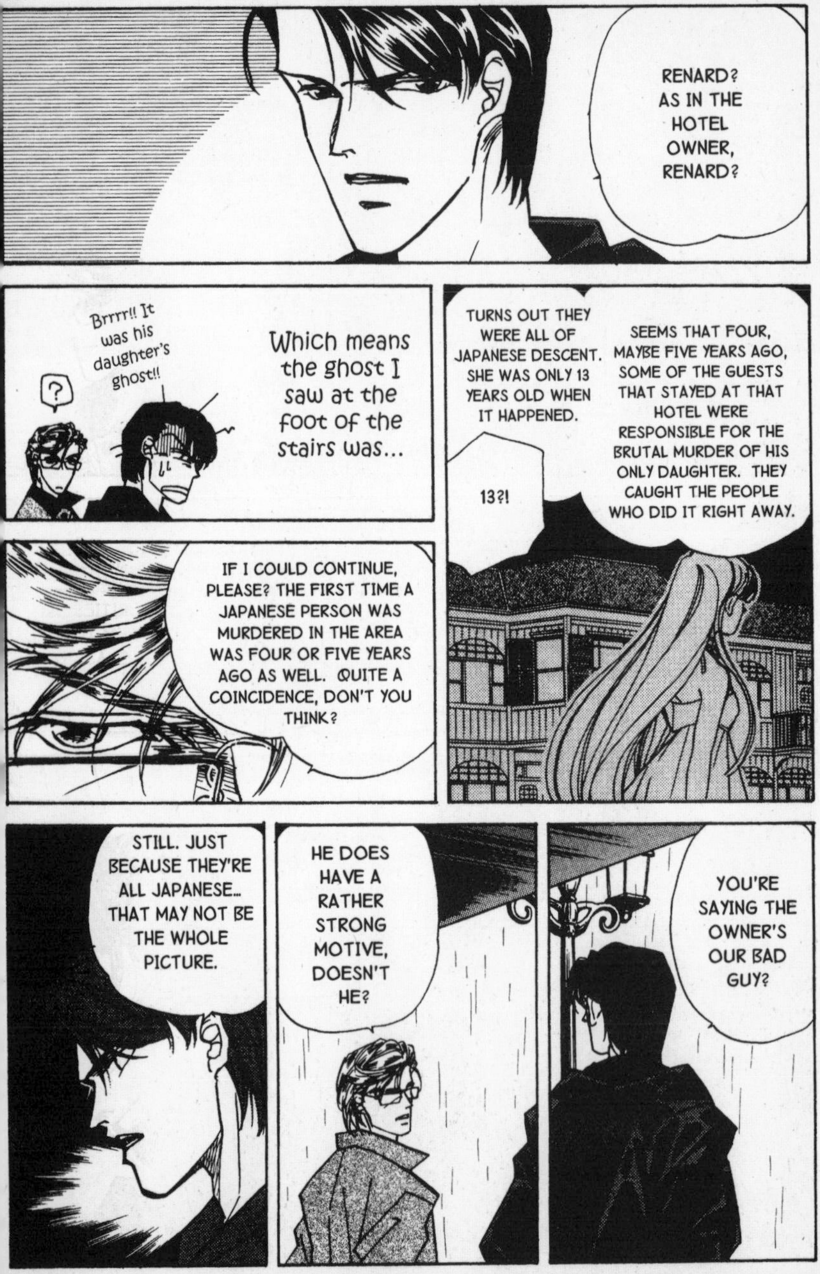
RENARD? AS IN THE HOTEL OWNER, RENARD?
SEEMS THAT FOUR, MAYBE FIVE YEARS AGO, SOME OF THE GUESTS THAT STAYED AT THAT HOTEL WERE RESPONSIBLE FOR THE BRUTAL MURDER OF HIS ONLY DAUGHTER. THEY CAUGHT THE PEOPLE WHO DID IT RIGHT AWAY.
TURNS OUT THEY WERE ALL OF JAPANESE DESCENT. SHE WAS ONLY 13 YEARS OLD WHEN IT HAPPENED.
13?!
Which means the ghost I saw at the foot of the stairs was...
Brrrr!! It was his daughter's ghost!!
?
IF I COULD CONTINUE, PLEASE? THE FIRST TIME A JAPANESE PERSON WAS MURDERED IN THE AREA WAS FOUR OR FIVE YEARS AGO AS WELL. QUITE A COINCIDENCE, DON'T YOU THINK?
YOU'RE SAYING THE OWNER'S OUR BAD GUY?
HE DOES HAVE A RATHER STRONG MOTIVE, DOESN'T HE?
STILL. JUST BECAUSE THEY'RE ALL JAPANESE... THAT MAY NOT BE THE WHOLE PICTURE.

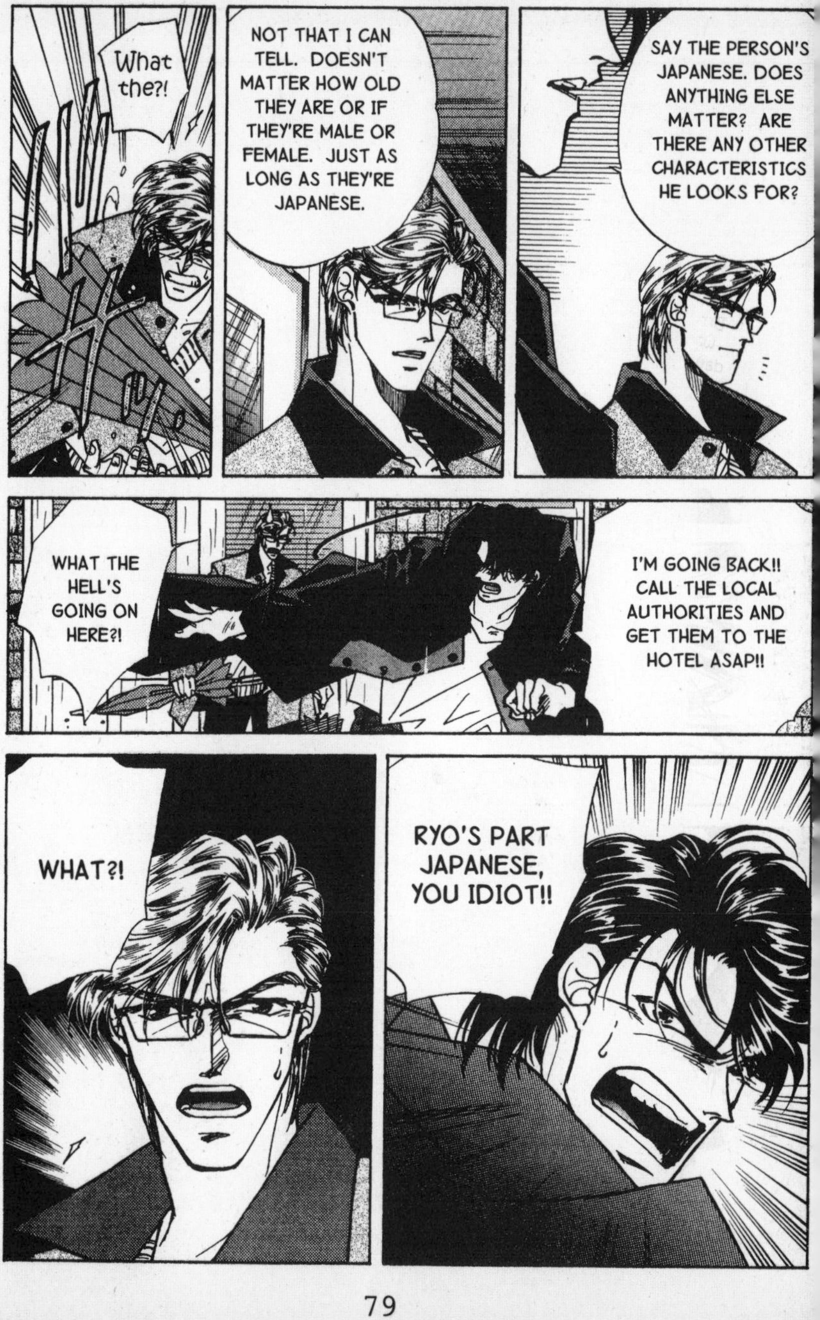
SAY THE PERSON'S JAPANESE. DOES ANYTHING ELSE MATTER? ARE THERE ANY OTHER CHARACTERISTICS HE LOOKS FOR?
NOT THAT I CAN TELL. DOESN'T MATTER HOW OLD THEY ARE OR IF THEY'RE MALE OR FEMALE. JUST AS LONG AS THEY'RE JAPANESE.
What the?!
I'M GOING BACK!! CALL THE LOCAL AUTHORITIES AND GET THEM TO THE HOTEL ASAP!!
WHAT THE HELL'S GOING ON HERE?!
RYO'S PART JAPANESE, YOU IDIOT!!
WHAT?!

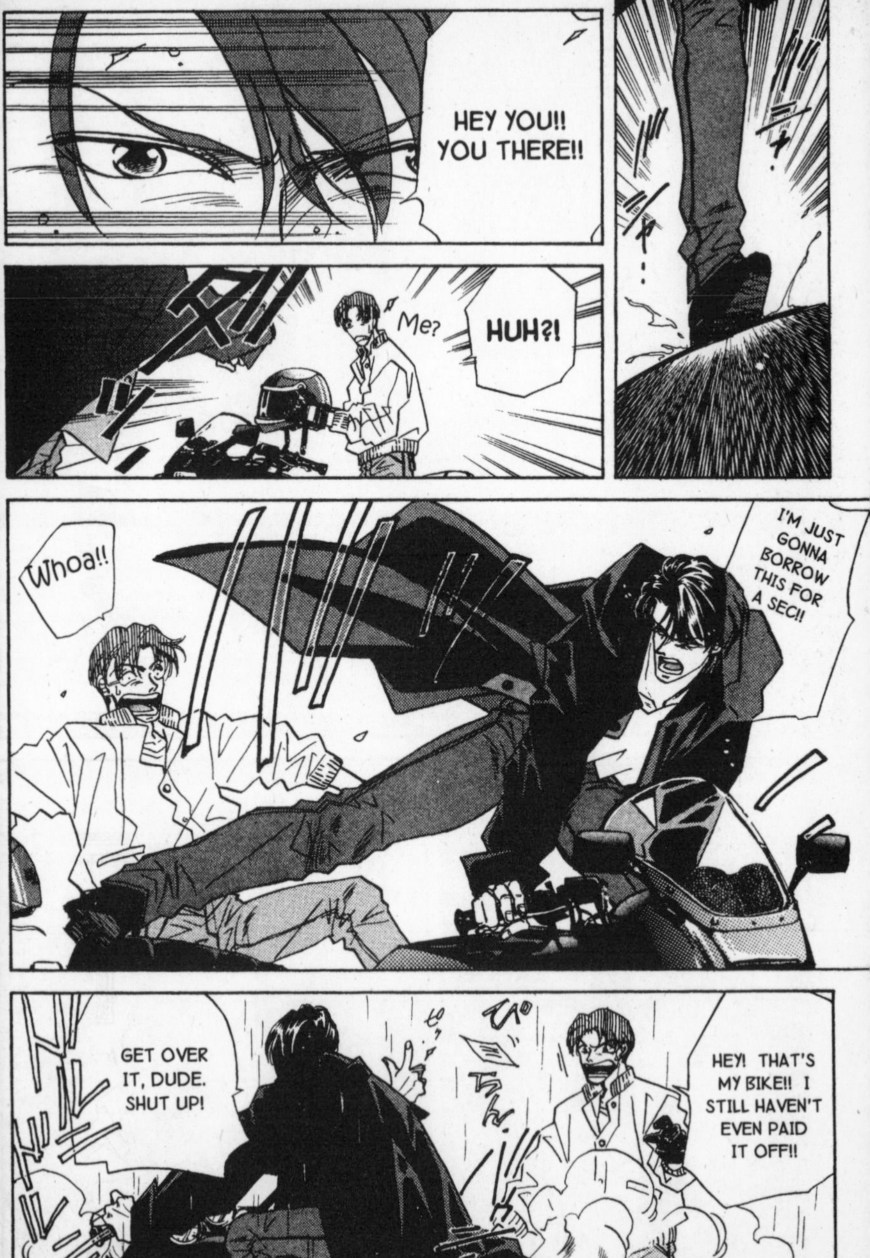
HEY YOU!! YOU THERE!!
HUH?!
Me?
I'M JUST GONNA BORROW THIS FOR A SEC!!
Whoa!!
HEY! THAT'S MY BIKE!! I STILL HAVEN'T EVEN PAID IT OFF!!
GET OVER IT, DUDE. SHUT UP!

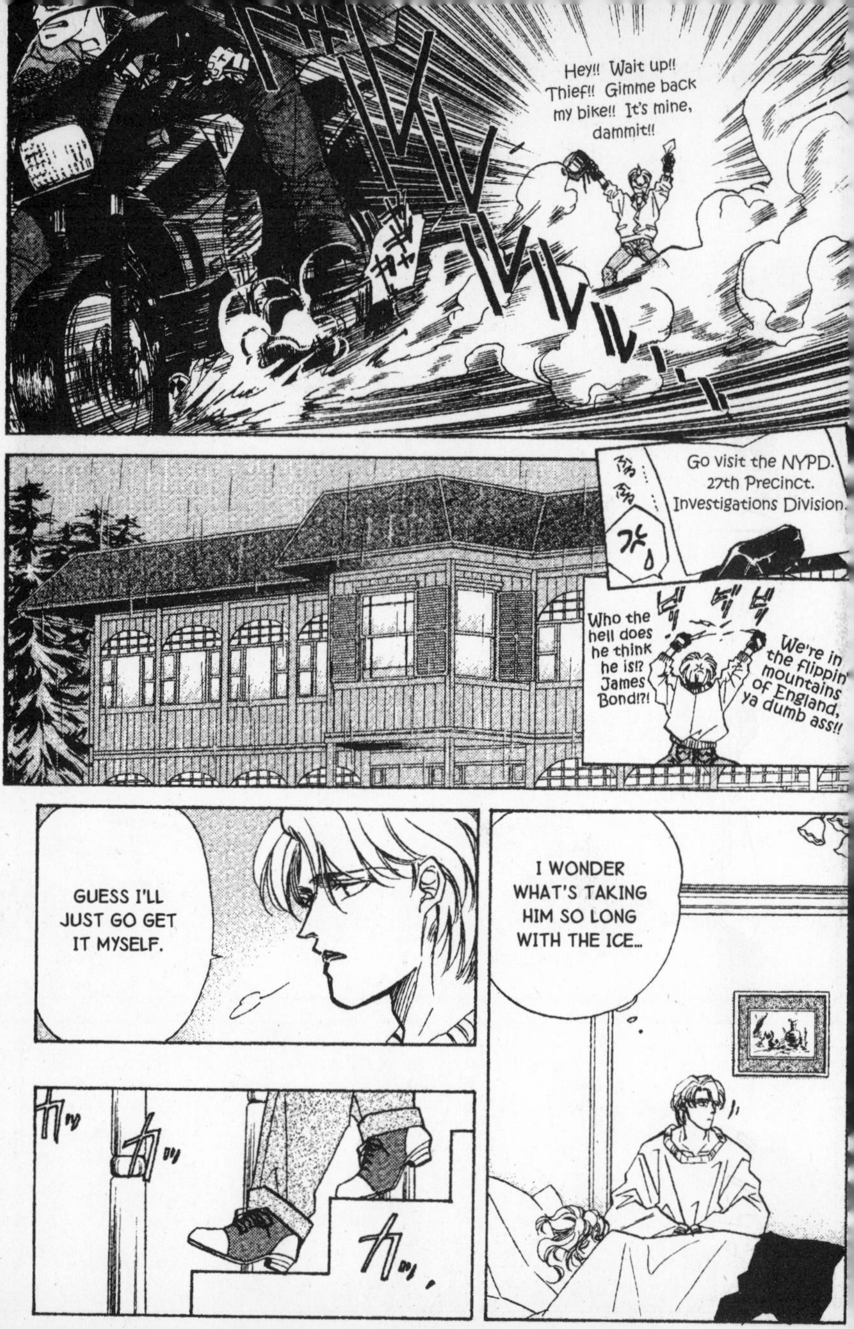
Hey!! Wait up!! Thief!! Gimme back my bike!! It's mine, dammit!!
Go visit the NYPD. 27th Precinct. Investigations Division.
We're in the flippin mountains of England, ya dumb ass!!
Who the hell does he think he is!? James Bond!?!
I WONDER WHAT'S TAKING HIM SO LONG WITH THE ICE...
GUESS I'LL JUST GO GET IT MYSELF.

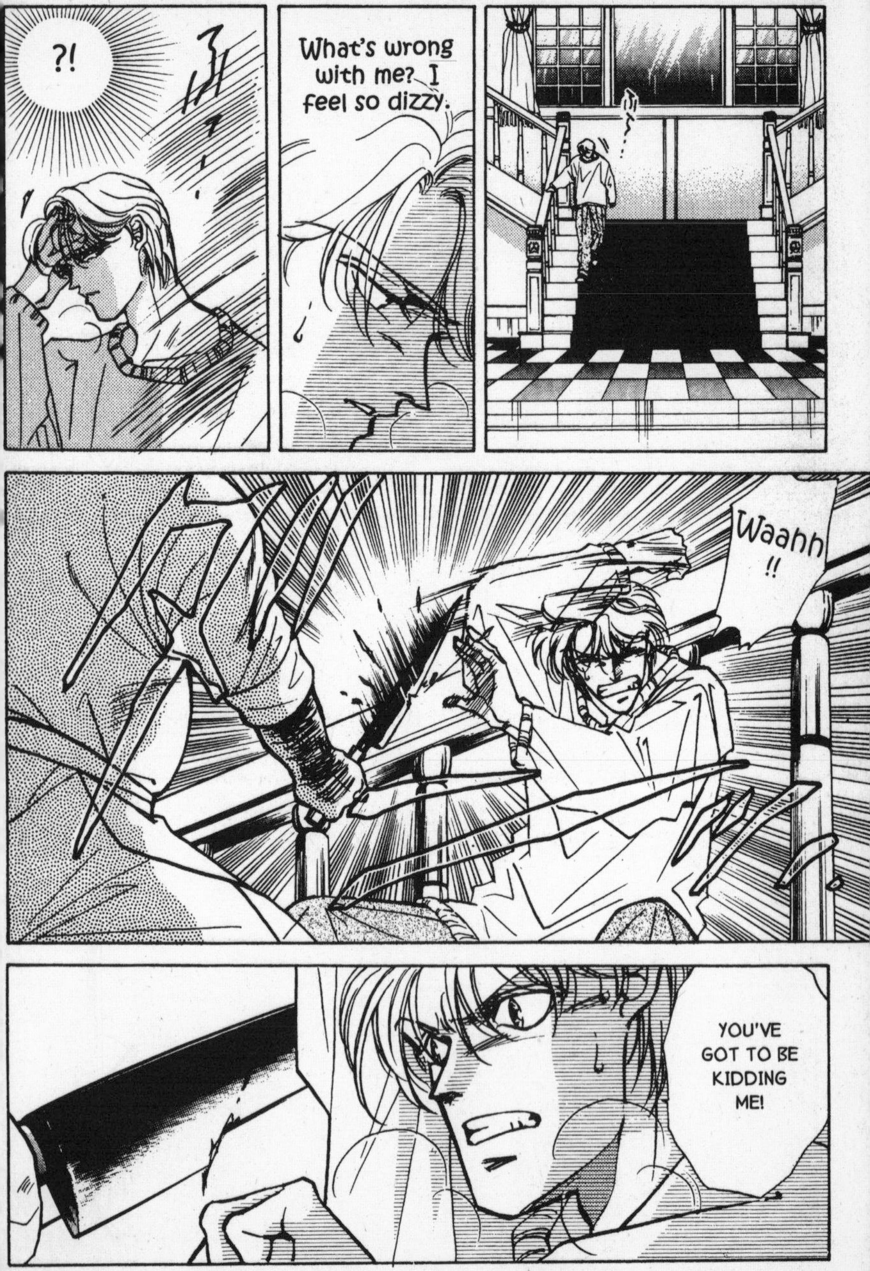
What's wrong with me? I feel so dizzy.
?!
Waahh !!
YOU'VE GOT TO BE KIDDING ME!

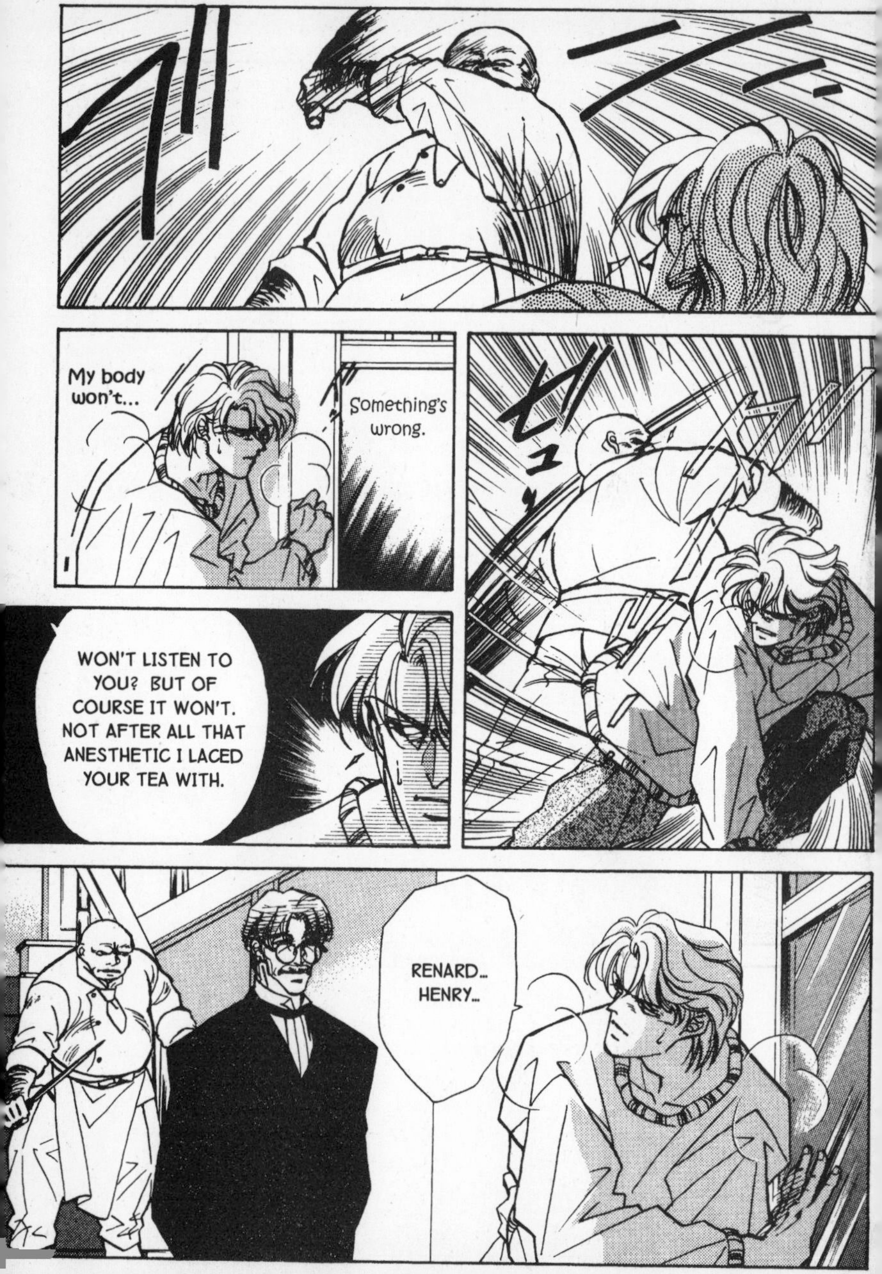
Something's wrong.
My body won't...
WON'T LISTEN TO YOU? BUT OF COURSE IT WON'T. NOT AFTER ALL THAT ANESTHETIC I LACED YOUR TEA WITH.
RENARD... HENRY...

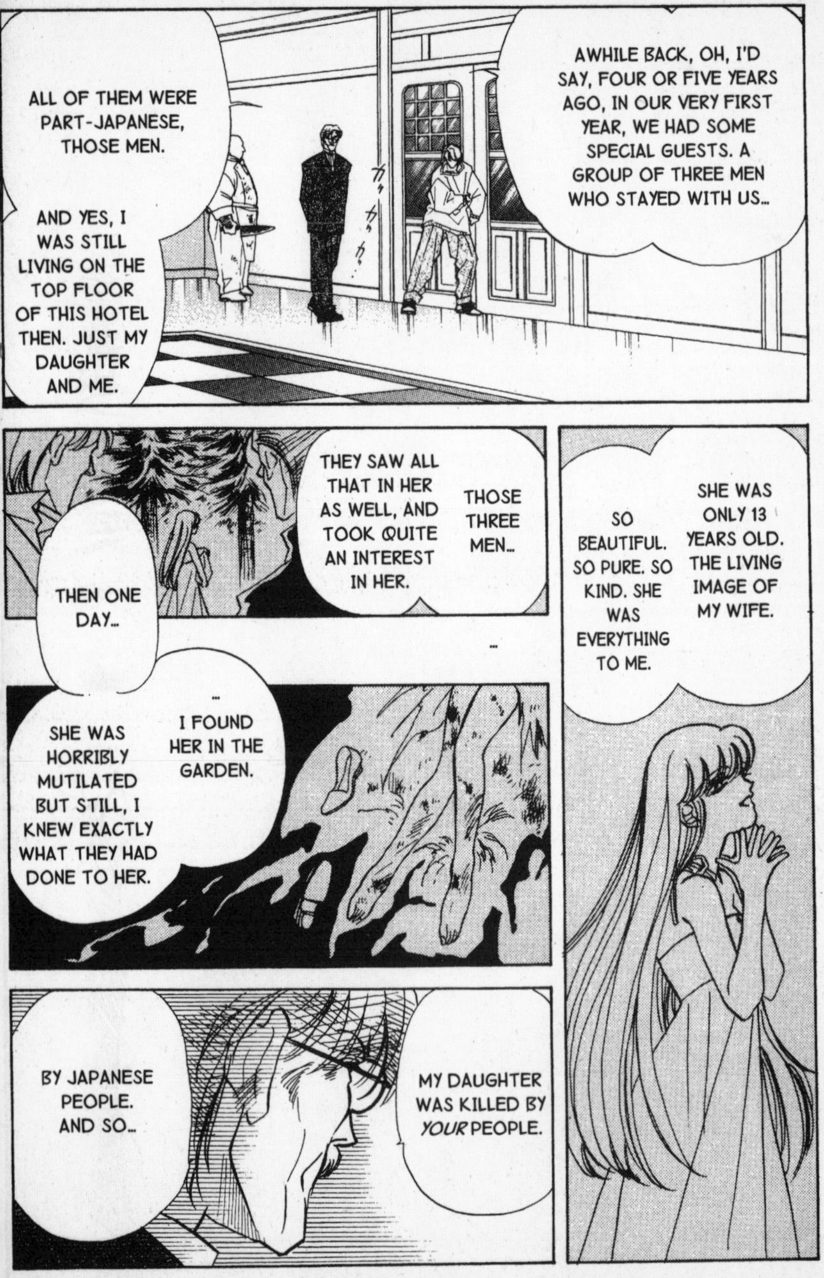
AWHILE BACK, OH, I'D SAY, FOUR OR FIVE YEARS AGO, IN OUR VERY FIRST YEAR, WE HAD SOME SPECIAL GUESTS. A GROUP OF THREE MEN WHO STAYED WITH US...
ALL OF THEM WERE PART-JAPANESE, THOSE MEN.
AND YES, I WAS STILL LIVING ON THE TOP FLOOR OF THIS HOTEL THEN. JUST MY DAUGHTER AND ME.
SHE WAS ONLY 13 YEARS OLD. THE LIVING IMAGE OF MY WIFE.
SO BEAUTIFUL. SO PURE. SO KIND. SHE WAS EVERYTHING TO ME.
THOSE THREE MEN...
THEY SAW ALL THAT IN HER AS WELL, AND TOOK QUITE AN INTEREST IN HER.
THEN ONE DAY...
...
...
I FOUND HER IN THE GARDEN.
SHE WAS HORRIBLY MUTILATED BUT STILL, I KNEW EXACTLY WHAT THEY HAD DONE TO HER.
MY DAUGHTER WAS KILLED BY *YOUR* PEOPLE.
BY JAPANESE PEOPLE. AND SO...

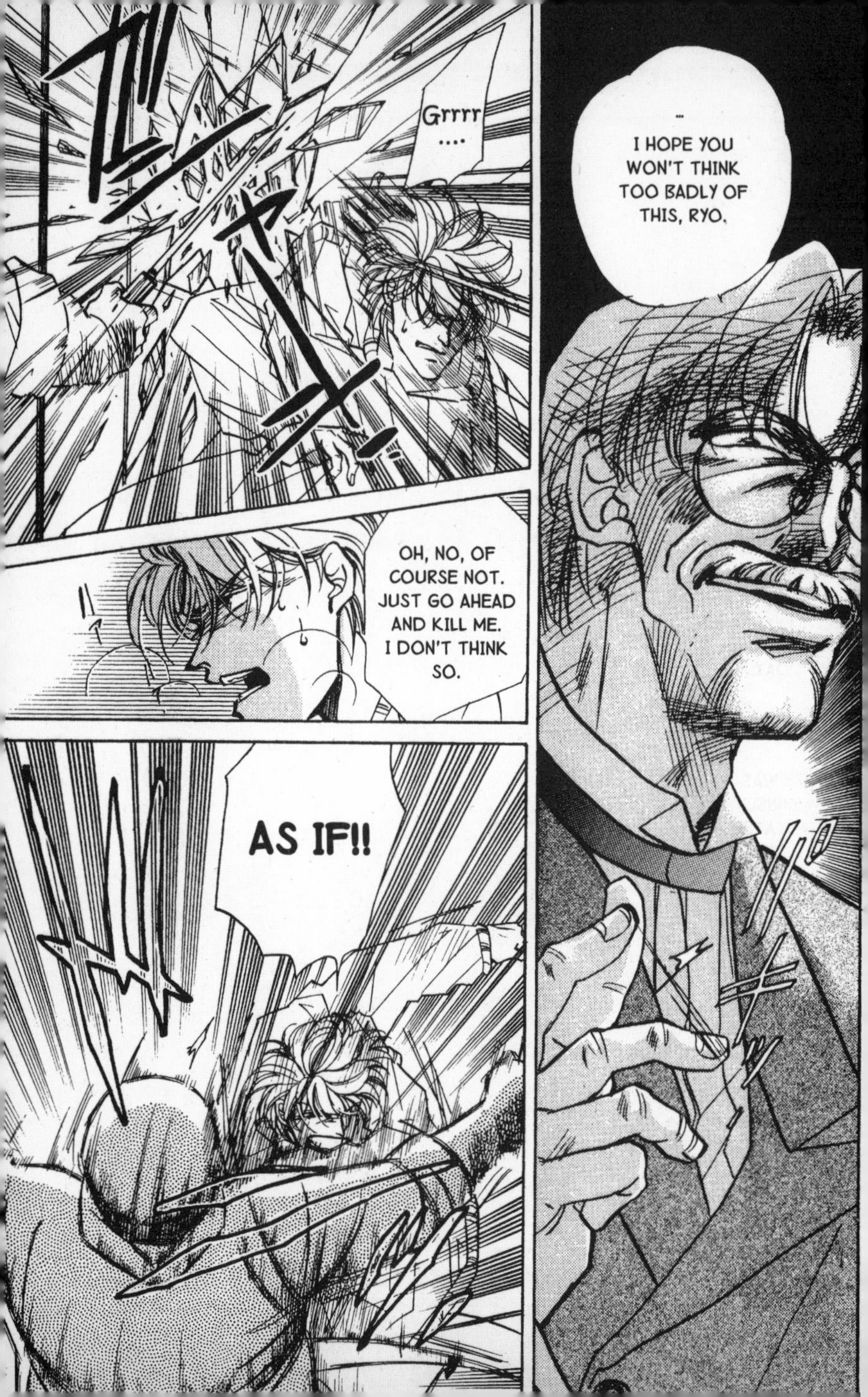
...
I HOPE YOU WON'T THINK TOO BADLY OF THIS, RYO.
Grrrr ....
OH, NO, OF COURSE NOT. JUST GO AHEAD AND KILL ME. I DON'T THINK SO.
AS IF!!

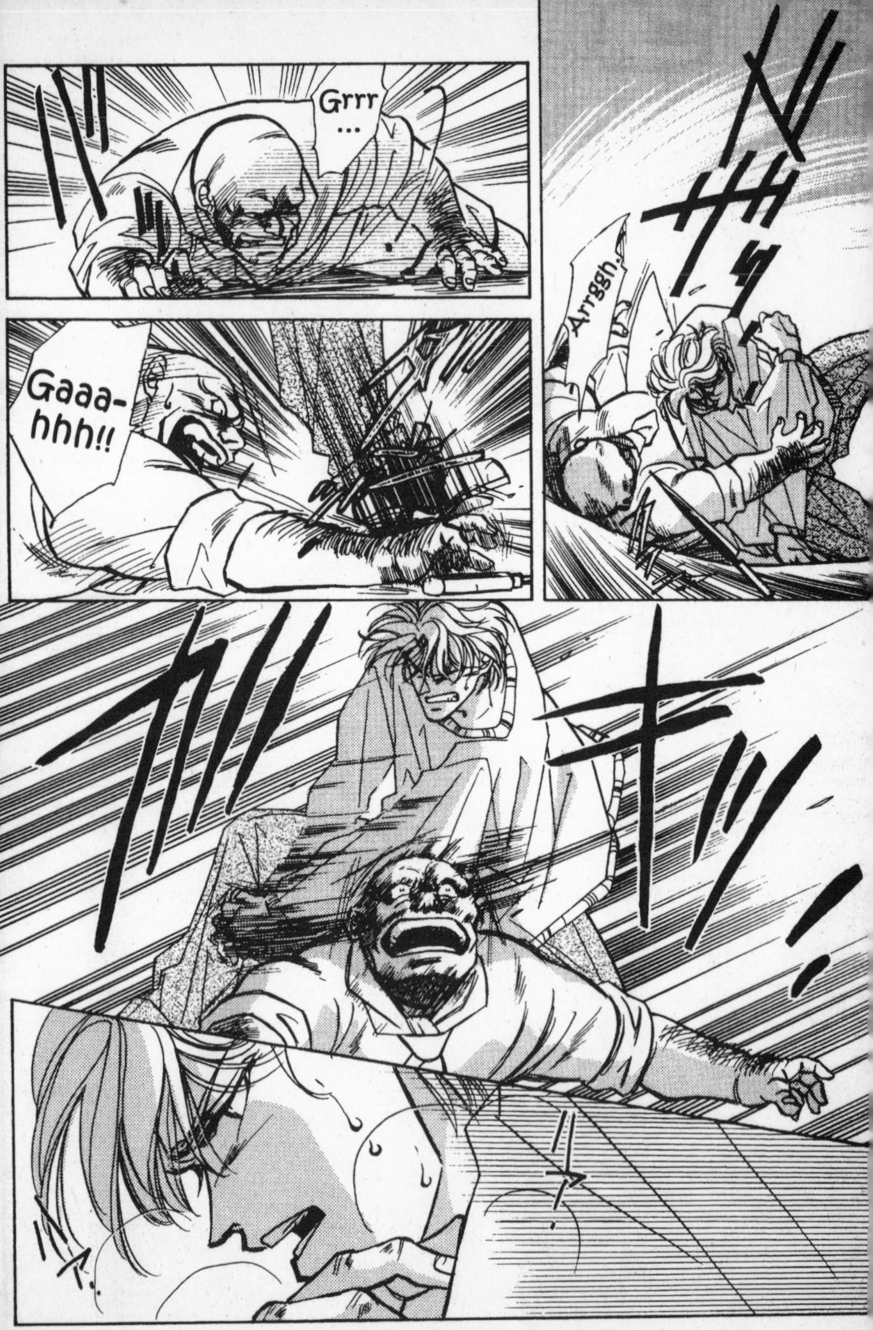
Arrggh.
Grrr ...
Gaaa-hhh!!

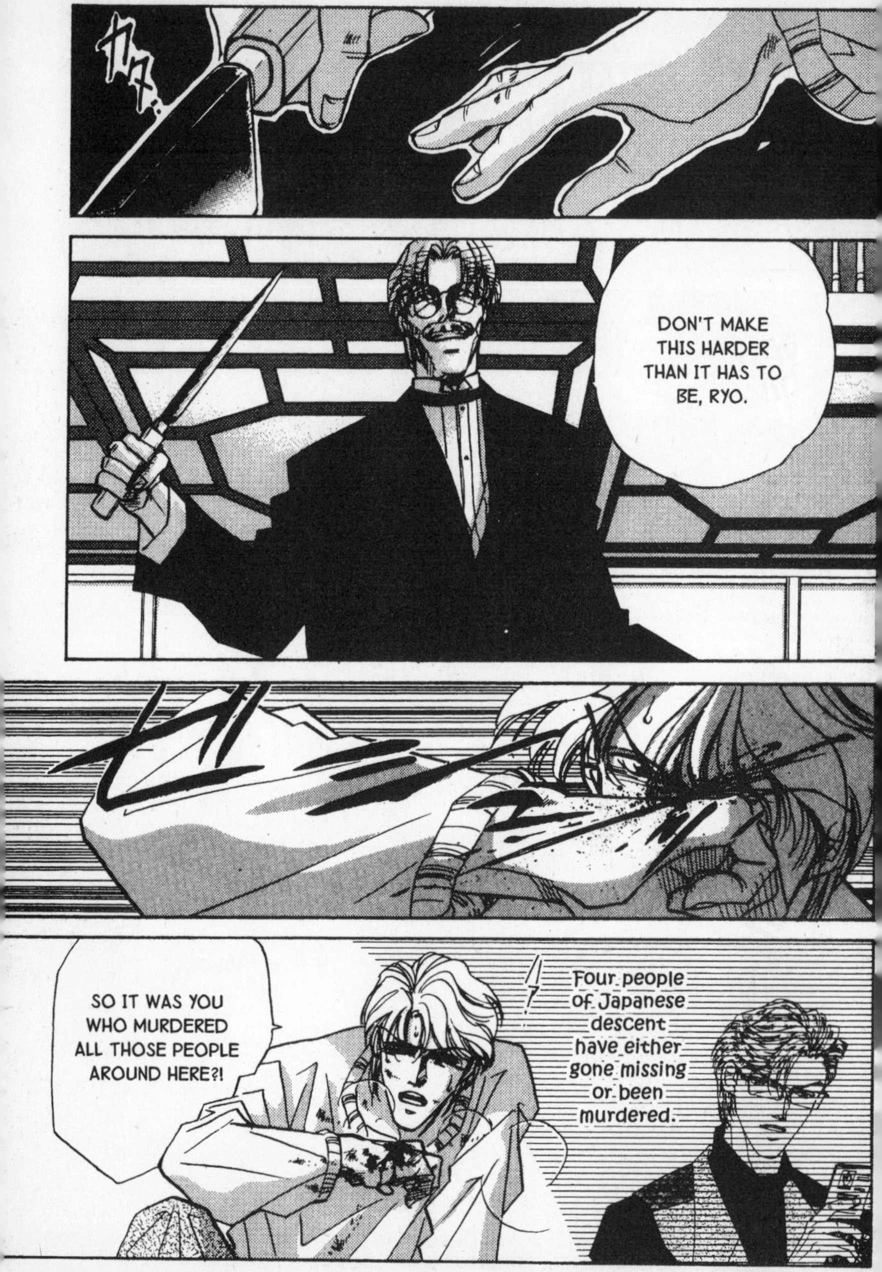
カァ…
DON'T MAKE THIS HARDER THAN IT HAS TO BE, RYO.
Four people of Japanese descent have either gone missing or been murdered.
SO IT WAS YOU WHO MURDERED ALL THOSE PEOPLE AROUND HERE?!

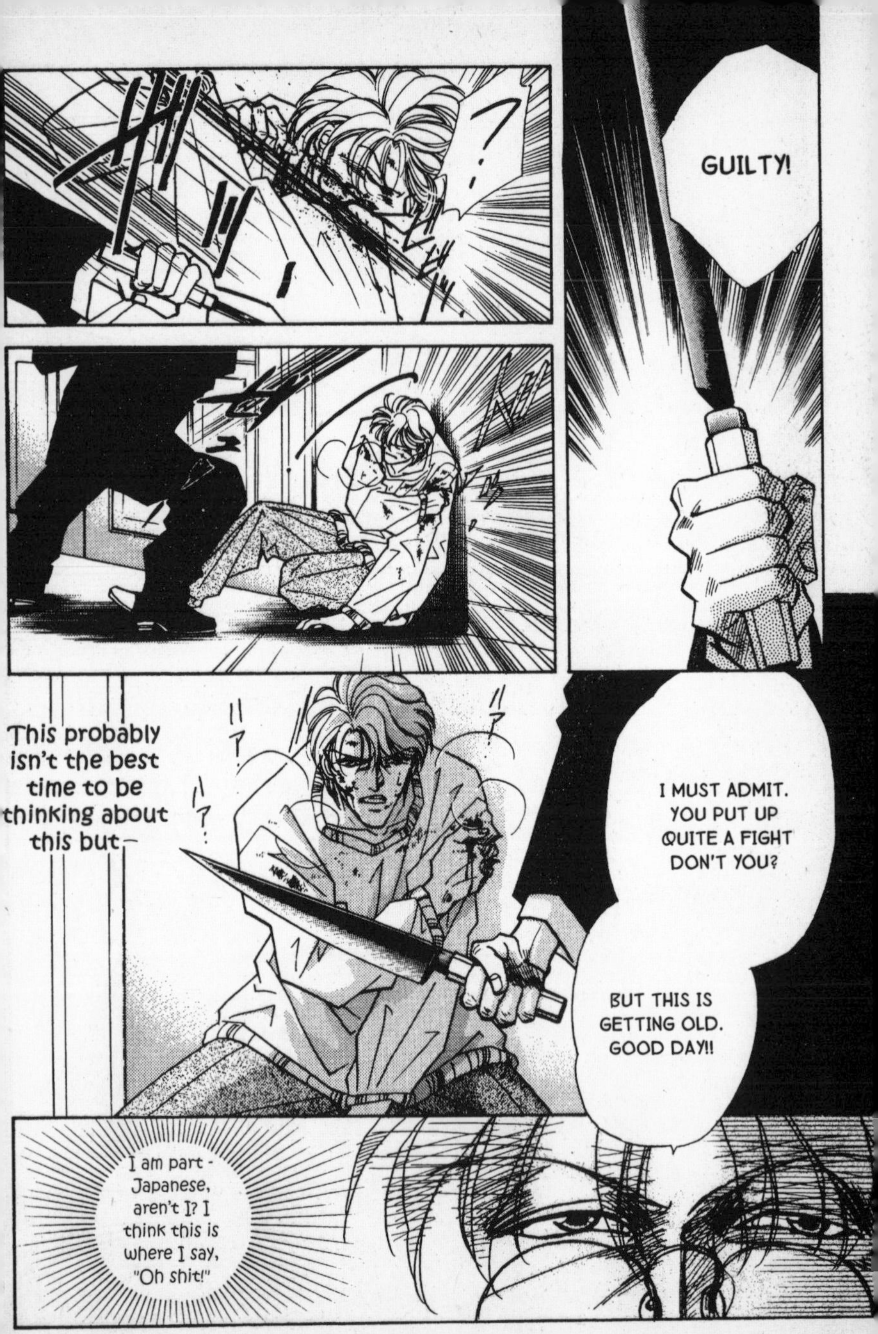
GUILTY!
I MUST ADMIT. YOU PUT UP QUITE A FIGHT DON'T YOU?
BUT THIS IS GETTING OLD. GOOD DAY!!
This probably isn't the best time to be thinking about this but–
I am part-Japanese, aren't I? I think this is where I say, "Oh shit!"

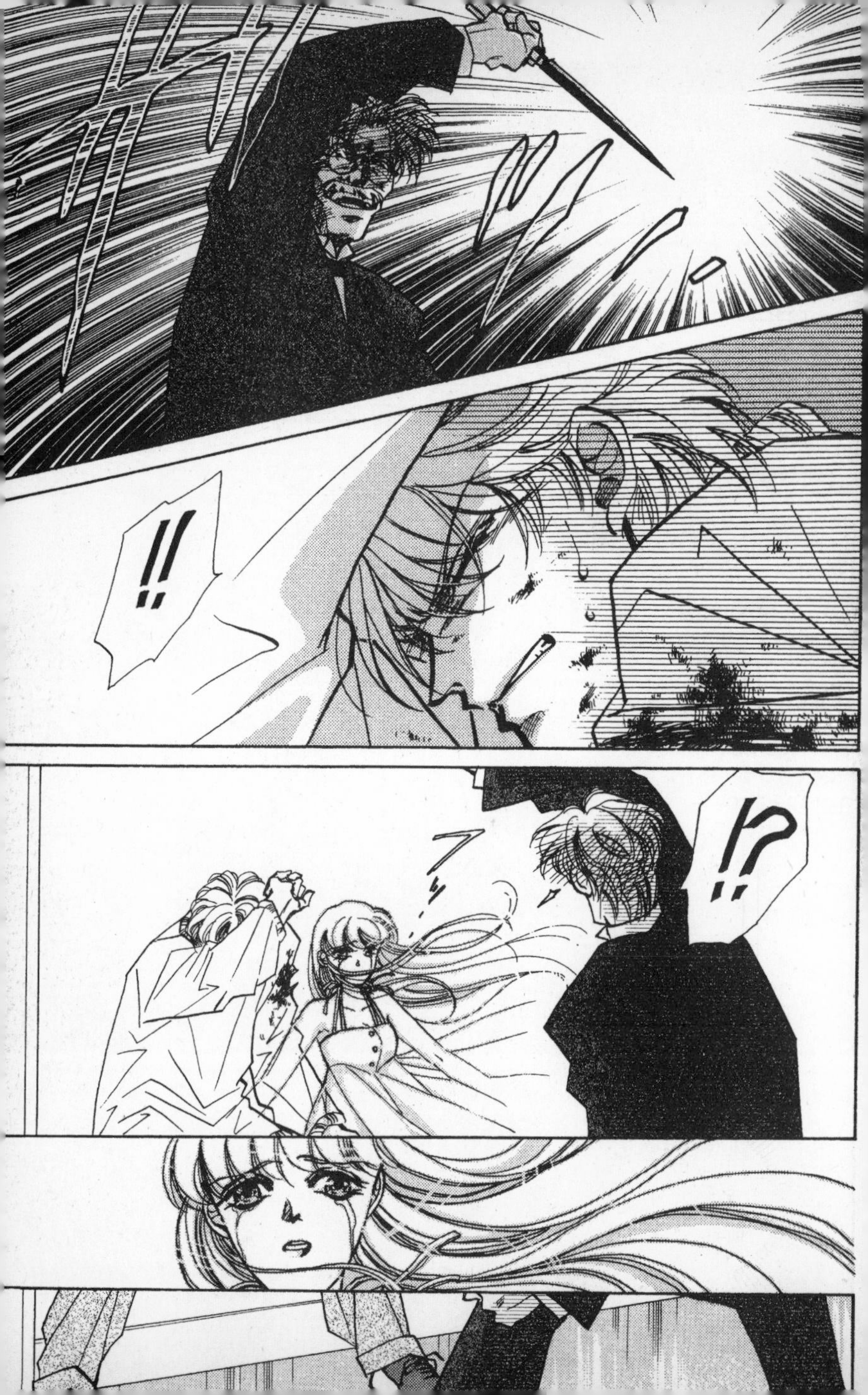

!!
!?

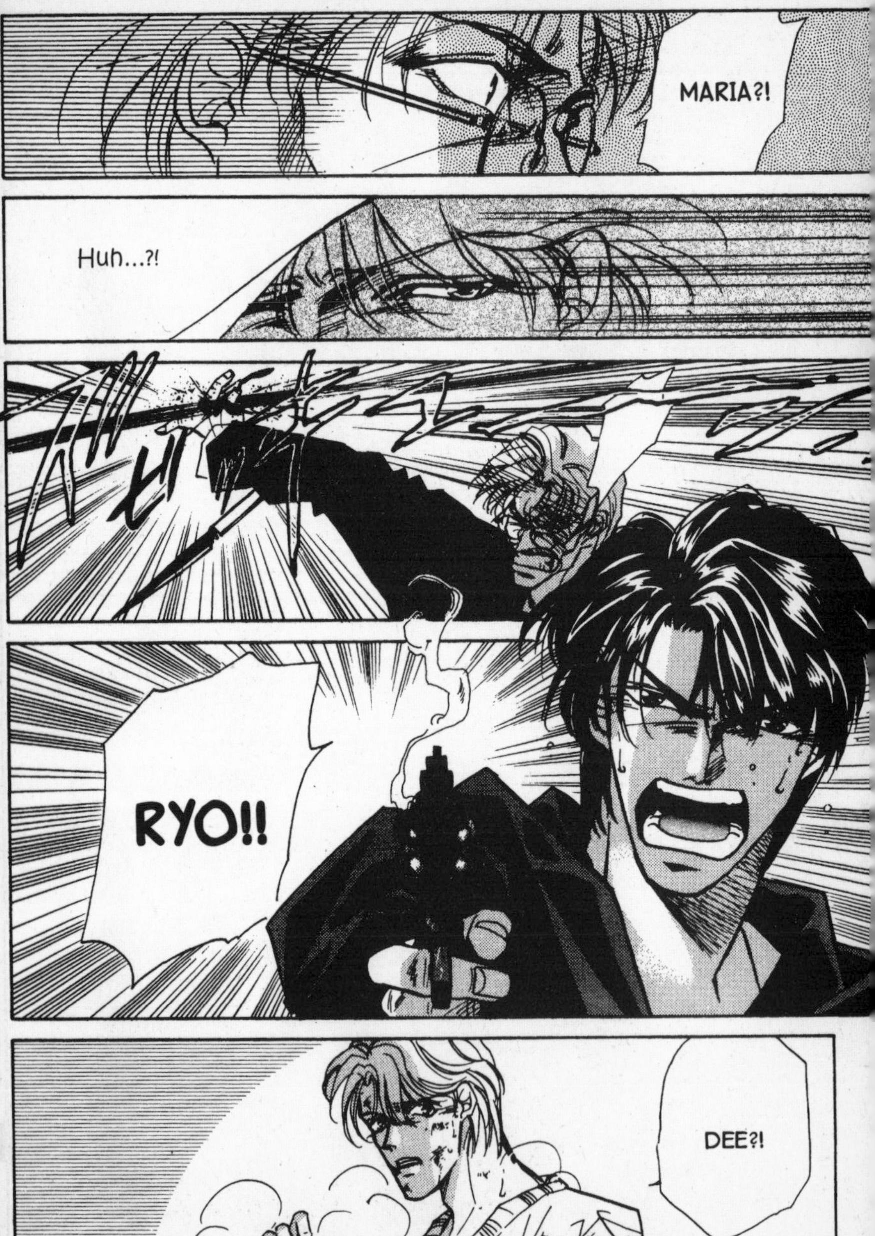
MARIA?!
Huh...?!
RYO!!
DEE?!

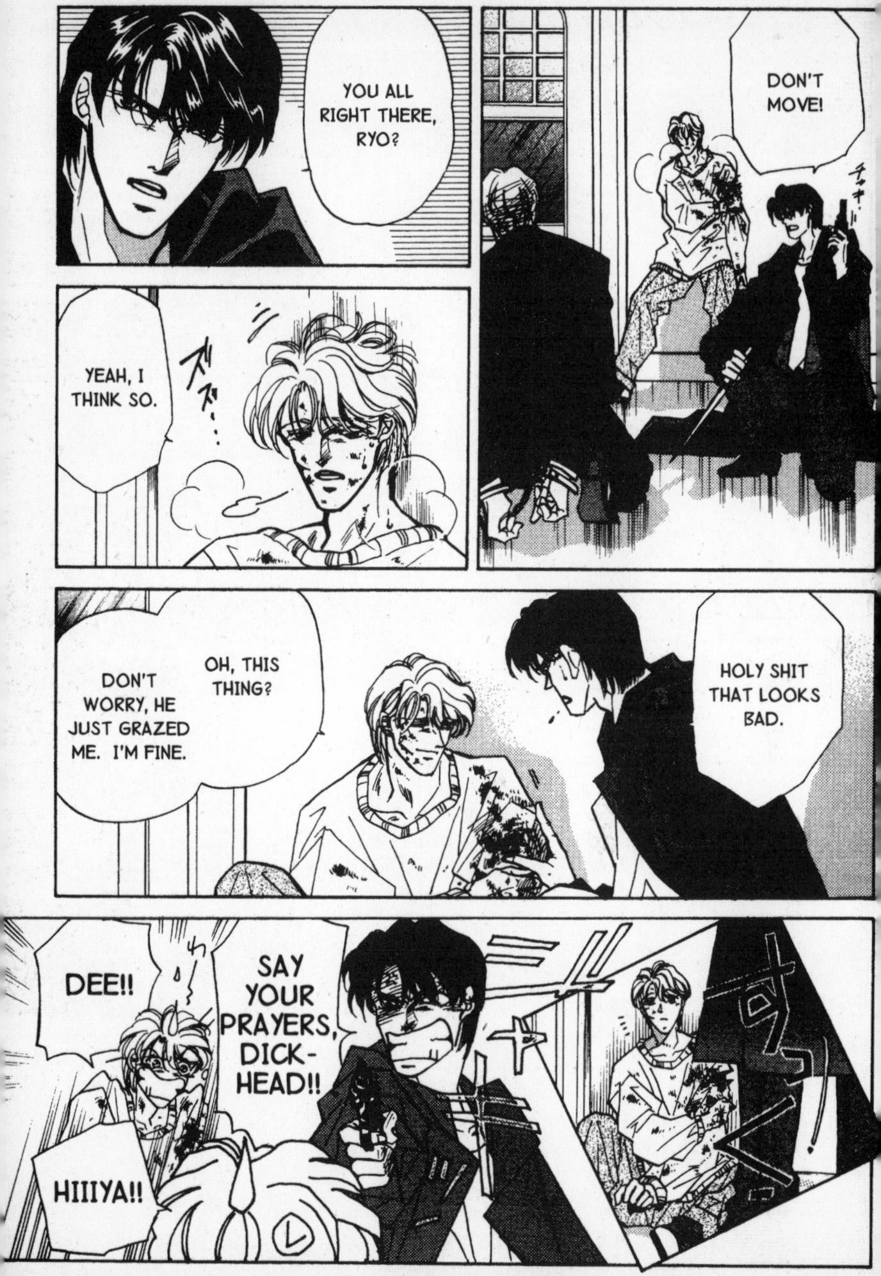
DON'T MOVE!
YOU ALL RIGHT THERE, RYO?
YEAH, I THINK SO.
HOLY SHIT THAT LOOKS BAD.
OH, THIS THING?
DON'T WORRY, HE JUST GRAZED ME. I'M FINE.
SAY YOUR PRAYERS, DICK-HEAD!!
DEE!!
HIIIYA!!

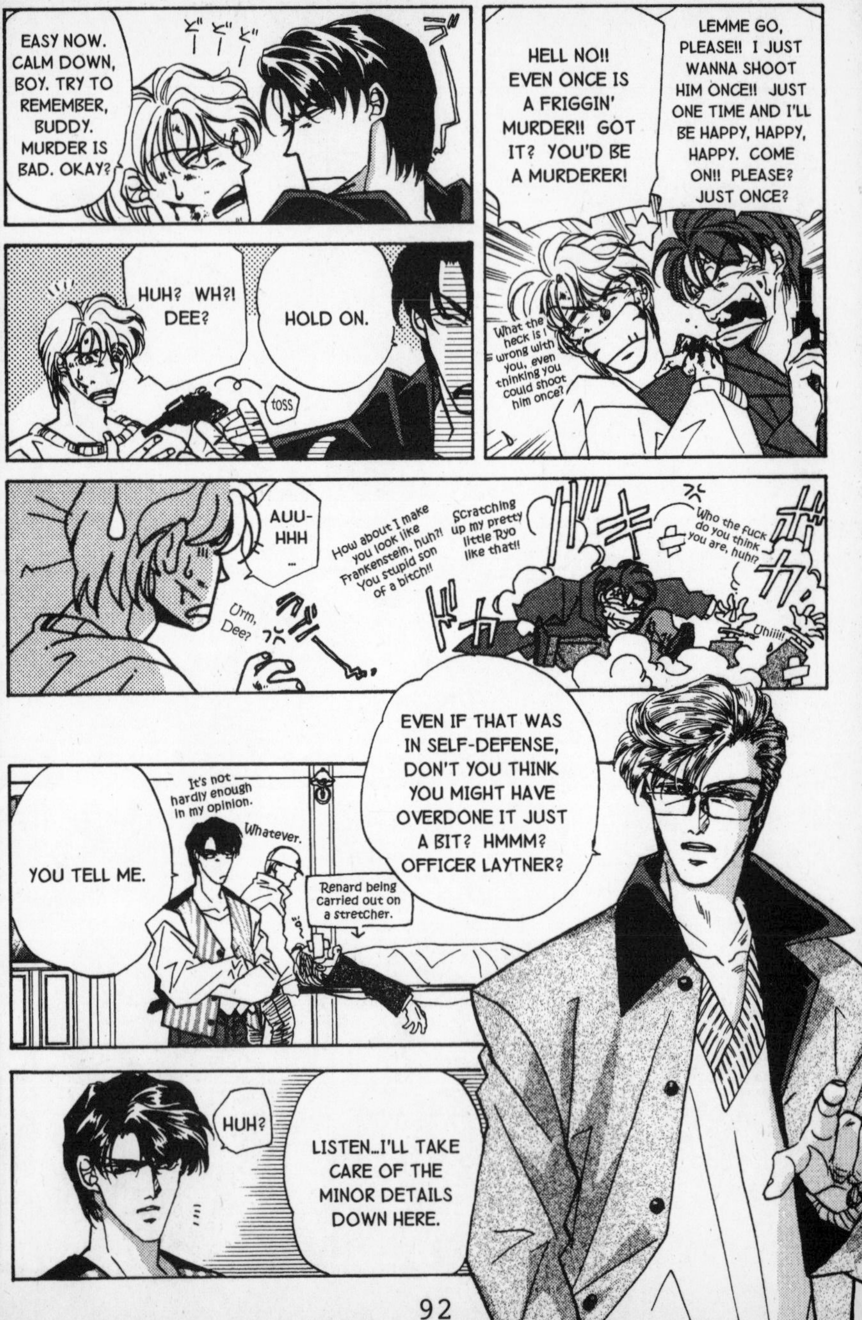
EASY NOW. CALM DOWN, BOY. TRY TO REMEMBER, BUDDY. MURDER IS BAD. OKAY?
LEMME GO, PLEASE!! I JUST WANNA SHOOT HIM ONCE!! JUST ONE TIME AND I'LL BE HAPPY, HAPPY, HAPPY. COME ON!! PLEASE? JUST ONCE?
HELL NO!! EVEN ONCE IS A FRIGGIN' MURDER!! GOT IT? YOU'D BE A MURDERER!
What the heck is wrong with you, even thinking you could shoot him once?
HUH? WH?! DEE?
HOLD ON.
toss
AUU-HHH ...
Urm, Dee?
How about I make you look like Frankenstein, huh?! You stupid son of a bitch!!
Scratching up my pretty little Ryo like that!!
Who the fuck do you think you are, huh!?
Uhiiii!
EVEN IF THAT WAS IN SELF-DEFENSE, DON'T YOU THINK YOU MIGHT HAVE OVERDONE IT JUST A BIT? HMMM? OFFICER LAYTNER?
YOU TELL ME.
It's not hardly enough in my opinion.
Whatever.
Renard being carried out on a stretcher.
HUH?
LISTEN...I'LL TAKE CARE OF THE MINOR DETAILS DOWN HERE.

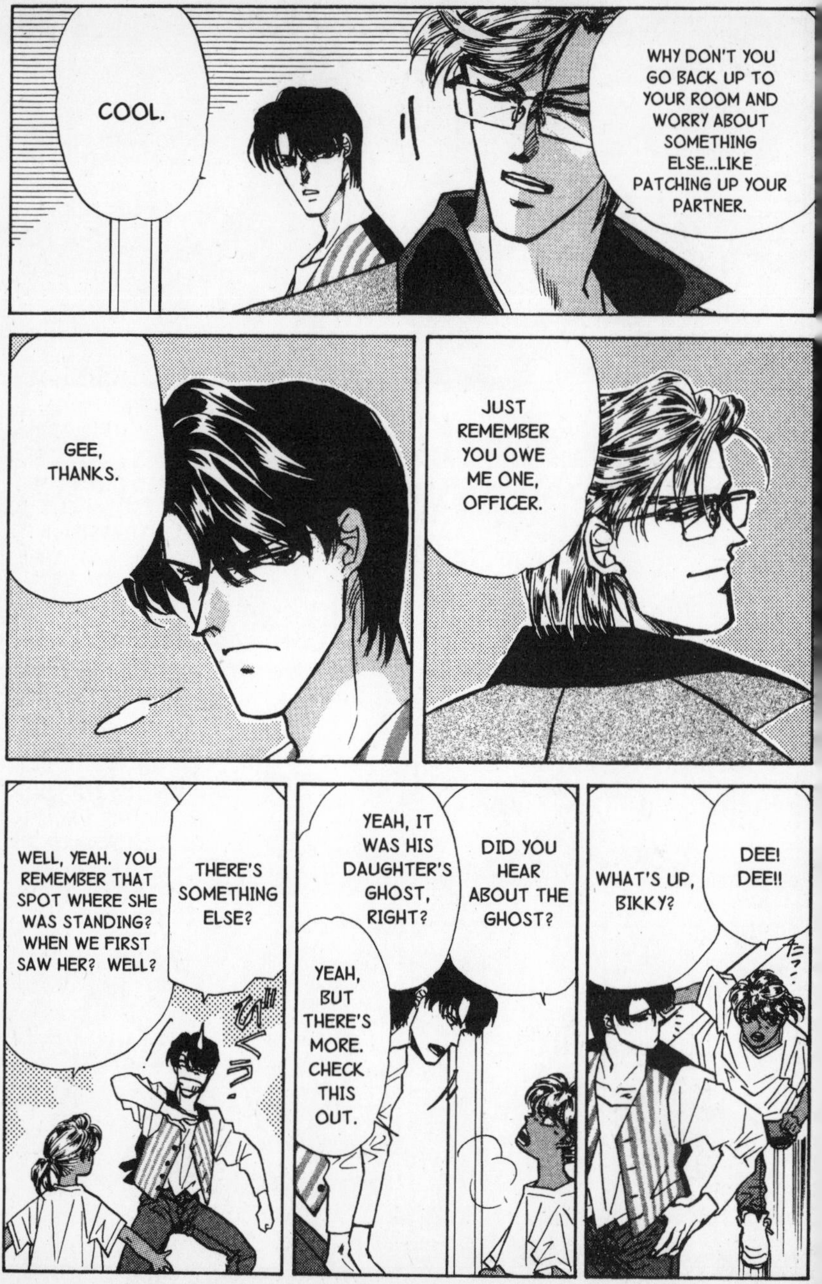
WHY DON'T YOU GO BACK UP TO YOUR ROOM AND WORRY ABOUT SOMETHING ELSE...LIKE PATCHING UP YOUR PARTNER.
COOL.
JUST REMEMBER YOU OWE ME ONE, OFFICER.
GEE, THANKS.
DEE! DEE!!
WHAT'S UP, BIKKY?
DID YOU HEAR ABOUT THE GHOST?
YEAH, IT WAS HIS DAUGHTER'S GHOST, RIGHT?
YEAH, BUT THERE'S MORE. CHECK THIS OUT.
THERE'S SOMETHING ELSE?
WELL, YEAH. YOU REMEMBER THAT SPOT WHERE SHE WAS STANDING? WHEN WE FIRST SAW HER? WELL?

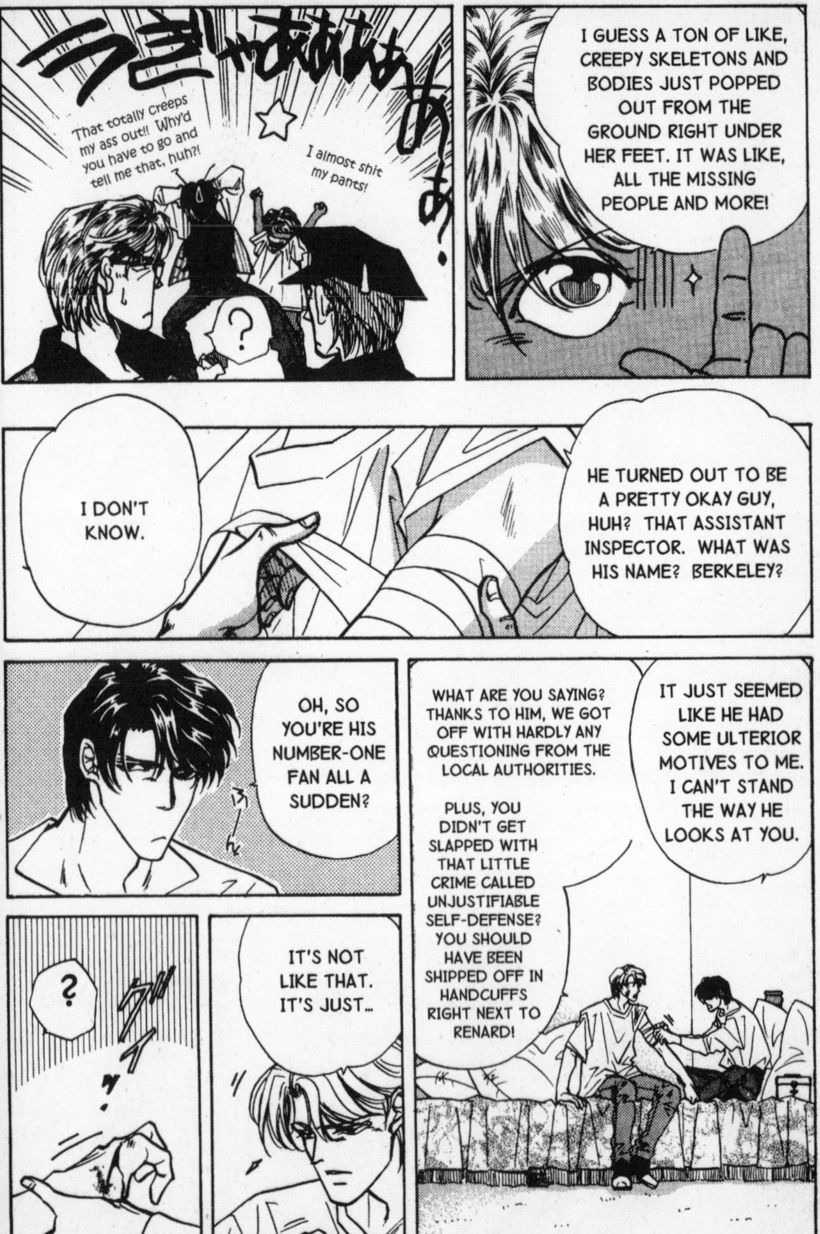
I GUESS A TON OF LIKE, CREEPY SKELETONS AND BODIES JUST POPPED OUT FROM THE GROUND RIGHT UNDER HER FEET. IT WAS LIKE, ALL THE MISSING PEOPLE AND MORE!
I almost shit my pants!
That totally creeps my ass out!! Why'd you have to go and tell me that, huh?!
?
HE TURNED OUT TO BE A PRETTY OKAY GUY, HUH? THAT ASSISTANT INSPECTOR. WHAT WAS HIS NAME? BERKELEY?
I DON'T KNOW.
OH, SO YOU'RE HIS NUMBER-ONE FAN ALL A SUDDEN?
WHAT ARE YOU SAYING? THANKS TO HIM, WE GOT OFF WITH HARDLY ANY QUESTIONING FROM THE LOCAL AUTHORITIES.
PLUS, YOU DIDN'T GET SLAPPED WITH THAT LITTLE CRIME CALLED UNJUSTIFIABLE SELF-DEFENSE? YOU SHOULD HAVE BEEN SHIPPED OFF IN HANDCUFFS RIGHT NEXT TO RENARD!
?
IT'S NOT LIKE THAT. IT'S JUST...
IT JUST SEEMED LIKE HE HAD SOME ULTERIOR MOTIVES TO ME. I CAN'T STAND THE WAY HE LOOKS AT YOU.

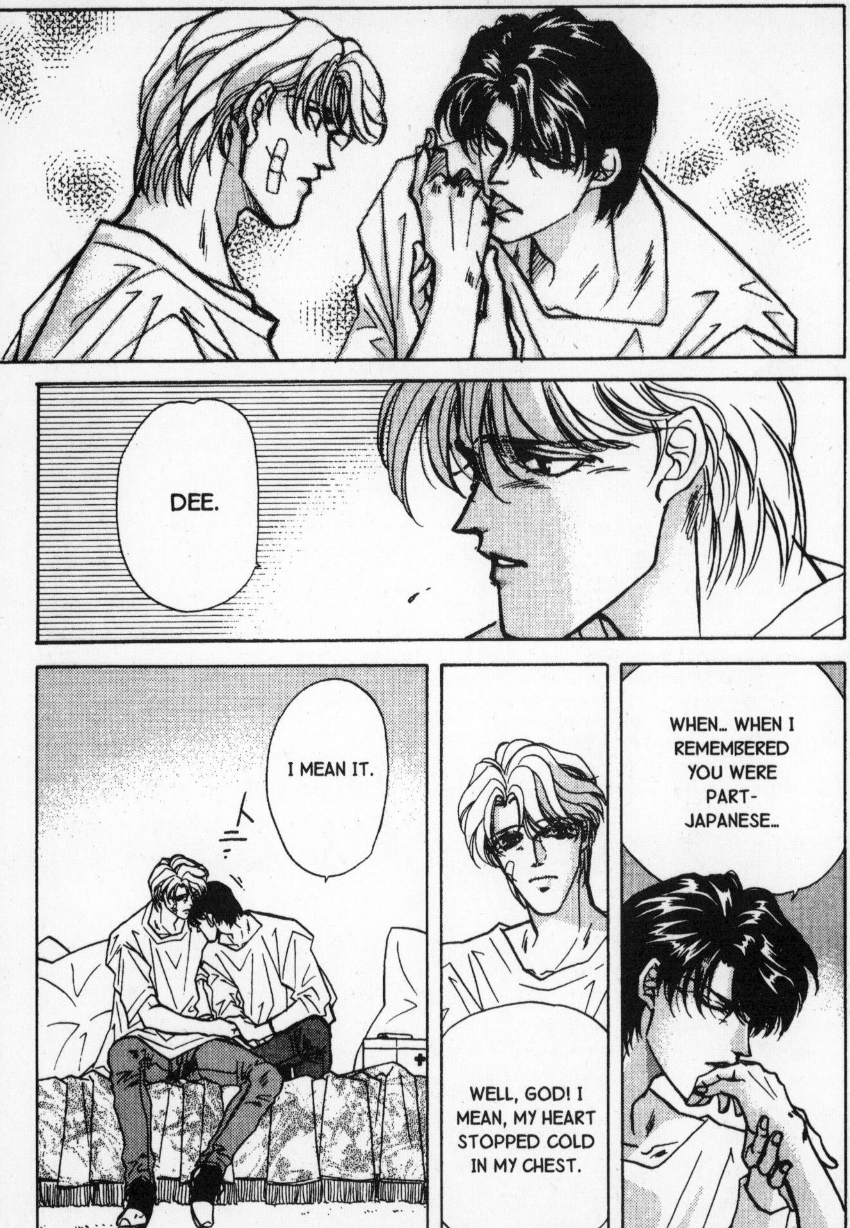
DEE.
WHEN... WHEN I REMEMBERED YOU WERE PART-JAPANESE...
WELL, GOD! I MEAN, MY HEART STOPPED COLD IN MY CHEST.
I MEAN IT.

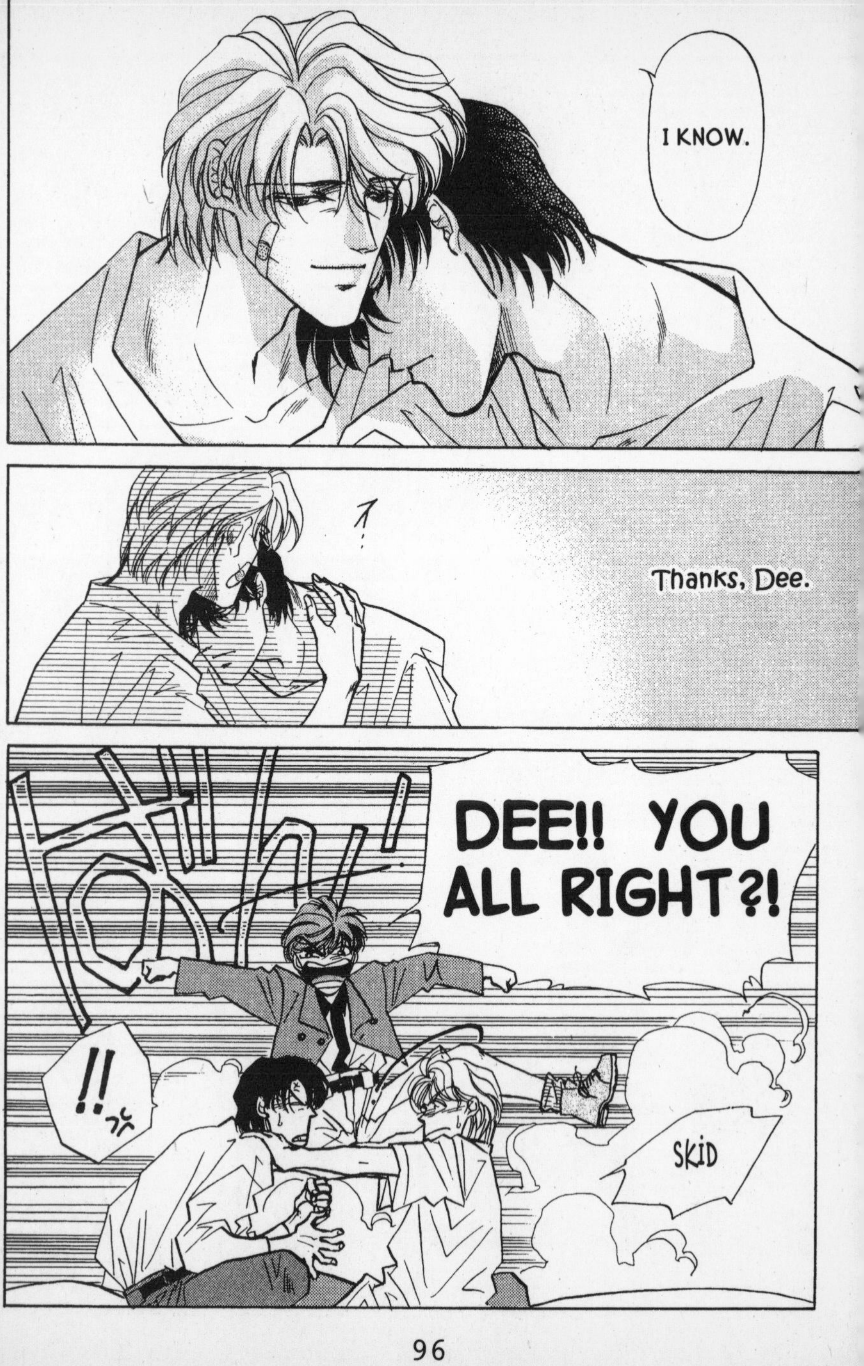
I KNOW.
Thanks, Dee.
DEE!! YOU ALL RIGHT?!
!!
SKID

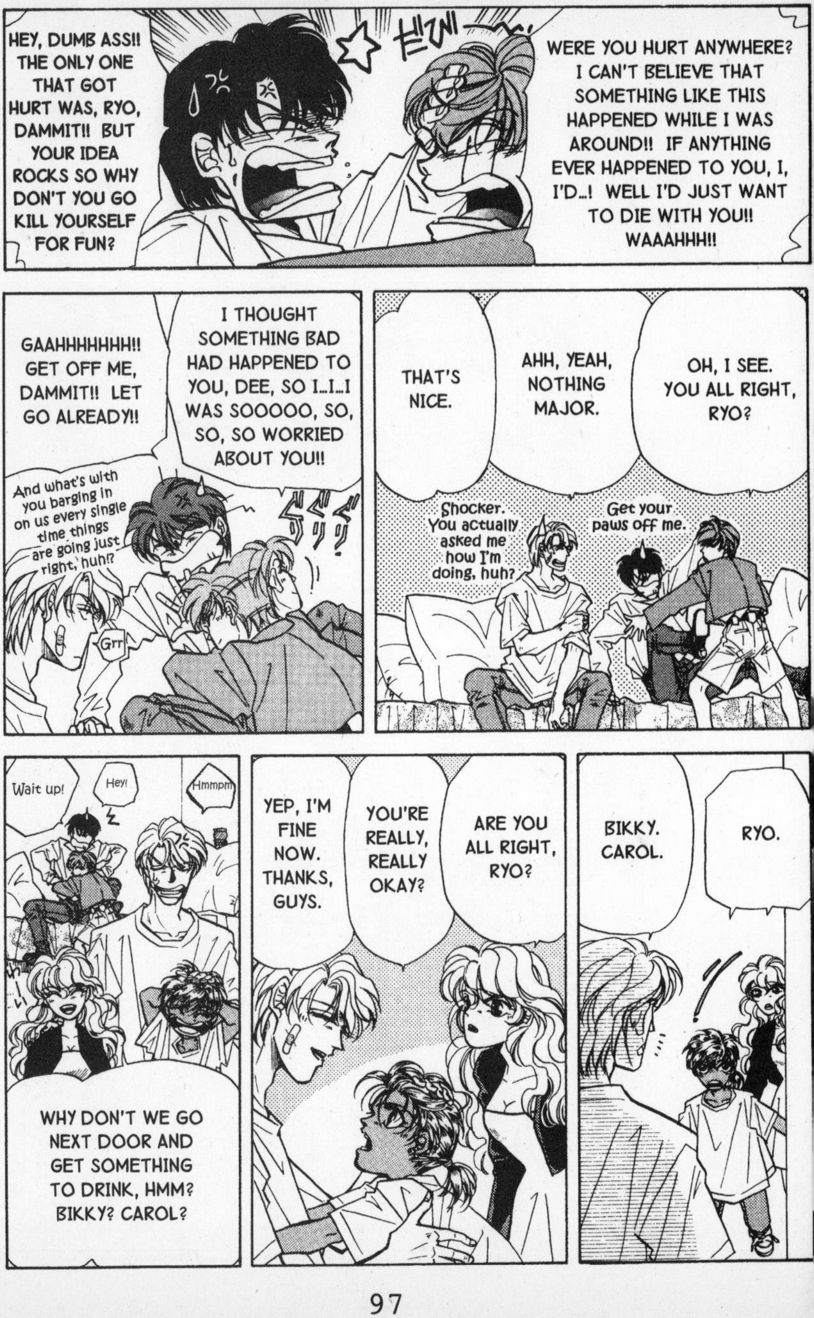
WERE YOU HURT ANYWHERE? I CAN'T BELIEVE THAT SOMETHING LIKE THIS HAPPENED WHILE I WAS AROUND!! IF ANYTHING EVER HAPPENED TO YOU, I, I'D...! WELL I'D JUST WANT TO DIE WITH YOU!! WAAAHHH!!
HEY, DUMB ASS!! THE ONLY ONE THAT GOT HURT WAS, RYO, DAMMIT!! BUT YOUR IDEA ROCKS SO WHY DON'T YOU GO KILL YOURSELF FOR FUN?
OH, I SEE. YOU ALL RIGHT, RYO?
AHH, YEAH, NOTHING MAJOR.
THAT'S NICE.
Get your paws off me.
Shocker. You actually asked me how I'm doing, huh?
I THOUGHT SOMETHING BAD HAD HAPPENED TO YOU, DEE, SO I...I...I WAS SOOOOO, SO, SO, SO WORRIED ABOUT YOU!!
GAAHHHHHHH!! GET OFF ME, DAMMIT!! LET GO ALREADY!!
And what's with you barging in on us every single time things are going just right, huh!?
Grr
RYO.
BIKKY. CAROL.
ARE YOU ALL RIGHT, RYO?
YOU'RE REALLY, REALLY OKAY?
YEP, I'M FINE NOW. THANKS, GUYS.
Hey!
Wait up!
WHY DON'T WE GO NEXT DOOR AND GET SOMETHING TO DRINK, HMM? BIKKY? CAROL?

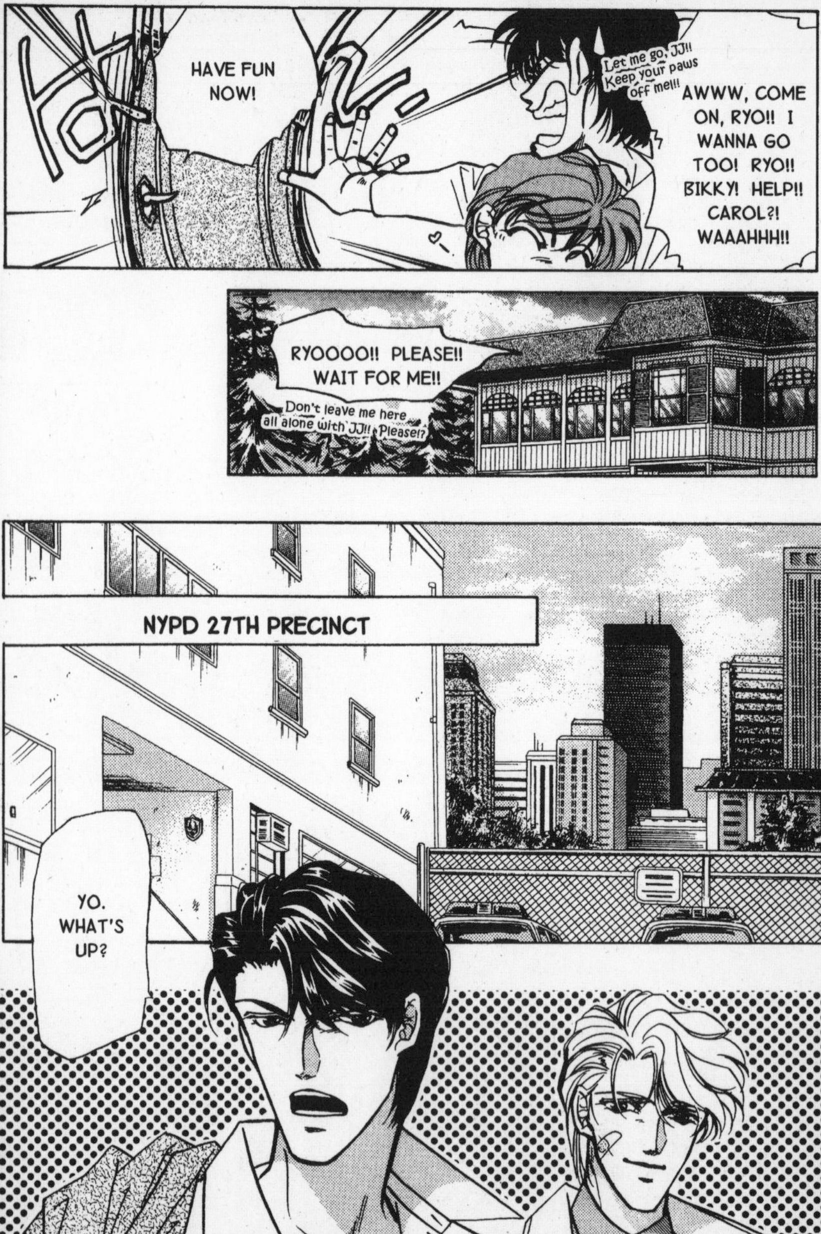
Let me go, JJ!! Keep your paws off me!!!
AWWW, COME ON, RYO!! I WANNA GO TOO! RYO!! BIKKY! HELP!! CAROL?! WAAAHHH!!
HAVE FUN NOW!
RYOOOO!! PLEASE!! WAIT FOR ME!!
Don't leave me here all alone with JJ!! Please!?
NYPD 27TH PRECINCT
YO. WHAT'S UP?

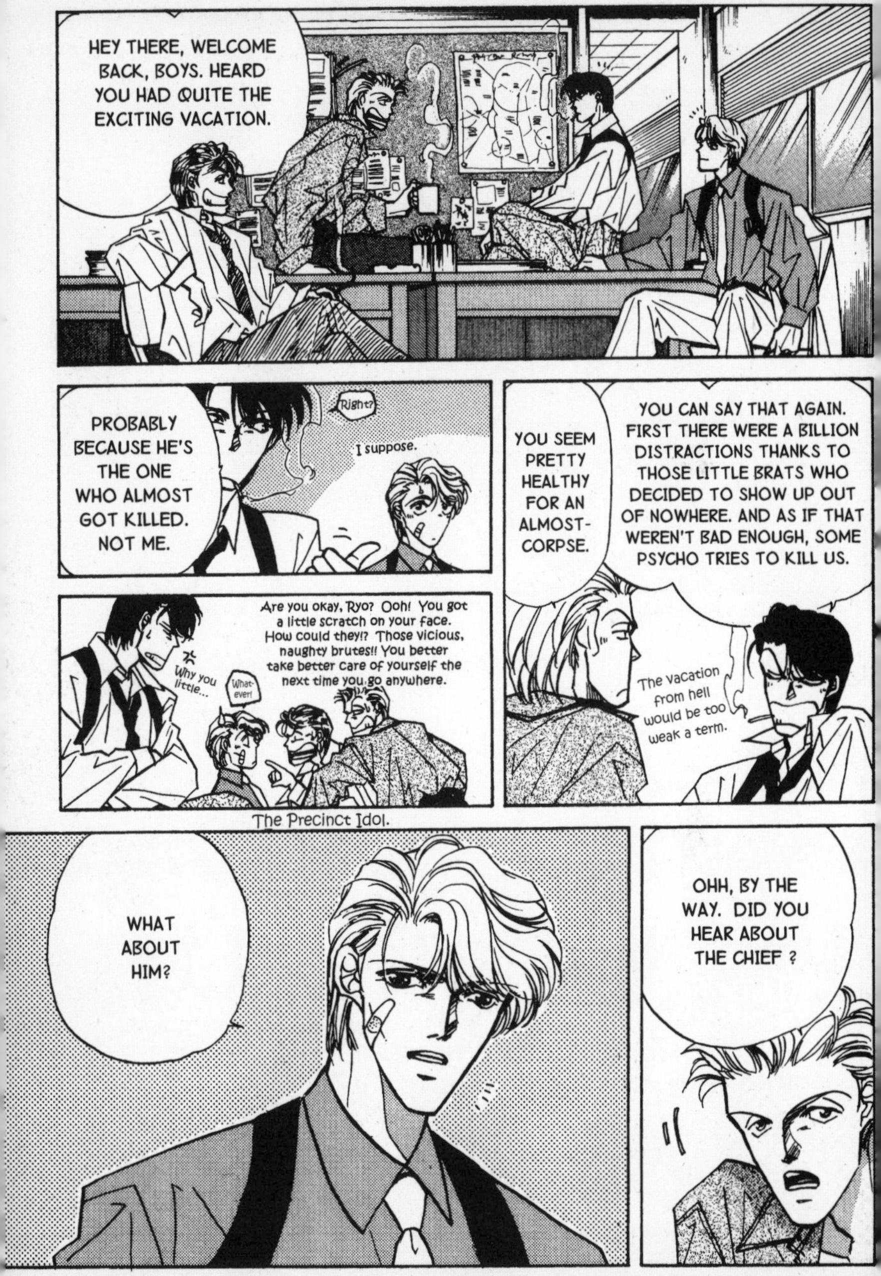
HEY THERE, WELCOME BACK, BOYS. HEARD YOU HAD QUITE THE EXCITING VACATION.
YOU CAN SAY THAT AGAIN. FIRST THERE WERE A BILLION DISTRACTIONS THANKS TO THOSE LITTLE BRATS WHO DECIDED TO SHOW UP OUT OF NOWHERE. AND AS IF THAT WEREN'T BAD ENOUGH, SOME PSYCHO TRIES TO KILL US.
YOU SEEM PRETTY HEALTHY FOR AN ALMOST-CORPSE.
The vacation from hell would be too weak a term.
PROBABLY BECAUSE HE'S THE ONE WHO ALMOST GOT KILLED. NOT ME.
Right?
I suppose.
Are you okay, Ryo? Ooh! You got a little scratch on your face. How could they!? Those vicious, naughty brutes!! You better take better care of yourself the next time you go anywhere.
Why you little...
What-ever!
The Precinct Idol.
OHH, BY THE WAY. DID YOU HEAR ABOUT THE CHIEF ?
WHAT ABOUT HIM?

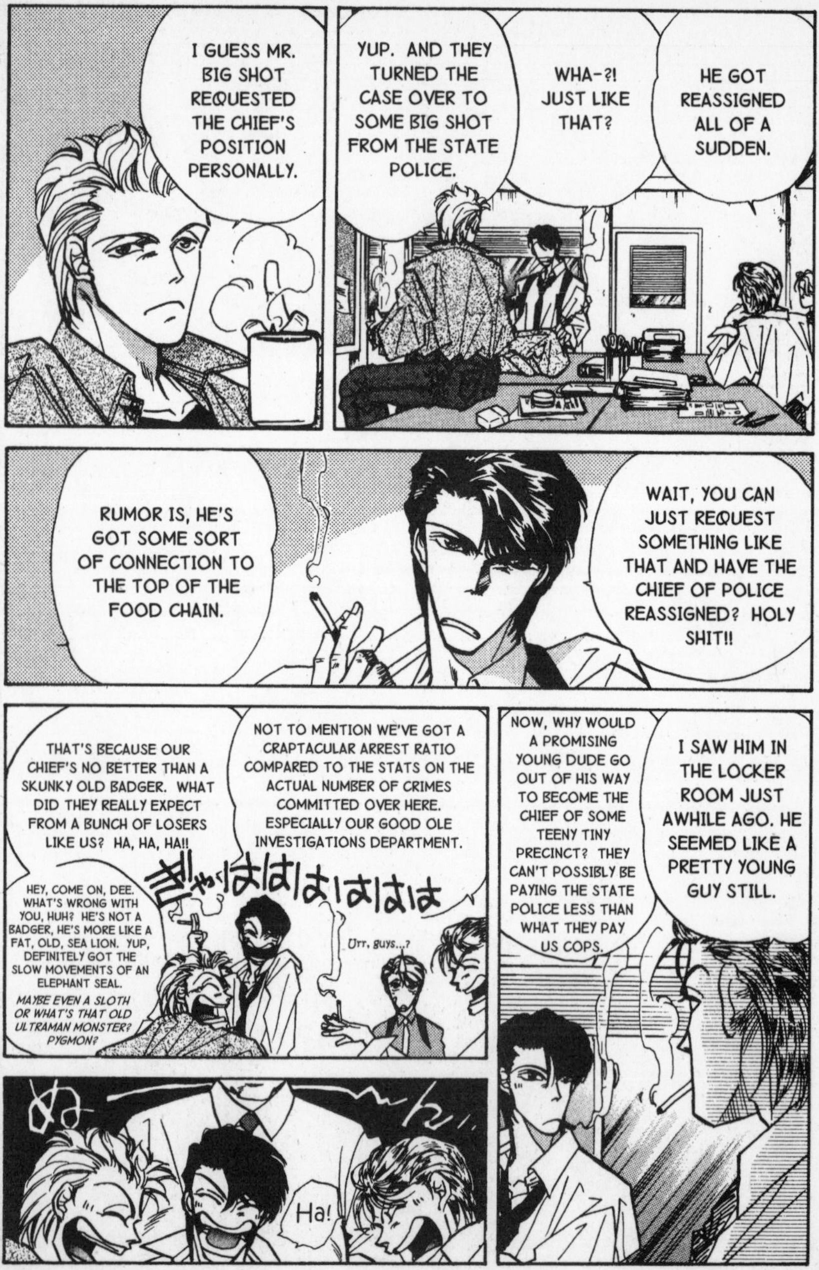
HE GOT REASSIGNED ALL OF A SUDDEN.
WHA-?! JUST LIKE THAT?
YUP. AND THEY TURNED THE CASE OVER TO SOME BIG SHOT FROM THE STATE POLICE.
I GUESS MR. BIG SHOT REQUESTED THE CHIEF'S POSITION PERSONALLY.
WAIT, YOU CAN JUST REQUEST SOMETHING LIKE THAT AND HAVE THE CHIEF OF POLICE REASSIGNED? HOLY SHIT!!
RUMOR IS, HE'S GOT SOME SORT OF CONNECTION TO THE TOP OF THE FOOD CHAIN.
I SAW HIM IN THE LOCKER ROOM JUST AWHILE AGO. HE SEEMED LIKE A PRETTY YOUNG GUY STILL.
NOW, WHY WOULD A PROMISING YOUNG DUDE GO OUT OF HIS WAY TO BECOME THE CHIEF OF SOME TEENY TINY PRECINCT? THEY CAN'T POSSIBLY BE PAYING THE STATE POLICE LESS THAN WHAT THEY PAY US COPS.
NOT TO MENTION WE'VE GOT A CRAPTACULAR ARREST RATIO COMPARED TO THE STATS ON THE ACTUAL NUMBER OF CRIMES COMMITTED OVER HERE. ESPECIALLY OUR GOOD OLE INVESTIGATIONS DEPARTMENT.
THAT'S BECAUSE OUR CHIEF'S NO BETTER THAN A SKUNKY OLD BADGER. WHAT DID THEY REALLY EXPECT FROM A BUNCH OF LOSERS LIKE US? HA, HA, HA!!
ぎゃはははははは
Urr, guys...?
HEY, COME ON, DEE. WHAT'S WRONG WITH YOU, HUH? HE'S NOT A BADGER, HE'S MORE LIKE A FAT, OLD, SEA LION. YUP, DEFINITELY GOT THE SLOW MOVEMENTS OF AN ELEPHANT SEAL.
MAYBE EVEN A SLOTH OR WHAT'S THAT OLD ULTRAMAN MONSTER? PYGMON?
ぬーーん
Ha!

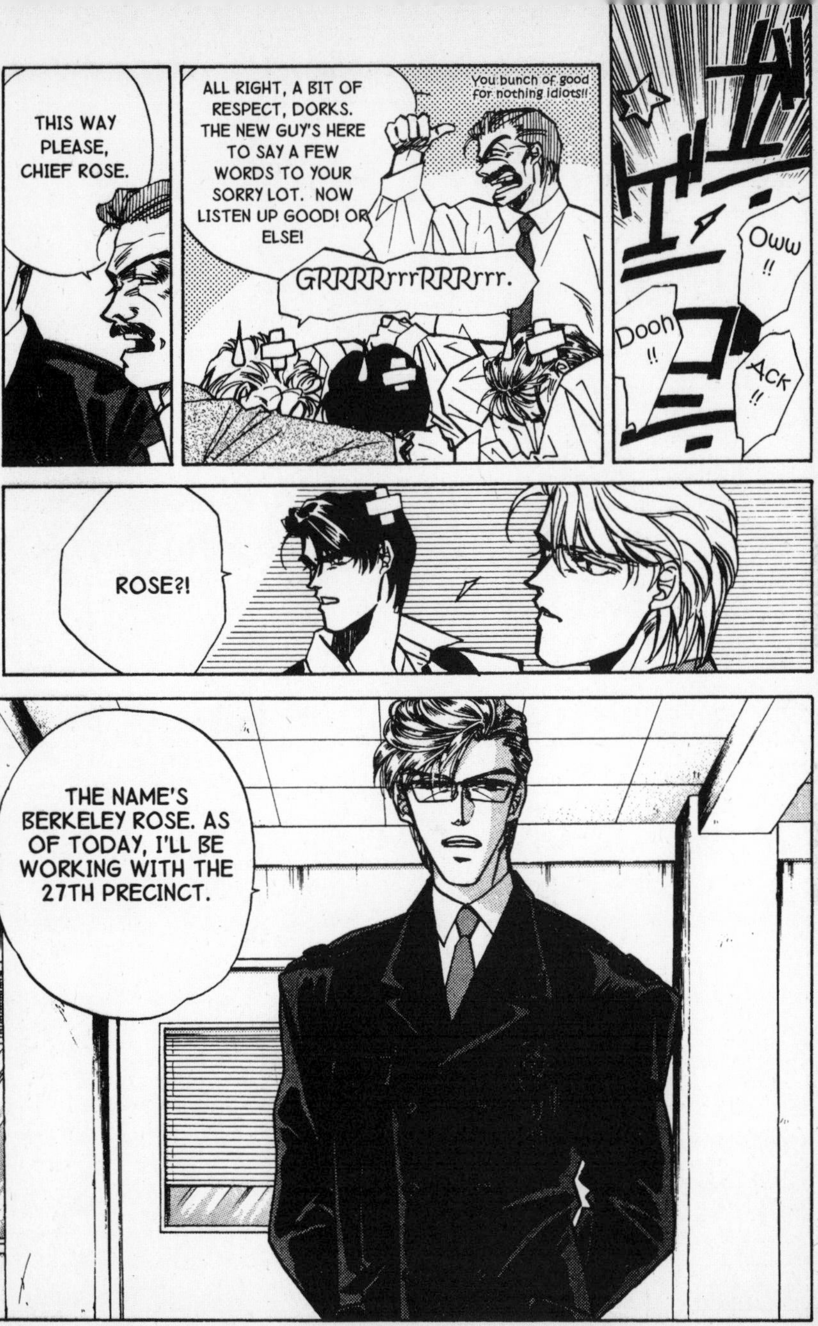
Oww !!
Dooh !!
Ack !!
You bunch of good for nothing idiots!!
ALL RIGHT, A BIT OF RESPECT, DORKS. THE NEW GUY'S HERE TO SAY A FEW WORDS TO YOUR SORRY LOT. NOW LISTEN UP GOOD! OR ELSE!
GRRRRrrrRRRrrr.
THIS WAY PLEASE, CHIEF ROSE.
ROSE?!
THE NAME'S BERKELEY ROSE. AS OF TODAY, I'LL BE WORKING WITH THE 27TH PRECINCT.

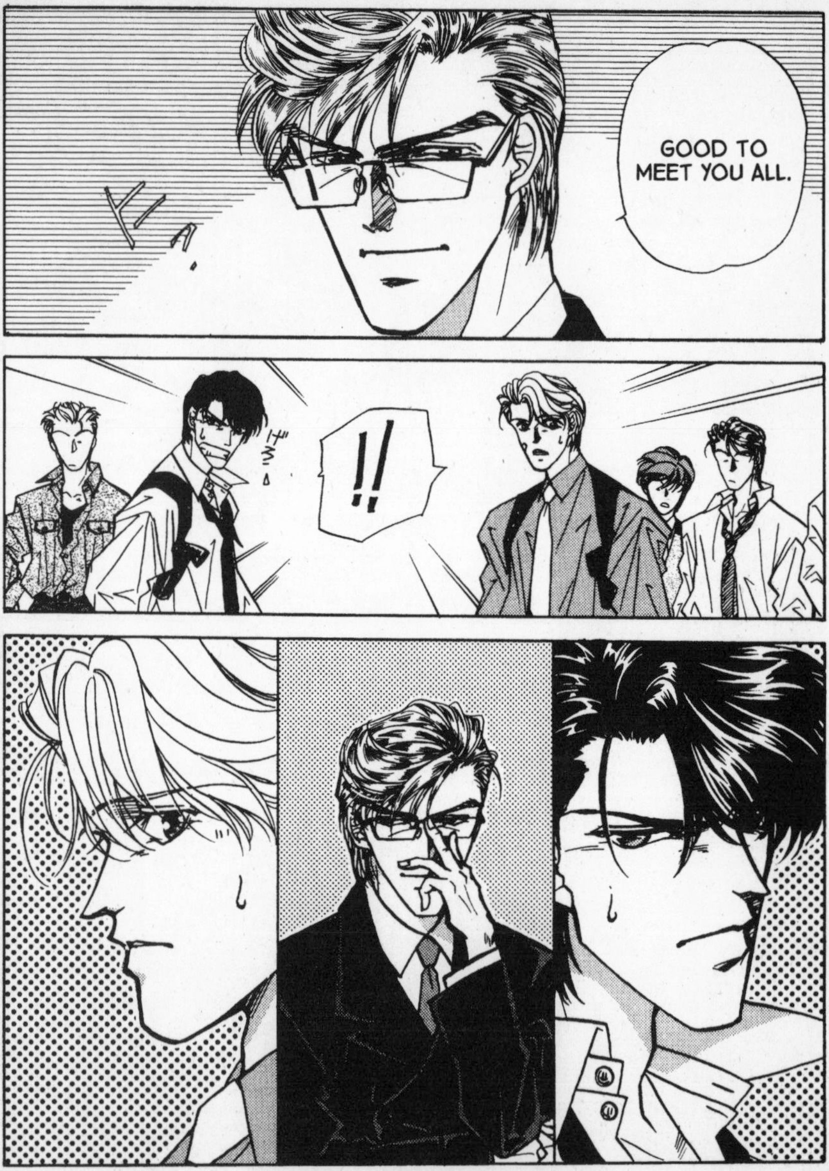
GOOD TO MEET YOU ALL.
!!
SEE YOU AGAIN.

FAKE act.5/The End.

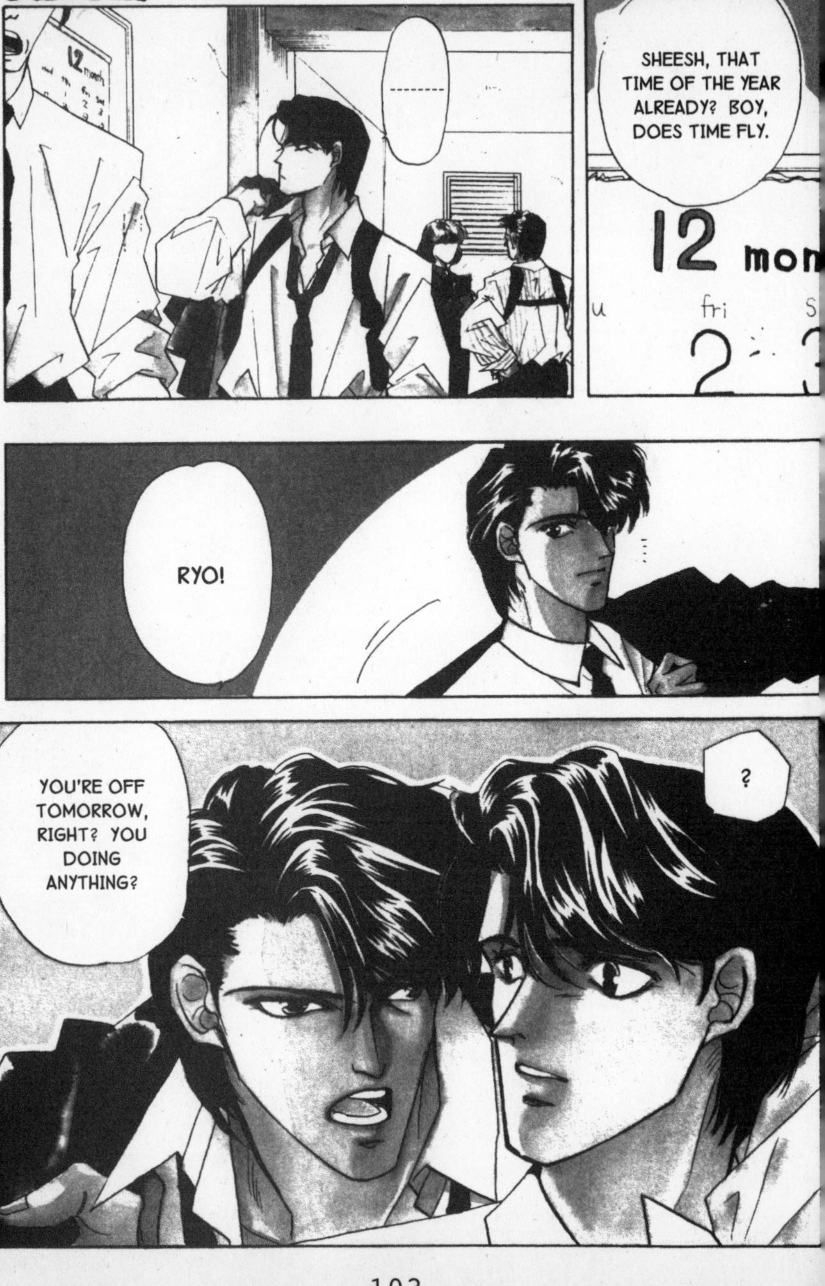
SHEESH, THAT TIME OF THE YEAR ALREADY? BOY, DOES TIME FLY.

RYO!
?
YOU'RE OFF TOMORROW, RIGHT? YOU DOING ANYTHING?

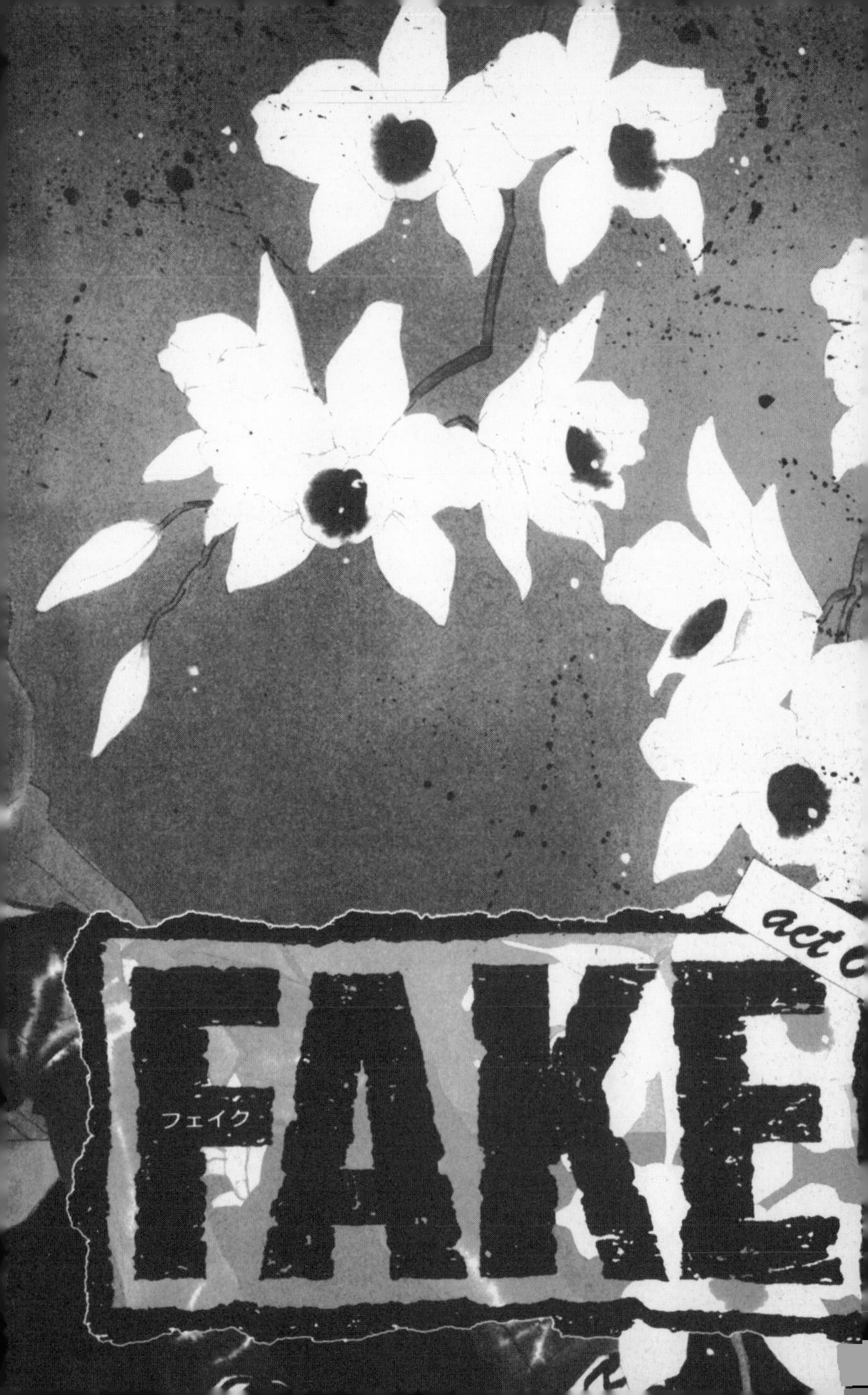
act
FAKE
フェイク

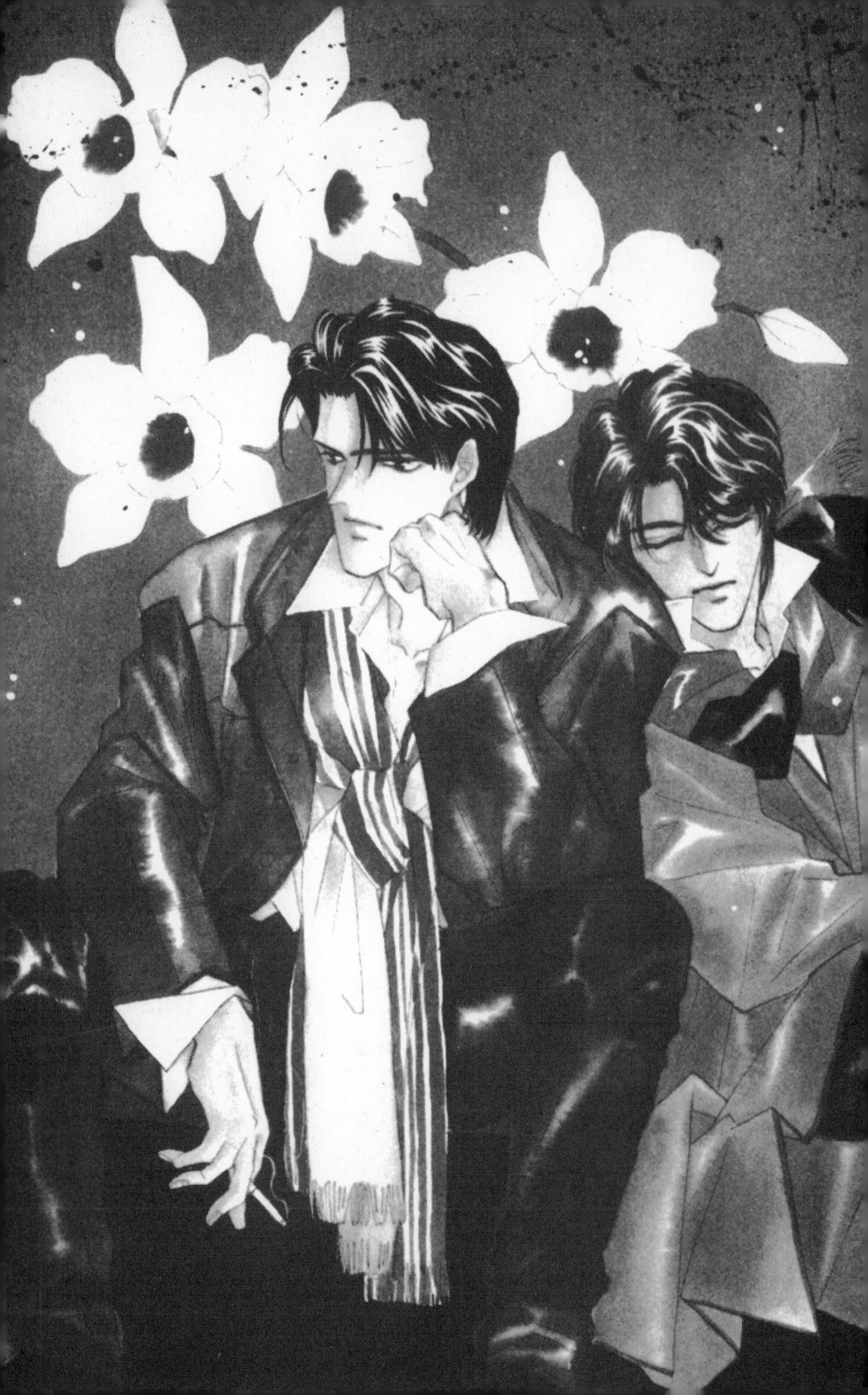

FAKE

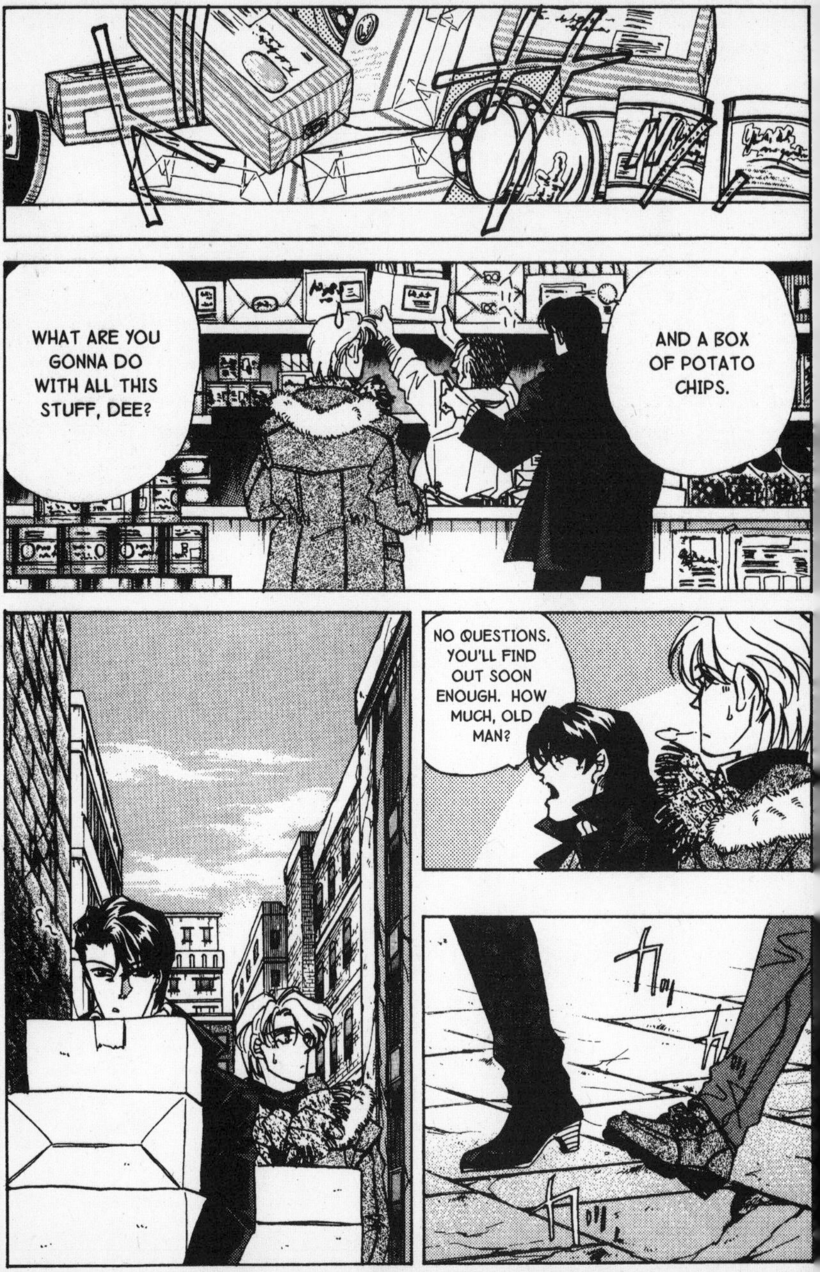
AND A BOX OF POTATO CHIPS.
WHAT ARE YOU GONNA DO WITH ALL THIS STUFF, DEE?
NO QUESTIONS. YOU'LL FIND OUT SOON ENOUGH. HOW MUCH, OLD MAN?

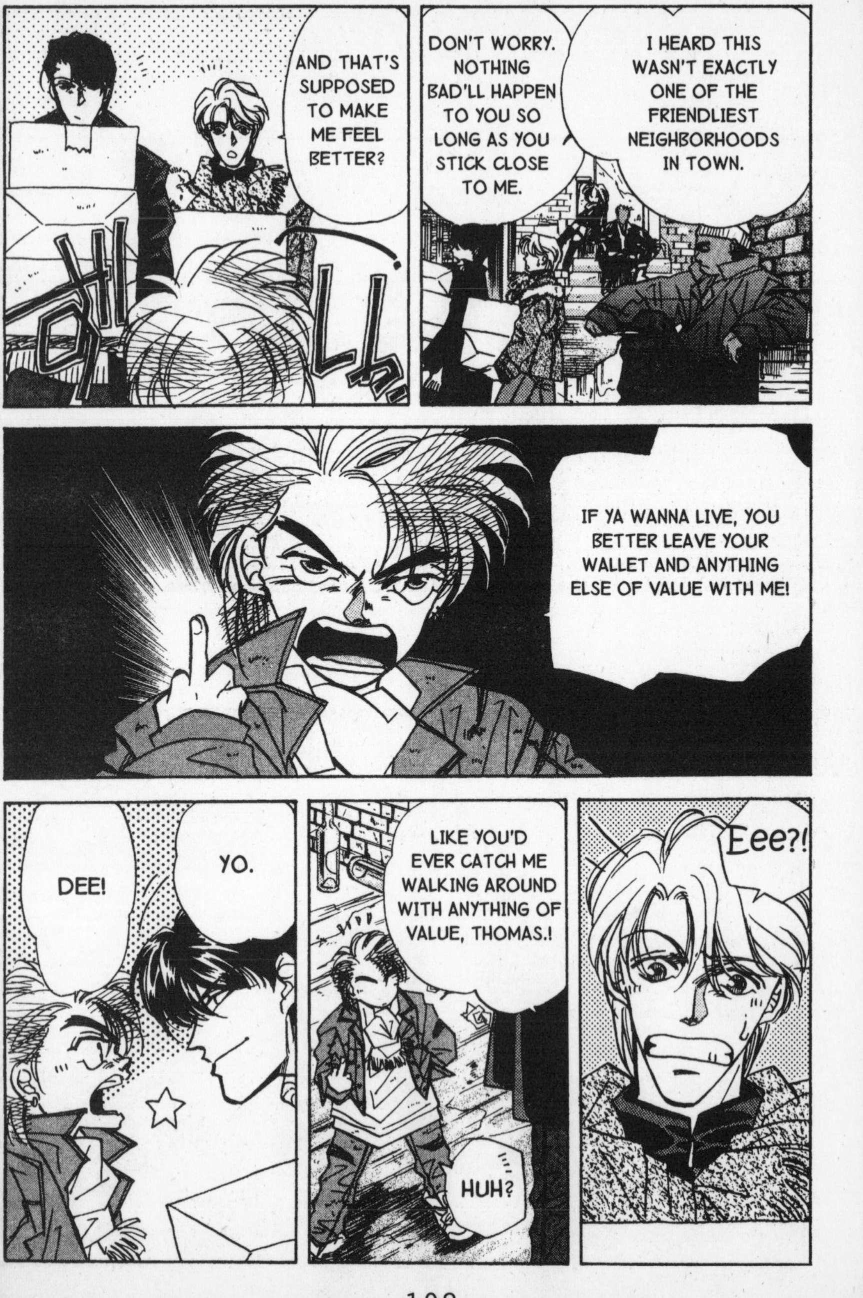
I HEARD THIS WASN'T EXACTLY ONE OF THE FRIENDLIEST NEIGHBORHOODS IN TOWN.
DON'T WORRY. NOTHING BAD'LL HAPPEN TO YOU SO LONG AS YOU STICK CLOSE TO ME.
AND THAT'S SUPPOSED TO MAKE ME FEEL BETTER?
IF YA WANNA LIVE, YOU BETTER LEAVE YOUR WALLET AND ANYTHING ELSE OF VALUE WITH ME!
Eee?!
LIKE YOU'D EVER CATCH ME WALKING AROUND WITH ANYTHING OF VALUE, THOMAS.!
HUH?
YO.
DEE!

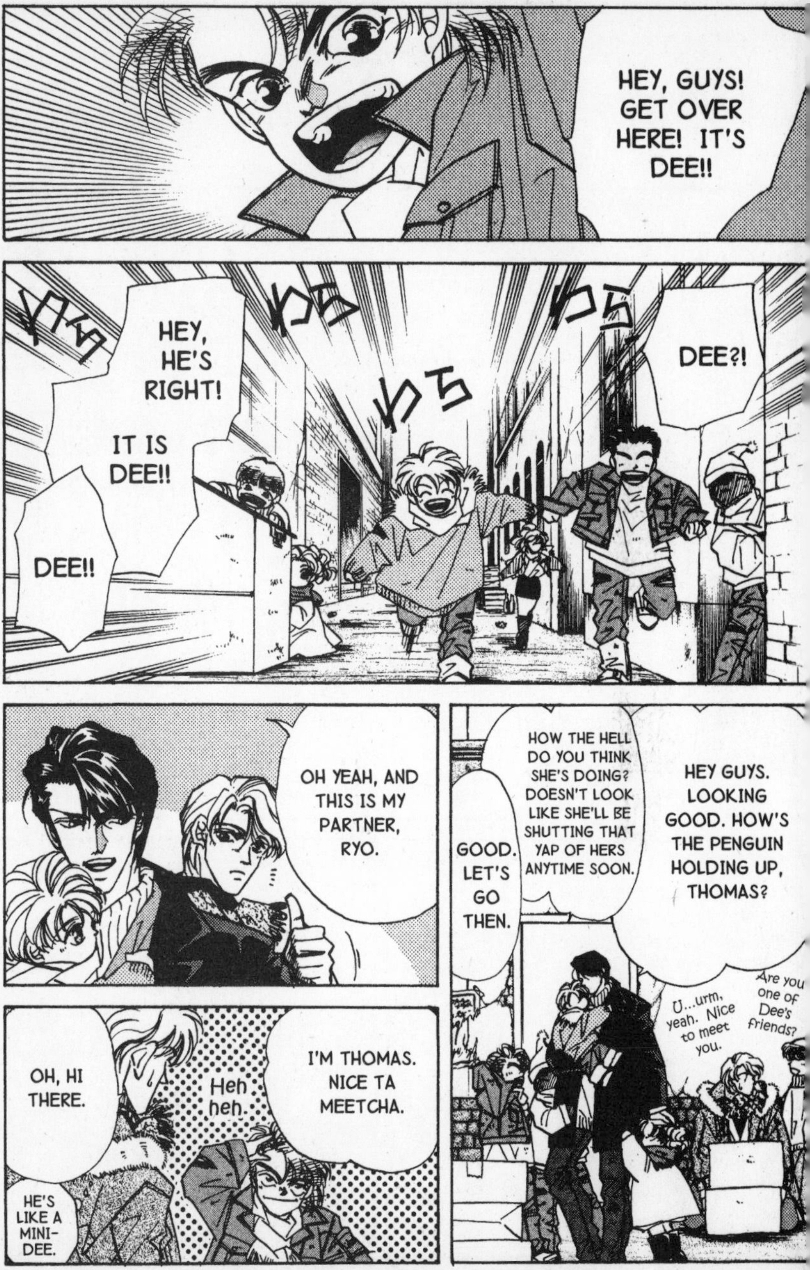
HEY, GUYS! GET OVER HERE! IT'S DEE!!
DEE?!
HEY, HE'S RIGHT!
IT IS DEE!!
DEE!!
HEY GUYS. LOOKING GOOD. HOW'S THE PENGUIN HOLDING UP, THOMAS?
HOW THE HELL DO YOU THINK SHE'S DOING? DOESN'T LOOK LIKE SHE'LL BE SHUTTING THAT YAP OF HERS ANYTIME SOON.
GOOD. LET'S GO THEN.
Are you one of Dee's friends?
U...urm, yeah. Nice to meet you.
OH YEAH, AND THIS IS MY PARTNER, RYO.
I'M THOMAS. NICE TA MEETCHA.
Heh heh.
OH, HI THERE.
HE'S LIKE A MINI-DEE.

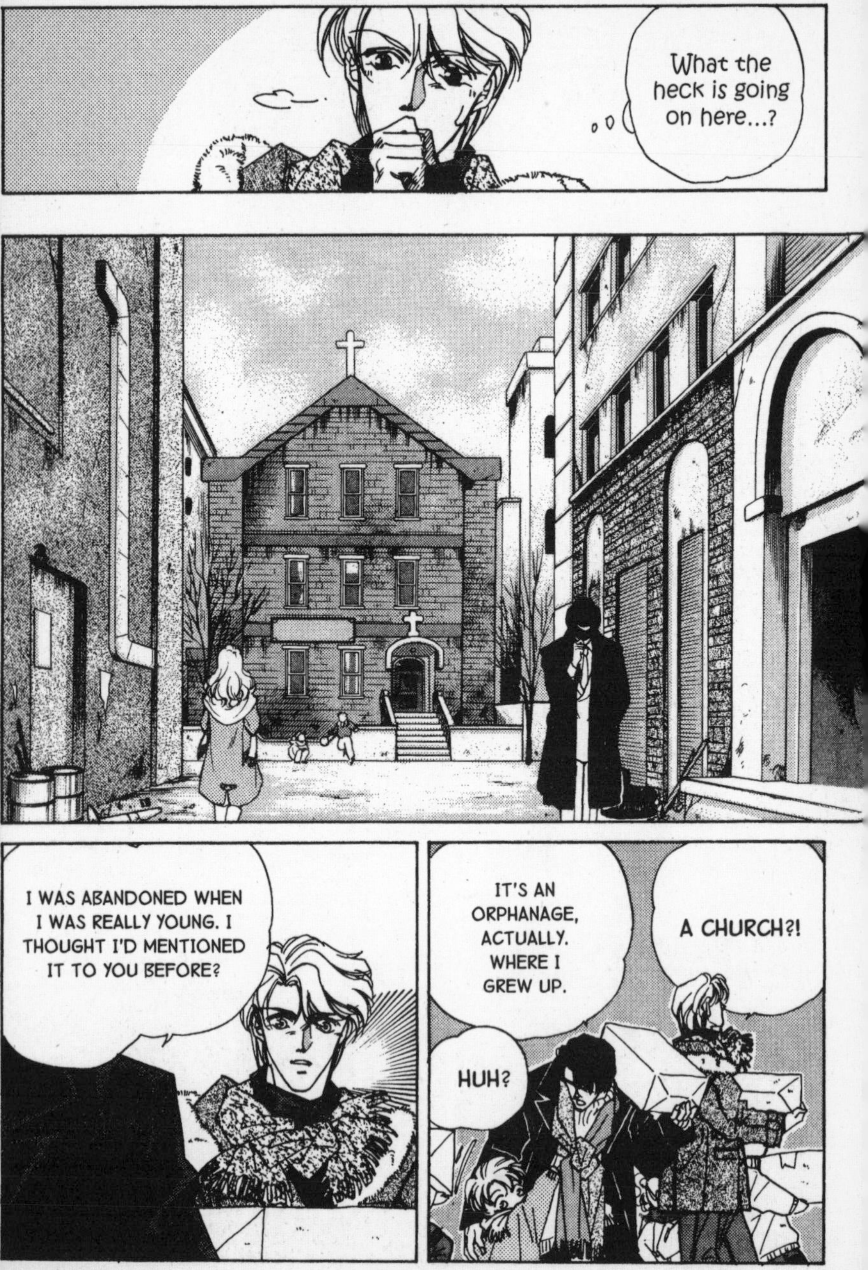
What the heck is going on here...?
A CHURCH?!
IT'S AN ORPHANAGE, ACTUALLY. WHERE I GREW UP.
HUH?
I WAS ABANDONED WHEN I WAS REALLY YOUNG. I THOUGHT I'D MENTIONED IT TO YOU BEFORE?

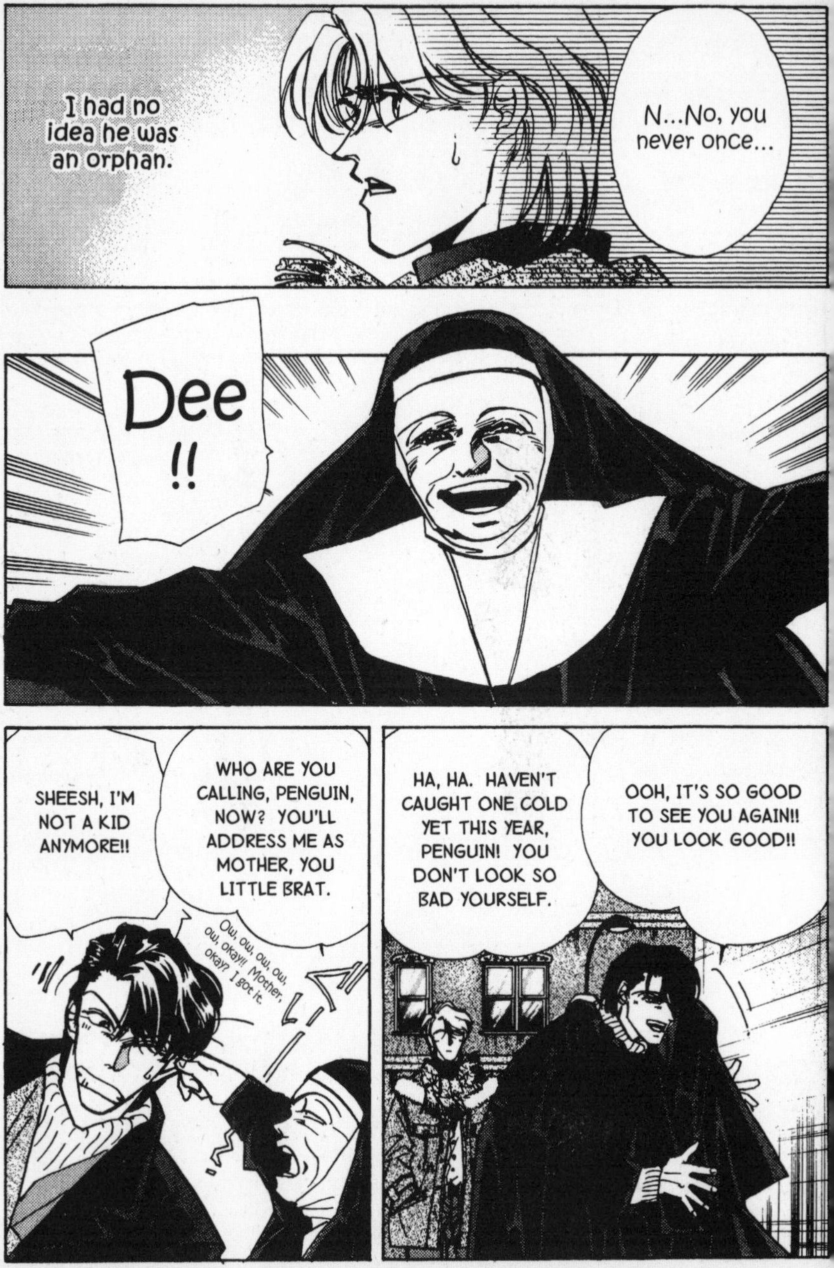
N...No, you never once...
I had no idea he was an orphan.
Dee !!
OOH, IT'S SO GOOD TO SEE YOU AGAIN!! YOU LOOK GOOD!!
HA, HA. HAVEN'T CAUGHT ONE COLD YET THIS YEAR, PENGUIN! YOU DON'T LOOK SO BAD YOURSELF.
WHO ARE YOU CALLING, PENGUIN, NOW? YOU'LL ADDRESS ME AS MOTHER, YOU LITTLE BRAT.
Ow, ow, ow, ow, ow, okay!! Mother, okay? I got it.
SHEESH, I'M NOT A KID ANYMORE!!

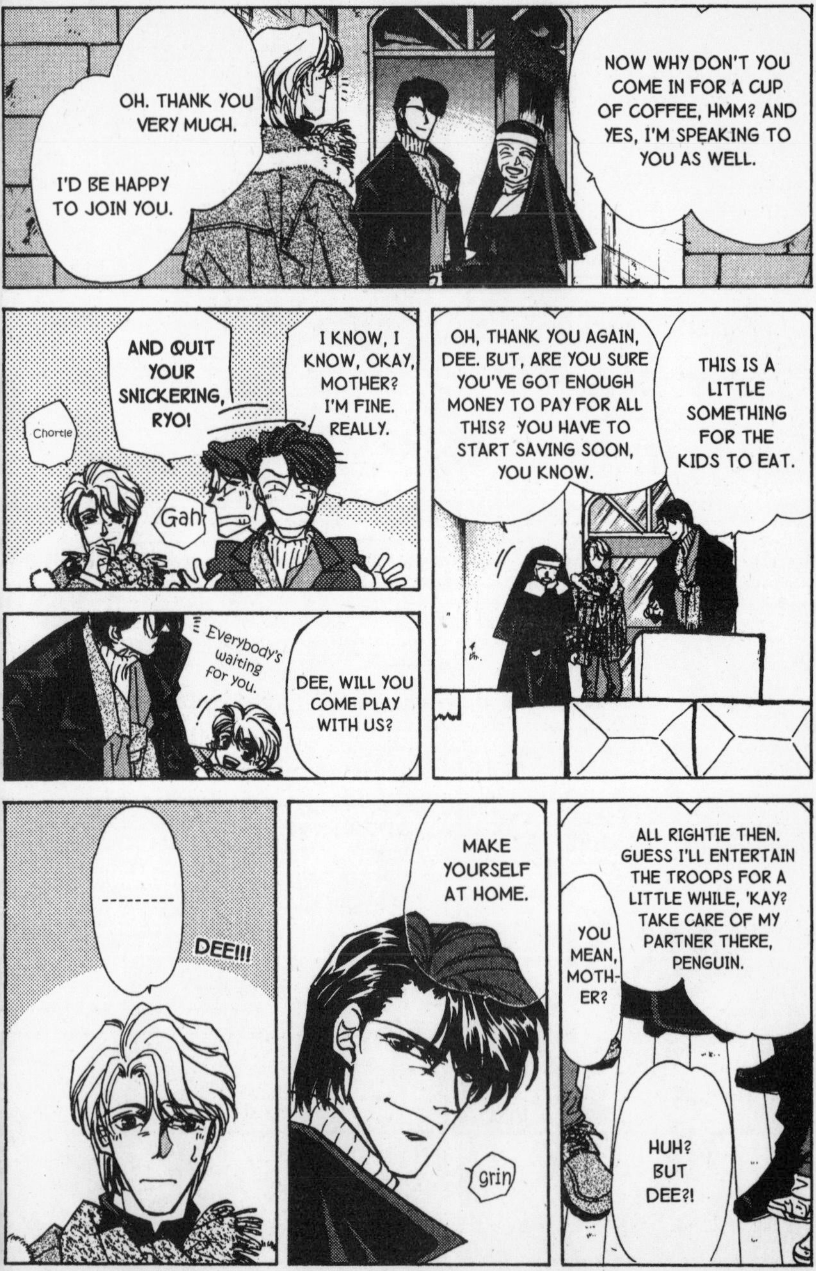
NOW WHY DON'T YOU COME IN FOR A CUP OF COFFEE, HMM? AND YES, I'M SPEAKING TO YOU AS WELL.
OH. THANK YOU VERY MUCH.
I'D BE HAPPY TO JOIN YOU.
THIS IS A LITTLE SOMETHING FOR THE KIDS TO EAT.
OH, THANK YOU AGAIN, DEE. BUT, ARE YOU SURE YOU'VE GOT ENOUGH MONEY TO PAY FOR ALL THIS? YOU HAVE TO START SAVING SOON, YOU KNOW.
I KNOW, I KNOW, OKAY, MOTHER? I'M FINE. REALLY.
AND QUIT YOUR SNICKERING, RYO!
Chortle
Gah
DEE, WILL YOU COME PLAY WITH US?
Everybody's waiting for you.
ALL RIGHTIE THEN. GUESS I'LL ENTERTAIN THE TROOPS FOR A LITTLE WHILE, 'KAY? TAKE CARE OF MY PARTNER THERE, PENGUIN.
YOU MEAN, MOTHER?
HUH? BUT DEE?!
MAKE YOURSELF AT HOME.
grin

DEE!!!

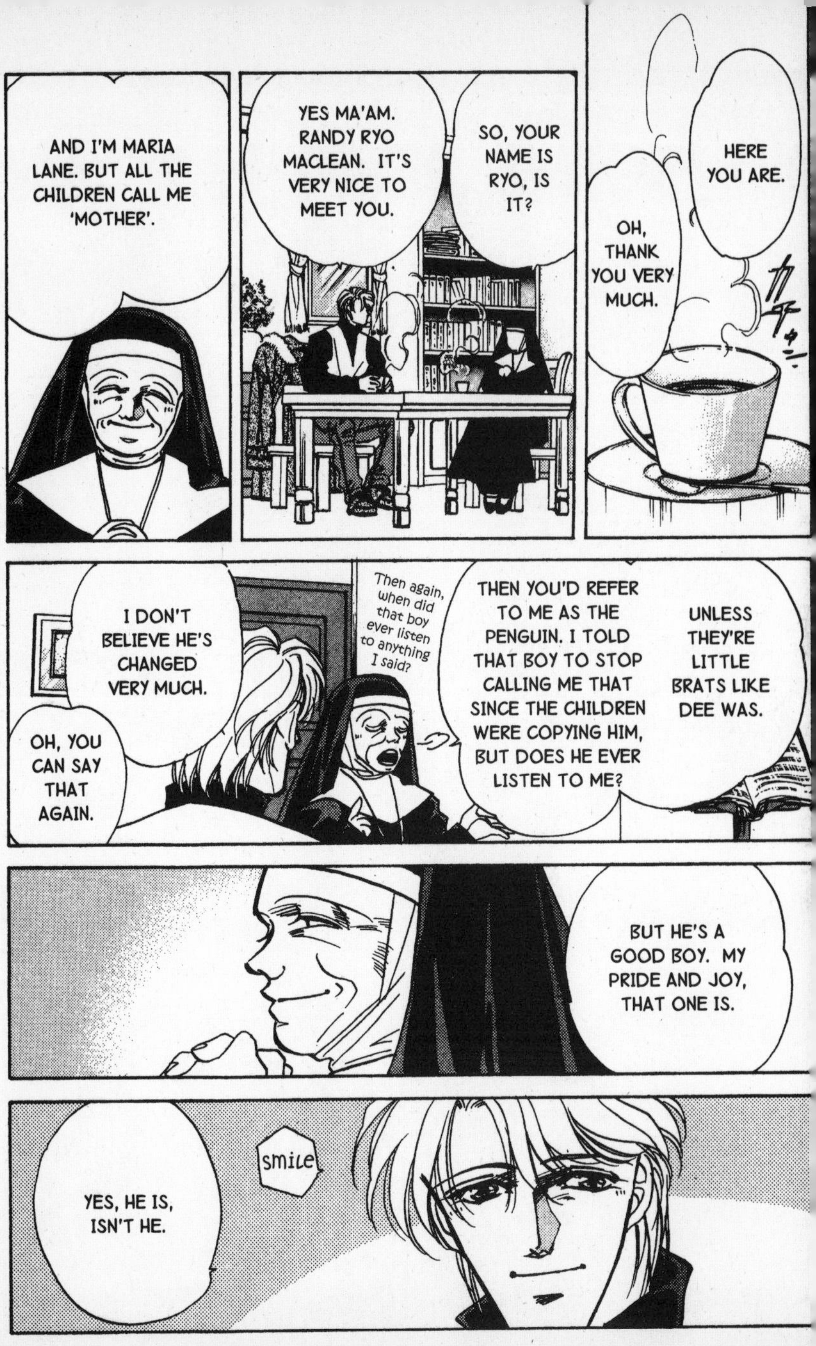
HERE YOU ARE.
OH, THANK YOU VERY MUCH.
SO, YOUR NAME IS RYO, IS IT?
YES MA'AM. RANDY RYO MACLEAN. IT'S VERY NICE TO MEET YOU.
AND I'M MARIA LANE. BUT ALL THE CHILDREN CALL ME 'MOTHER'.
UNLESS THEY'RE LITTLE BRATS LIKE DEE WAS.
THEN YOU'D REFER TO ME AS THE PENGUIN. I TOLD THAT BOY TO STOP CALLING ME THAT SINCE THE CHILDREN WERE COPYING HIM, BUT DOES HE EVER LISTEN TO ME?
Then again, when did that boy ever listen to anything I said?
I DON'T BELIEVE HE'S CHANGED VERY MUCH.
OH, YOU CAN SAY THAT AGAIN.
BUT HE'S A GOOD BOY. MY PRIDE AND JOY, THAT ONE IS.
smile
YES, HE IS, ISN'T HE.

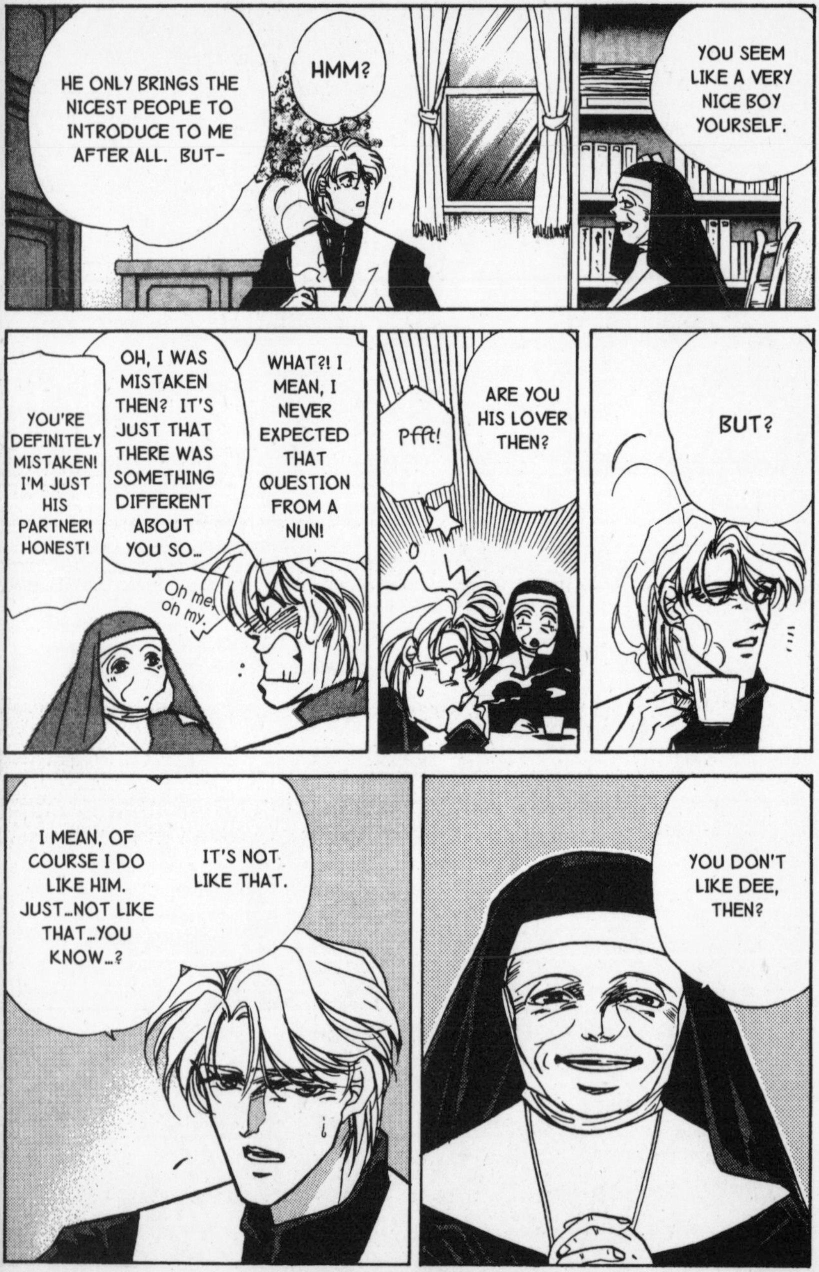
YOU SEEM LIKE A VERY NICE BOY YOURSELF.
HE ONLY BRINGS THE NICEST PEOPLE TO INTRODUCE TO ME AFTER ALL. BUT-
HMM?
BUT?
ARE YOU HIS LOVER THEN?
Pfft!
WHAT?! I MEAN, I NEVER EXPECTED THAT QUESTION FROM A NUN!
OH, I WAS MISTAKEN THEN? IT'S JUST THAT THERE WAS SOMETHING DIFFERENT ABOUT YOU SO...
YOU'RE DEFINITELY MISTAKEN! I'M JUST HIS PARTNER! HONEST!
Oh me, oh my.
YOU DON'T LIKE DEE, THEN?
IT'S NOT LIKE THAT.
I MEAN, OF COURSE I DO LIKE HIM. JUST...NOT LIKE THAT...YOU KNOW...?

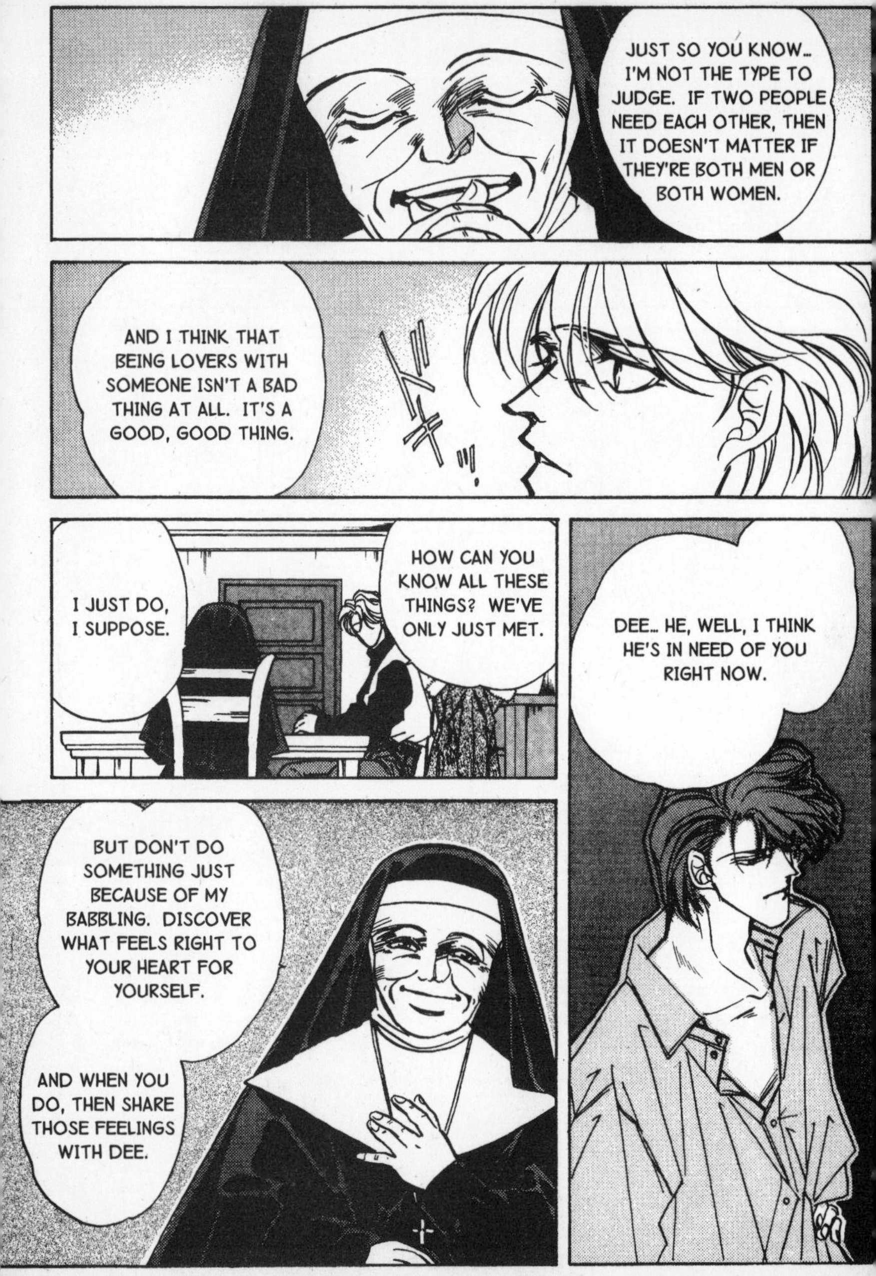
JUST SO YOU KNOW... I'M NOT THE TYPE TO JUDGE. IF TWO PEOPLE NEED EACH OTHER, THEN IT DOESN'T MATTER IF THEY'RE BOTH MEN OR BOTH WOMEN.
AND I THINK THAT BEING LOVERS WITH SOMEONE ISN'T A BAD THING AT ALL. IT'S A GOOD, GOOD THING.
DEE... HE, WELL, I THINK HE'S IN NEED OF YOU RIGHT NOW.
HOW CAN YOU KNOW ALL THESE THINGS? WE'VE ONLY JUST MET.
I JUST DO, I SUPPOSE.
BUT DON'T DO SOMETHING JUST BECAUSE OF MY BABBLING. DISCOVER WHAT FEELS RIGHT TO YOUR HEART FOR YOURSELF.
AND WHEN YOU DO, THEN SHARE THOSE FEELINGS WITH DEE.

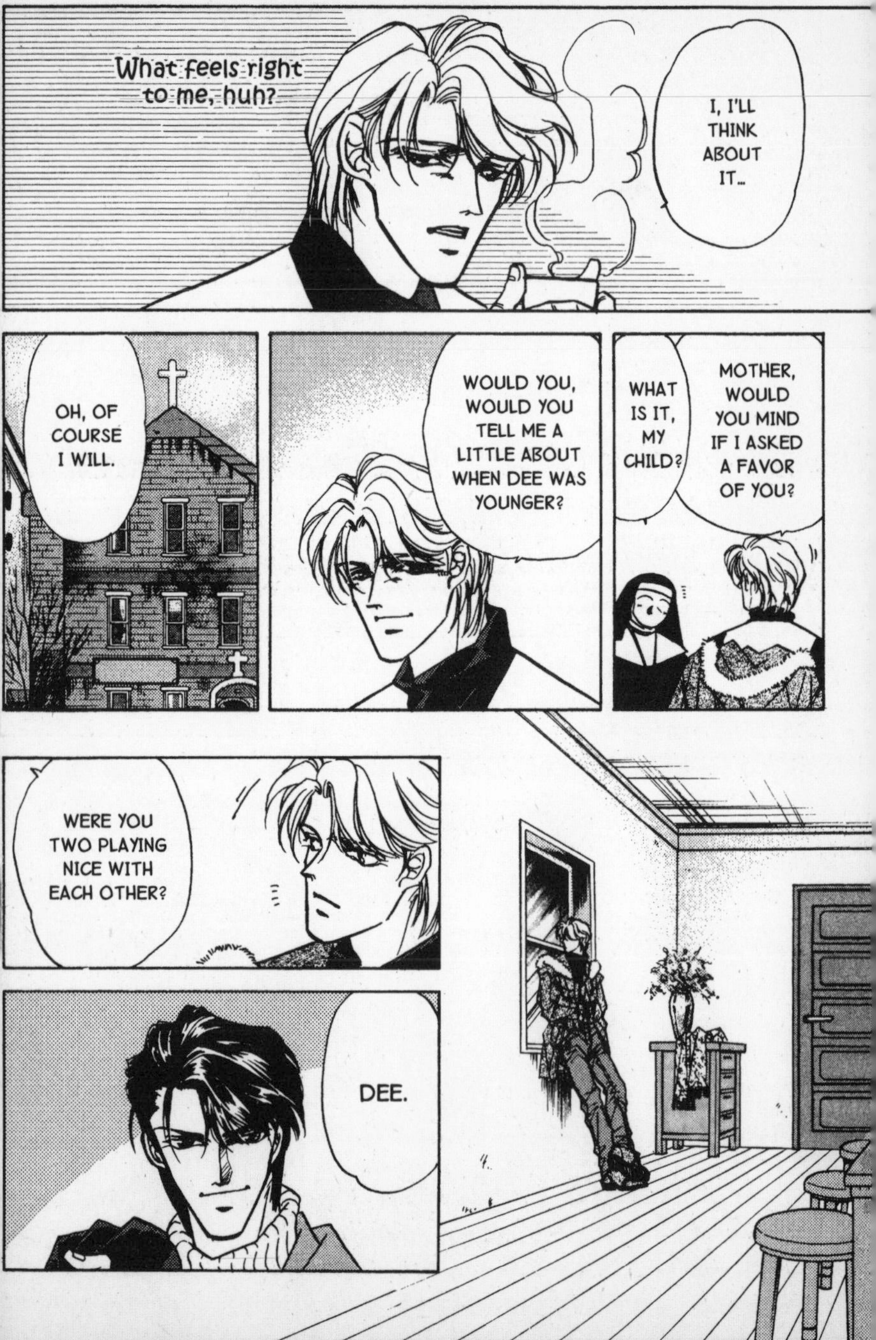
I, I'LL THINK ABOUT IT...
What feels right to me, huh?
MOTHER, WOULD YOU MIND IF I ASKED A FAVOR OF YOU?
WHAT IS IT, MY CHILD?
WOULD YOU, WOULD YOU TELL ME A LITTLE ABOUT WHEN DEE WAS YOUNGER?
OH, OF COURSE I WILL.
WERE YOU TWO PLAYING NICE WITH EACH OTHER?
DEE.

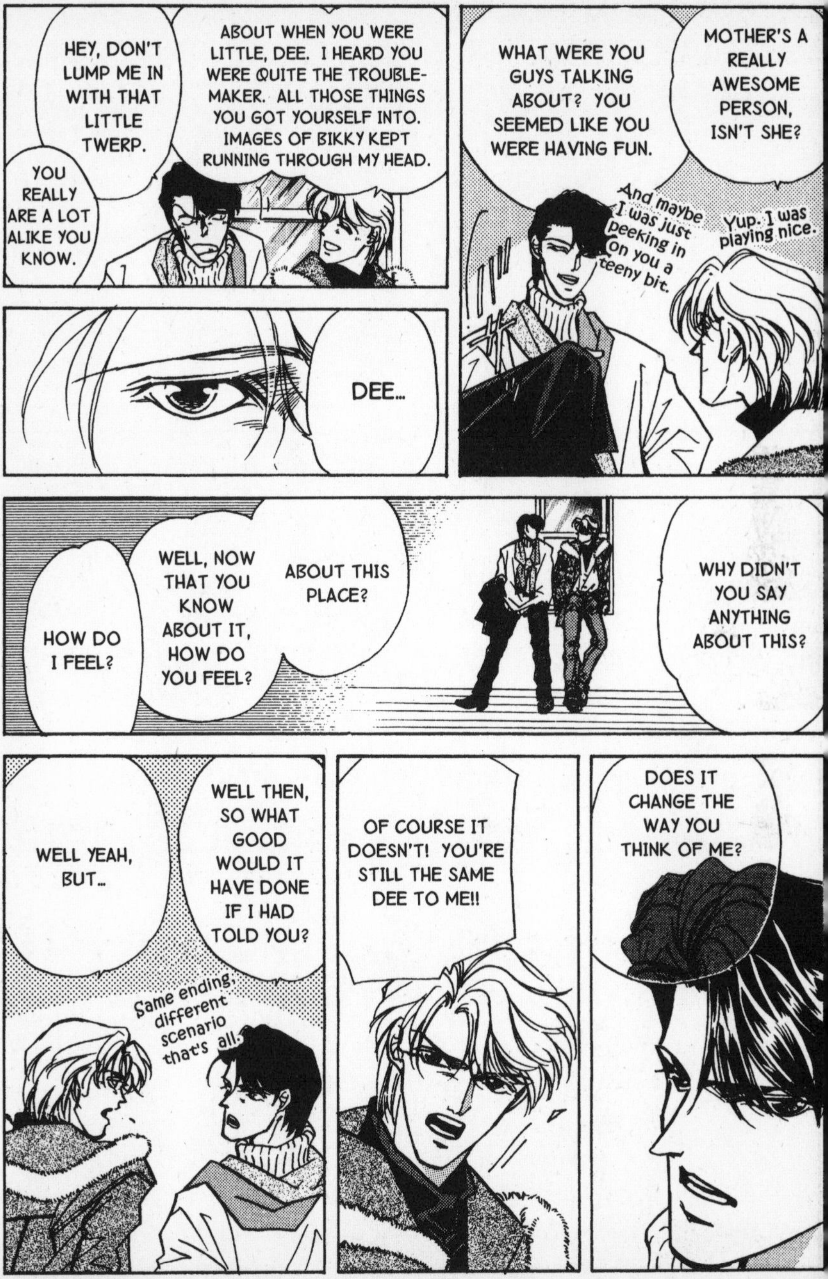
MOTHER'S A REALLY AWESOME PERSON, ISN'T SHE?
WHAT WERE YOU GUYS TALKING ABOUT? YOU SEEMED LIKE YOU WERE HAVING FUN.
Yup. I was playing nice.
And maybe I was just peeking in on you a teeny bit.
ABOUT WHEN YOU WERE LITTLE, DEE. I HEARD YOU WERE QUITE THE TROUBLE-MAKER. ALL THOSE THINGS YOU GOT YOURSELF INTO. IMAGES OF BIKKY KEPT RUNNING THROUGH MY HEAD.
YOU REALLY ARE A LOT ALIKE YOU KNOW.
HEY, DON'T LUMP ME IN WITH THAT LITTLE TWERP.
DEE...
WHY DIDN'T YOU SAY ANYTHING ABOUT THIS?
ABOUT THIS PLACE?
WELL, NOW THAT YOU KNOW ABOUT IT, HOW DO YOU FEEL?
HOW DO I FEEL?
DOES IT CHANGE THE WAY YOU THINK OF ME?
OF COURSE IT DOESN'T! YOU'RE STILL THE SAME DEE TO ME!!
WELL THEN, SO WHAT GOOD WOULD IT HAVE DONE IF I HAD TOLD YOU?
WELL YEAH, BUT...
Same ending, different scenario that's all.

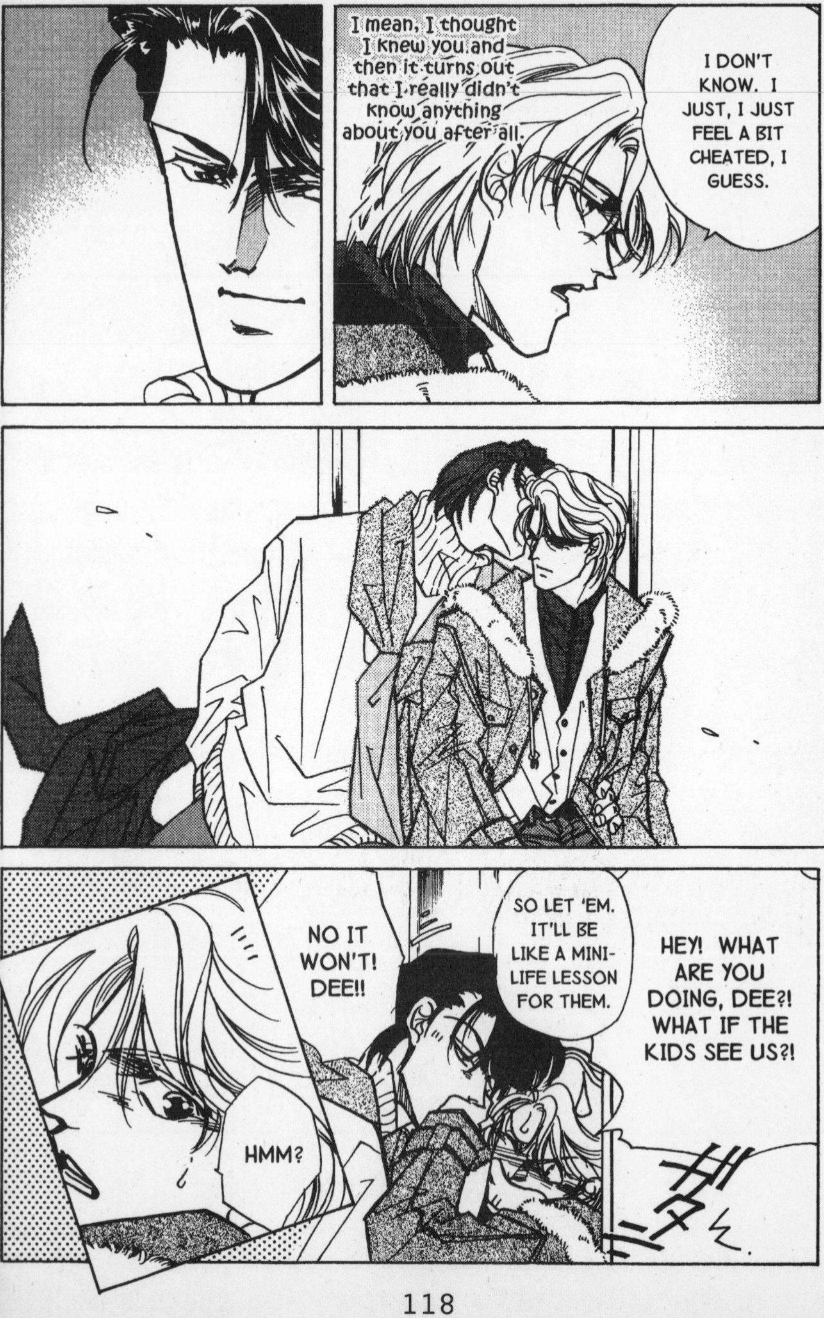
I DON'T KNOW. I JUST, I JUST FEEL A BIT CHEATED, I GUESS.
I mean, I thought I knew you and then it turns out that I really didn't know anything about you after all.
HEY! WHAT ARE YOU DOING, DEE?! WHAT IF THE KIDS SEE US?!
SO LET 'EM. IT'LL BE LIKE A MINI-LIFE LESSON FOR THEM.
NO IT WON'T! DEE!!
HMM?

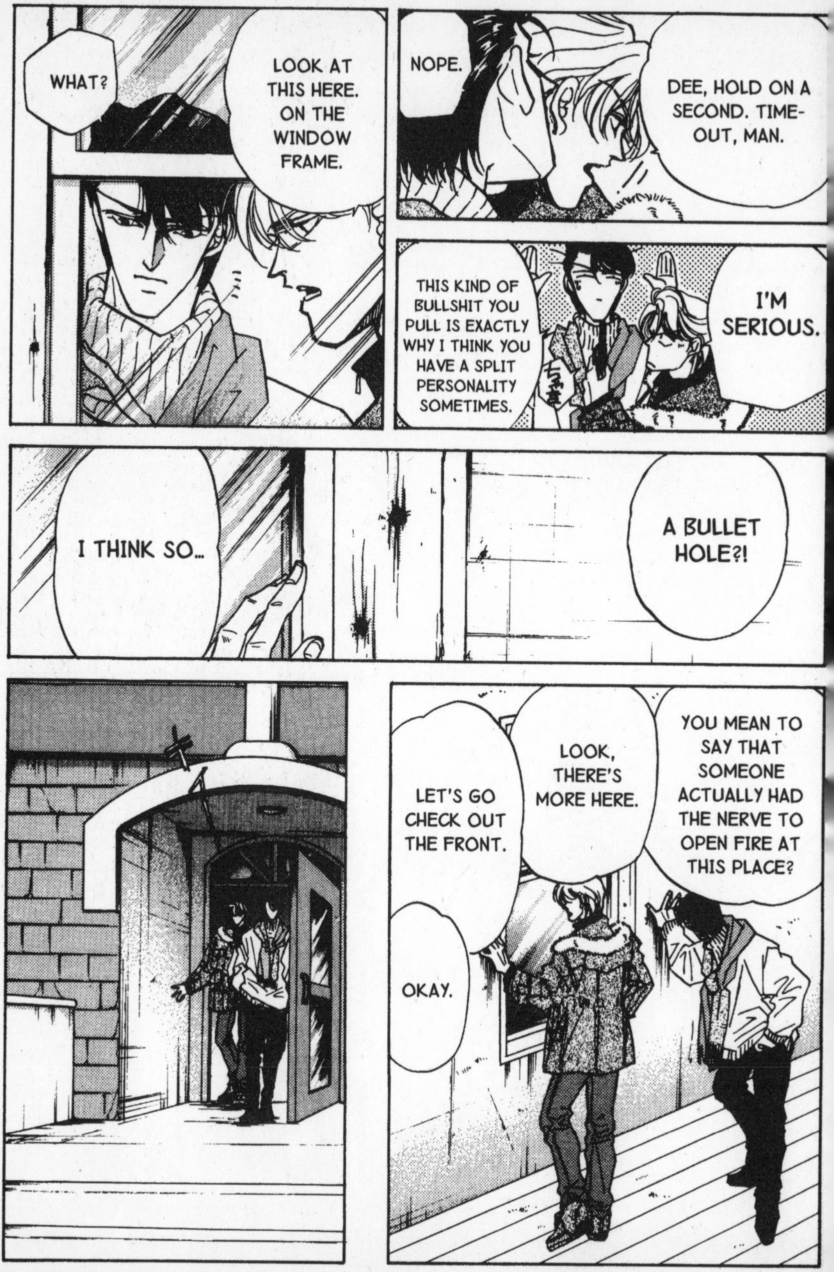
DEE, HOLD ON A SECOND. TIME-OUT, MAN.
NOPE.
I'M SERIOUS.
THIS KIND OF BULLSHIT YOU PULL IS EXACTLY WHY I THINK YOU HAVE A SPLIT PERSONALITY SOMETIMES.
LOOK AT THIS HERE. ON THE WINDOW FRAME.
WHAT?
A BULLET HOLE?!
I THINK SO...
YOU MEAN TO SAY THAT SOMEONE ACTUALLY HAD THE NERVE TO OPEN FIRE AT THIS PLACE?
LOOK, THERE'S MORE HERE.
LET'S GO CHECK OUT THE FRONT.
OKAY.

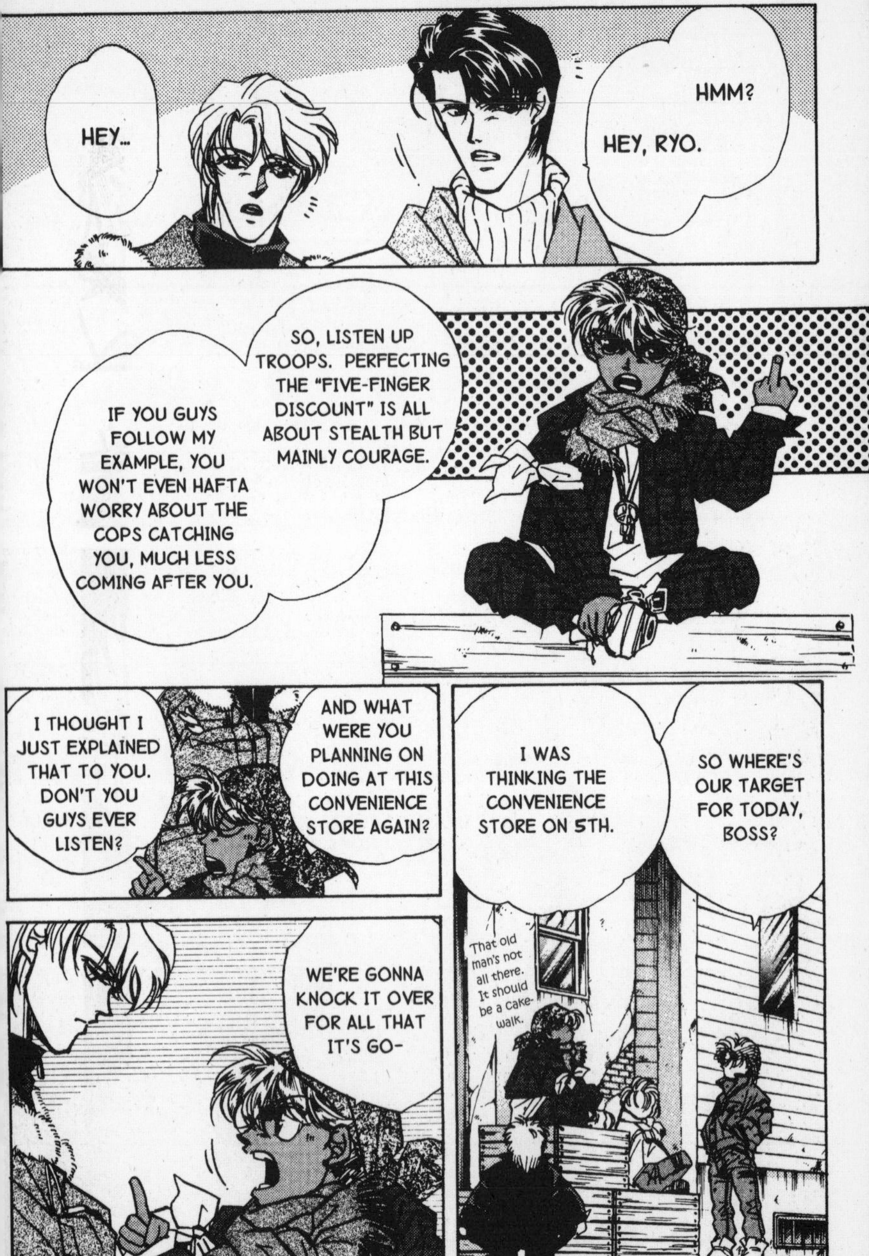
HMM? HEY, RYO.
HEY...
SO, LISTEN UP TROOPS. PERFECTING THE "FIVE-FINGER DISCOUNT" IS ALL ABOUT STEALTH BUT MAINLY COURAGE.
IF YOU GUYS FOLLOW MY EXAMPLE, YOU WON'T EVEN HAFTA WORRY ABOUT THE COPS CATCHING YOU, MUCH LESS COMING AFTER YOU.
SO WHERE'S OUR TARGET FOR TODAY, BOSS?
I WAS THINKING THE CONVENIENCE STORE ON 5TH.
That old man's not all there. It should be a cake-walk.
AND WHAT WERE YOU PLANNING ON DOING AT THIS CONVENIENCE STORE AGAIN?
I THOUGHT I JUST EXPLAINED THAT TO YOU. DON'T YOU GUYS EVER LISTEN?
WE'RE GONNA KNOCK IT OVER FOR ALL THAT IT'S GO-

Hey geek, feel like a loser much?

what an idiot!

Crap! I'm sorry!!

Bikky !!

ACK!! Ryo?!

Hmm?

What's that dude up to?

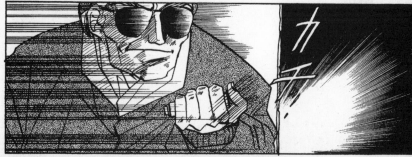

121

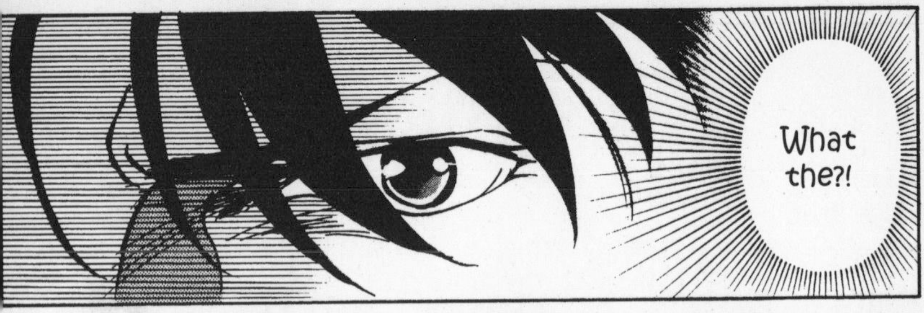
What the?!

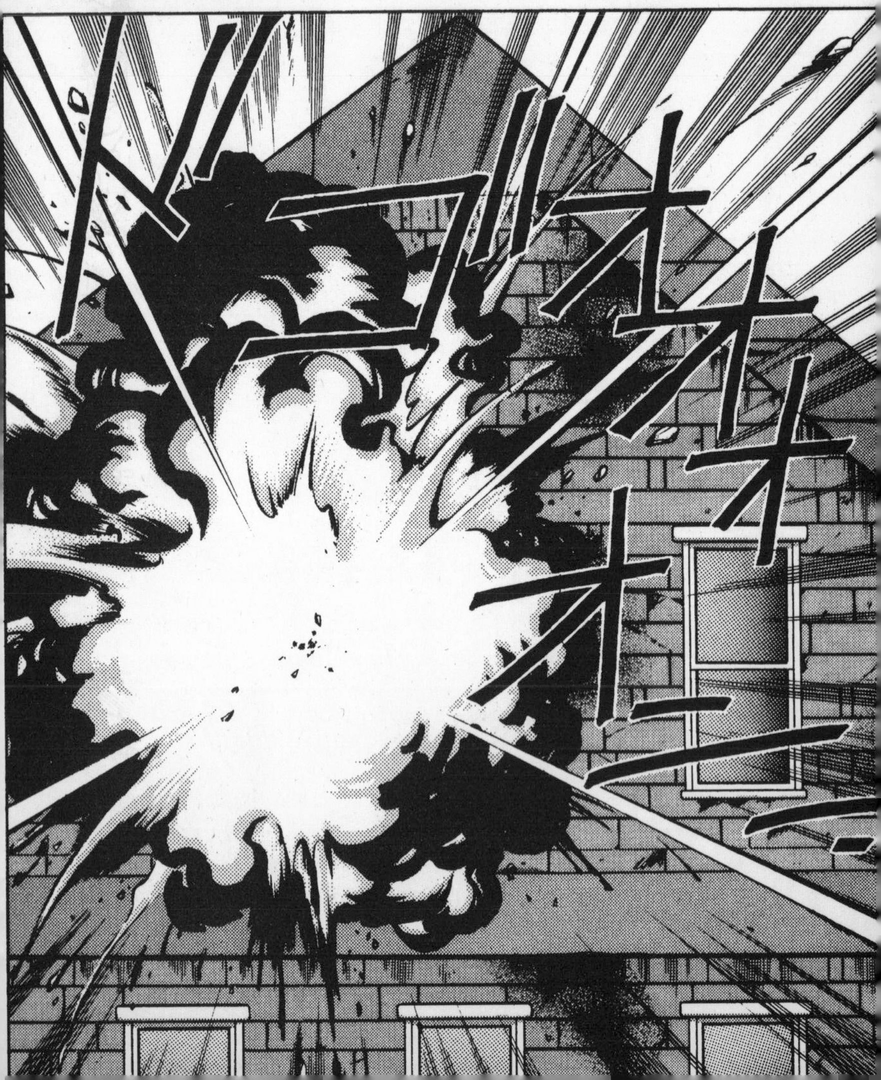

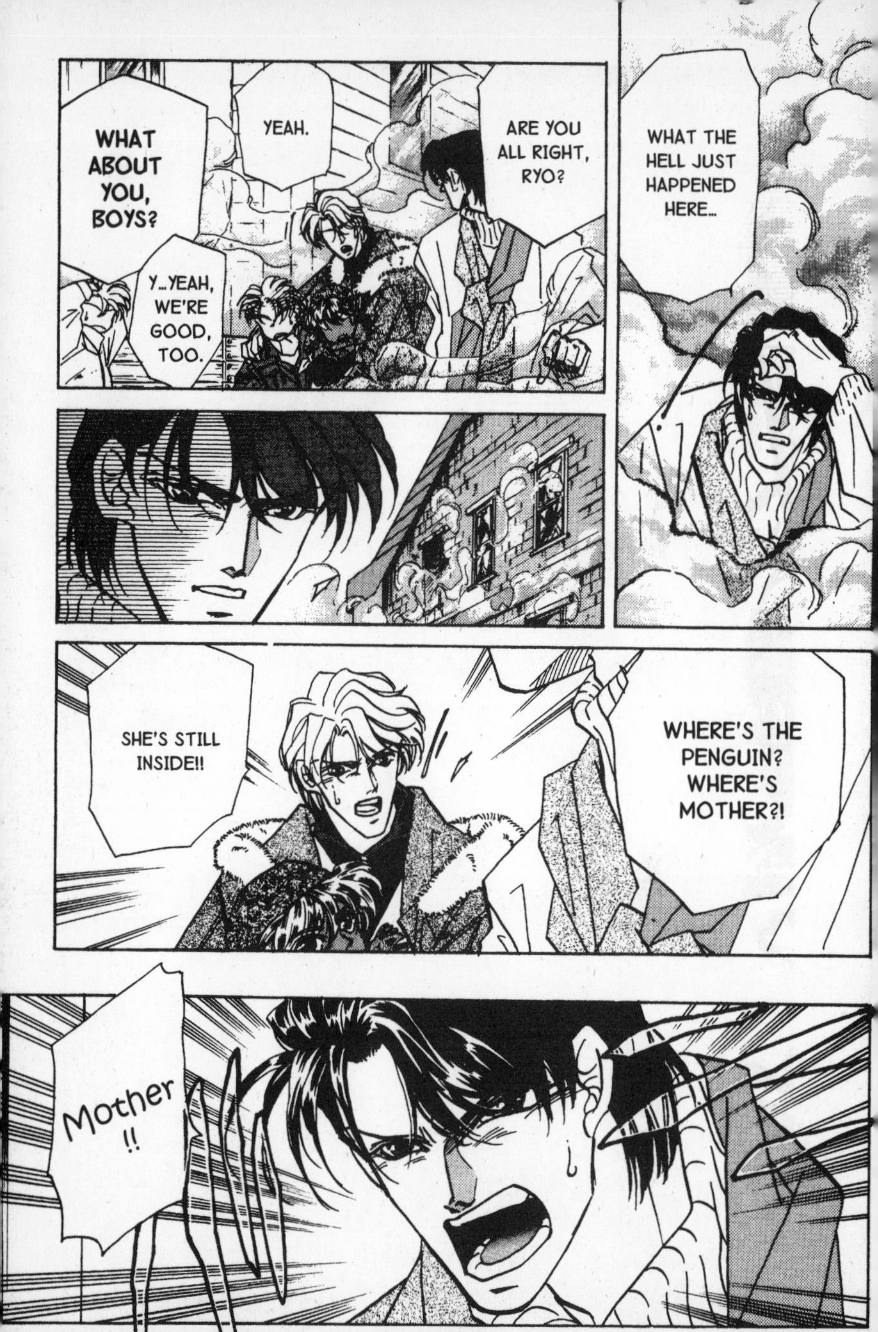
WHAT THE HELL JUST HAPPENED HERE...
ARE YOU ALL RIGHT, RYO?
YEAH.
WHAT ABOUT YOU, BOYS?
Y...YEAH, WE'RE GOOD, TOO.
WHERE'S THE PENGUIN? WHERE'S MOTHER?!
SHE'S STILL INSIDE!!
Mother !!

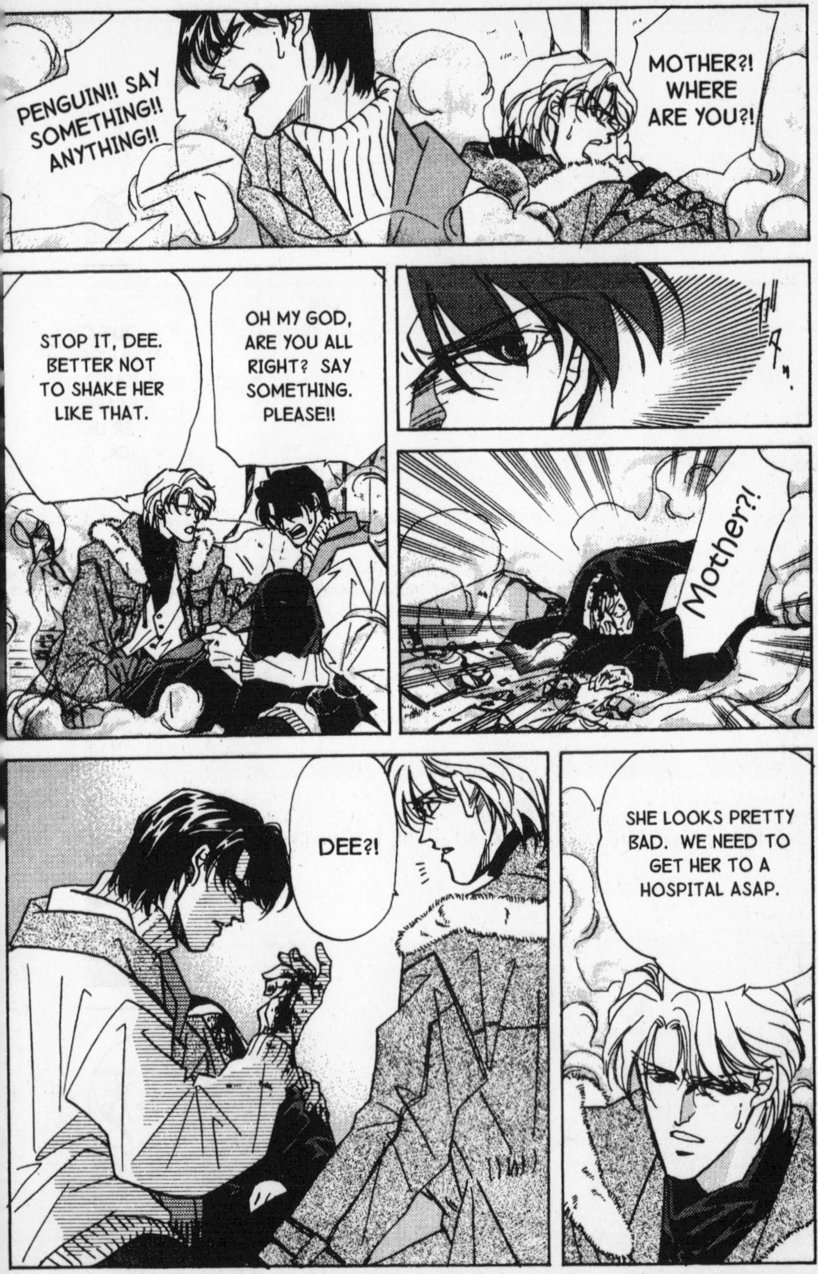
MOTHER?! WHERE ARE YOU?!
PENGUIN!! SAY SOMETHING!! ANYTHING!!
Mother?!
OH MY GOD, ARE YOU ALL RIGHT? SAY SOMETHING. PLEASE!!
STOP IT, DEE. BETTER NOT TO SHAKE HER LIKE THAT.
SHE LOOKS PRETTY BAD. WE NEED TO GET HER TO A HOSPITAL ASAP.
DEE?!

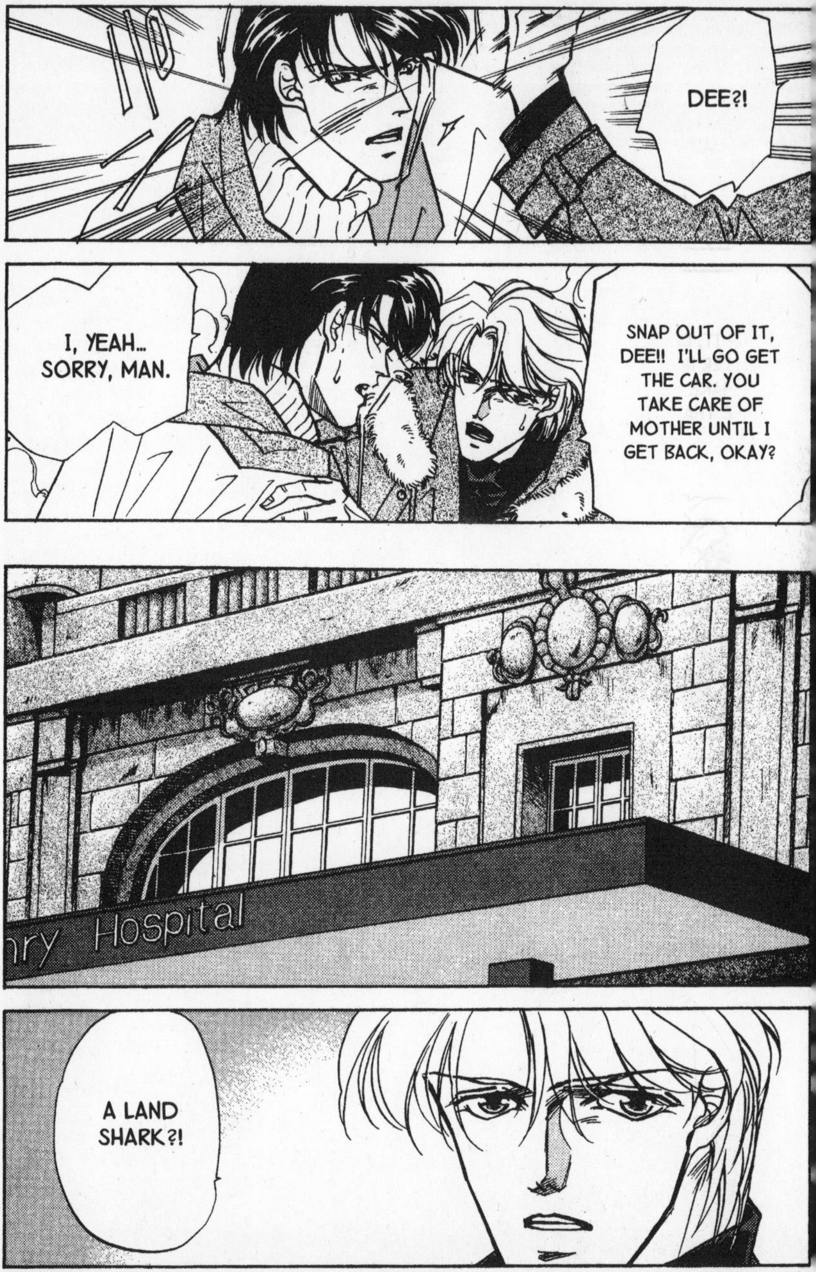
DEE?!
SNAP OUT OF IT, DEE!! I'LL GO GET THE CAR. YOU TAKE CARE OF MOTHER UNTIL I GET BACK, OKAY?
I, YEAH... SORRY, MAN.
...nry Hospital
A LAND SHARK?!

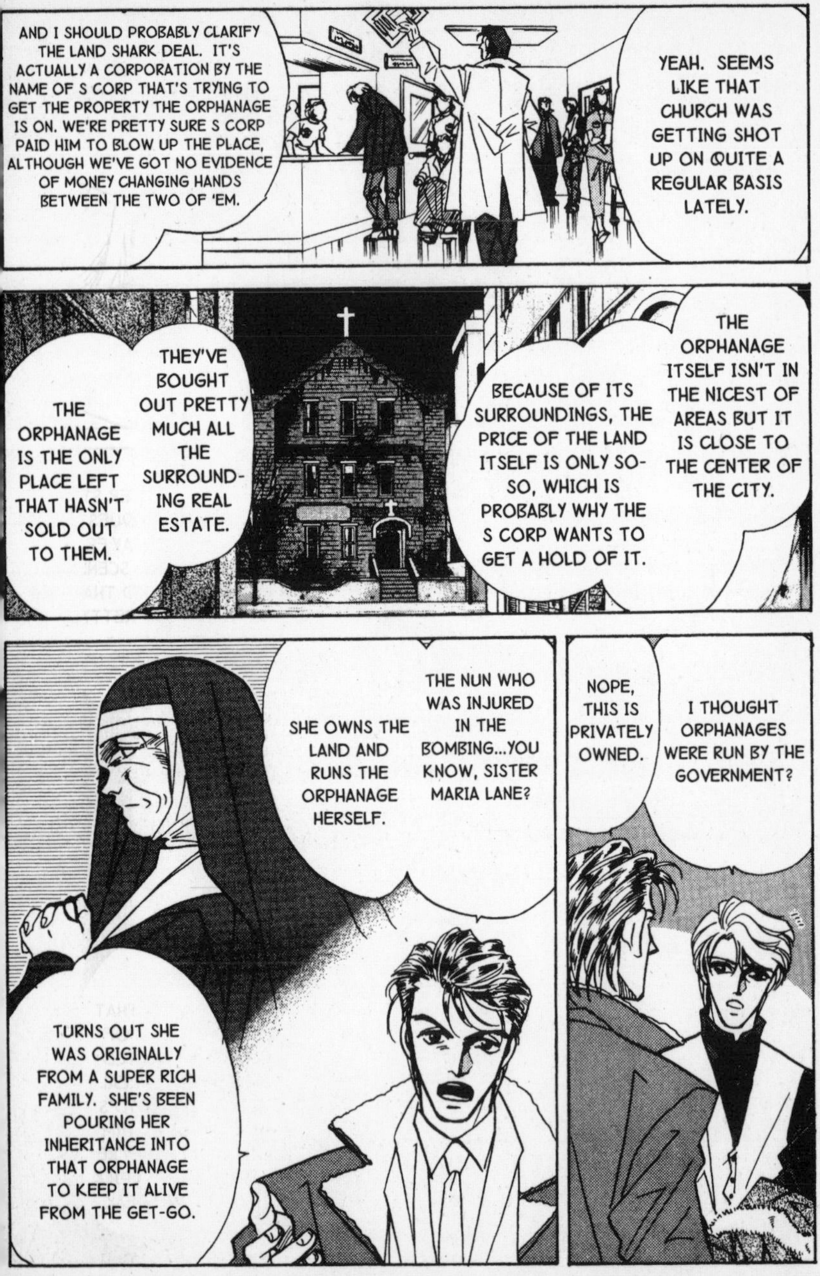
YEAH. SEEMS LIKE THAT CHURCH WAS GETTING SHOT UP ON QUITE A REGULAR BASIS LATELY.
AND I SHOULD PROBABLY CLARIFY THE LAND SHARK DEAL. IT'S ACTUALLY A CORPORATION BY THE NAME OF S CORP THAT'S TRYING TO GET THE PROPERTY THE ORPHANAGE IS ON. WE'RE PRETTY SURE S CORP PAID HIM TO BLOW UP THE PLACE, ALTHOUGH WE'VE GOT NO EVIDENCE OF MONEY CHANGING HANDS BETWEEN THE TWO OF 'EM.
THE ORPHANAGE ITSELF ISN'T IN THE NICEST OF AREAS BUT IT IS CLOSE TO THE CENTER OF THE CITY.
BECAUSE OF ITS SURROUNDINGS, THE PRICE OF THE LAND ITSELF IS ONLY SO-SO, WHICH IS PROBABLY WHY THE S CORP WANTS TO GET A HOLD OF IT.
THEY'VE BOUGHT OUT PRETTY MUCH ALL THE SURROUND-ING REAL ESTATE.
THE ORPHANAGE IS THE ONLY PLACE LEFT THAT HASN'T SOLD OUT TO THEM.
I THOUGHT ORPHANAGES WERE RUN BY THE GOVERNMENT?
NOPE, THIS IS PRIVATELY OWNED.
THE NUN WHO WAS INJURED IN THE BOMBING...YOU KNOW, SISTER MARIA LANE?
SHE OWNS THE LAND AND RUNS THE ORPHANAGE HERSELF.
TURNS OUT SHE WAS ORIGINALLY FROM A SUPER RICH FAMILY. SHE'S BEEN POURING HER INHERITANCE INTO THAT ORPHANAGE TO KEEP IT ALIVE FROM THE GET-GO.

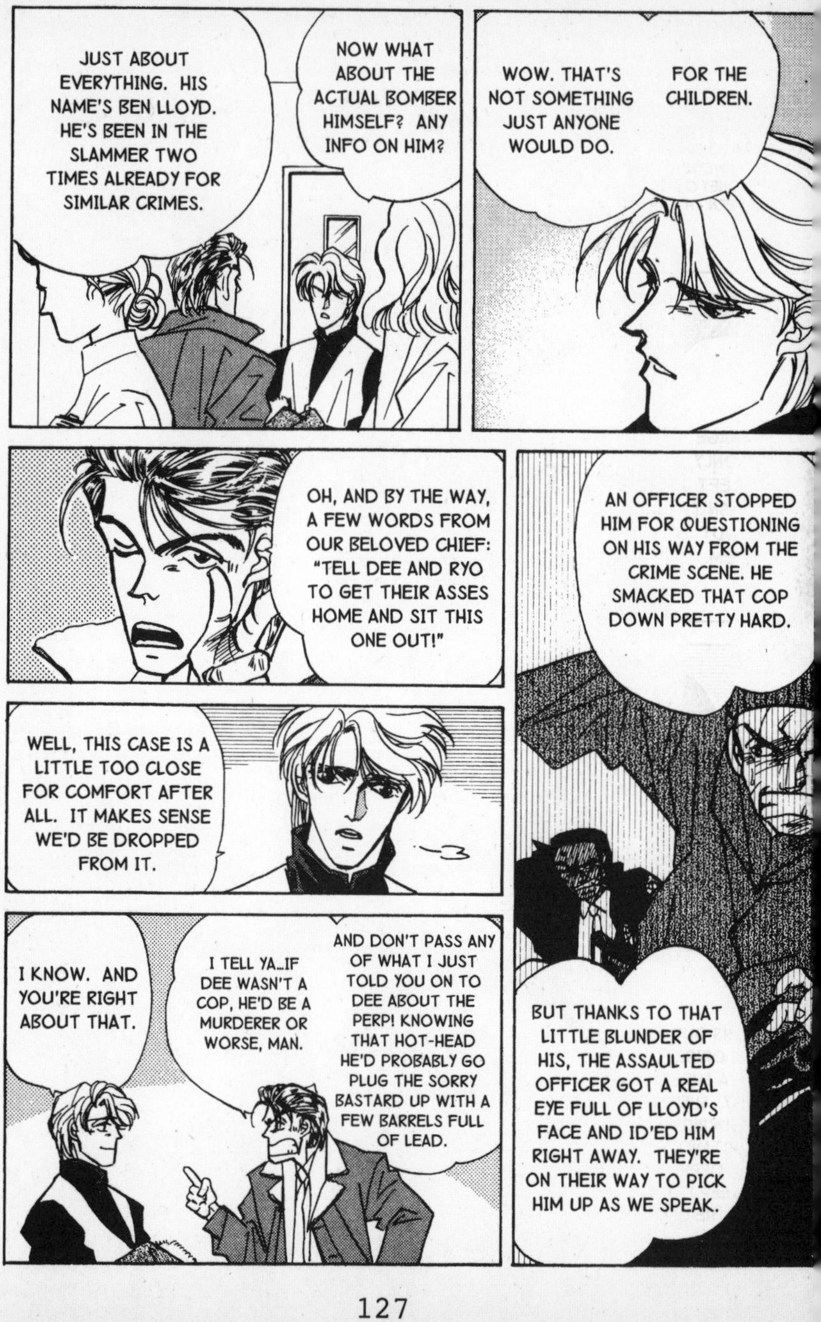
WOW. THAT'S NOT SOMETHING JUST ANYONE WOULD DO.
FOR THE CHILDREN.
NOW WHAT ABOUT THE ACTUAL BOMBER HIMSELF? ANY INFO ON HIM?
JUST ABOUT EVERYTHING. HIS NAME'S BEN LLOYD. HE'S BEEN IN THE SLAMMER TWO TIMES ALREADY FOR SIMILAR CRIMES.
AN OFFICER STOPPED HIM FOR QUESTIONING ON HIS WAY FROM THE CRIME SCENE. HE SMACKED THAT COP DOWN PRETTY HARD.
BUT THANKS TO THAT LITTLE BLUNDER OF HIS, THE ASSAULTED OFFICER GOT A REAL EYE FULL OF LLOYD'S FACE AND ID'ED HIM RIGHT AWAY. THEY'RE ON THEIR WAY TO PICK HIM UP AS WE SPEAK.
OH, AND BY THE WAY, A FEW WORDS FROM OUR BELOVED CHIEF: "TELL DEE AND RYO TO GET THEIR ASSES HOME AND SIT THIS ONE OUT!"
WELL, THIS CASE IS A LITTLE TOO CLOSE FOR COMFORT AFTER ALL. IT MAKES SENSE WE'D BE DROPPED FROM IT.
AND DON'T PASS ANY OF WHAT I JUST TOLD YOU ON TO DEE ABOUT THE PERP! KNOWING THAT HOT-HEAD HE'D PROBABLY GO PLUG THE SORRY BASTARD UP WITH A FEW BARRELS FULL OF LEAD.
I TELL YA...IF DEE WASN'T A COP, HE'D BE A MURDERER OR WORSE, MAN.
I KNOW. AND YOU'RE RIGHT ABOUT THAT.

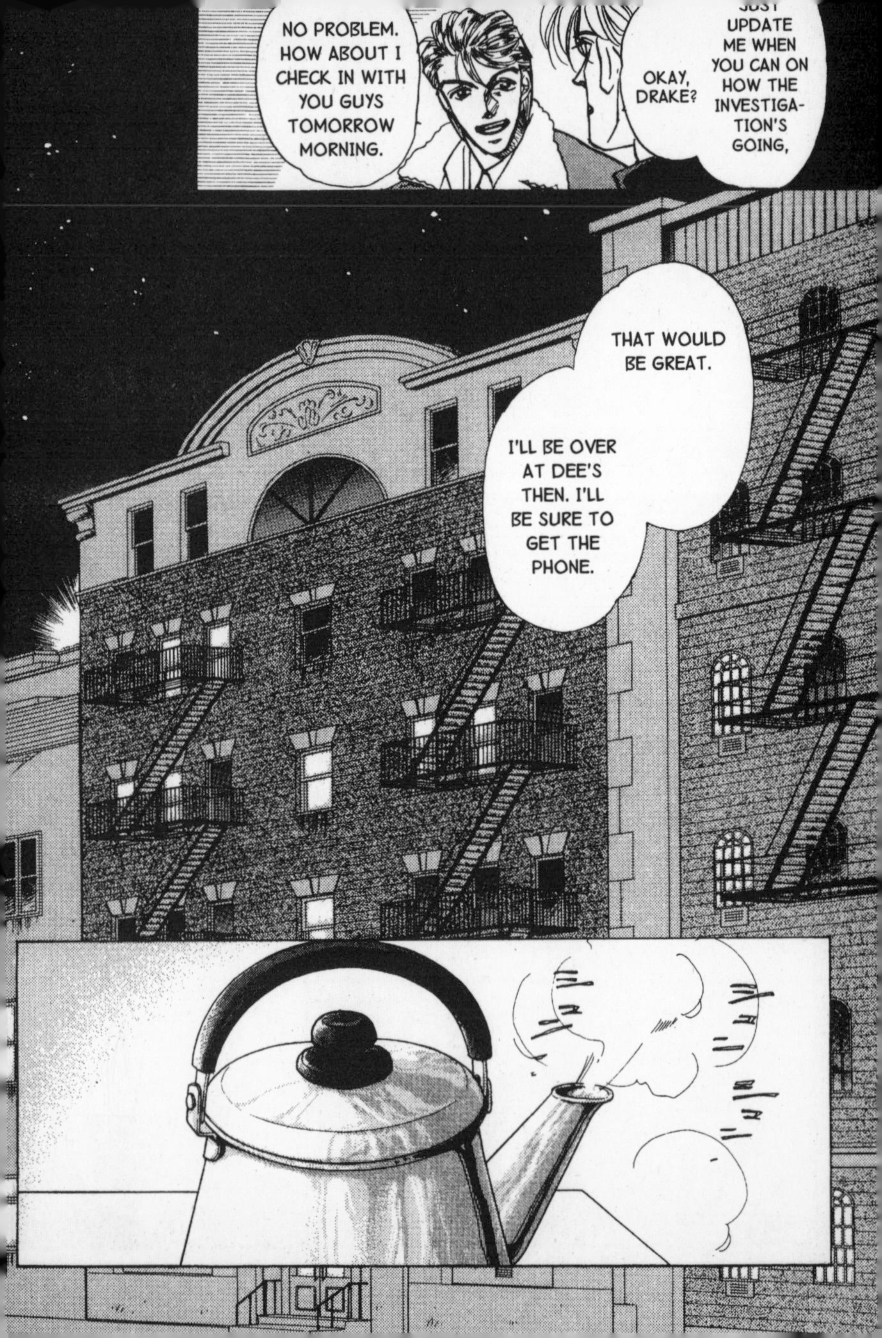
UPDATE ME WHEN YOU CAN ON HOW THE INVESTIGATION'S GOING,
OKAY, DRAKE?
NO PROBLEM. HOW ABOUT I CHECK IN WITH YOU GUYS TOMORROW MORNING.
THAT WOULD BE GREAT.
I'LL BE OVER AT DEE'S THEN. I'LL BE SURE TO GET THE PHONE.

Now that I think about it, this is the first time I've ever been to Dee's place.

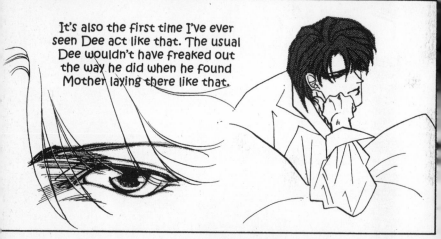

It's also the first time I've ever seen Dee act like that. The usual Dee wouldn't have freaked out the way he did when he found Mother laying there like that.

But then again, how the hell was I expecting him to be? It's his 'mother' for crying out loud.

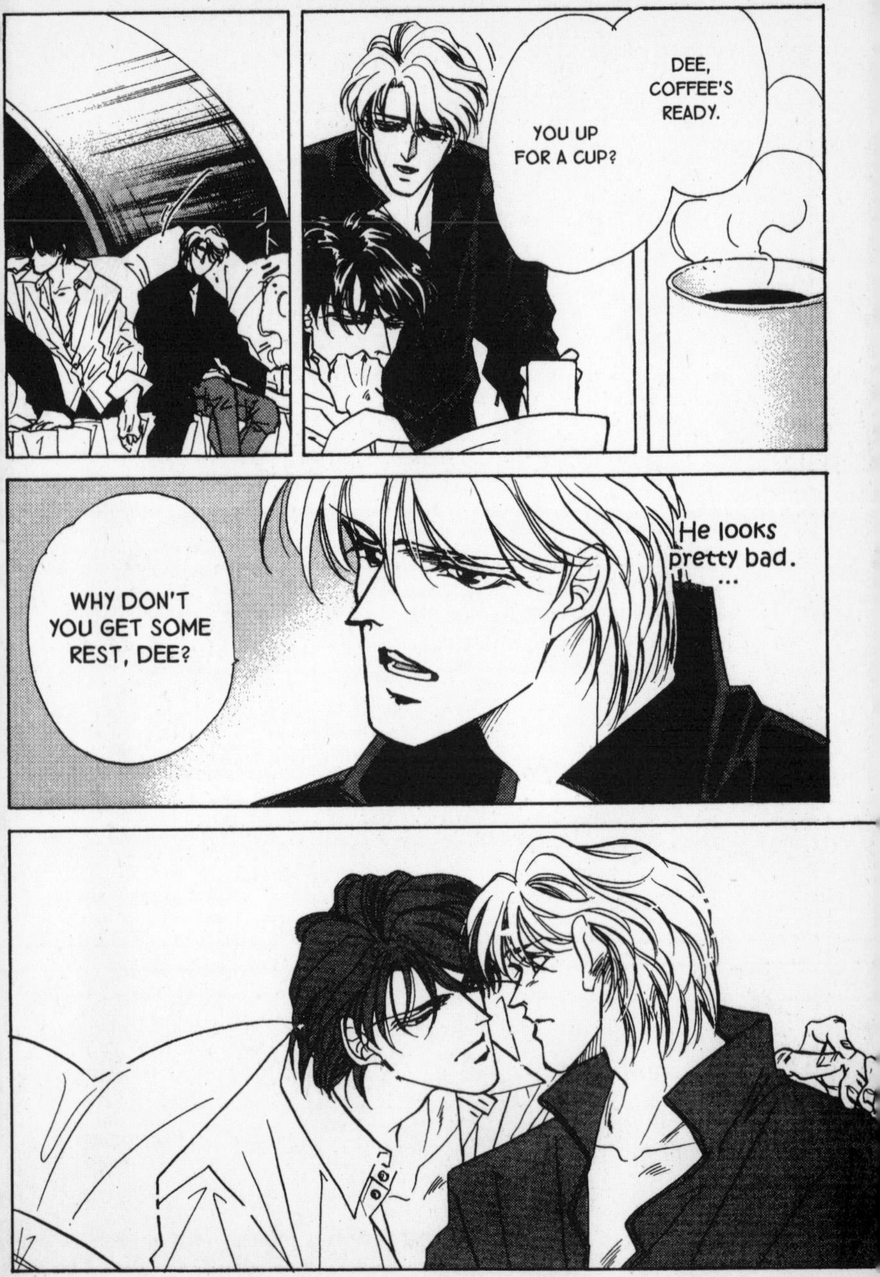
DEE, COFFEE'S READY.
YOU UP FOR A CUP?
He looks pretty bad.
...
WHY DON'T YOU GET SOME REST, DEE?

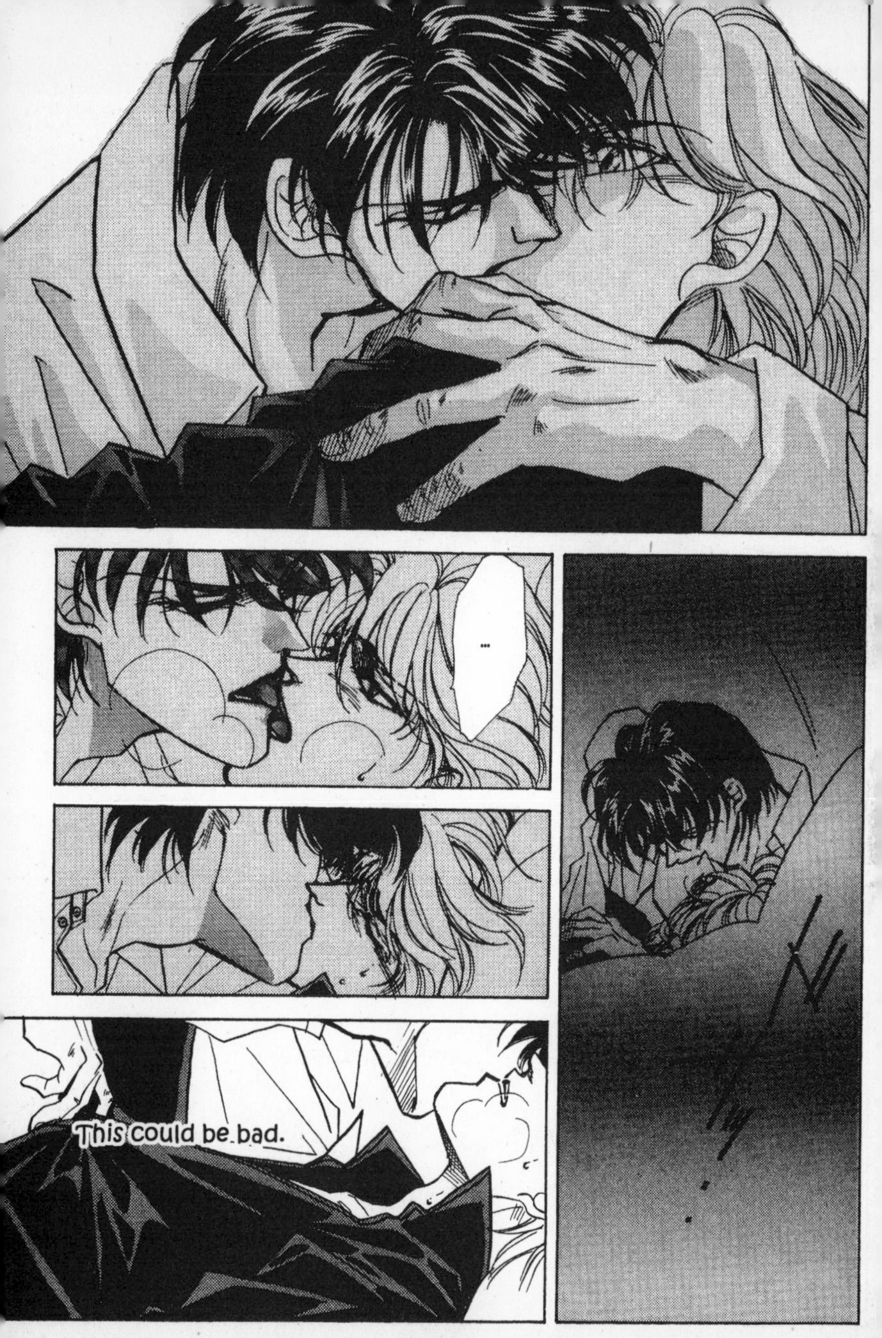
...
This could be bad.

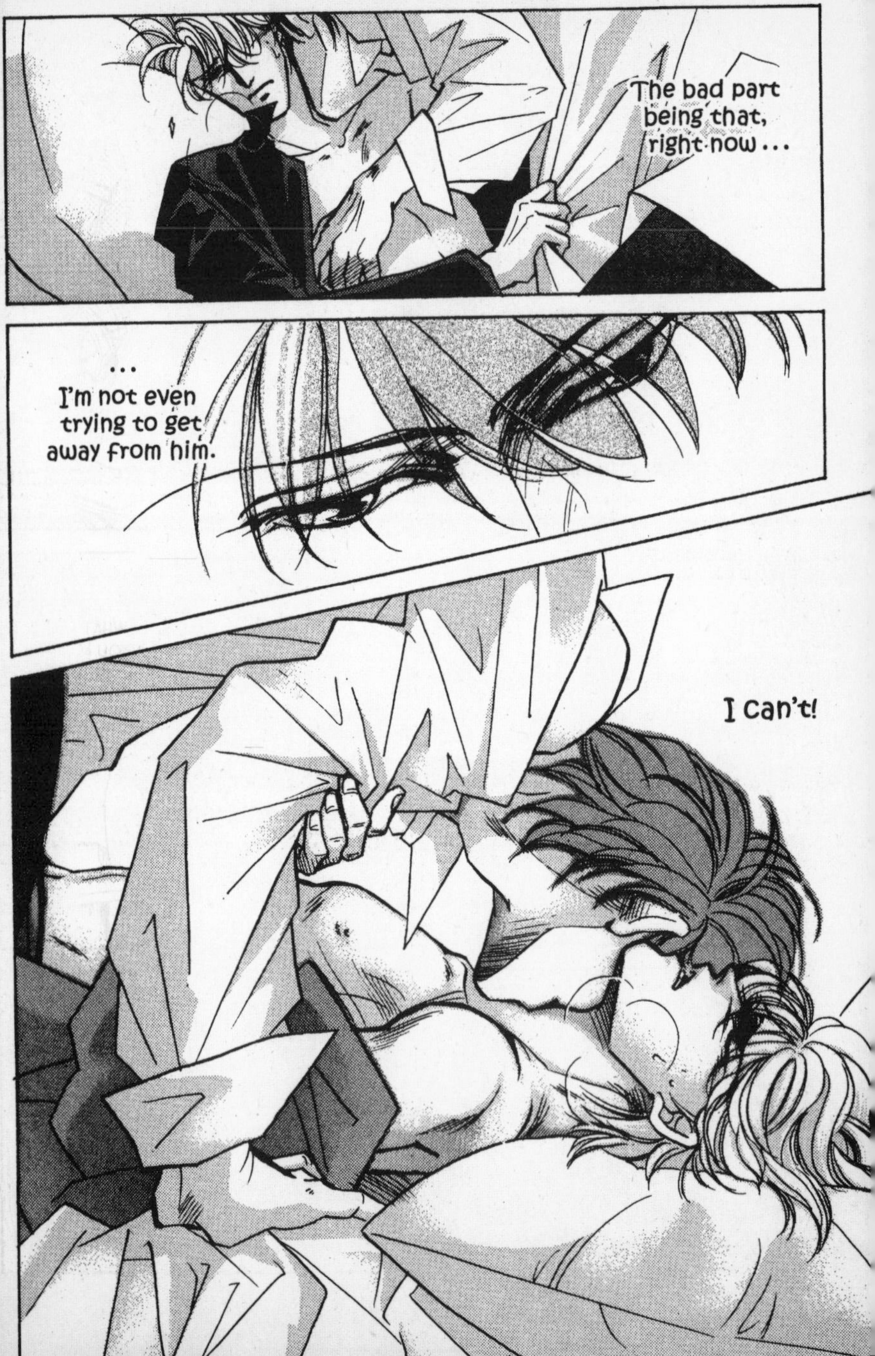
The bad part being that, right now . . .
. . .
I'm not even trying to get away from him.
I can't!

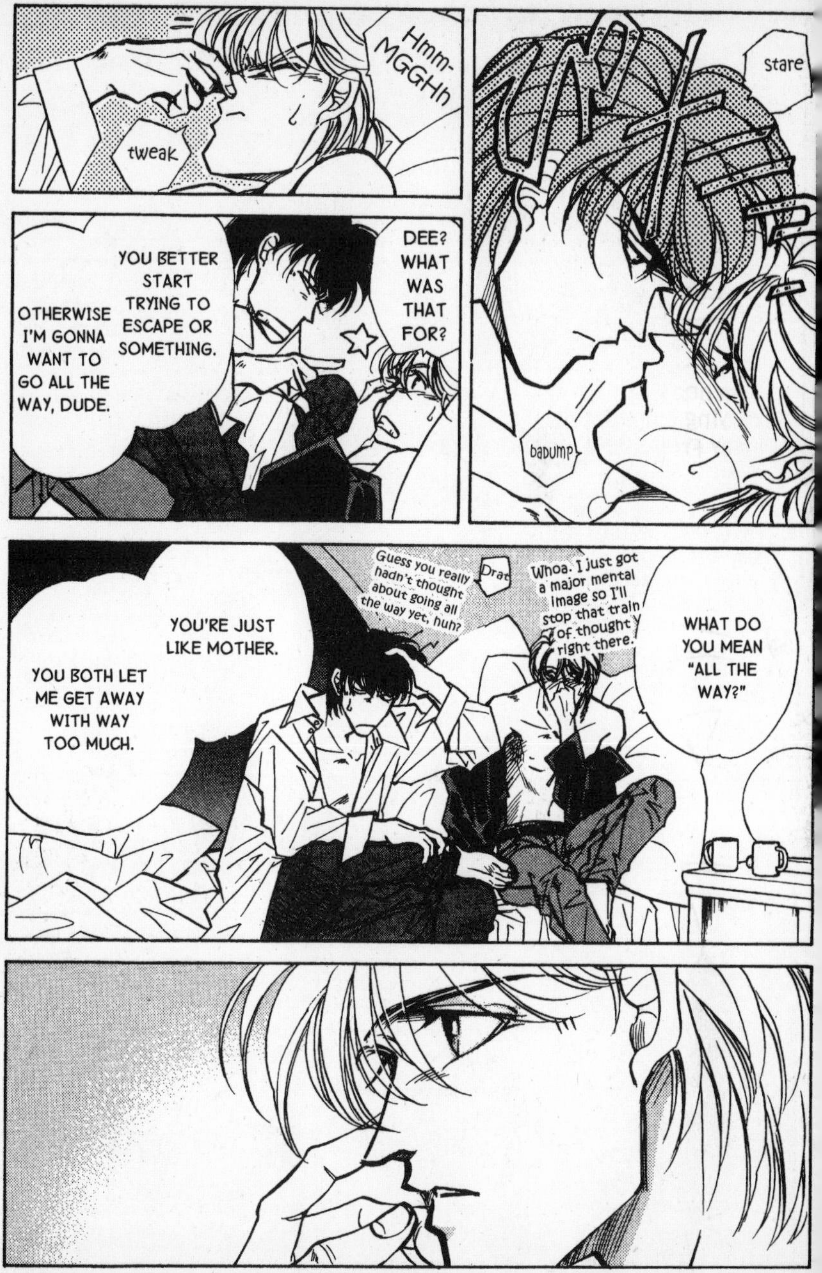
stare
badump
Hmm-MGGHh
tweak
DEE? WHAT WAS THAT FOR?
YOU BETTER START TRYING TO ESCAPE OR SOMETHING.
OTHERWISE I'M GONNA WANT TO GO ALL THE WAY, DUDE.
WHAT DO YOU MEAN "ALL THE WAY?"
Whoa. I just got a major mental image so I'll stop that train of thought right there.
Drat
Guess you really hadn't thought about going all the way yet, huh?
YOU'RE JUST LIKE MOTHER.
YOU BOTH LET ME GET AWAY WITH WAY TOO MUCH.

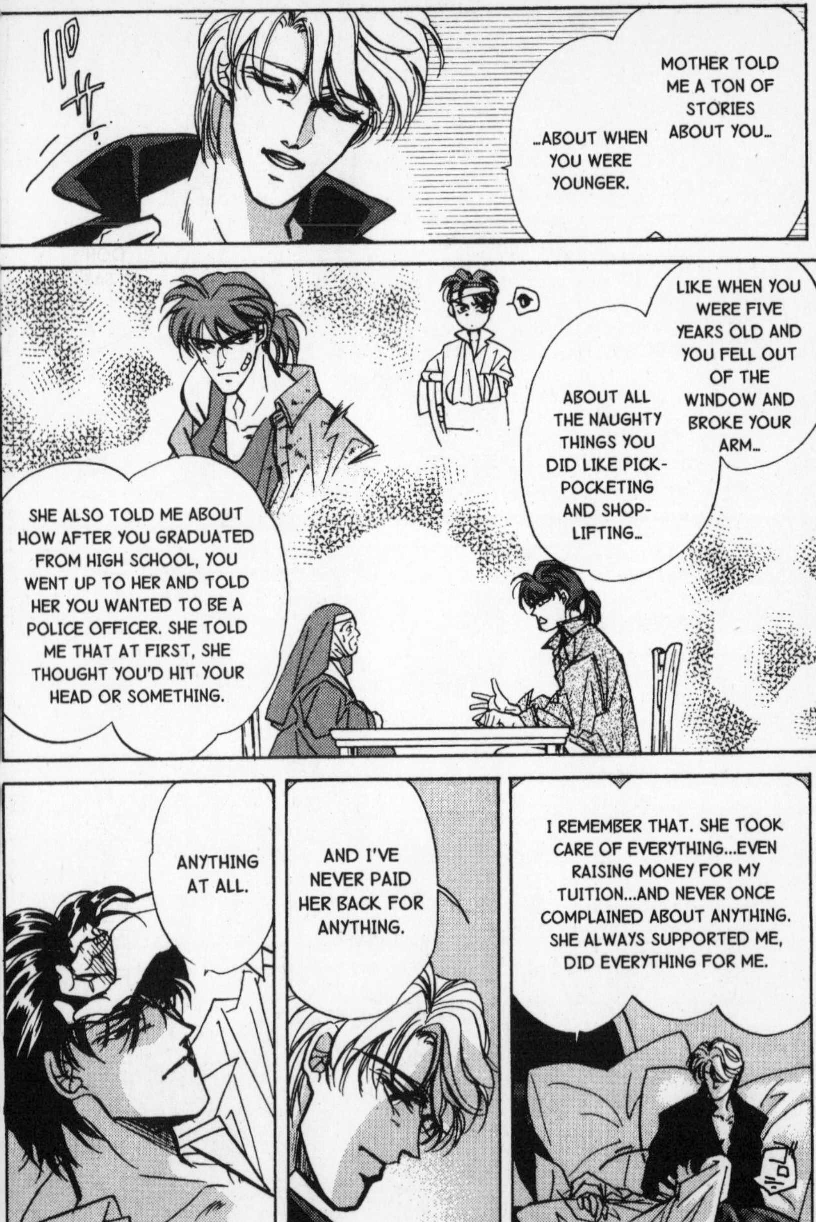
MOTHER TOLD ME A TON OF STORIES ABOUT YOU...
...ABOUT WHEN YOU WERE YOUNGER.
LIKE WHEN YOU WERE FIVE YEARS OLD AND YOU FELL OUT OF THE WINDOW AND BROKE YOUR ARM...
ABOUT ALL THE NAUGHTY THINGS YOU DID LIKE PICK-POCKETING AND SHOP-LIFTING...
SHE ALSO TOLD ME ABOUT HOW AFTER YOU GRADUATED FROM HIGH SCHOOL, YOU WENT UP TO HER AND TOLD HER YOU WANTED TO BE A POLICE OFFICER. SHE TOLD ME THAT AT FIRST, SHE THOUGHT YOU'D HIT YOUR HEAD OR SOMETHING.
I REMEMBER THAT. SHE TOOK CARE OF EVERYTHING...EVEN RAISING MONEY FOR MY TUITION...AND NEVER ONCE COMPLAINED ABOUT ANYTHING. SHE ALWAYS SUPPORTED ME, DID EVERYTHING FOR ME.
AND I'VE NEVER PAID HER BACK FOR ANYTHING.
ANYTHING AT ALL.

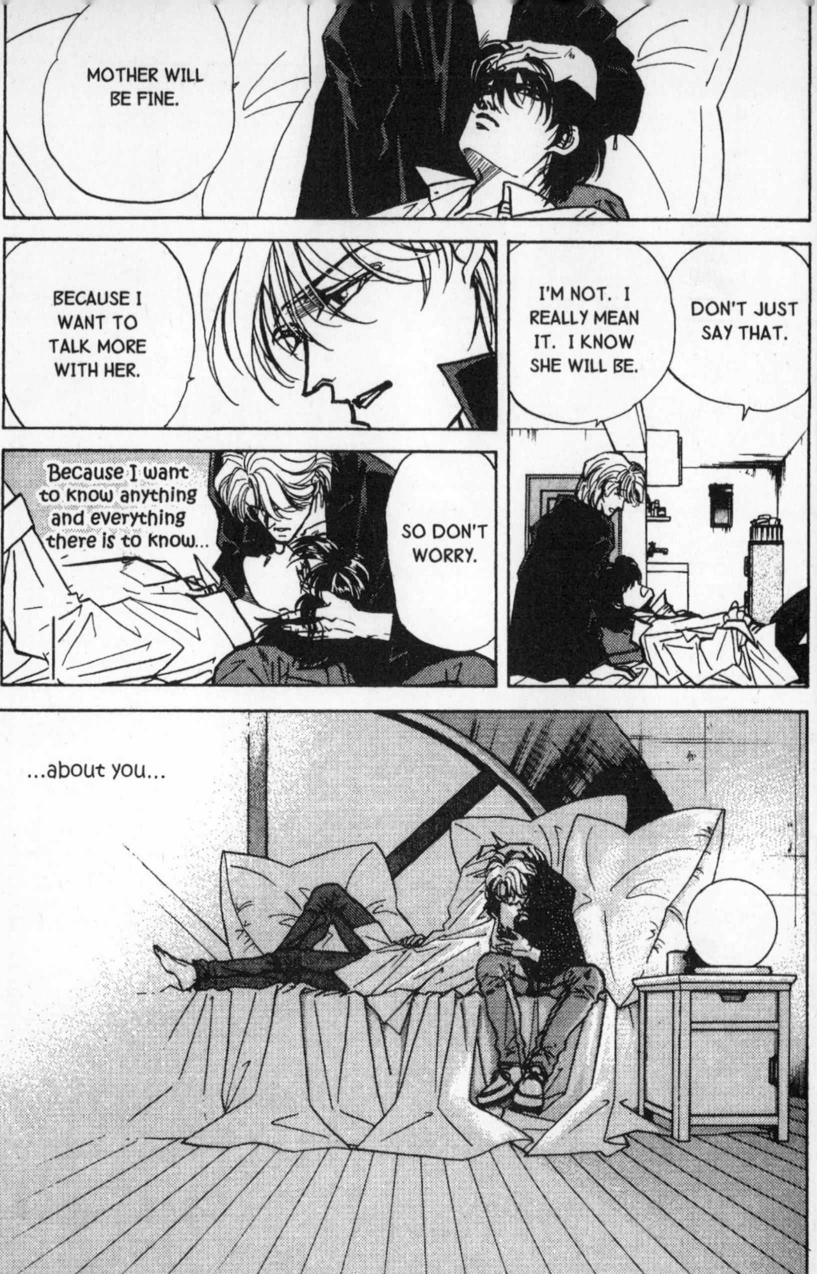
MOTHER WILL BE FINE.
DON'T JUST SAY THAT.
I'M NOT. I REALLY MEAN IT. I KNOW SHE WILL BE.
BECAUSE I WANT TO TALK MORE WITH HER.
SO DON'T WORRY.
Because I want to know anything and everything there is to know...
...about you...

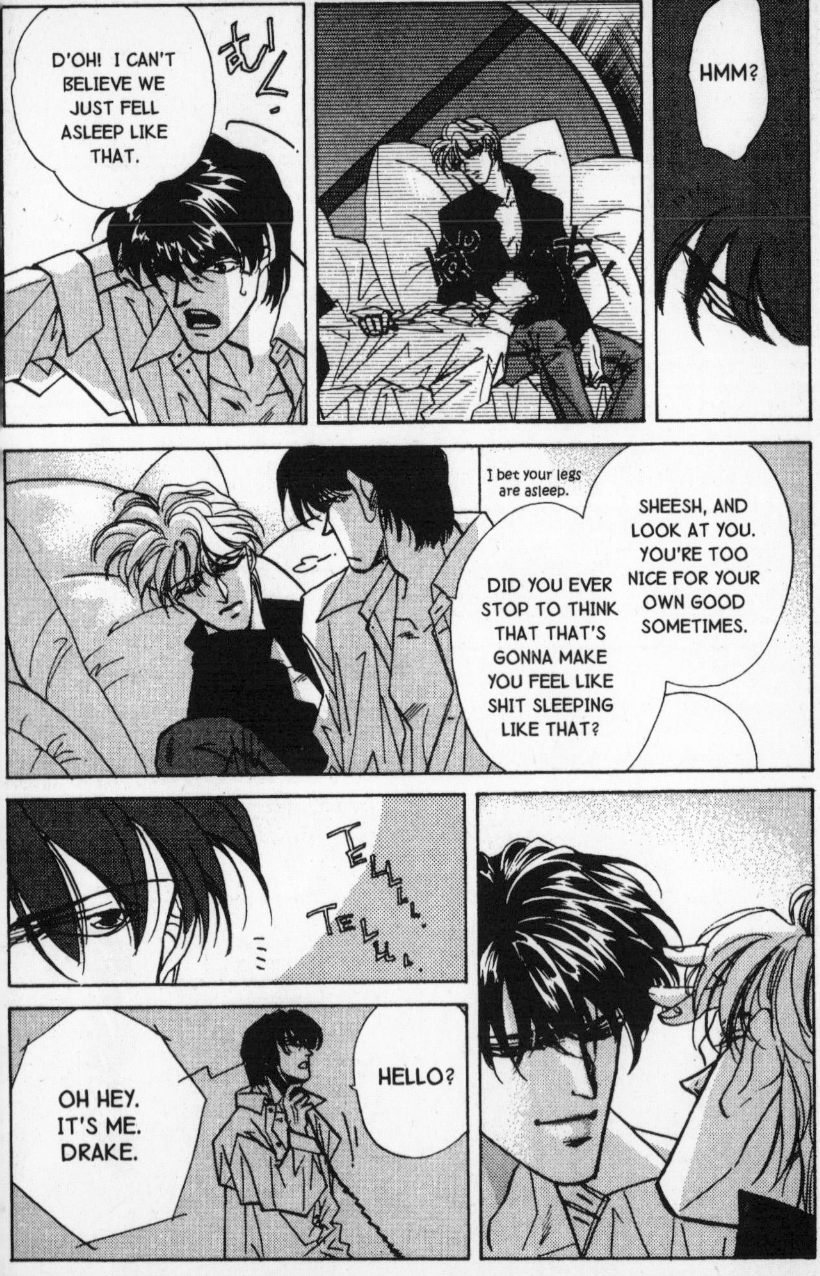
HMM?
D'OH! I CAN'T BELIEVE WE JUST FELL ASLEEP LIKE THAT.
SHEESH, AND LOOK AT YOU. YOU'RE TOO NICE FOR YOUR OWN GOOD SOMETIMES.
DID YOU EVER STOP TO THINK THAT THAT'S GONNA MAKE YOU FEEL LIKE SHIT SLEEPING LIKE THAT?
I bet your legs are asleep.
HELLO?
OH HEY. IT'S ME. DRAKE.

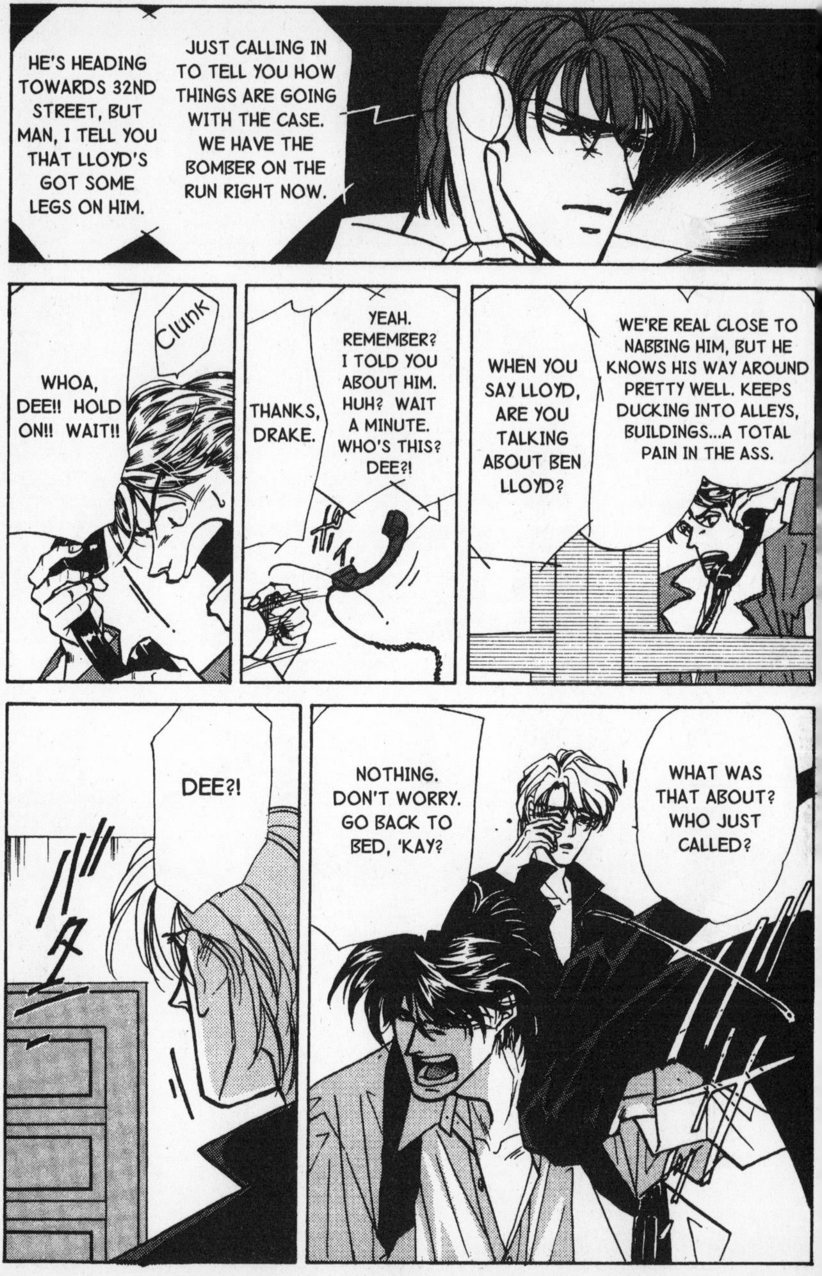
JUST CALLING IN TO TELL YOU HOW THINGS ARE GOING WITH THE CASE. WE HAVE THE BOMBER ON THE RUN RIGHT NOW.
HE'S HEADING TOWARDS 32ND STREET, BUT MAN, I TELL YOU THAT LLOYD'S GOT SOME LEGS ON HIM.
WE'RE REAL CLOSE TO NABBING HIM, BUT HE KNOWS HIS WAY AROUND PRETTY WELL. KEEPS DUCKING INTO ALLEYS, BUILDINGS...A TOTAL PAIN IN THE ASS.
WHEN YOU SAY LLOYD, ARE YOU TALKING ABOUT BEN LLOYD?
YEAH. REMEMBER? I TOLD YOU ABOUT HIM. HUH? WAIT A MINUTE. WHO'S THIS? DEE?!
THANKS, DRAKE.
Clunk
WHOA, DEE!! HOLD ON!! WAIT!!
WHAT WAS THAT ABOUT? WHO JUST CALLED?
NOTHING. DON'T WORRY. GO BACK TO BED, 'KAY?
DEE?!

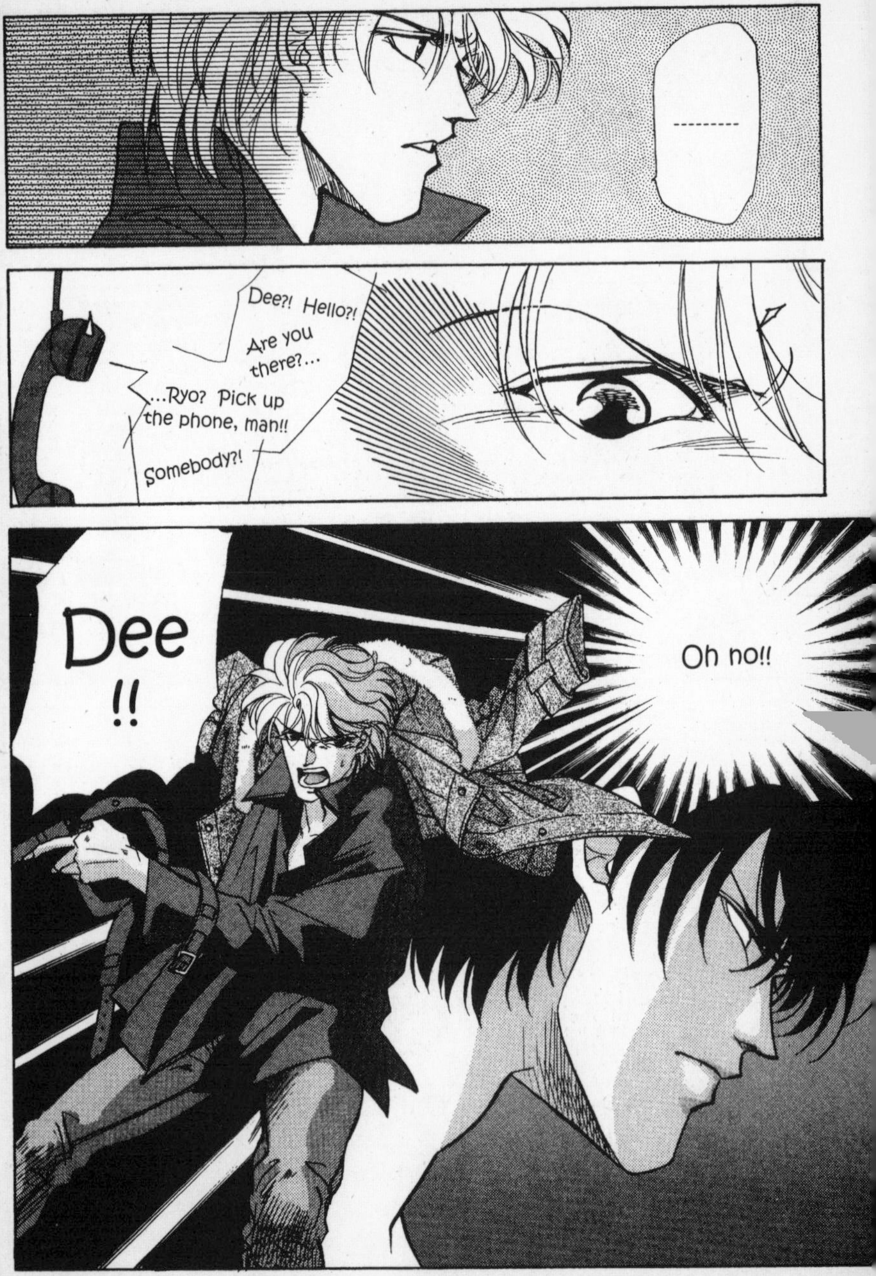

Dee?! Hello?!
Are you there?...
...Ryo? Pick up the phone, man!!
Somebody?!
Oh no!!
Dee !!

FAKE

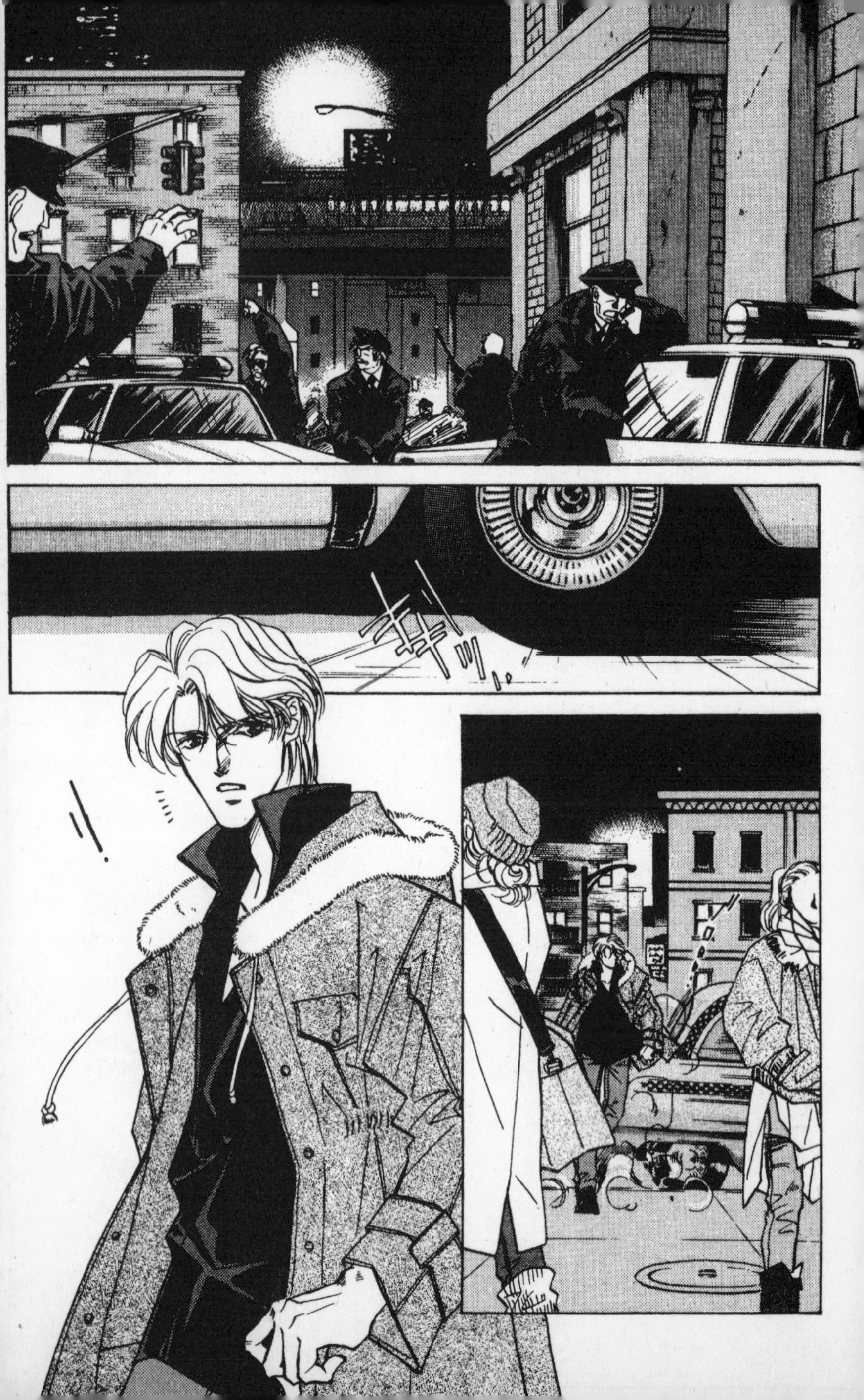
キキッ

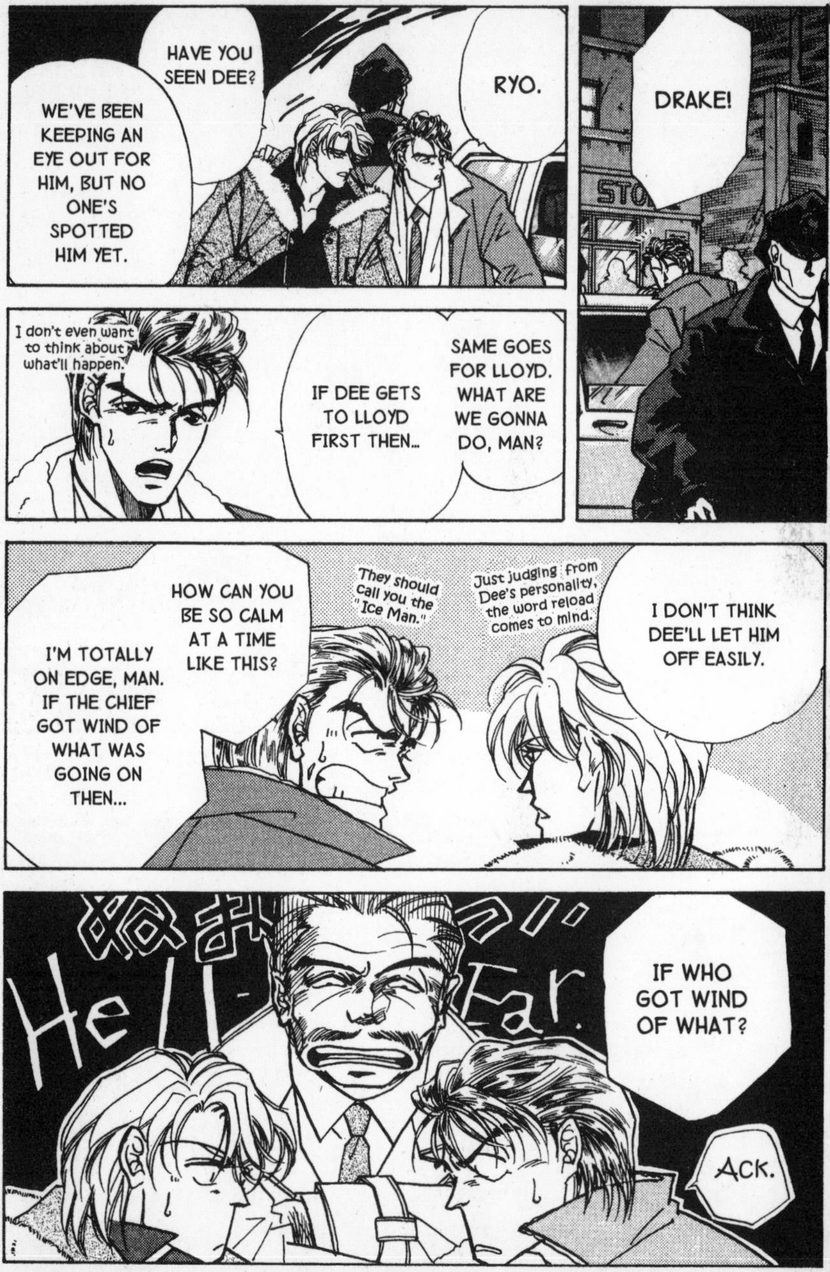
DRAKE!
RYO.
HAVE YOU SEEN DEE?
WE'VE BEEN KEEPING AN EYE OUT FOR HIM, BUT NO ONE'S SPOTTED HIM YET.
SAME GOES FOR LLOYD. WHAT ARE WE GONNA DO, MAN?
IF DEE GETS TO LLOYD FIRST THEN...
I don't even want to think about what'll happen.
I DON'T THINK DEE'LL LET HIM OFF EASILY.
Just judging from Dee's personality, the word reload comes to mind.
They should call you the "Ice Man."
HOW CAN YOU BE SO CALM AT A TIME LIKE THIS?
I'M TOTALLY ON EDGE, MAN. IF THE CHIEF GOT WIND OF WHAT WAS GOING ON THEN...
IF WHO GOT WIND OF WHAT?
Hell-Ear.
ACK.

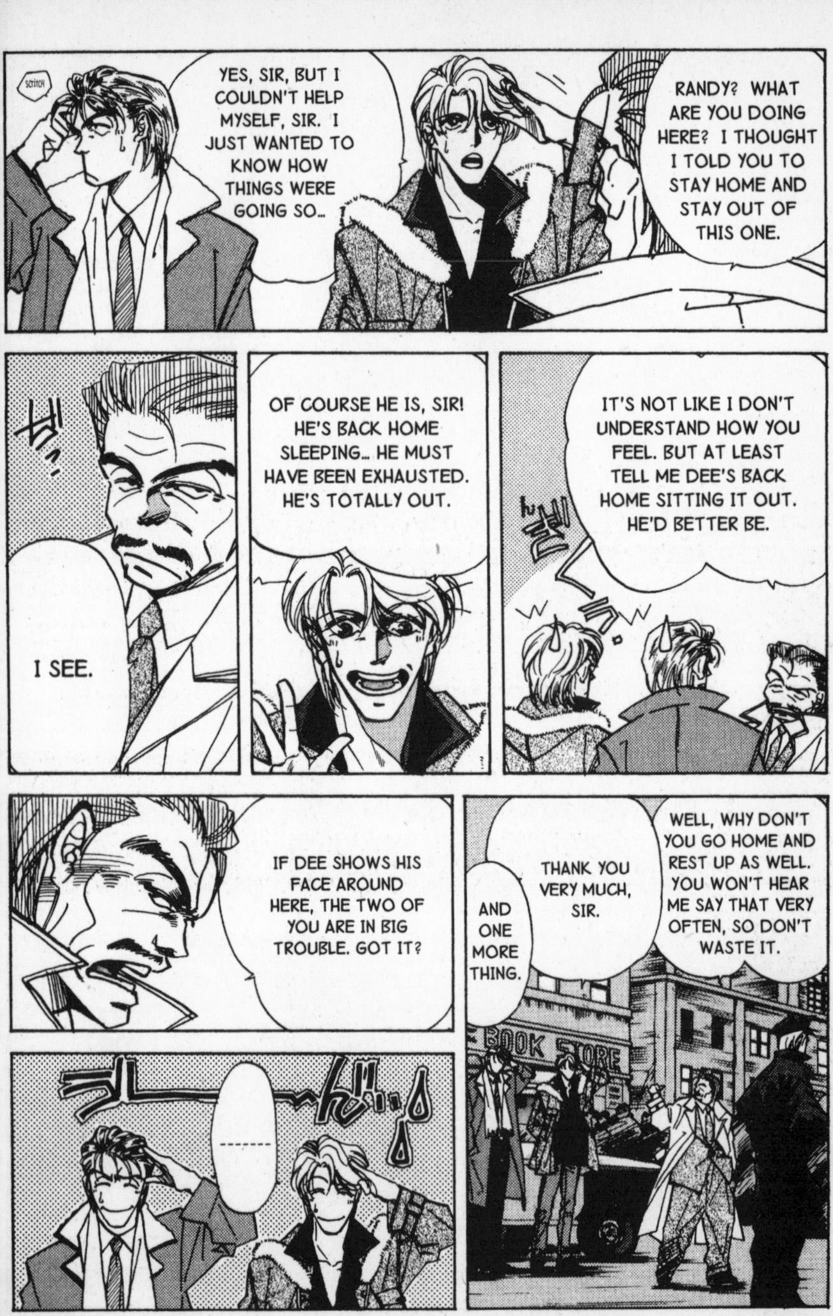
RANDY? WHAT ARE YOU DOING HERE? I THOUGHT I TOLD YOU TO STAY HOME AND STAY OUT OF THIS ONE.
scritch
YES, SIR, BUT I COULDN'T HELP MYSELF, SIR. I JUST WANTED TO KNOW HOW THINGS WERE GOING SO...
IT'S NOT LIKE I DON'T UNDERSTAND HOW YOU FEEL. BUT AT LEAST TELL ME DEE'S BACK HOME SITTING IT OUT. HE'D BETTER BE.
OF COURSE HE IS, SIR! HE'S BACK HOME SLEEPING... HE MUST HAVE BEEN EXHAUSTED. HE'S TOTALLY OUT.
I SEE.
WELL, WHY DON'T YOU GO HOME AND REST UP AS WELL. YOU WON'T HEAR ME SAY THAT VERY OFTEN, SO DON'T WASTE IT.
THANK YOU VERY MUCH, SIR.
AND ONE MORE THING.
BOOK STORE
IF DEE SHOWS HIS FACE AROUND HERE, THE TWO OF YOU ARE IN BIG TROUBLE. GOT IT?

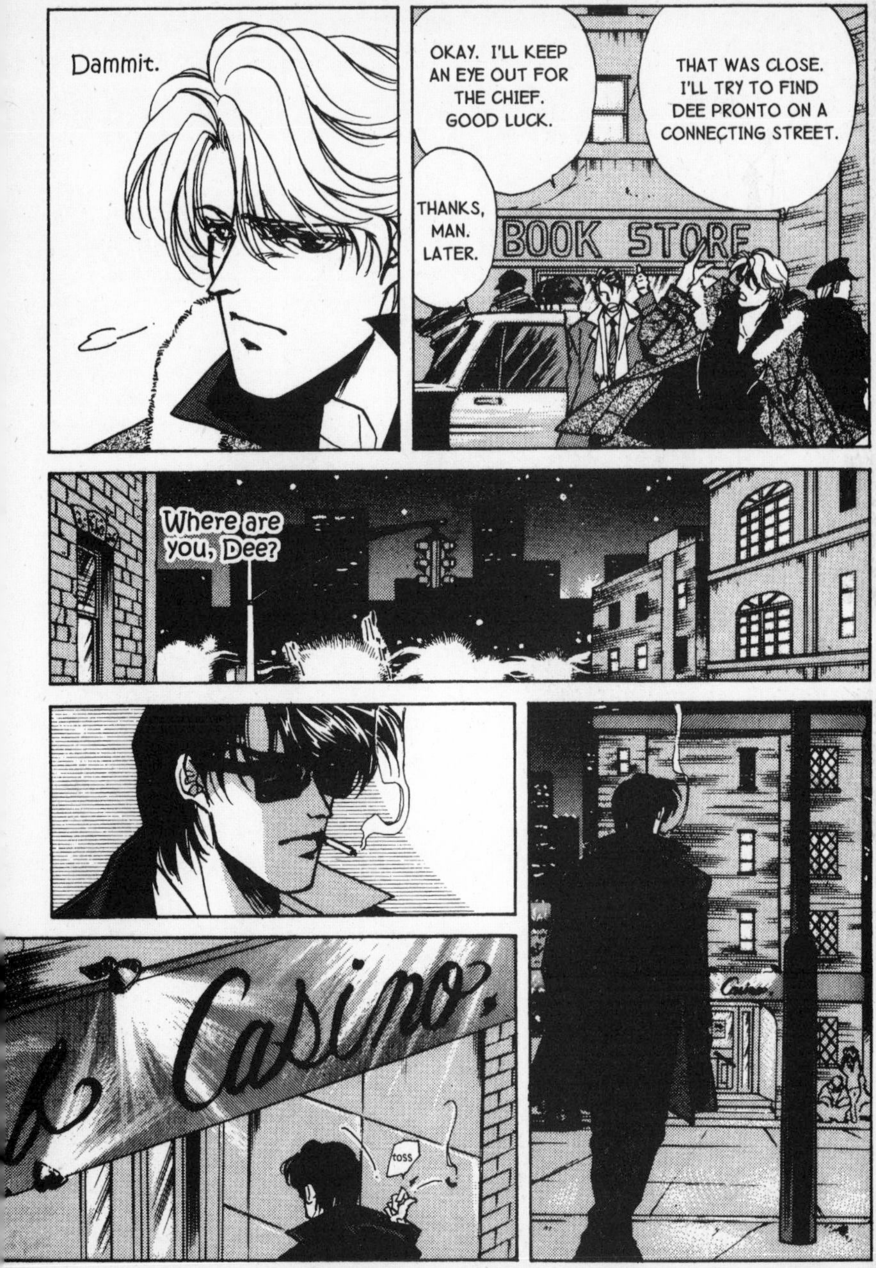
THAT WAS CLOSE. I'LL TRY TO FIND DEE PRONTO ON A CONNECTING STREET.
OKAY. I'LL KEEP AN EYE OUT FOR THE CHIEF. GOOD LUCK.
THANKS, MAN. LATER.
BOOK STORE
Dammit.
Where are you, Dee?
Casino
Casino.
toss

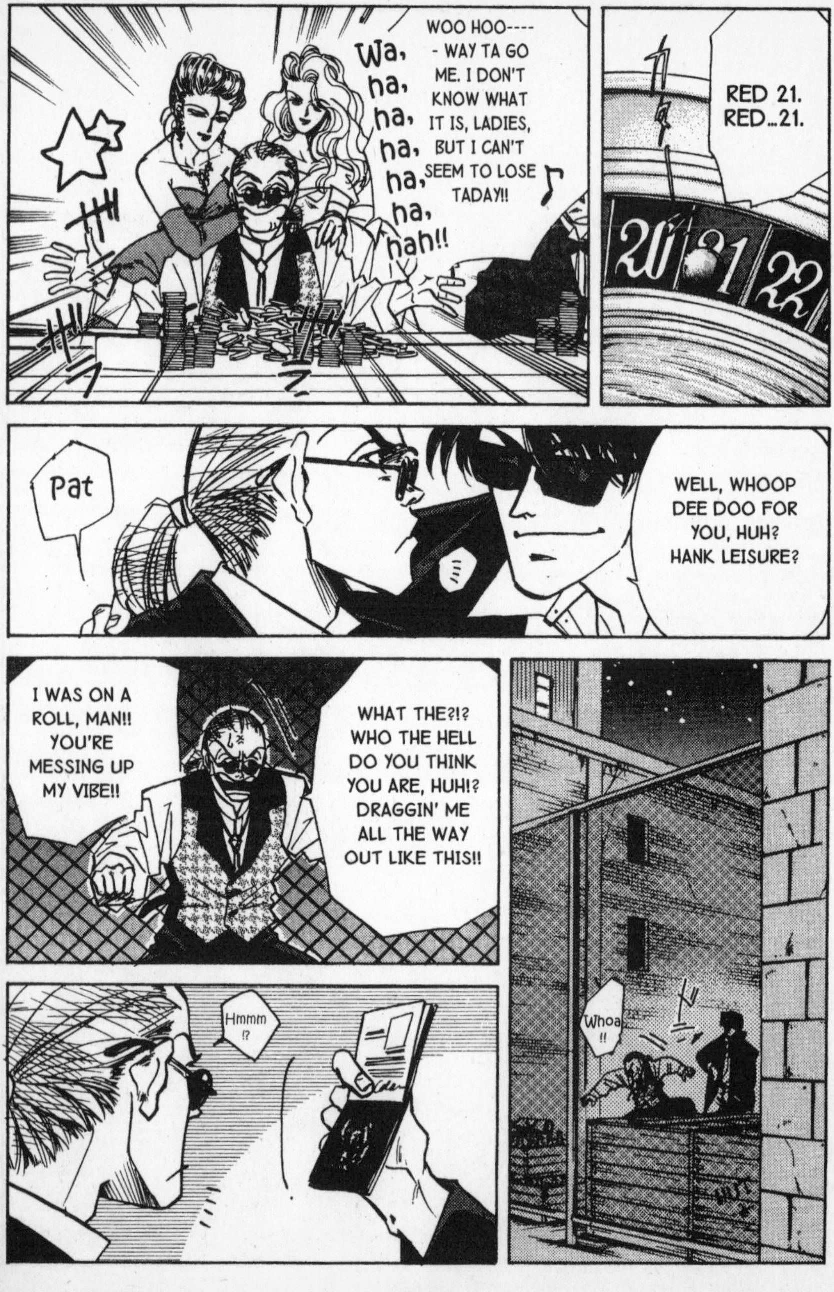
RED 21. RED...21.
WOO HOO---- - WAY TA GO ME. I DON'T KNOW WHAT IT IS, LADIES, BUT I CAN'T SEEM TO LOSE TADAY!!
Wa, ha, ha, ha, ha, ha, hah!!
WELL, WHOOP DEE DOO FOR YOU, HUH? HANK LEISURE?
Pat
Whoa!!
WHAT THE?!? WHO THE HELL DO YOU THINK YOU ARE, HUH!? DRAGGIN' ME ALL THE WAY OUT LIKE THIS!!
I WAS ON A ROLL, MAN!! YOU'RE MESSING UP MY VIBE!!
Hmmm !?

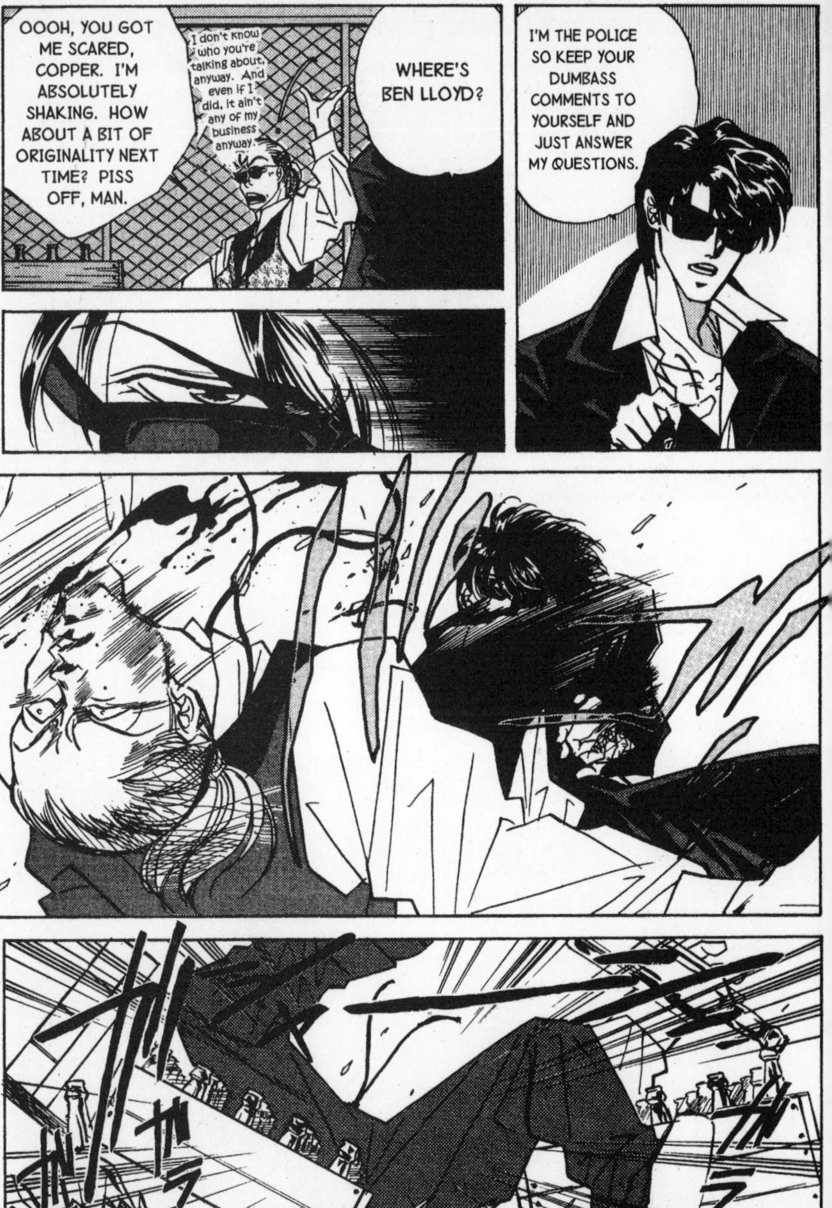
I'M THE POLICE SO KEEP YOUR DUMBASS COMMENTS TO YOURSELF AND JUST ANSWER MY QUESTIONS.
WHERE'S BEN LLOYD?
I don't know who you're talking about, anyway. And even if I did, it ain't any of my business anyway.
OOOH, YOU GOT ME SCARED, COPPER. I'M ABSOLUTELY SHAKING. HOW ABOUT A BIT OF ORIGINALITY NEXT TIME? PISS OFF, MAN.
ガラ
ガラ

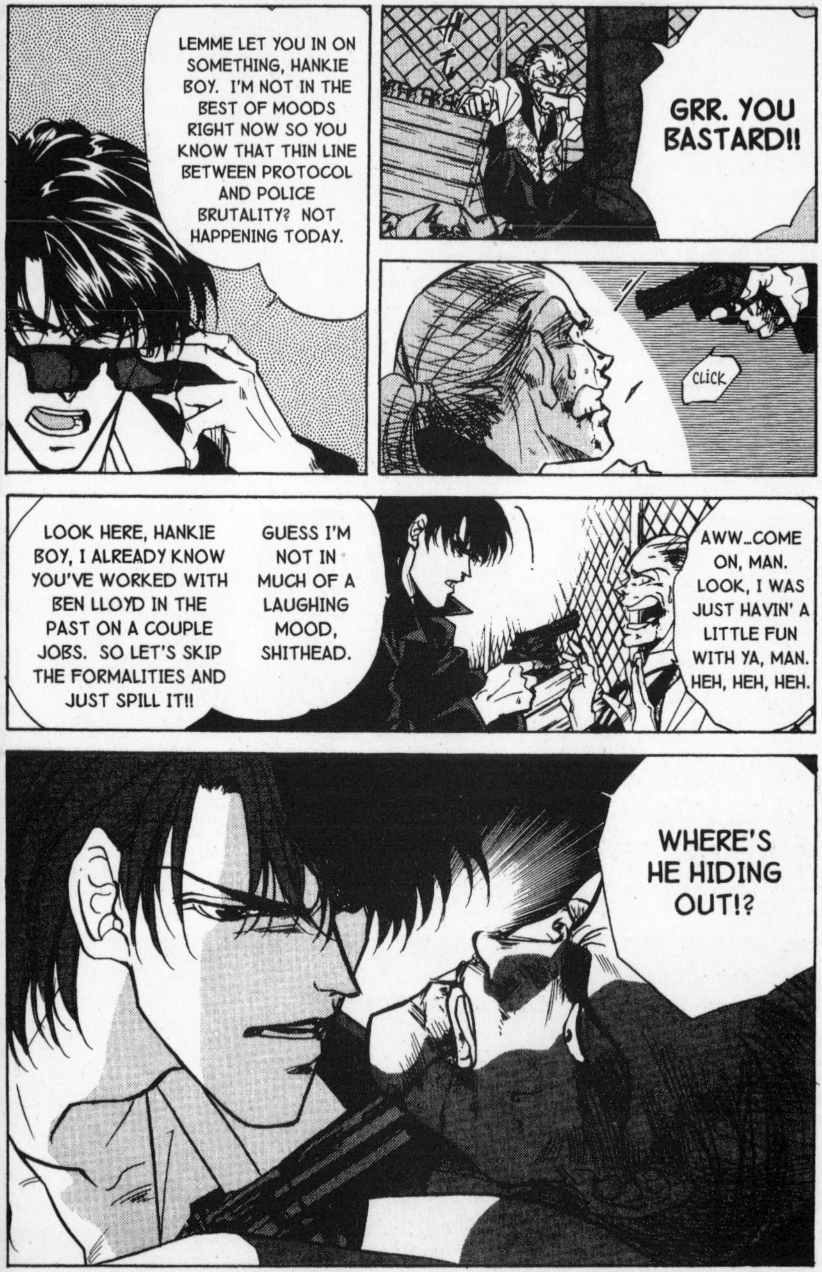
GRR. YOU BASTARD!!
CLICK
LEMME LET YOU IN ON SOMETHING, HANKIE BOY. I'M NOT IN THE BEST OF MOODS RIGHT NOW SO YOU KNOW THAT THIN LINE BETWEEN PROTOCOL AND POLICE BRUTALITY? NOT HAPPENING TODAY.
AWW...COME ON, MAN. LOOK, I WAS JUST HAVIN' A LITTLE FUN WITH YA, MAN. HEH, HEH, HEH.
GUESS I'M NOT IN MUCH OF A LAUGHING MOOD, SHITHEAD.
LOOK HERE, HANKIE BOY, I ALREADY KNOW YOU'VE WORKED WITH BEN LLOYD IN THE PAST ON A COUPLE JOBS. SO LET'S SKIP THE FORMALITIES AND JUST SPILL IT!!
WHERE'S HE HIDING OUT!?

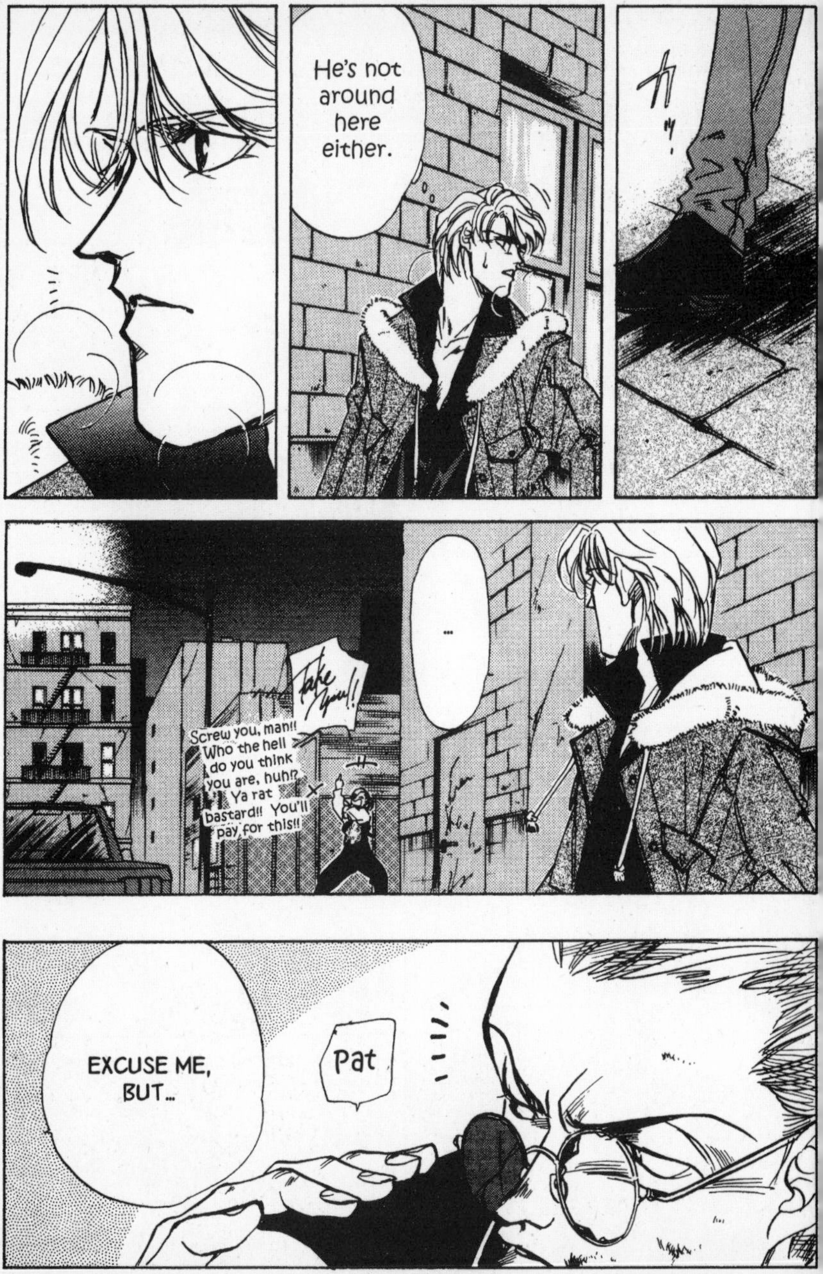
カッ
He's not around here either.
...
Screw you, man!! Who the hell do you think you are, huh!? Ya rat bastard!! You'll pay for this!!
Pat
EXCUSE ME, BUT...

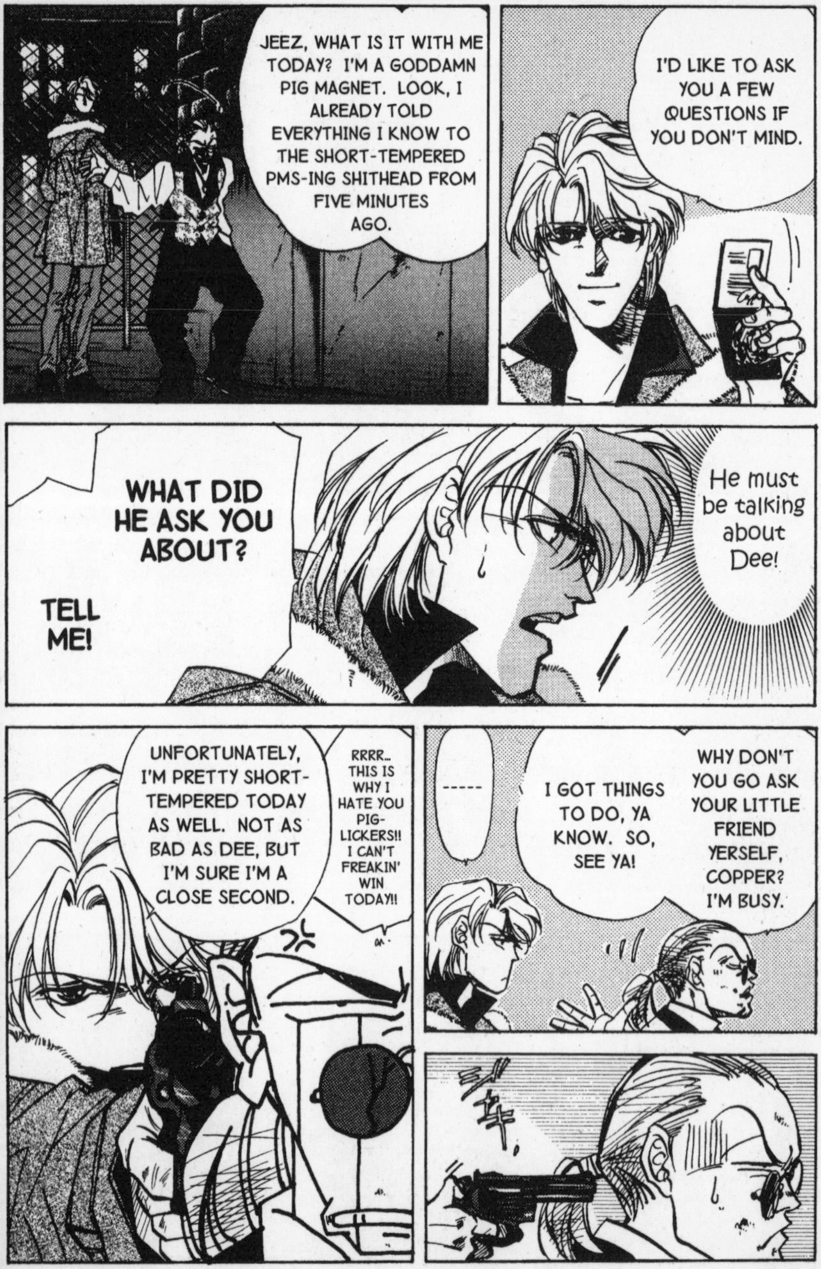
I'D LIKE TO ASK YOU A FEW QUESTIONS IF YOU DON'T MIND.
JEEZ, WHAT IS IT WITH ME TODAY? I'M A GODDAMN PIG MAGNET. LOOK, I ALREADY TOLD EVERYTHING I KNOW TO THE SHORT-TEMPERED PMS-ING SHITHEAD FROM FIVE MINUTES AGO.
He must be talking about Dee!
WHAT DID HE ASK YOU ABOUT?
TELL ME!
WHY DON'T YOU GO ASK YOUR LITTLE FRIEND YERSELF, COPPER? I'M BUSY.
I GOT THINGS TO DO, YA KNOW. SO, SEE YA!

RRRR... THIS IS WHY I HATE YOU PIG-LICKERS!! I CAN'T FREAKIN' WIN TODAY!!
UNFORTUNATELY, I'M PRETTY SHORT-TEMPERED TODAY AS WELL. NOT AS BAD AS DEE, BUT I'M SURE I'M A CLOSE SECOND.

Turn the third corner from the main street. Then look for the second red brick apartment complex. Ben Lloyd should be hiding out up in the attic there.

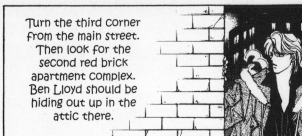

And if he ain't there then I have no freakin' clue where else he could be, okay? I swear, man.

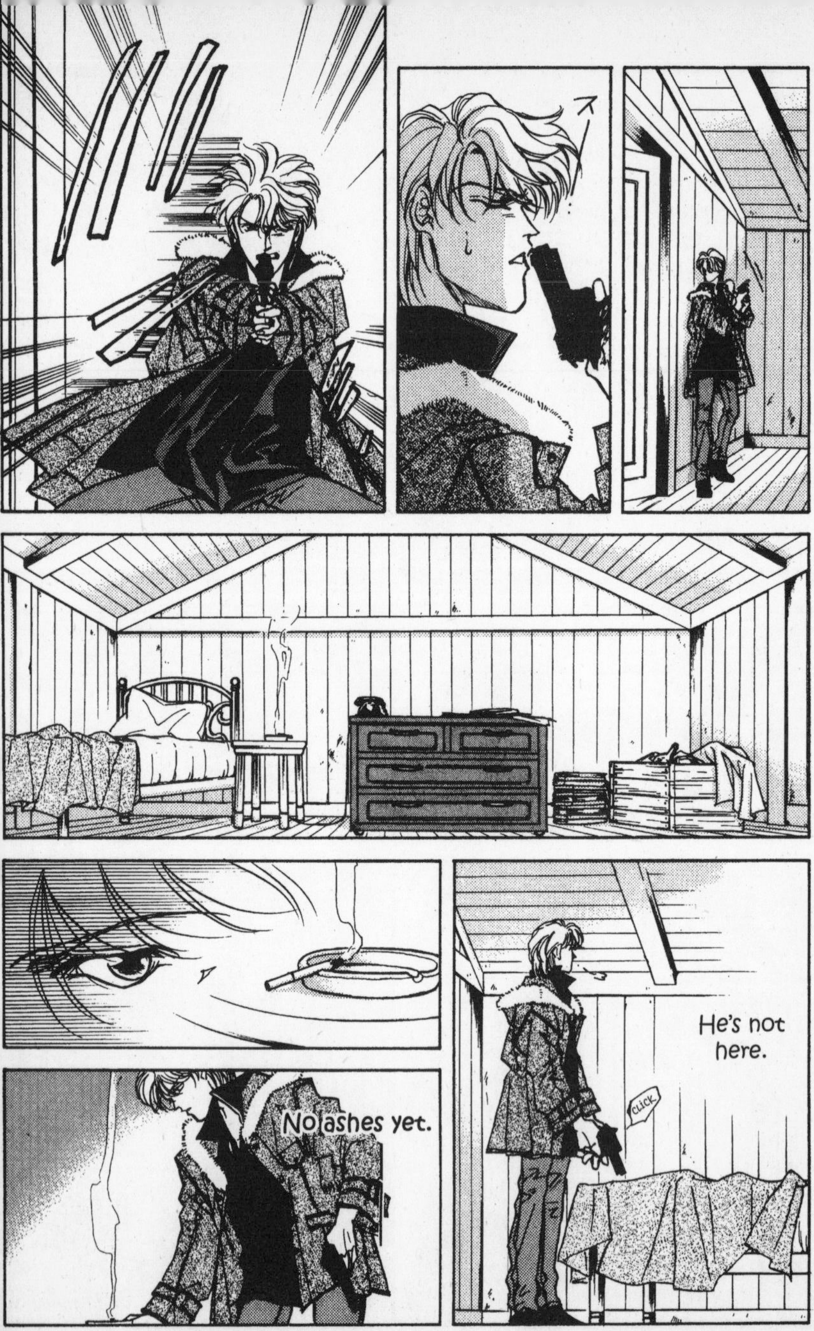
He's not here.
CLICK
No ashes yet.

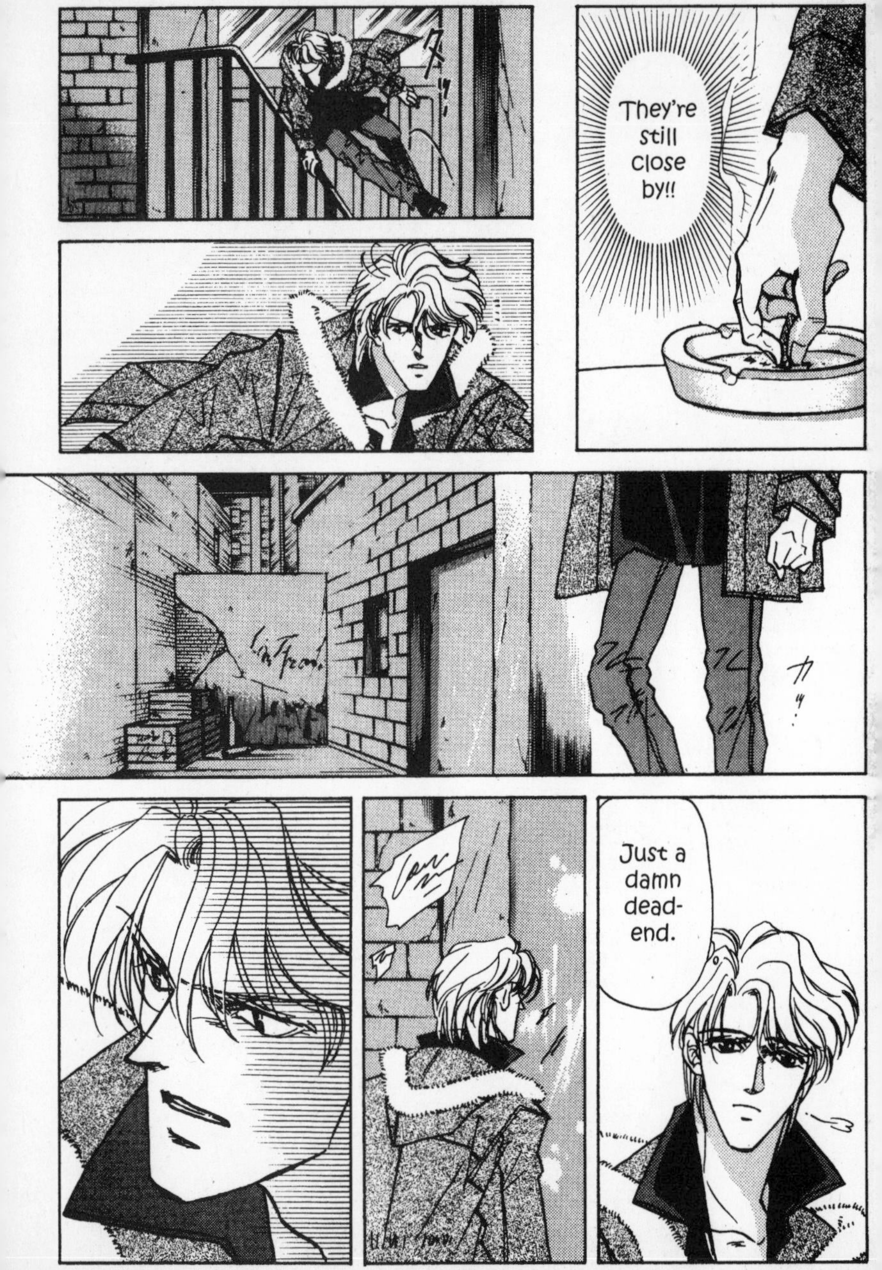
They're still close by!!
Just a damn dead-end.

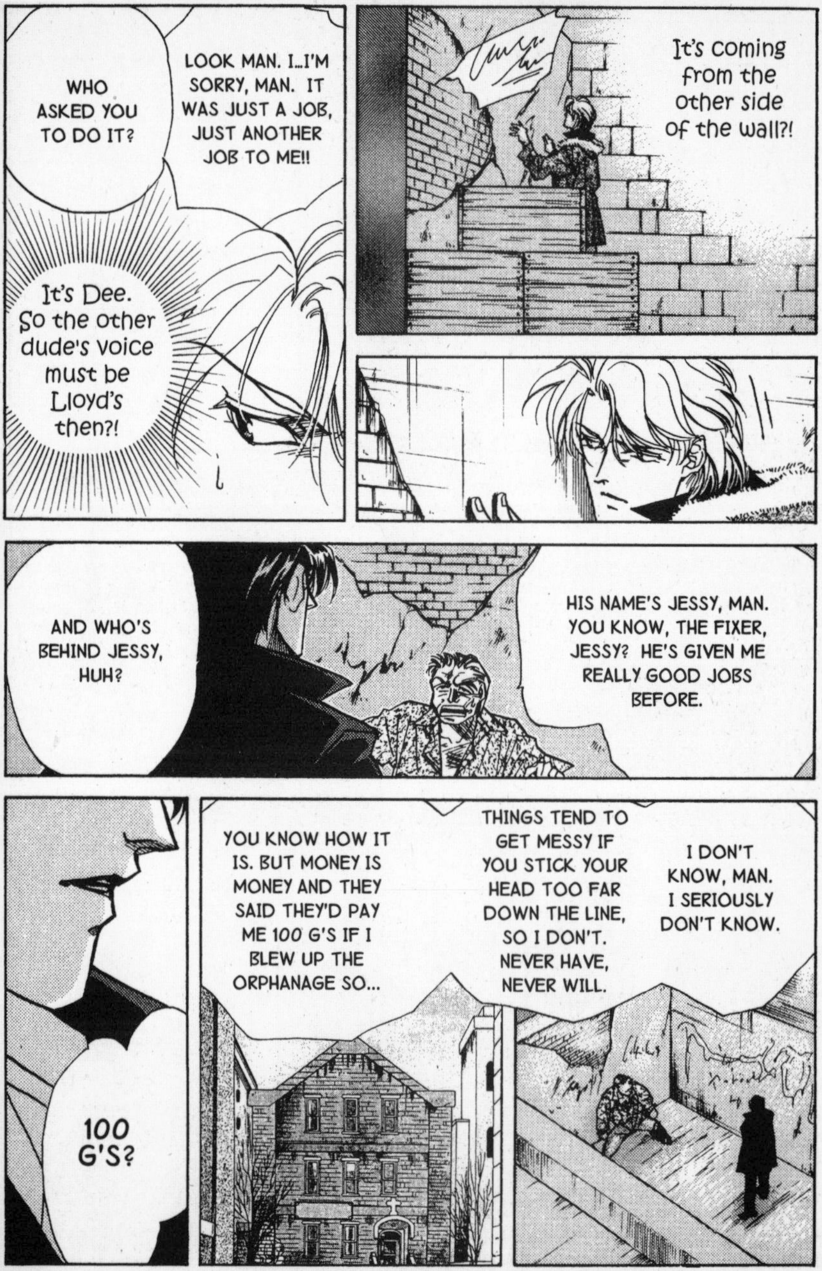
It's coming from the other side of the wall?!
LOOK MAN. I...I'M SORRY, MAN. IT WAS JUST A JOB, JUST ANOTHER JOB TO ME!!
WHO ASKED YOU TO DO IT?
It's Dee. So the other dude's voice must be Lloyd's then?!
HIS NAME'S JESSY, MAN. YOU KNOW, THE FIXER, JESSY? HE'S GIVEN ME REALLY GOOD JOBS BEFORE.
AND WHO'S BEHIND JESSY, HUH?
I DON'T KNOW, MAN. I SERIOUSLY DON'T KNOW.
THINGS TEND TO GET MESSY IF YOU STICK YOUR HEAD TOO FAR DOWN THE LINE, SO I DON'T. NEVER HAVE, NEVER WILL.
YOU KNOW HOW IT IS. BUT MONEY IS MONEY AND THEY SAID THEY'D PAY ME 100 G'S IF I BLEW UP THE ORPHANAGE SO...
100 G'S?

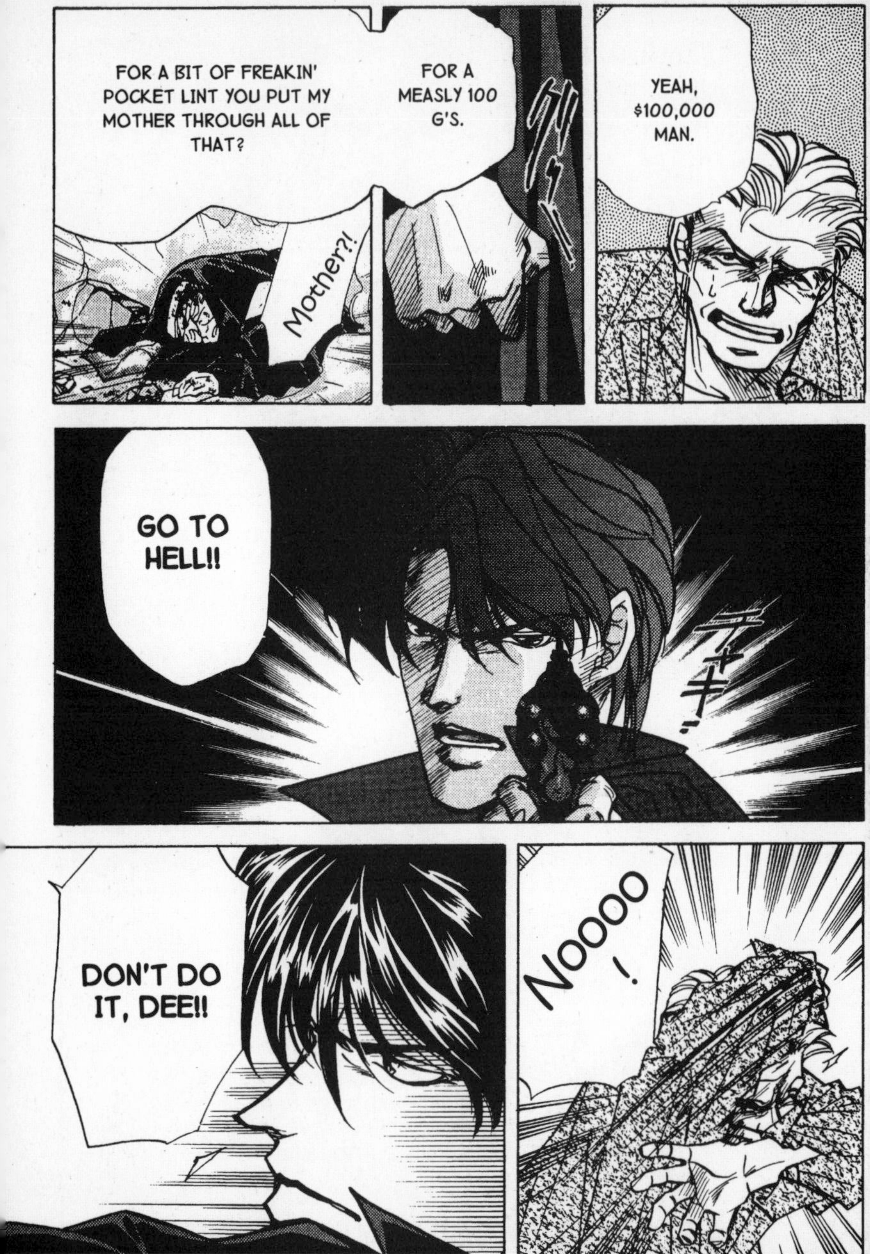
FOR A BIT OF FREAKIN' POCKET LINT YOU PUT MY MOTHER THROUGH ALL OF THAT?
Mother?!
FOR A MEASLY 100 G'S.
YEAH, $100,000 MAN.
GO TO HELL!!
DON'T DO IT, DEE!!
Noooo!

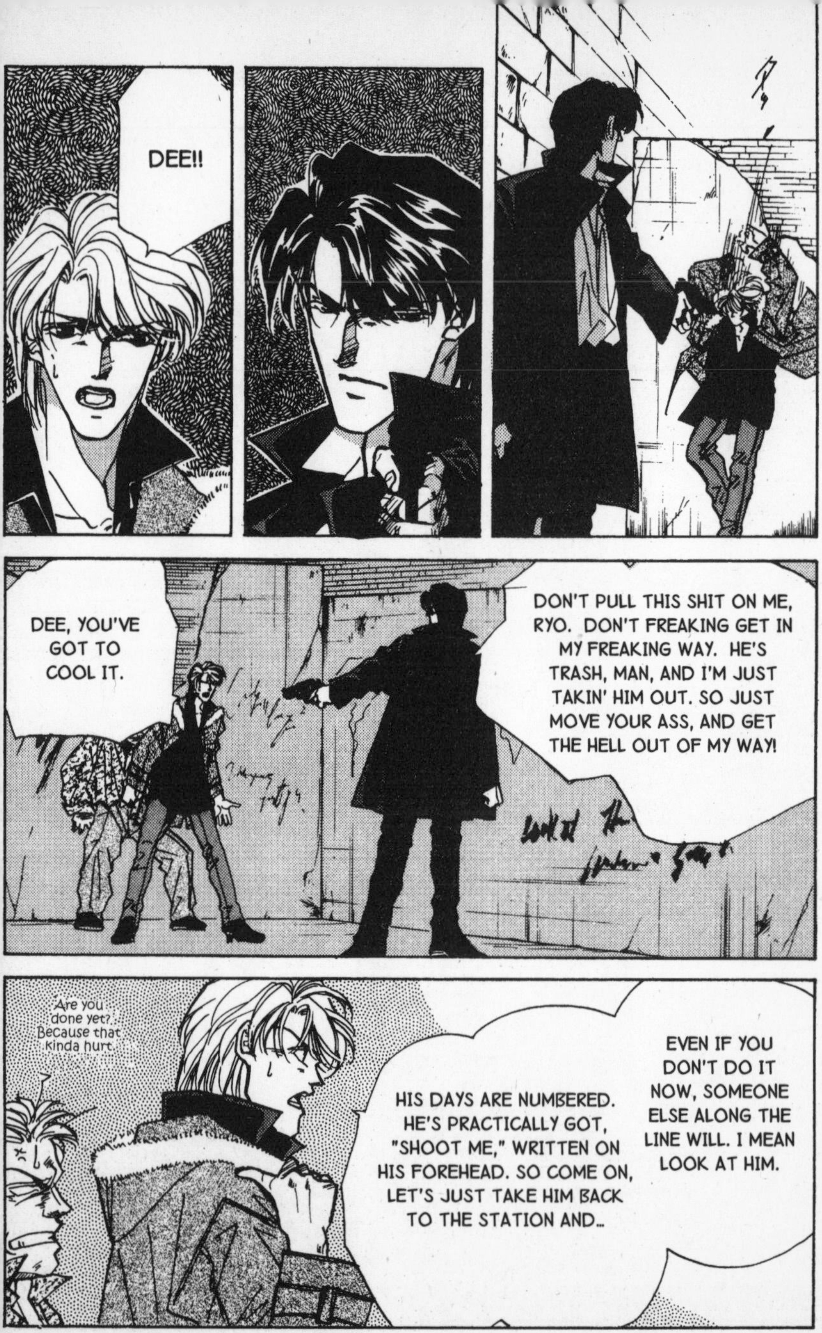

DEE!!
DON'T PULL THIS SHIT ON ME, RYO. DON'T FREAKING GET IN MY FREAKING WAY. HE'S TRASH, MAN, AND I'M JUST TAKIN' HIM OUT. SO JUST MOVE YOUR ASS, AND GET THE HELL OUT OF MY WAY!
DEE, YOU'VE GOT TO COOL IT.
EVEN IF YOU DON'T DO IT NOW, SOMEONE ELSE ALONG THE LINE WILL. I MEAN LOOK AT HIM.
HIS DAYS ARE NUMBERED. HE'S PRACTICALLY GOT, "SHOOT ME," WRITTEN ON HIS FOREHEAD. SO COME ON, LET'S JUST TAKE HIM BACK TO THE STATION AND...
Are you done yet? Because that kinda hurt.

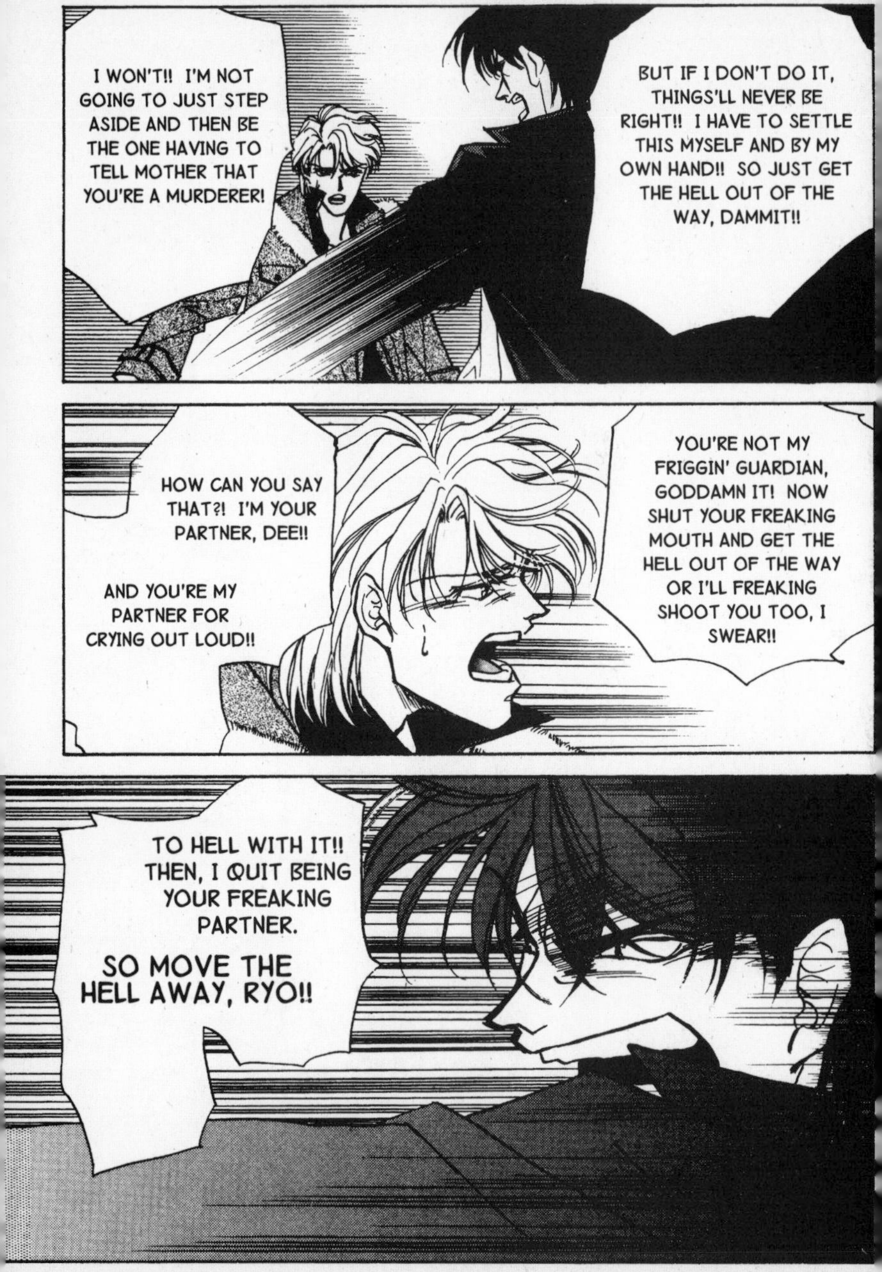
BUT IF I DON'T DO IT, THINGS'LL NEVER BE RIGHT!! I HAVE TO SETTLE THIS MYSELF AND BY MY OWN HAND!! SO JUST GET THE HELL OUT OF THE WAY, DAMMIT!!
I WON'T!! I'M NOT GOING TO JUST STEP ASIDE AND THEN BE THE ONE HAVING TO TELL MOTHER THAT YOU'RE A MURDERER!
YOU'RE NOT MY FRIGGIN' GUARDIAN, GODDAMN IT! NOW SHUT YOUR FREAKING MOUTH AND GET THE HELL OUT OF THE WAY OR I'LL FREAKING SHOOT YOU TOO, I SWEAR!!
HOW CAN YOU SAY THAT?! I'M YOUR PARTNER, DEE!!
AND YOU'RE MY PARTNER FOR CRYING OUT LOUD!!
TO HELL WITH IT!! THEN, I QUIT BEING YOUR FREAKING PARTNER.
SO MOVE THE HELL AWAY, RYO!!

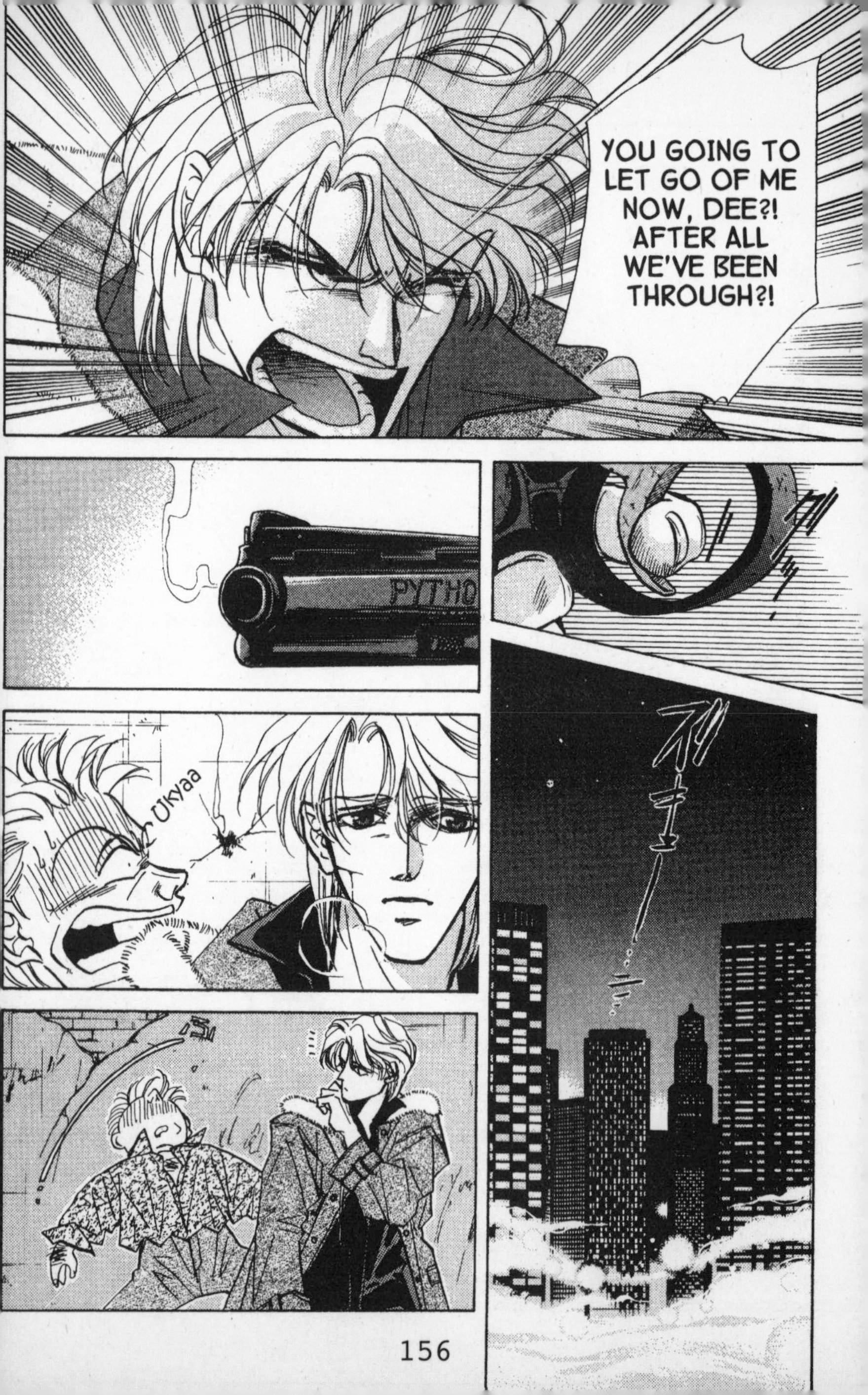
YOU GOING TO LET GO OF ME NOW, DEE?! AFTER ALL WE'VE BEEN THROUGH?!
PYTHO
Ukyaa

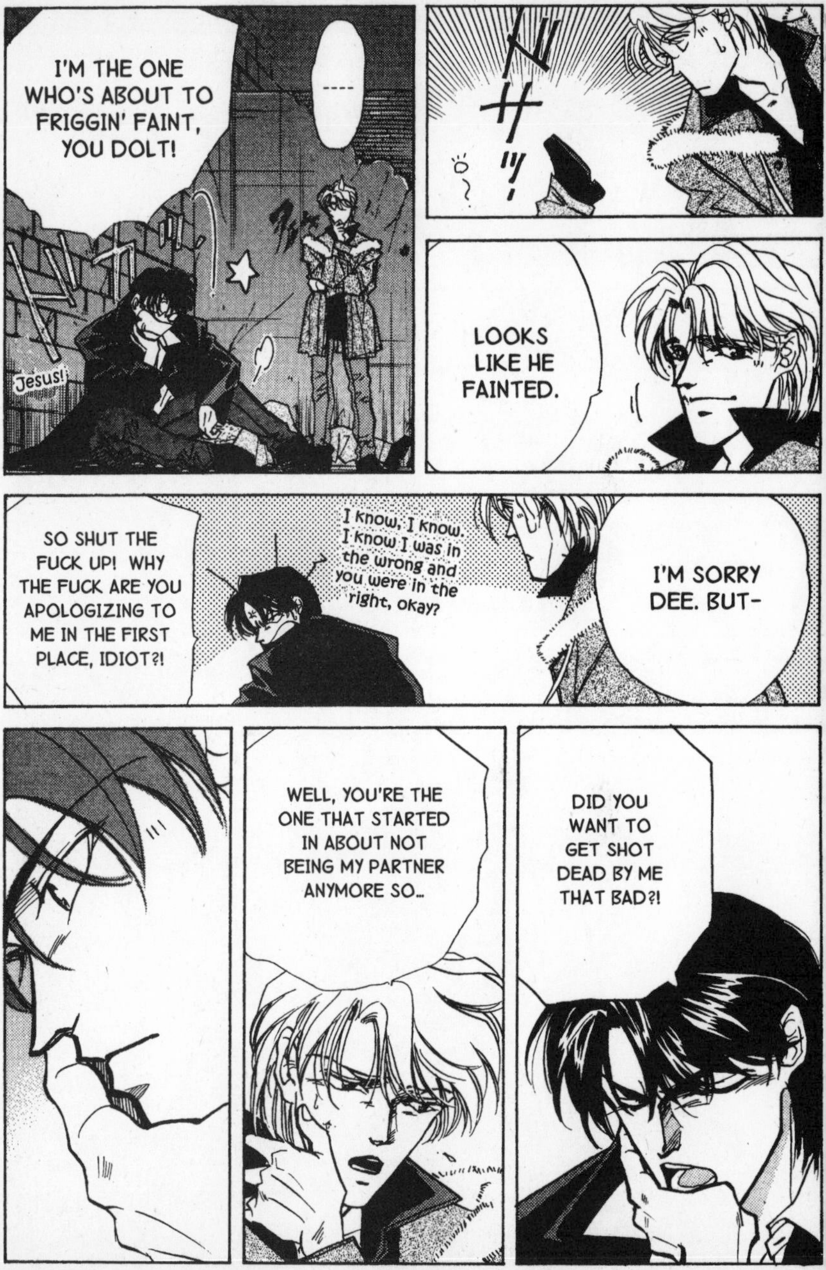
LOOKS LIKE HE FAINTED.

I'M THE ONE WHO'S ABOUT TO FRIGGIN' FAINT, YOU DOLT!
Jesus!
I'M SORRY DEE. BUT-
I know, I know. I know I was in the wrong and you were in the right, okay?
SO SHUT THE FUCK UP! WHY THE FUCK ARE YOU APOLOGIZING TO ME IN THE FIRST PLACE, IDIOT?!
DID YOU WANT TO GET SHOT DEAD BY ME THAT BAD?!
WELL, YOU'RE THE ONE THAT STARTED IN ABOUT NOT BEING MY PARTNER ANYMORE SO...

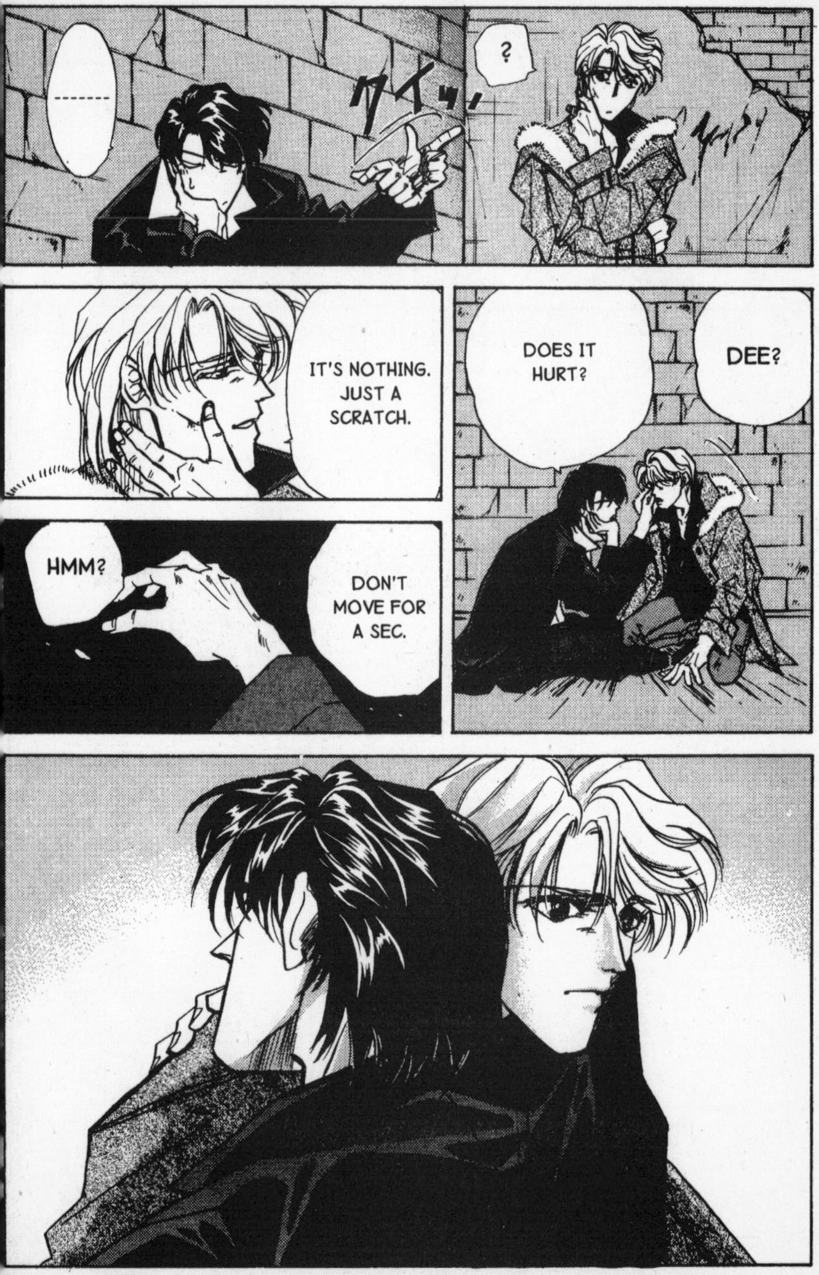
?
クイッ

DEE?
DOES IT HURT?
IT'S NOTHING. JUST A SCRATCH.
DON'T MOVE FOR A SEC.
HMM?

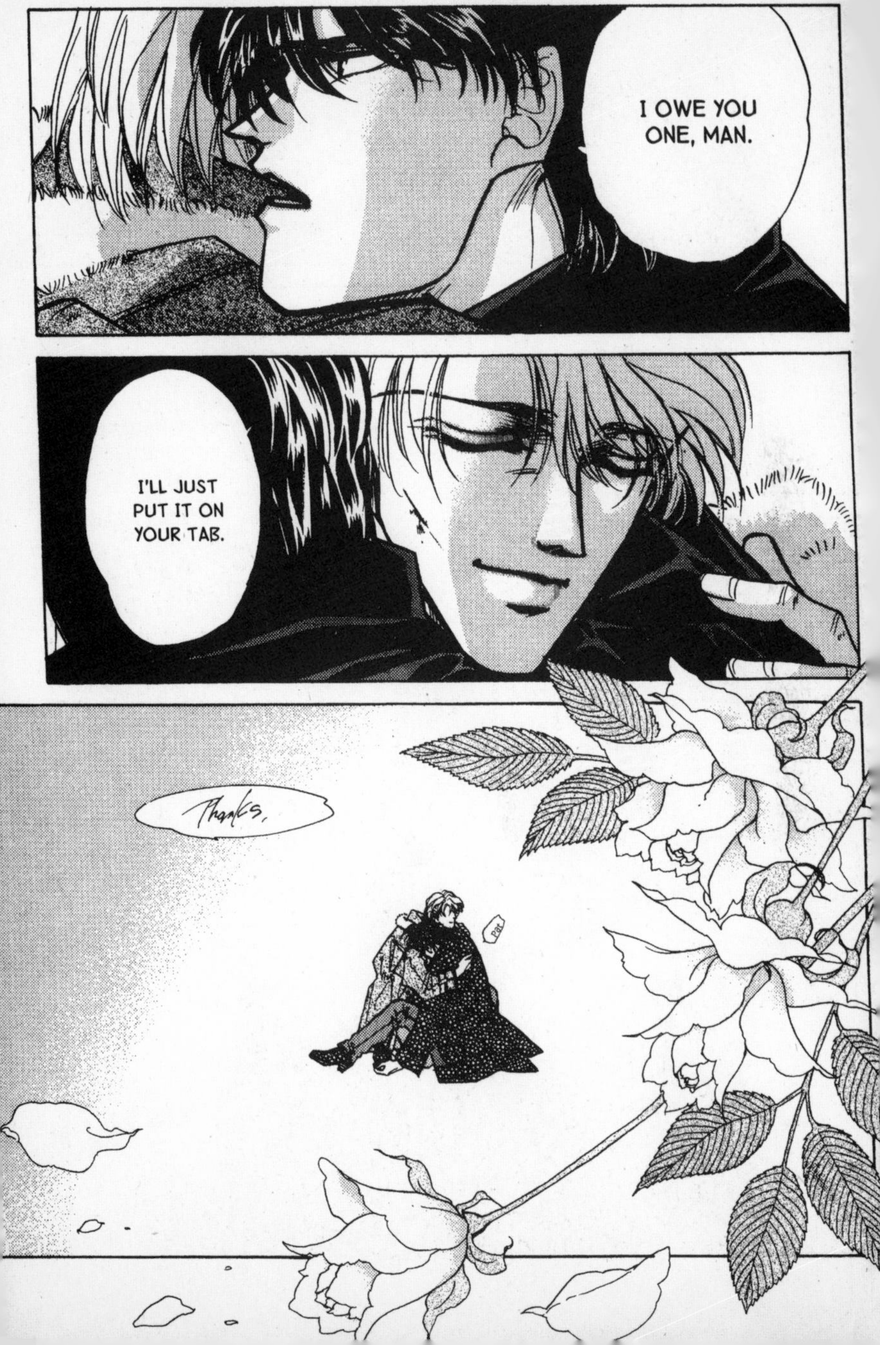
I OWE YOU ONE, MAN.
I'LL JUST PUT IT ON YOUR TAB.
Thanks,

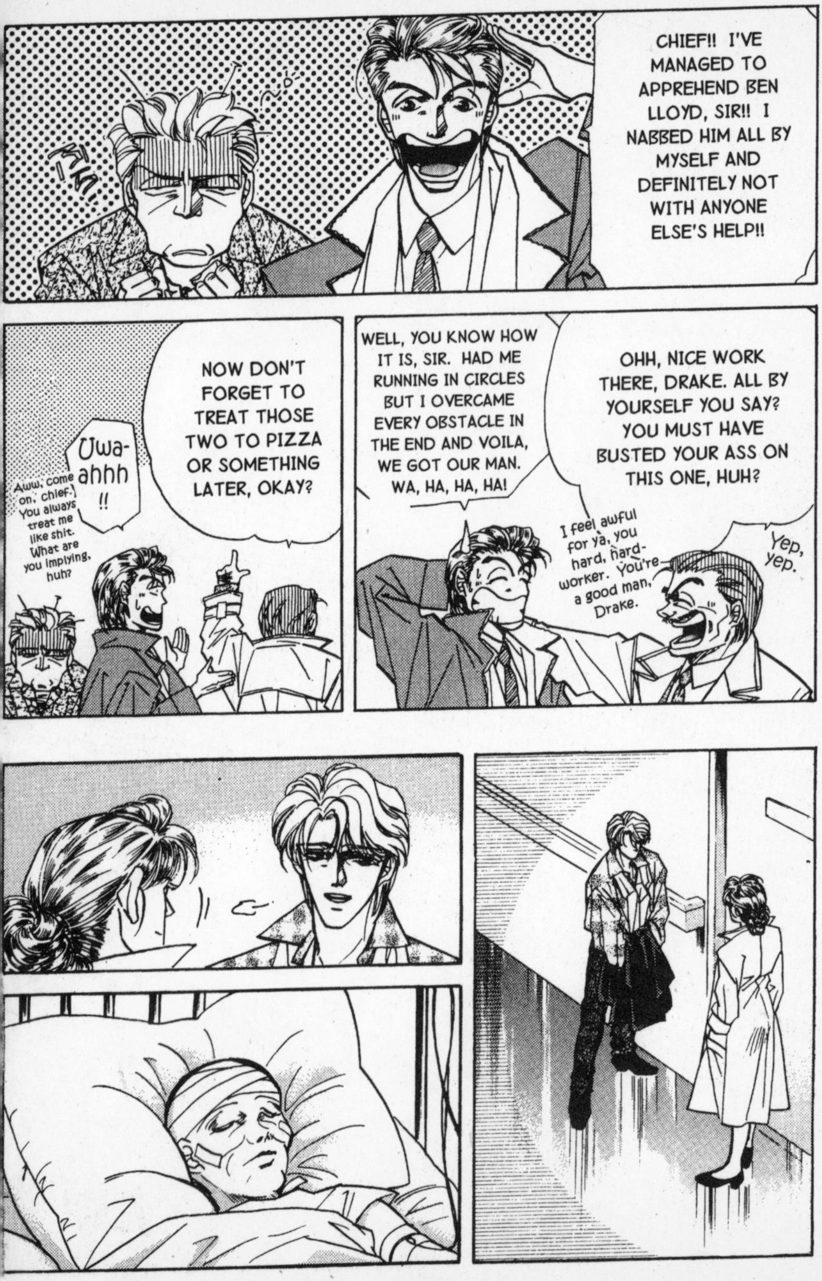

CHIEF!! I'VE MANAGED TO APPREHEND BEN LLOYD, SIR!! I NABBED HIM ALL BY MYSELF AND DEFINITELY NOT WITH ANYONE ELSE'S HELP!!
OHH, NICE WORK THERE, DRAKE. ALL BY YOURSELF YOU SAY? YOU MUST HAVE BUSTED YOUR ASS ON THIS ONE, HUH?
WELL, YOU KNOW HOW IT IS, SIR. HAD ME RUNNING IN CIRCLES BUT I OVERCAME EVERY OBSTACLE IN THE END AND VOILA, WE GOT OUR MAN. WA, HA, HA, HA!
Yep, yep.
I feel awful for ya, you hard, hard-worker. You're a good man, Drake.
NOW DON'T FORGET TO TREAT THOSE TWO TO PIZZA OR SOMETHING LATER, OKAY?
Uwa-ahhh !!
Aww, come on, chief. You always treat me like shit. What are you implying, huh?

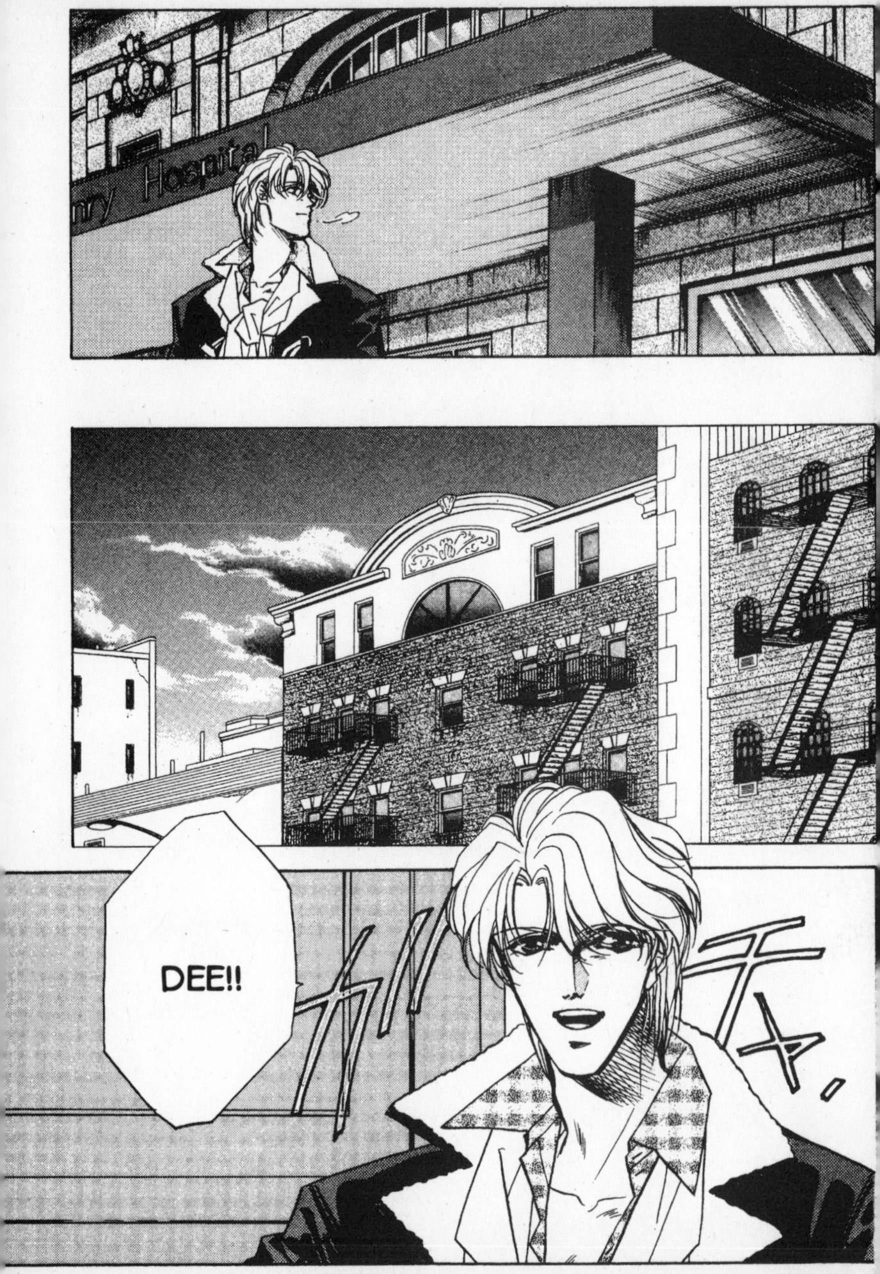
Hospital
DEE!!

Dee—who's under house arrest for firing his weapon (the chief found out)—and Ryo on their day off.

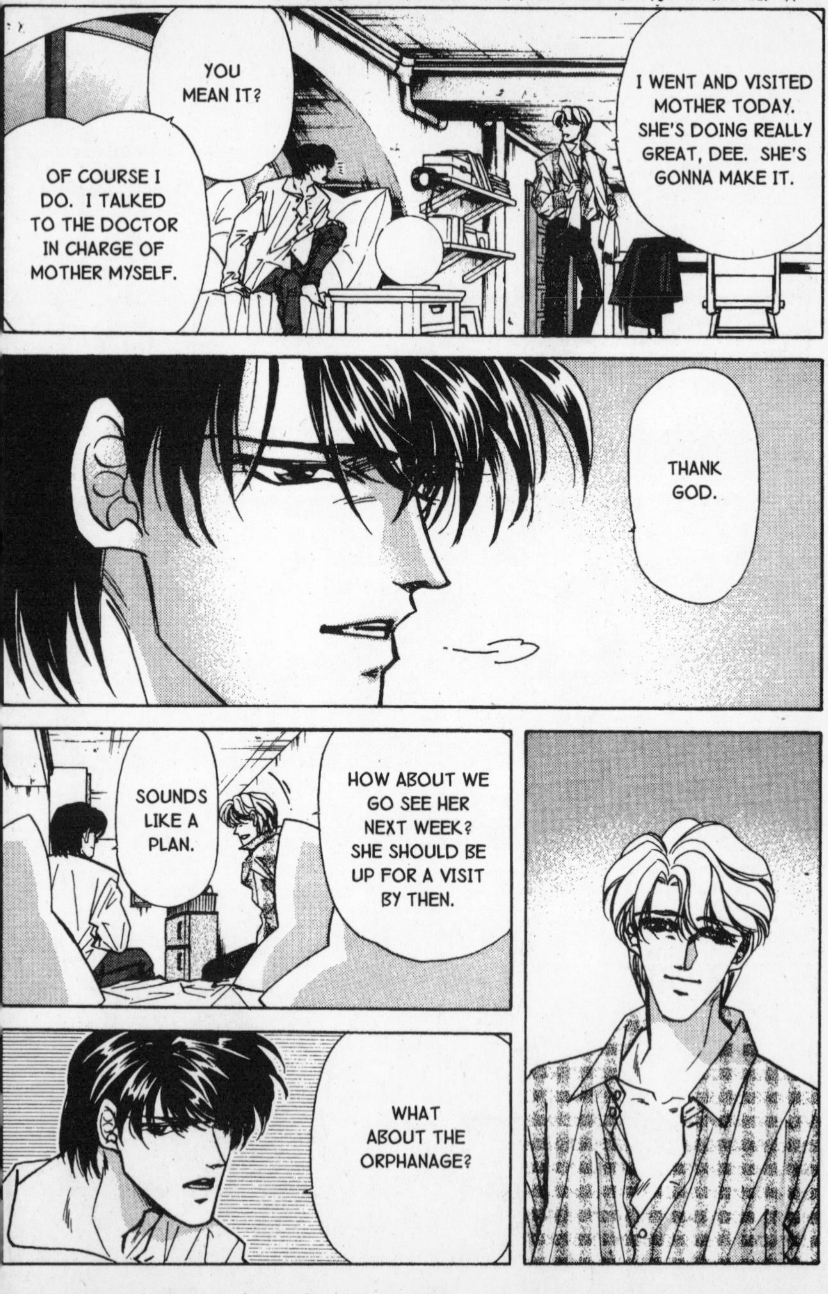
I WENT AND VISITED MOTHER TODAY. SHE'S DOING REALLY GREAT, DEE. SHE'S GONNA MAKE IT.
YOU MEAN IT?
OF COURSE I DO. I TALKED TO THE DOCTOR IN CHARGE OF MOTHER MYSELF.
THANK GOD.
HOW ABOUT WE GO SEE HER NEXT WEEK? SHE SHOULD BE UP FOR A VISIT BY THEN.
SOUNDS LIKE A PLAN.
WHAT ABOUT THE ORPHANAGE?

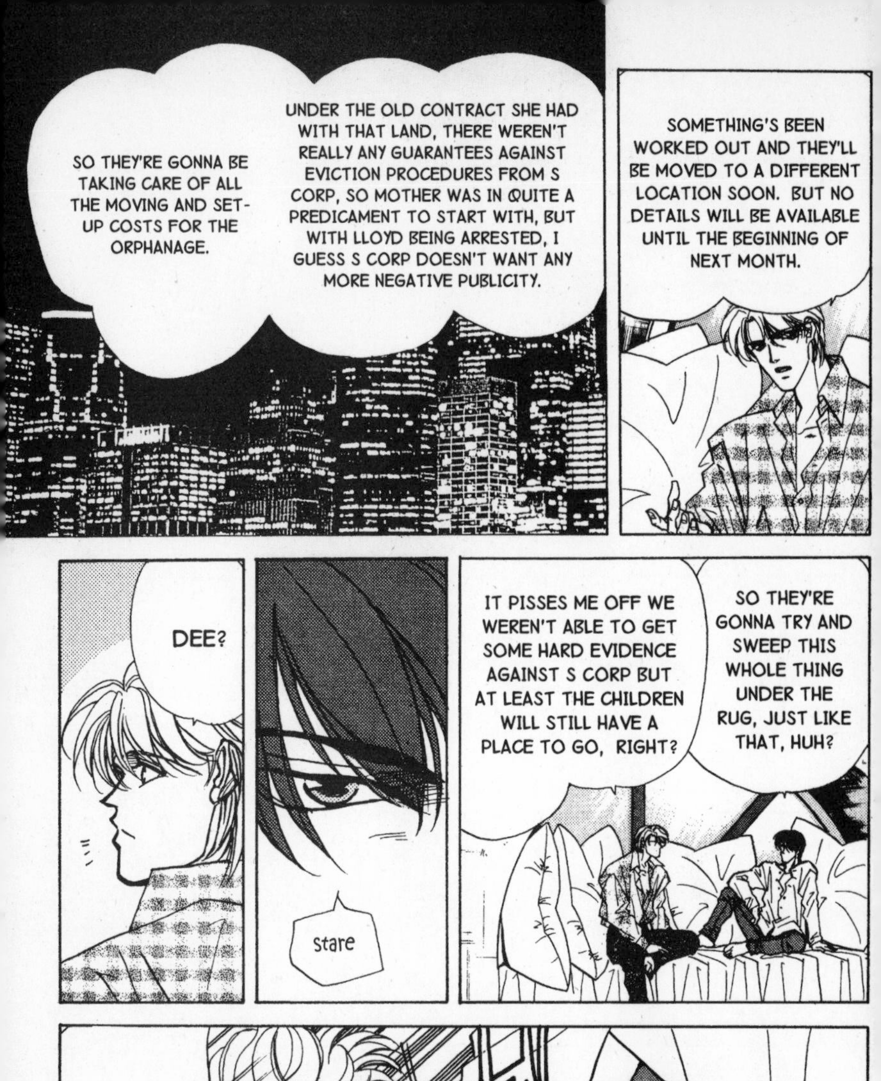
SOMETHING'S BEEN WORKED OUT AND THEY'LL BE MOVED TO A DIFFERENT LOCATION SOON. BUT NO DETAILS WILL BE AVAILABLE UNTIL THE BEGINNING OF NEXT MONTH.
UNDER THE OLD CONTRACT SHE HAD WITH THAT LAND, THERE WEREN'T REALLY ANY GUARANTEES AGAINST EVICTION PROCEDURES FROM S CORP, SO MOTHER WAS IN QUITE A PREDICAMENT TO START WITH, BUT WITH LLOYD BEING ARRESTED, I GUESS S CORP DOESN'T WANT ANY MORE NEGATIVE PUBLICITY.
SO THEY'RE GONNA BE TAKING CARE OF ALL THE MOVING AND SET-UP COSTS FOR THE ORPHANAGE.
SO THEY'RE GONNA TRY AND SWEEP THIS WHOLE THING UNDER THE RUG, JUST LIKE THAT, HUH?
IT PISSES ME OFF WE WEREN'T ABLE TO GET SOME HARD EVIDENCE AGAINST S CORP BUT AT LEAST THE CHILDREN WILL STILL HAVE A PLACE TO GO, RIGHT?
stare
DEE?
WAAHH !?

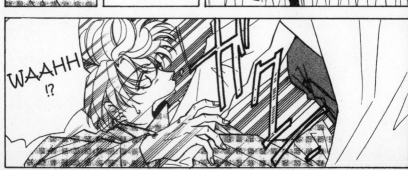

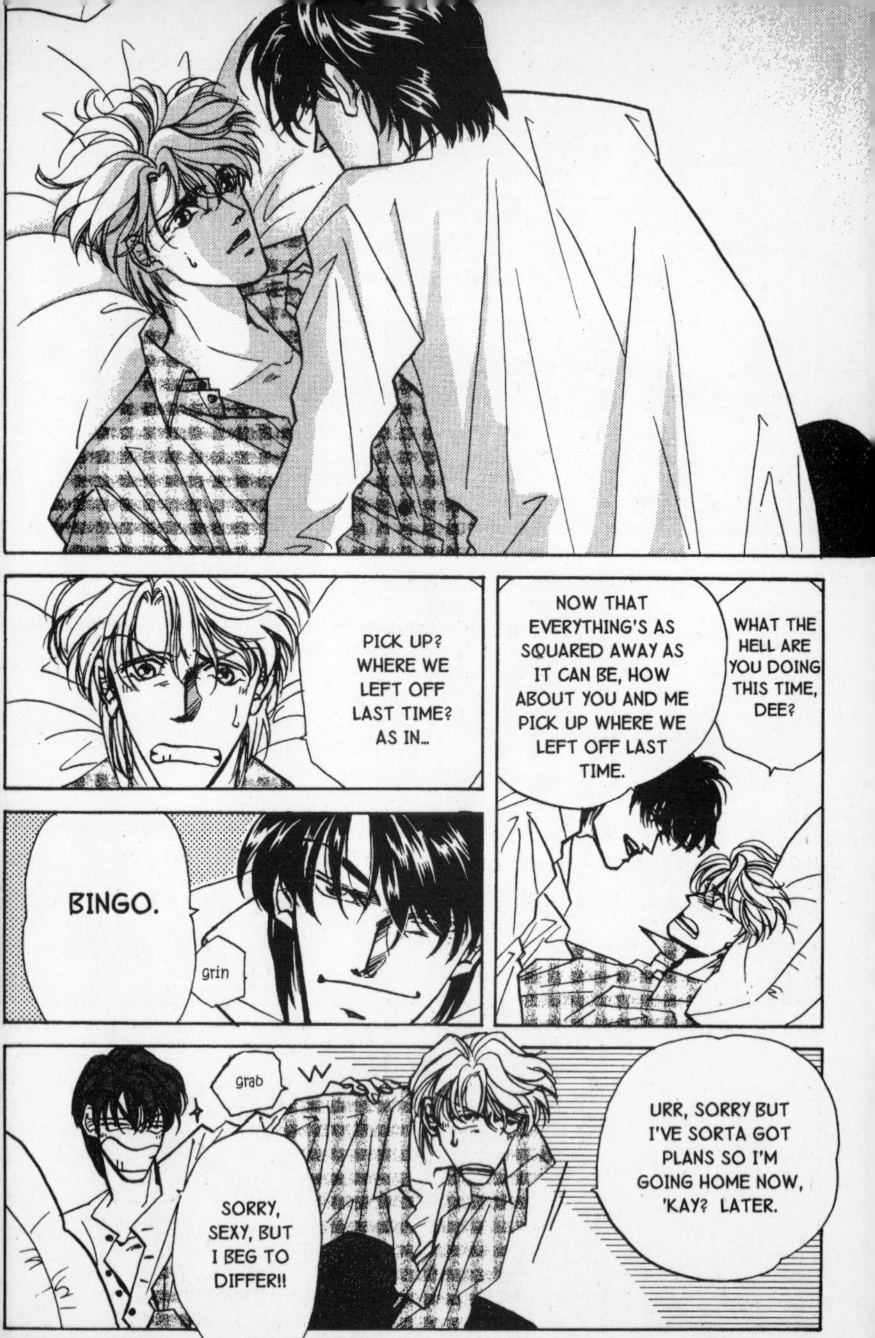
WHAT THE HELL ARE YOU DOING THIS TIME, DEE?
NOW THAT EVERYTHING'S AS SQUARED AWAY AS IT CAN BE, HOW ABOUT YOU AND ME PICK UP WHERE WE LEFT OFF LAST TIME.
PICK UP? WHERE WE LEFT OFF LAST TIME? AS IN...
BINGO.
grin
URR, SORRY BUT I'VE SORTA GOT PLANS SO I'M GOING HOME NOW, 'KAY? LATER.
grab
SORRY, SEXY, BUT I BEG TO DIFFER!!

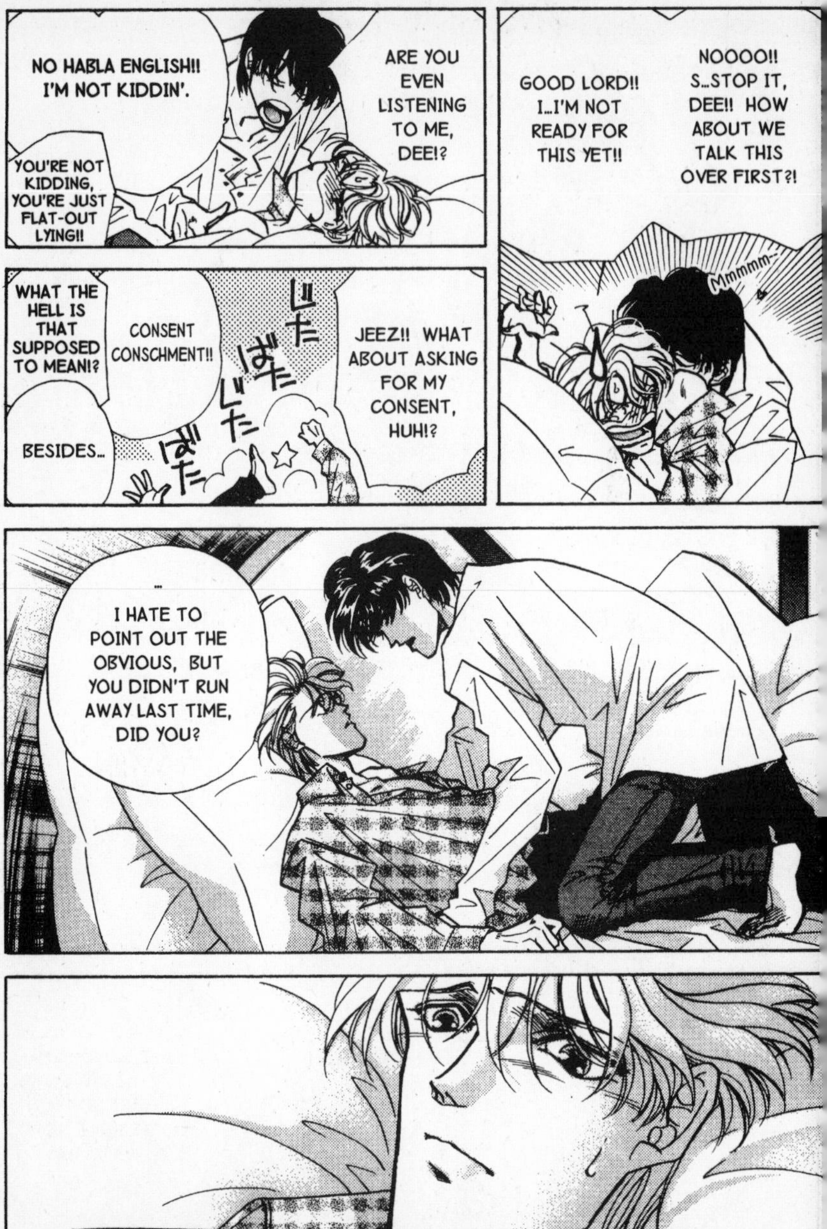
NOOOO!! S...STOP IT, DEE!! HOW ABOUT WE TALK THIS OVER FIRST?!
GOOD LORD!! I...I'M NOT READY FOR THIS YET!!
Mmmmm
ARE YOU EVEN LISTENING TO ME, DEE!?
NO HABLA ENGLISH!! I'M NOT KIDDIN'.
YOU'RE NOT KIDDING, YOU'RE JUST FLAT-OUT LYING!!
JEEZ!! WHAT ABOUT ASKING FOR MY CONSENT, HUH!?
じた ばた じた ばた
CONSENT CONSCHMENT!!
WHAT THE HELL IS THAT SUPPOSED TO MEAN!?
BESIDES...
... I HATE TO POINT OUT THE OBVIOUS, BUT YOU DIDN'T RUN AWAY LAST TIME, DID YOU?

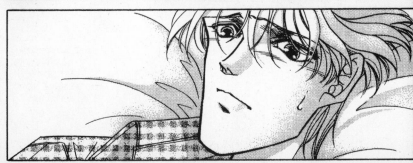

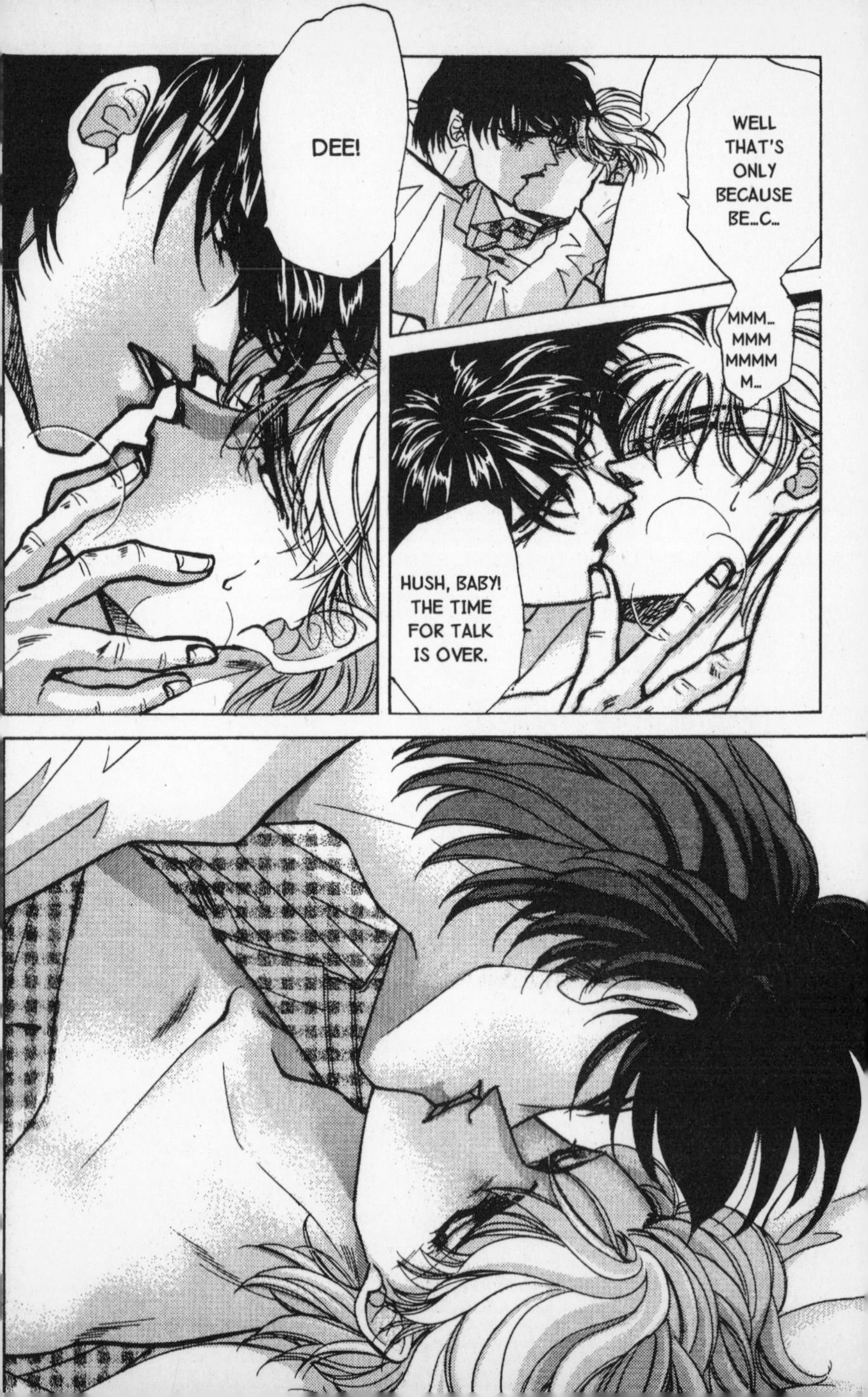
WELL THAT'S ONLY BECAUSE BE...C...
MMM... MMM MMMM M...
HUSH, BABY! THE TIME FOR TALK IS OVER.
DEE!

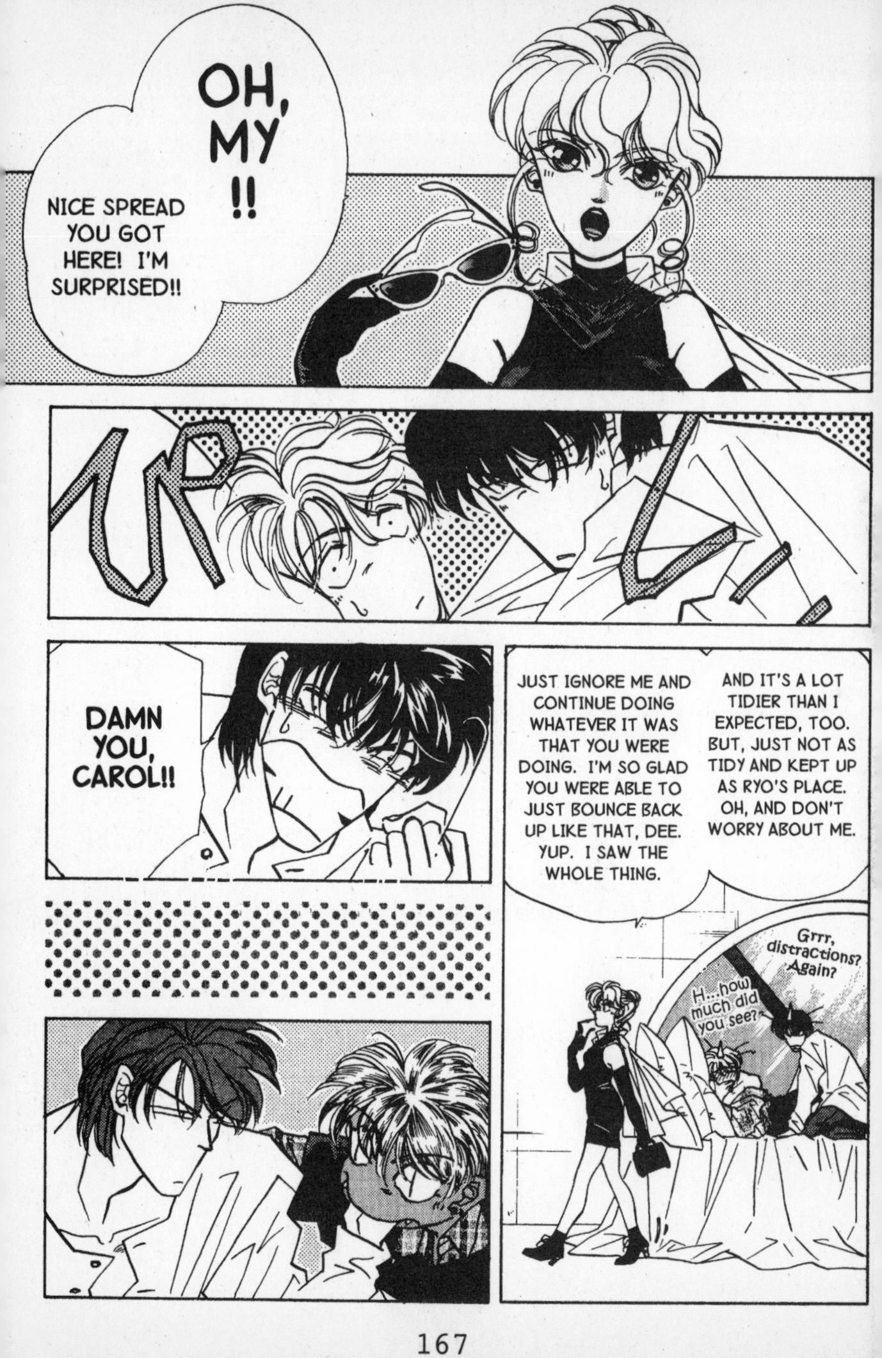
OH, MY!!
NICE SPREAD YOU GOT HERE! I'M SURPRISED!!
AND IT'S A LOT TIDIER THAN I EXPECTED, TOO. BUT, JUST NOT AS TIDY AND KEPT UP AS RYO'S PLACE. OH, AND DON'T WORRY ABOUT ME.
JUST IGNORE ME AND CONTINUE DOING WHATEVER IT WAS THAT YOU WERE DOING. I'M SO GLAD YOU WERE ABLE TO JUST BOUNCE BACK UP LIKE THAT, DEE. YUP. I SAW THE WHOLE THING.
Grrr, distractions? Again?
H...how much did you see?
DAMN YOU, CAROL!!

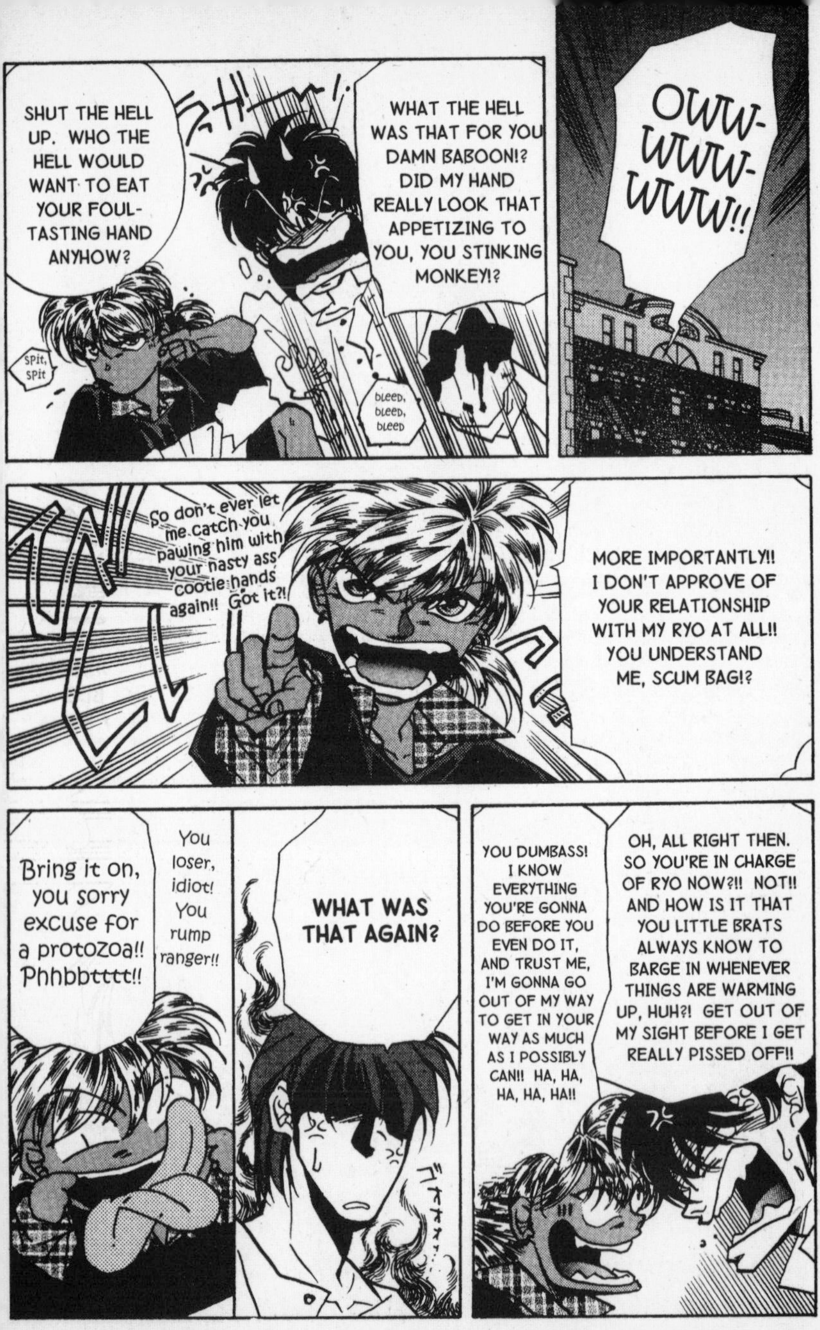
OWW-WWW-WWW!!
WHAT THE HELL WAS THAT FOR YOU DAMN BABOON!? DID MY HAND REALLY LOOK THAT APPETIZING TO YOU, YOU STINKING MONKEY!?
bleed, bleed, bleed
SHUT THE HELL UP. WHO THE HELL WOULD WANT TO EAT YOUR FOUL-TASTING HAND ANYHOW?
Spit, spit
MORE IMPORTANTLY!! I DON'T APPROVE OF YOUR RELATIONSHIP WITH MY RYO AT ALL!! YOU UNDERSTAND ME, SCUM BAG!?
So don't ever let me catch you pawing him with your nasty ass cootie hands again!! Got it?!
OH, ALL RIGHT THEN. SO YOU'RE IN CHARGE OF RYO NOW?!! NOT!! AND HOW IS IT THAT YOU LITTLE BRATS ALWAYS KNOW TO BARGE IN WHENEVER THINGS ARE WARMING UP, HUH?! GET OUT OF MY SIGHT BEFORE I GET REALLY PISSED OFF!!
YOU DUMBASS! I KNOW EVERYTHING YOU'RE GONNA DO BEFORE YOU EVEN DO IT, AND TRUST ME, I'M GONNA GO OUT OF MY WAY TO GET IN YOUR WAY AS MUCH AS I POSSIBLY CAN!! HA, HA, HA, HA, HA!!
WHAT WAS THAT AGAIN?
You loser, idiot! You rump ranger!!
Bring it on, you sorry excuse for a protozoa!! Phhbbtttt!!

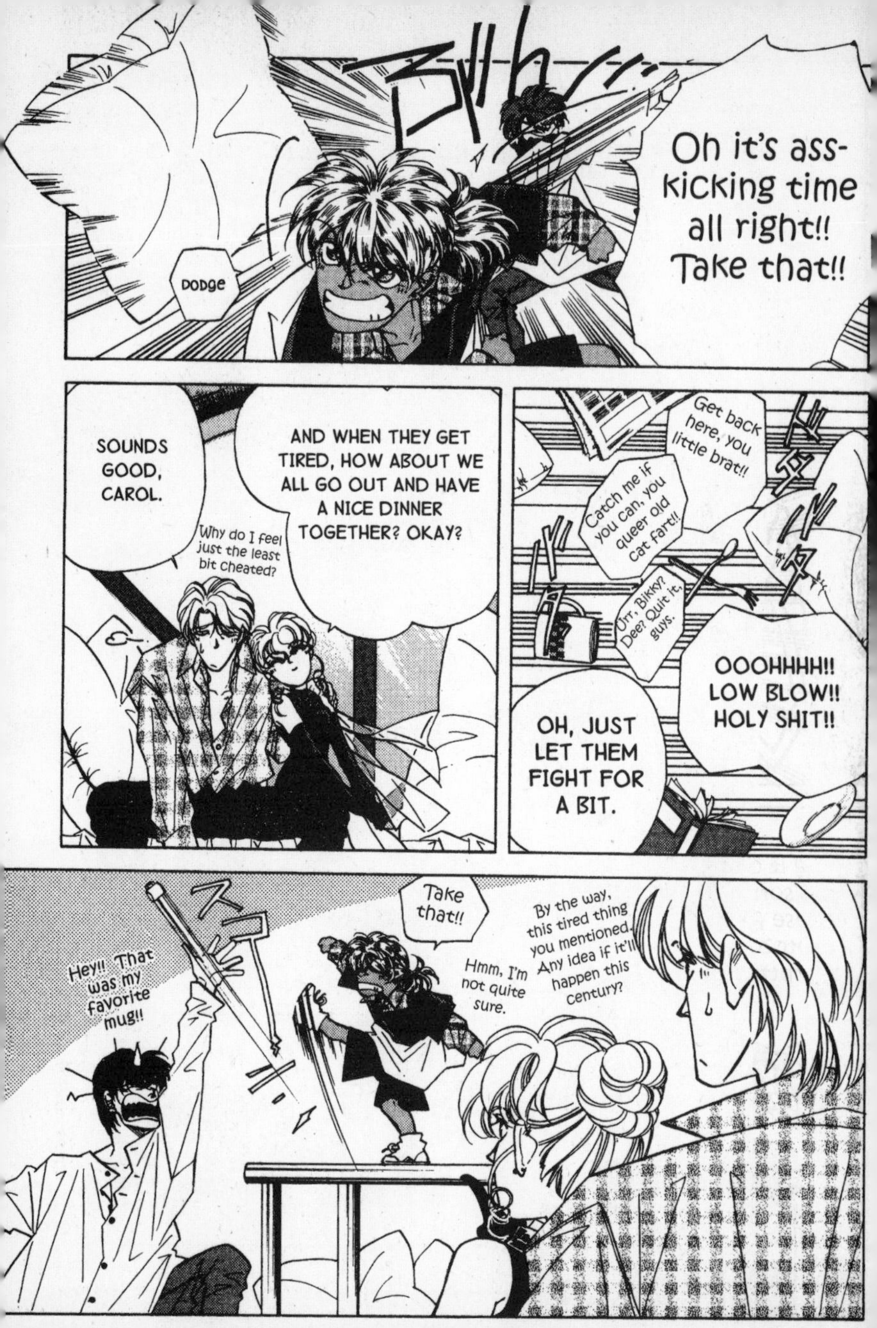
Oh it's ass-kicking time all right!! Take that!!
DODGE
Get back here, you little brat!!
Catch me if you can, you queer old cat fart!!
Urr, Bikky? Dee? Quit it, guys.
OOOHHHH!! LOW BLOW!! HOLY SHIT!!
OH, JUST LET THEM FIGHT FOR A BIT.
AND WHEN THEY GET TIRED, HOW ABOUT WE ALL GO OUT AND HAVE A NICE DINNER TOGETHER? OKAY?
SOUNDS GOOD, CAROL.
Why do I feel just the least bit cheated?
By the way, this tired thing you mentioned. Any idea if it'll happen this century?
Hmm, I'm not quite sure.
Take that!!
Hey!! That was my favorite mug!!

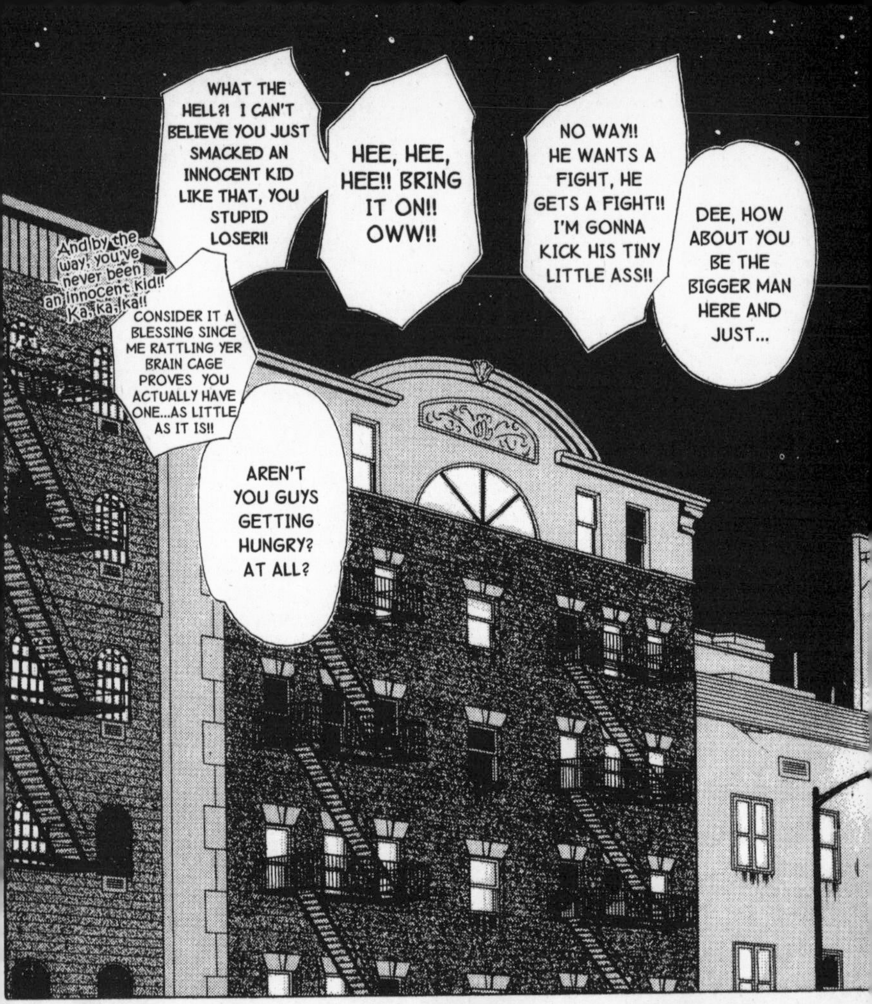
DEE, HOW ABOUT YOU BE THE BIGGER MAN HERE AND JUST...
NO WAY!! HE WANTS A FIGHT, HE GETS A FIGHT!! I'M GONNA KICK HIS TINY LITTLE ASS!!
HEE, HEE, HEE!! BRING IT ON!! OWW!!
WHAT THE HELL?! I CAN'T BELIEVE YOU JUST SMACKED AN INNOCENT KID LIKE THAT, YOU STUPID LOSER!!
And by the way, you've never been an innocent kid!! Ka, ka, ka!!
CONSIDER IT A BLESSING SINCE ME RATTLING YER BRAIN CAGE PROVES YOU ACTUALLY HAVE ONE...AS LITTLE AS IT IS!!
AREN'T YOU GUYS GETTING HUNGRY? AT ALL?

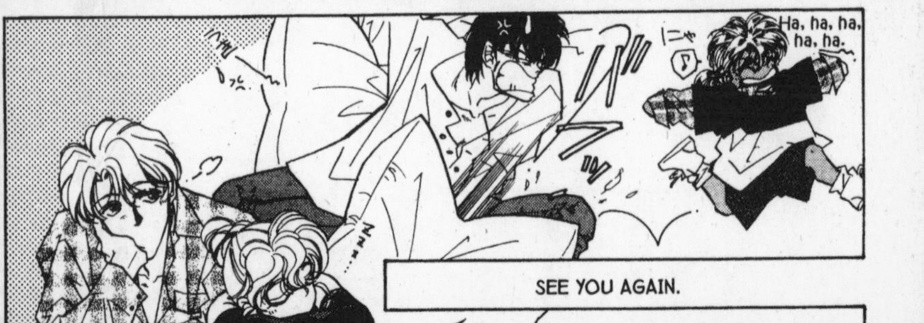
Ha, ha, ha, ha, ha.
SEE YOU AGAIN.

FAKE act.6/End.

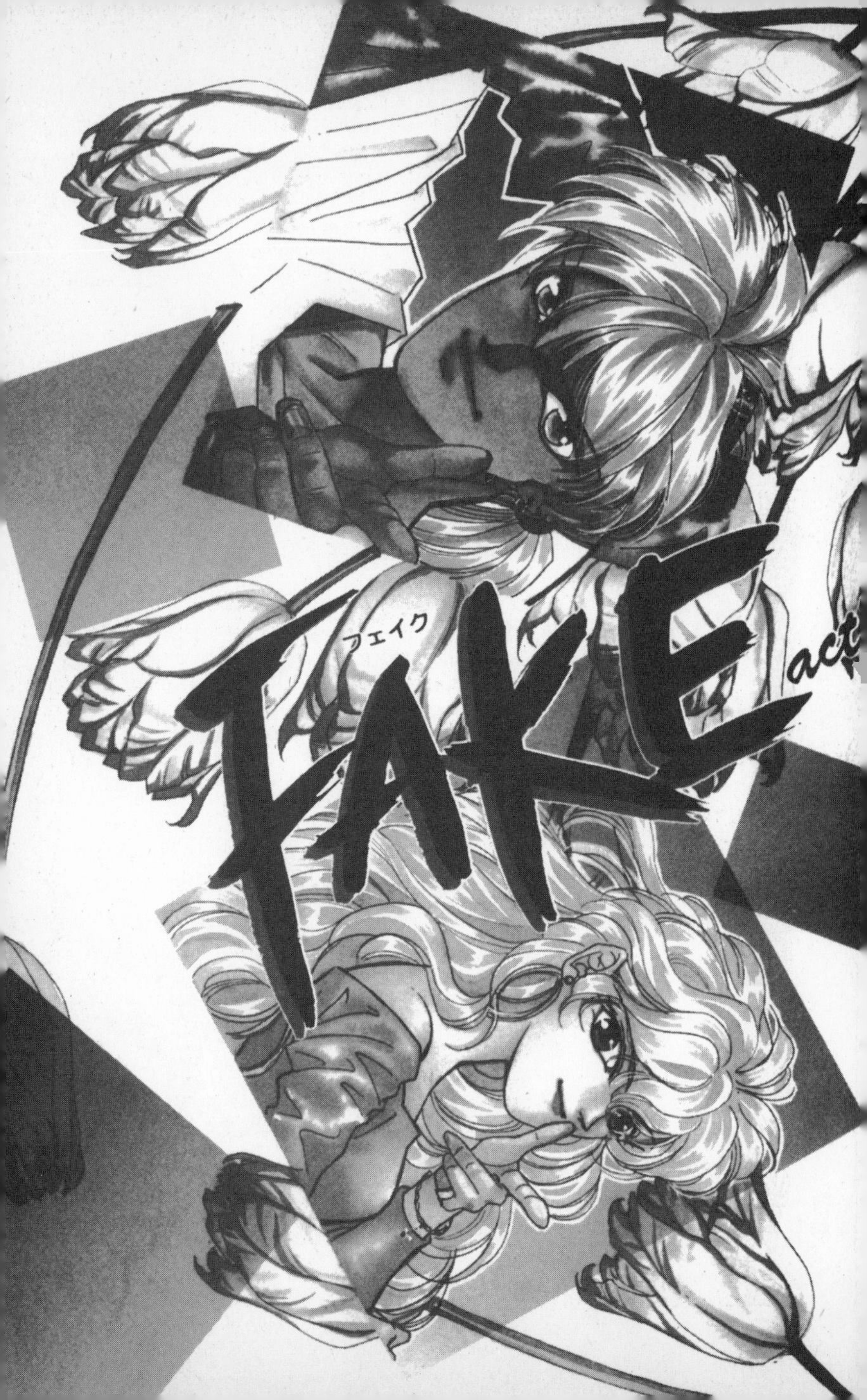
FAKE
フェイク
act

FAKE

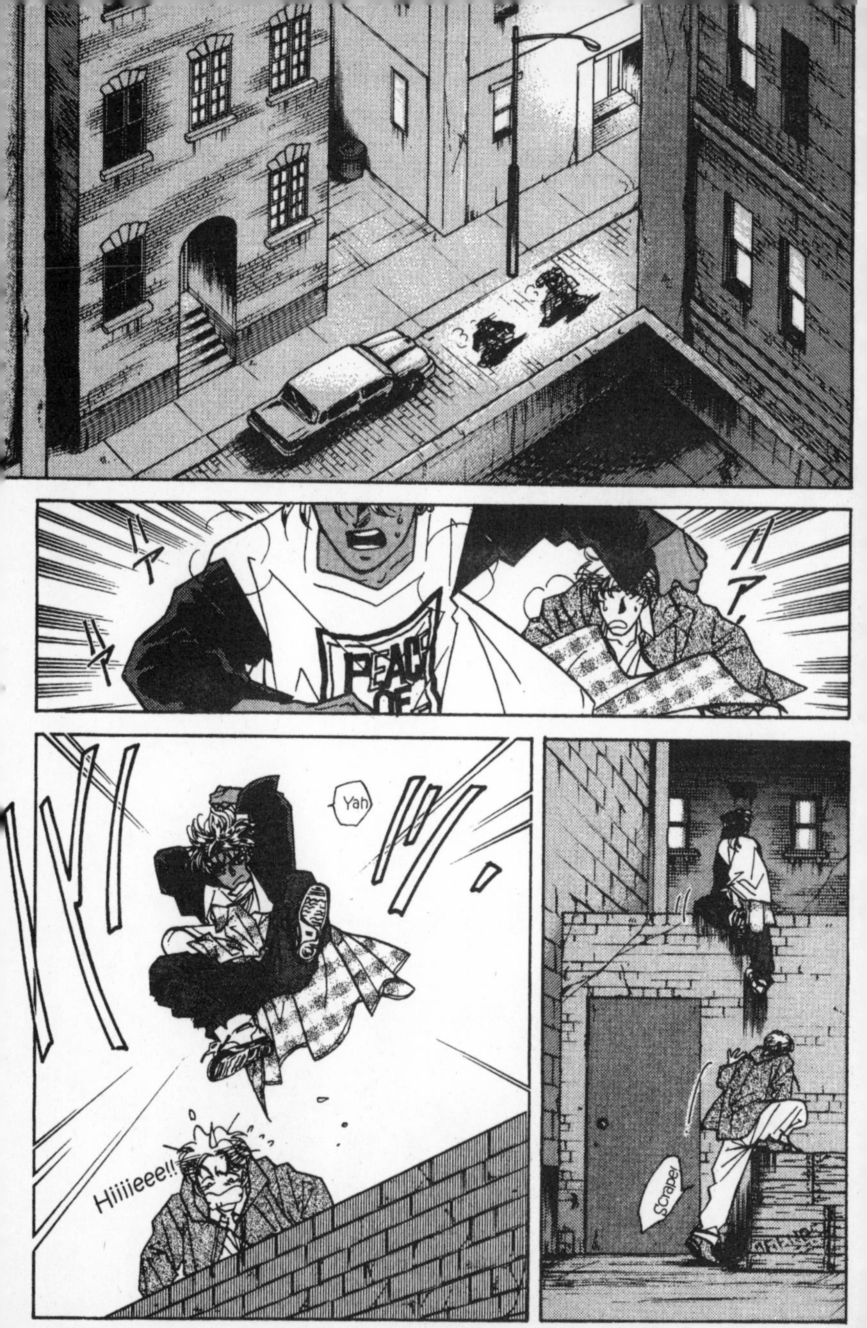
ハア
ハア
ハア
Scrape!
Yah
Hiiiieee!!

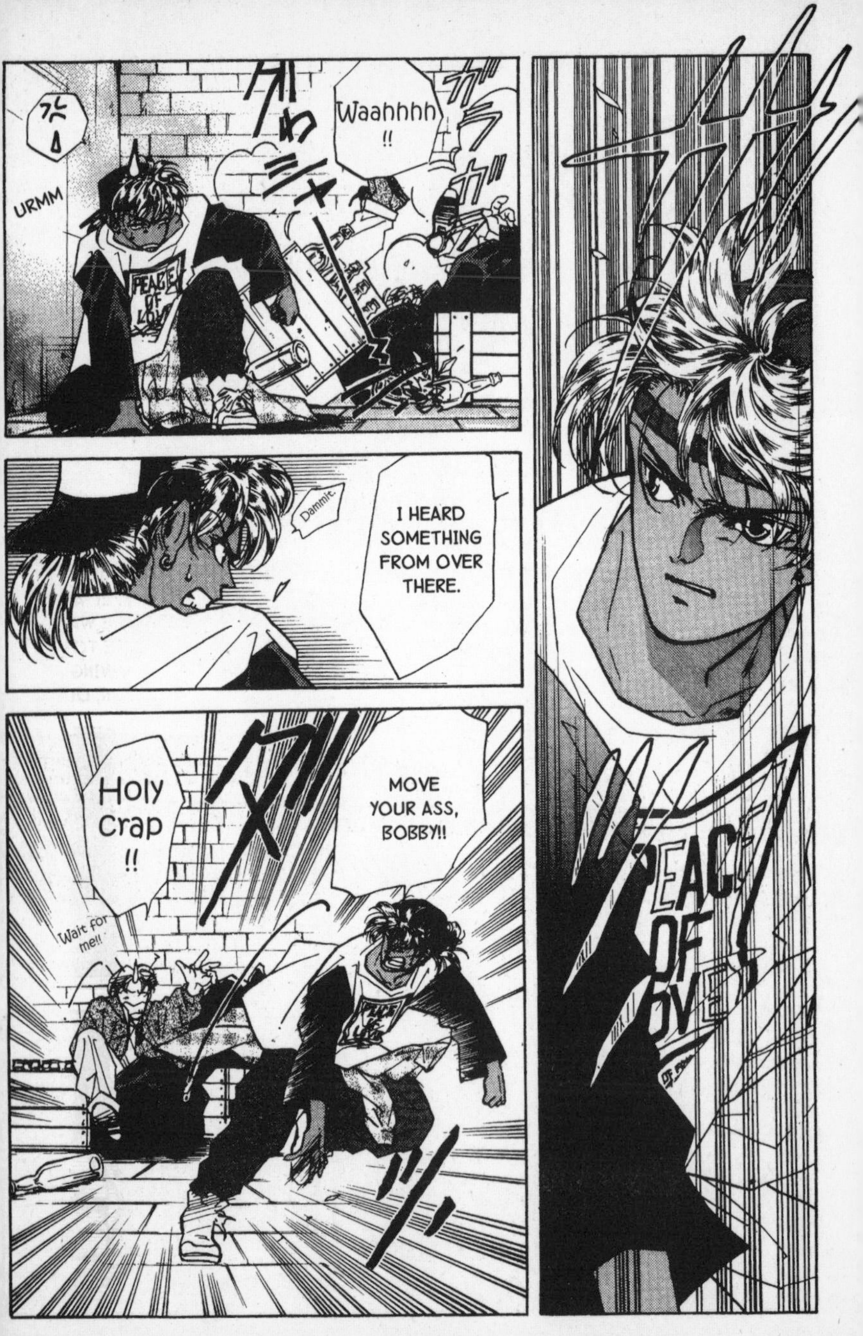
Waahhhh!!
URMM
Dammit.
I HEARD SOMETHING FROM OVER THERE.
MOVE YOUR ASS, BOBBY!!
Holy Crap!!
Wait for me!!

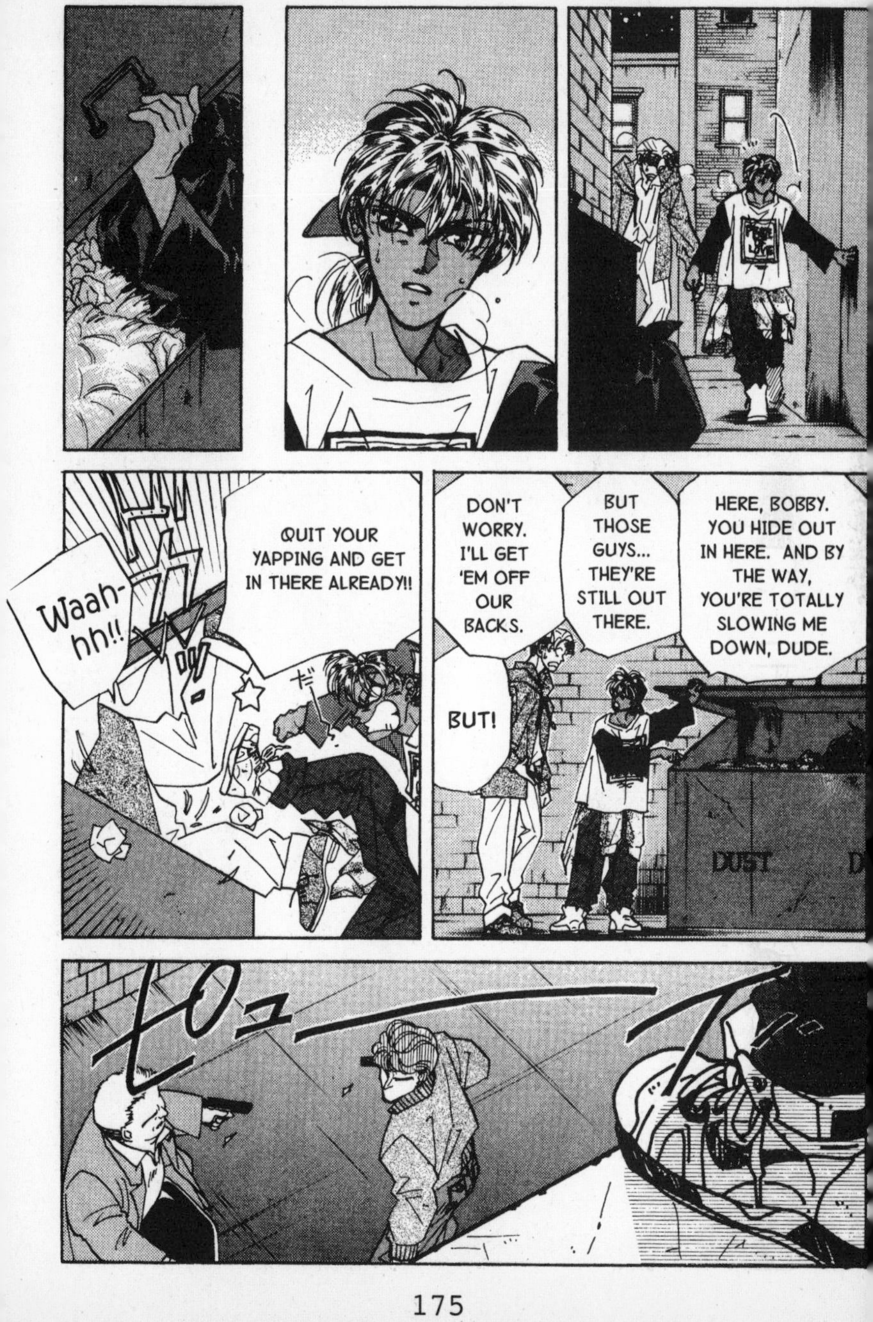
HERE, BOBBY. YOU HIDE OUT IN HERE. AND BY THE WAY, YOU'RE TOTALLY SLOWING ME DOWN, DUDE.
BUT THOSE GUYS... THEY'RE STILL OUT THERE.
DON'T WORRY. I'LL GET 'EM OFF OUR BACKS.
BUT!
DUST
QUIT YOUR YAPPING AND GET IN THERE ALREADY!!
Waah-hh!!

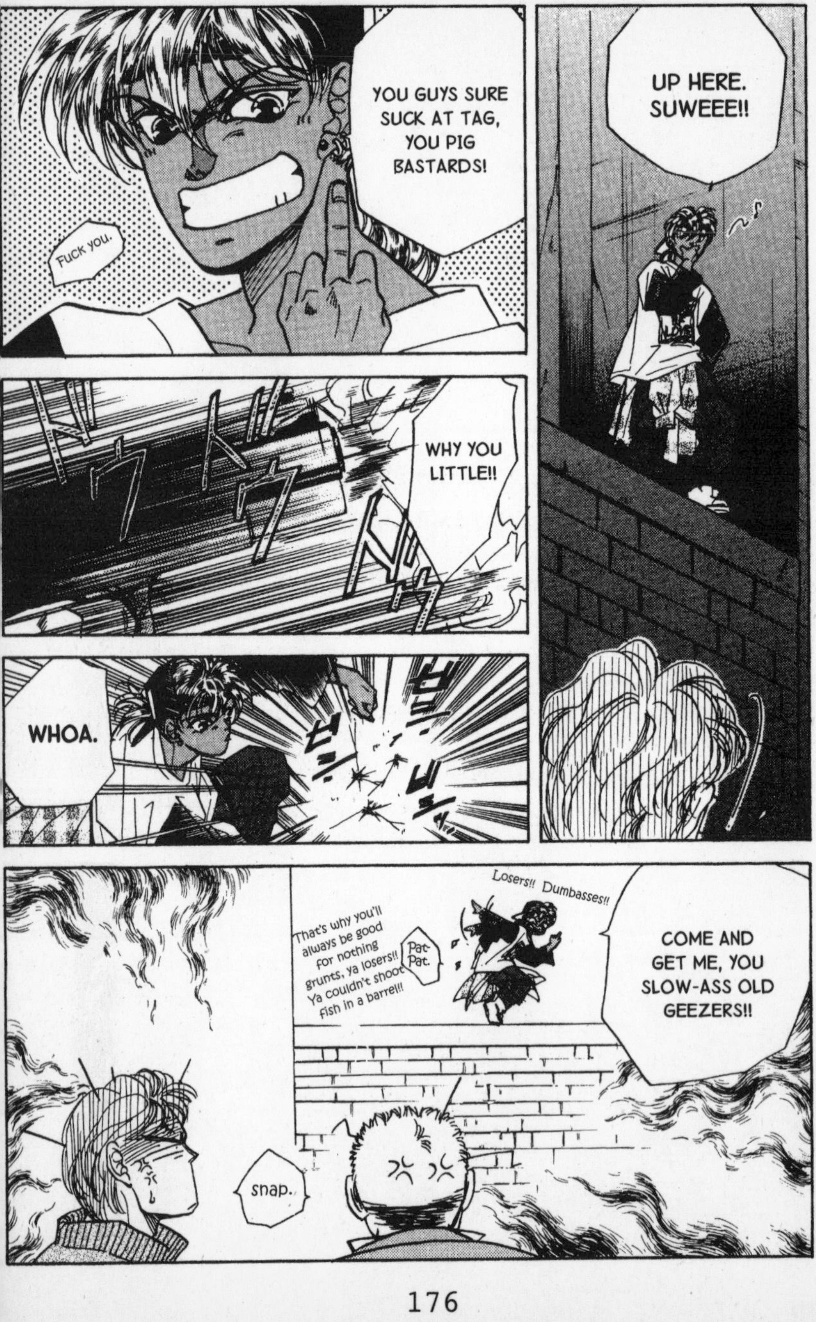
YOU GUYS SURE SUCK AT TAG, YOU PIG BASTARDS!
Fuck you.
UP HERE. SUWEEE!!
WHY YOU LITTLE!!
WHOA.
That's why you'll always be good for nothing grunts, ya losers!! Ya couldn't shoot fish in a barrel!!
Pat-Pat.
Losers!! Dumbasses!!
COME AND GET ME, YOU SLOW-ASS OLD GEEZERS!!
snap.

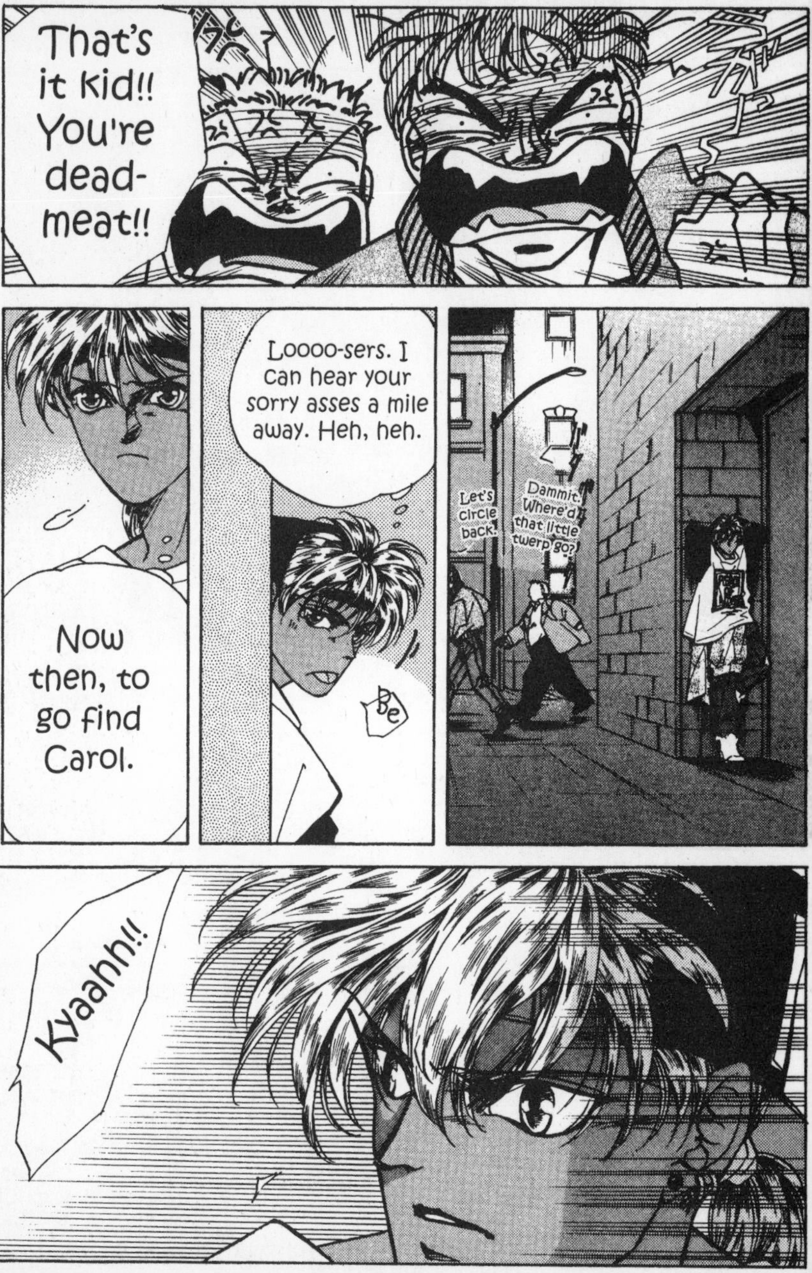
That's it kid!! You're dead-meat!!
Dammit. Where'd that little twerp go?
Let's circle back.
Loooo-sers. I can hear your sorry asses a mile away. Heh, heh.
Be
Now then, to go find Carol.
Kyaahh!!

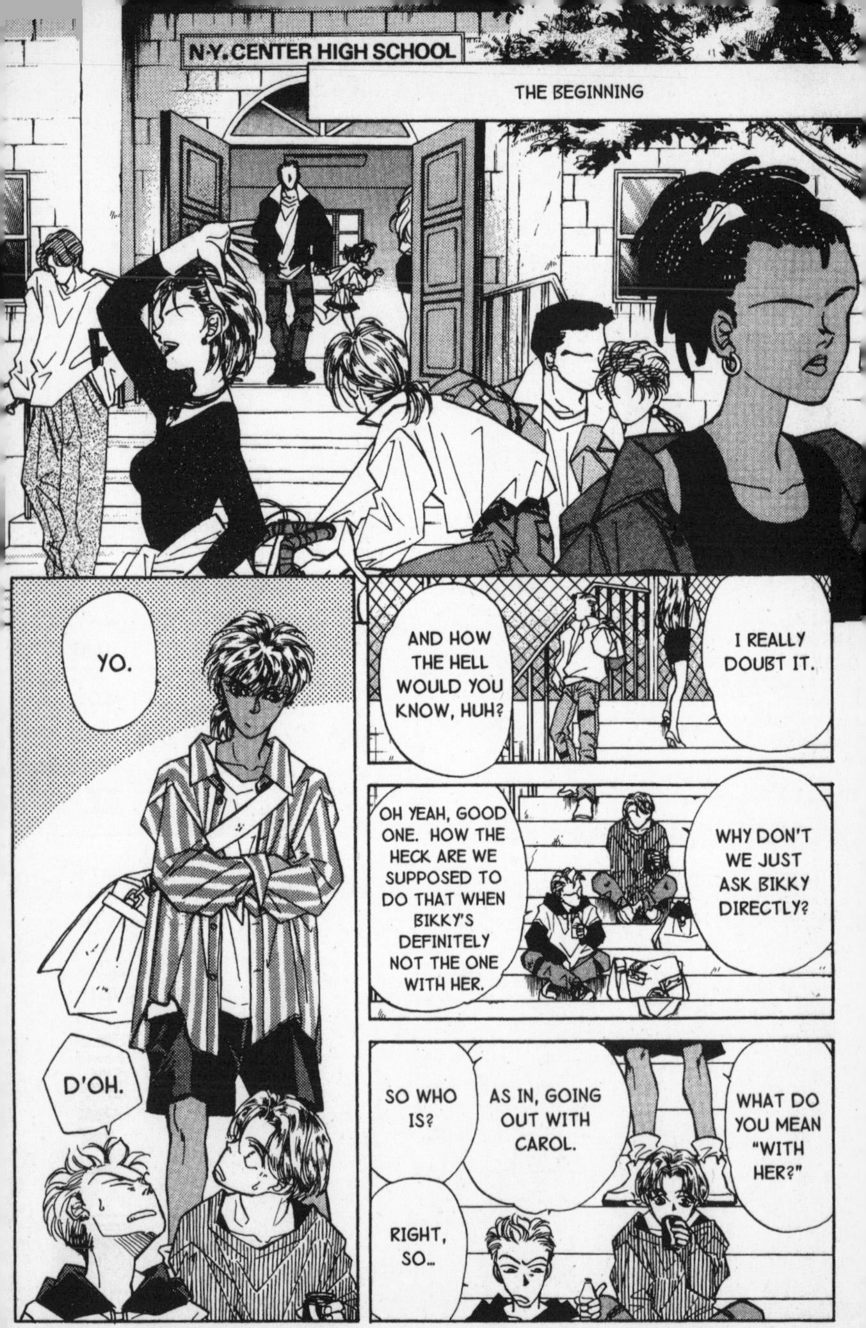
N·Y. CENTER HIGH SCHOOL
THE BEGINNING
I REALLY DOUBT IT.
AND HOW THE HELL WOULD YOU KNOW, HUH?
WHY DON'T WE JUST ASK BIKKY DIRECTLY?
OH YEAH, GOOD ONE. HOW THE HECK ARE WE SUPPOSED TO DO THAT WHEN BIKKY'S DEFINITELY NOT THE ONE WITH HER.
WHAT DO YOU MEAN "WITH HER?"
AS IN, GOING OUT WITH CAROL.
SO WHO IS?
RIGHT, SO...
YO.
D'OH.

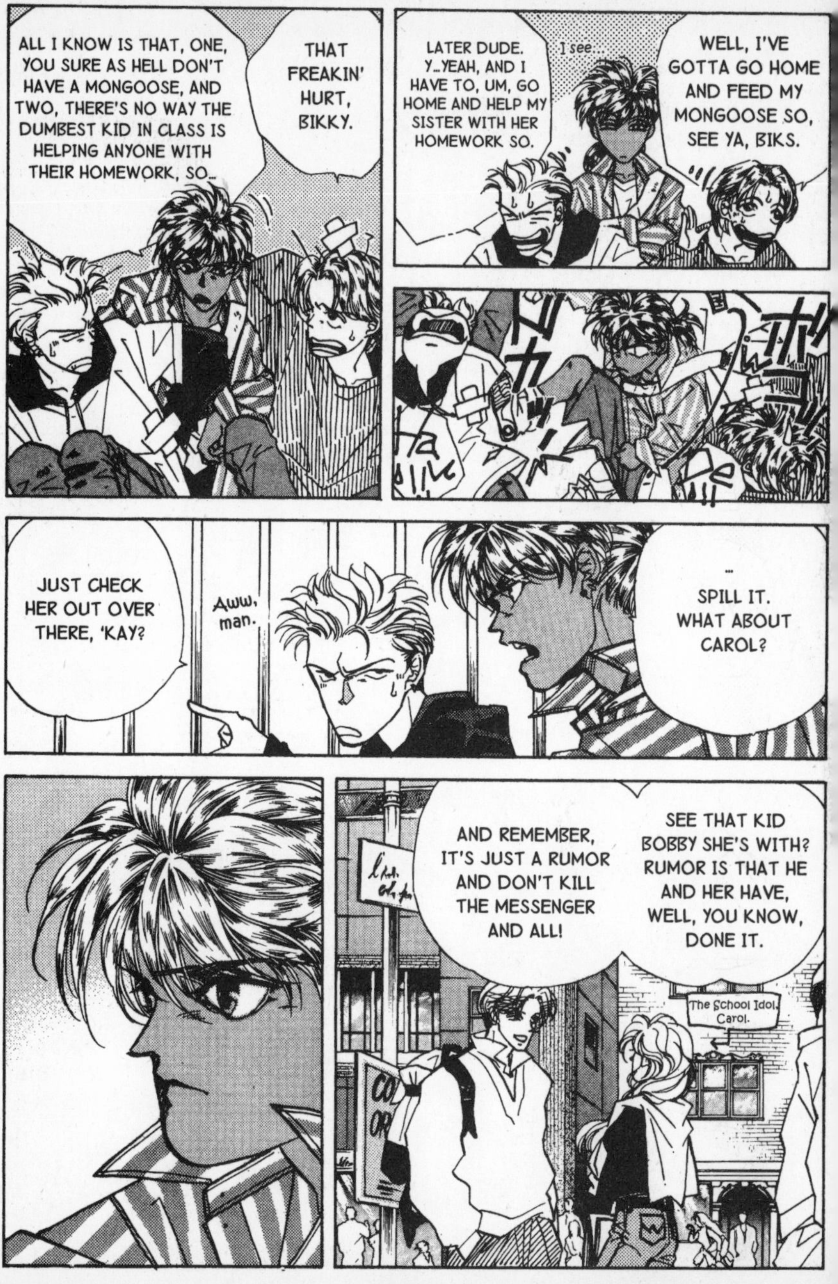
WELL, I'VE GOTTA GO HOME AND FEED MY MONGOOSE SO, SEE YA, BIKS.
I see...
LATER DUDE. Y...YEAH, AND I HAVE TO, UM, GO HOME AND HELP MY SISTER WITH HER HOMEWORK SO.
THAT FREAKIN' HURT, BIKKY.
ALL I KNOW IS THAT, ONE, YOU SURE AS HELL DON'T HAVE A MONGOOSE, AND TWO, THERE'S NO WAY THE DUMBEST KID IN CLASS IS HELPING ANYONE WITH THEIR HOMEWORK, SO...
... SPILL IT. WHAT ABOUT CAROL?
Aww, man.
JUST CHECK HER OUT OVER THERE, 'KAY?
SEE THAT KID BOBBY SHE'S WITH? RUMOR IS THAT HE AND HER HAVE, WELL, YOU KNOW, DONE IT.
AND REMEMBER, IT'S JUST A RUMOR AND DON'T KILL THE MESSENGER AND ALL!
The School Idol, Carol.

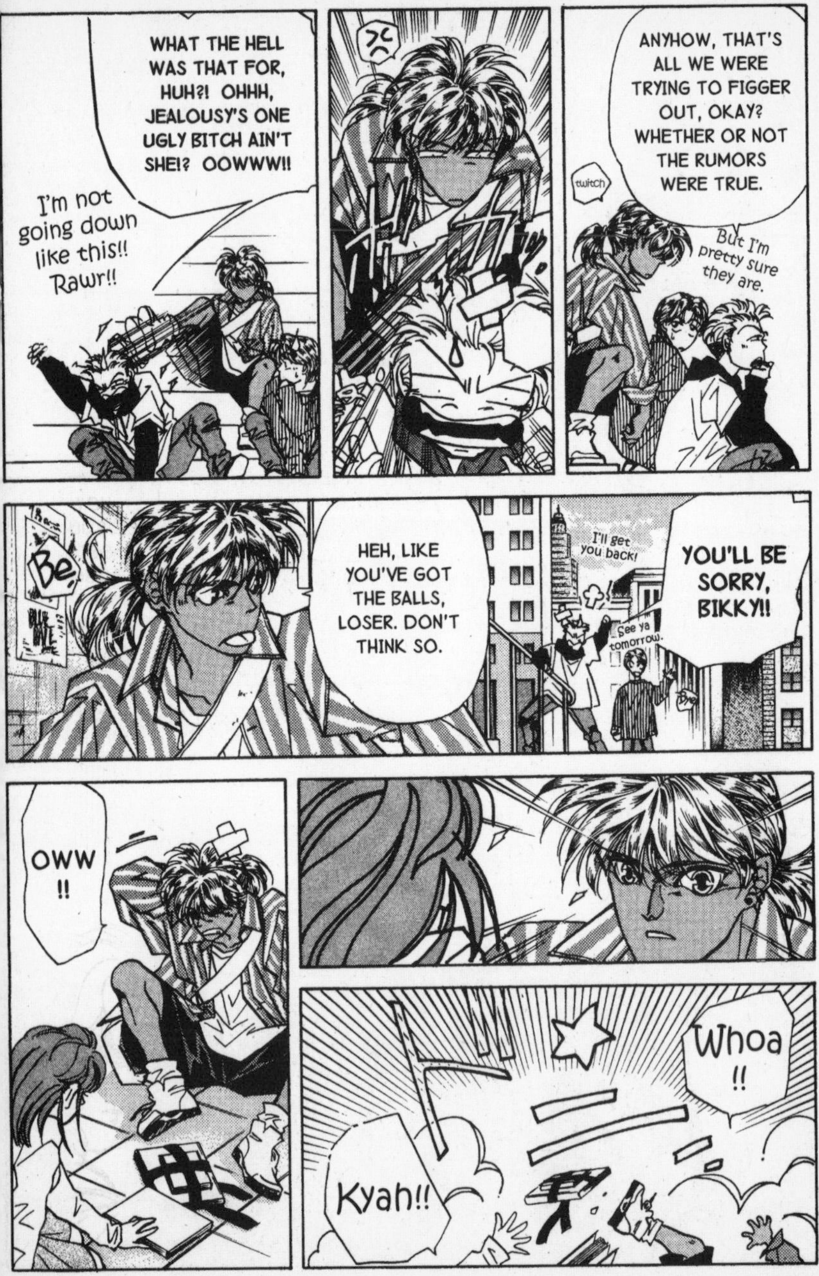
ANYHOW, THAT'S ALL WE WERE TRYING TO FIGGER OUT, OKAY? WHETHER OR NOT THE RUMORS WERE TRUE.
twitch
But I'm pretty sure they are.
WHAT THE HELL WAS THAT FOR, HUH?! OHHH, JEALOUSY'S ONE UGLY BITCH AIN'T SHE!? OOWWW!!
I'm not going down like this!! Rawr!!
YOU'LL BE SORRY, BIKKY!!
I'll get you back!
See ya tomorrow.
Bye
HEH, LIKE YOU'VE GOT THE BALLS, LOSER. DON'T THINK SO.
Whoa !!
Kyah!!
OWW !!

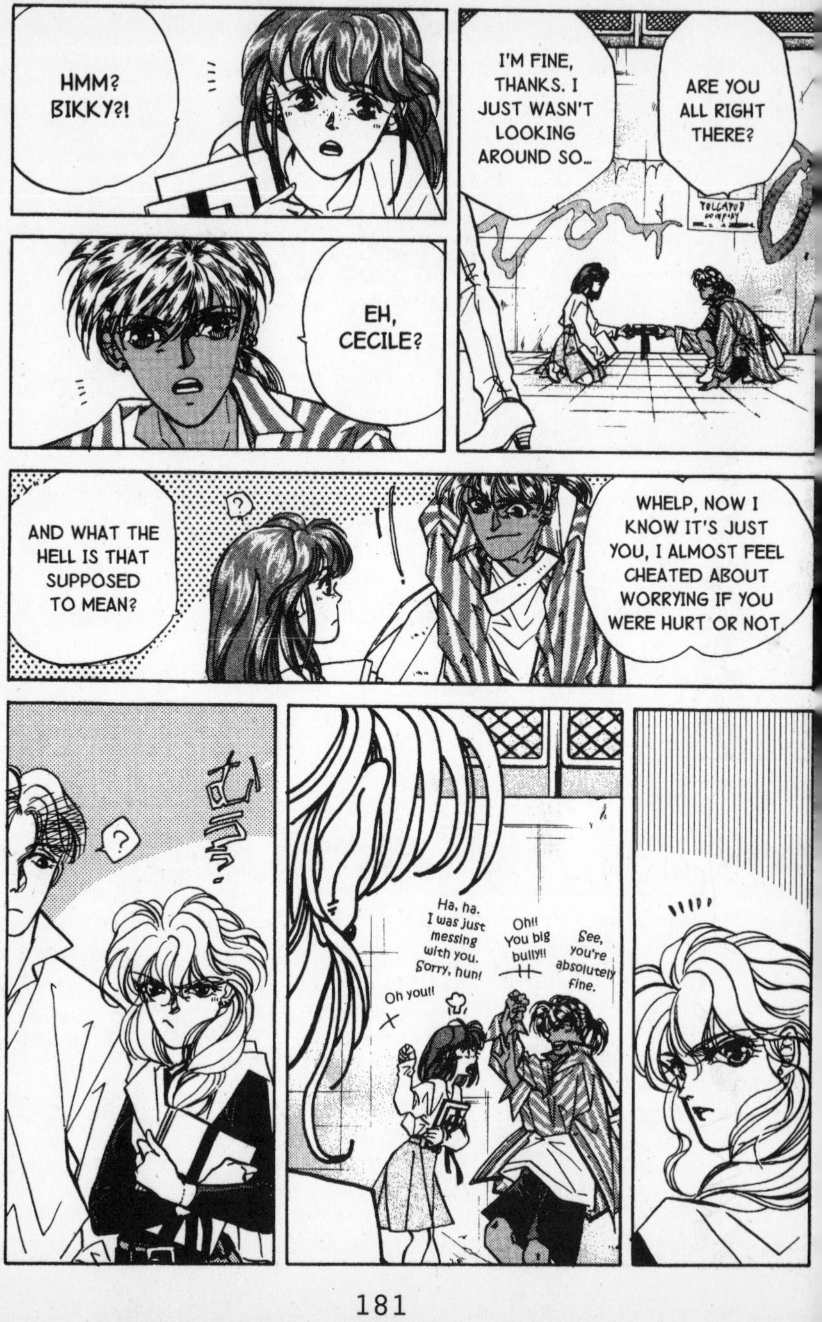
ARE YOU ALL RIGHT THERE?
I'M FINE, THANKS. I JUST WASN'T LOOKING AROUND SO...
HMM? BIKKY?!
EH, CECILE?
WHELP, NOW I KNOW IT'S JUST YOU, I ALMOST FEEL CHEATED ABOUT WORRYING IF YOU WERE HURT OR NOT.
AND WHAT THE HELL IS THAT SUPPOSED TO MEAN?
See, you're absolutely fine.
Oh!! You big bully!!
Ha, ha. I was just messing with you. Sorry, hun!
Oh you!!

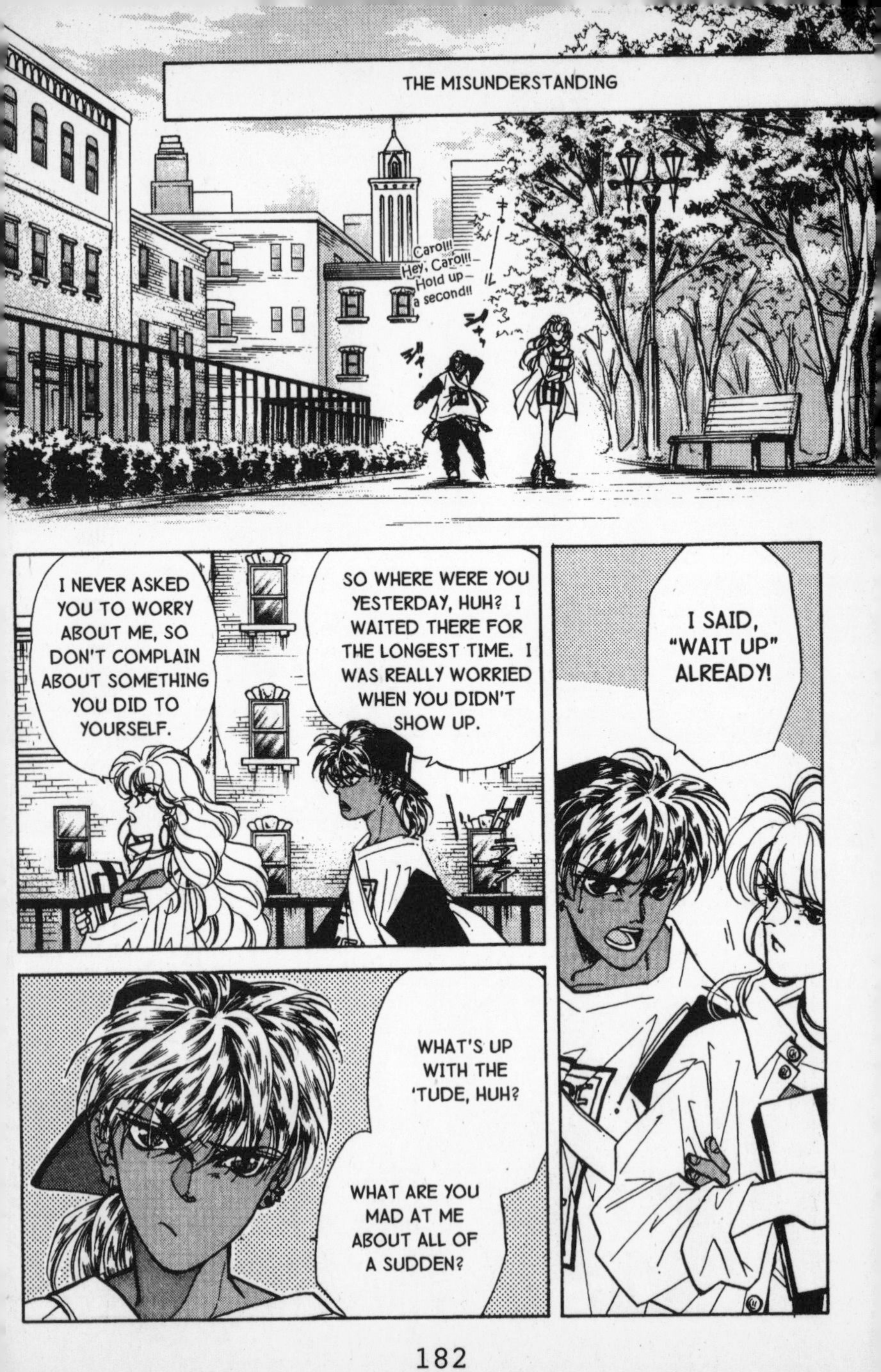
THE MISUNDERSTANDING
Carol!! Hey, Carol!! Hold up— a second!!
I SAID, "WAIT UP" ALREADY!
SO WHERE WERE YOU YESTERDAY, HUH? I WAITED THERE FOR THE LONGEST TIME. I WAS REALLY WORRIED WHEN YOU DIDN'T SHOW UP.
I NEVER ASKED YOU TO WORRY ABOUT ME, SO DON'T COMPLAIN ABOUT SOMETHING YOU DID TO YOURSELF.
WHAT'S UP WITH THE 'TUDE, HUH?
WHAT ARE YOU MAD AT ME ABOUT ALL OF A SUDDEN?

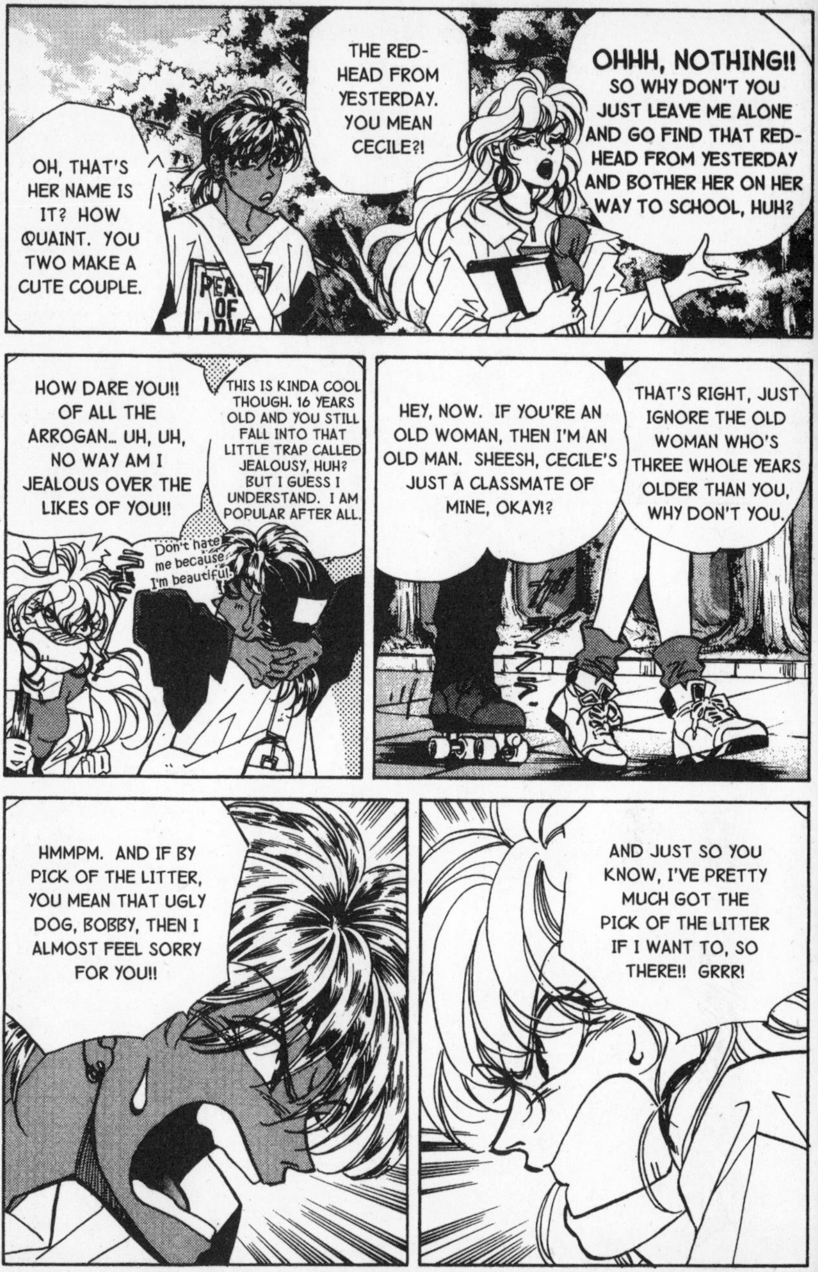
OHHH, NOTHING!! SO WHY DON'T YOU JUST LEAVE ME ALONE AND GO FIND THAT RED-HEAD FROM YESTERDAY AND BOTHER HER ON HER WAY TO SCHOOL, HUH?
THE RED-HEAD FROM YESTERDAY. YOU MEAN CECILE?!
OH, THAT'S HER NAME IS IT? HOW QUAINT. YOU TWO MAKE A CUTE COUPLE.
THAT'S RIGHT, JUST IGNORE THE OLD WOMAN WHO'S THREE WHOLE YEARS OLDER THAN YOU, WHY DON'T YOU.
HEY, NOW. IF YOU'RE AN OLD WOMAN, THEN I'M AN OLD MAN. SHEESH, CECILE'S JUST A CLASSMATE OF MINE, OKAY!?
THIS IS KINDA COOL THOUGH. 16 YEARS OLD AND YOU STILL FALL INTO THAT LITTLE TRAP CALLED JEALOUSY, HUH? BUT I GUESS I UNDERSTAND. I AM POPULAR AFTER ALL.
Don't hate me because I'm beautiful.
HOW DARE YOU!! OF ALL THE ARROGAN... UH, UH, NO WAY AM I JEALOUS OVER THE LIKES OF YOU!!
AND JUST SO YOU KNOW, I'VE PRETTY MUCH GOT THE PICK OF THE LITTER IF I WANT TO, SO THERE!! GRRR!
HMMPM. AND IF BY PICK OF THE LITTER, YOU MEAN THAT UGLY DOG, BOBBY, THEN I ALMOST FEEL SORRY FOR YOU!!

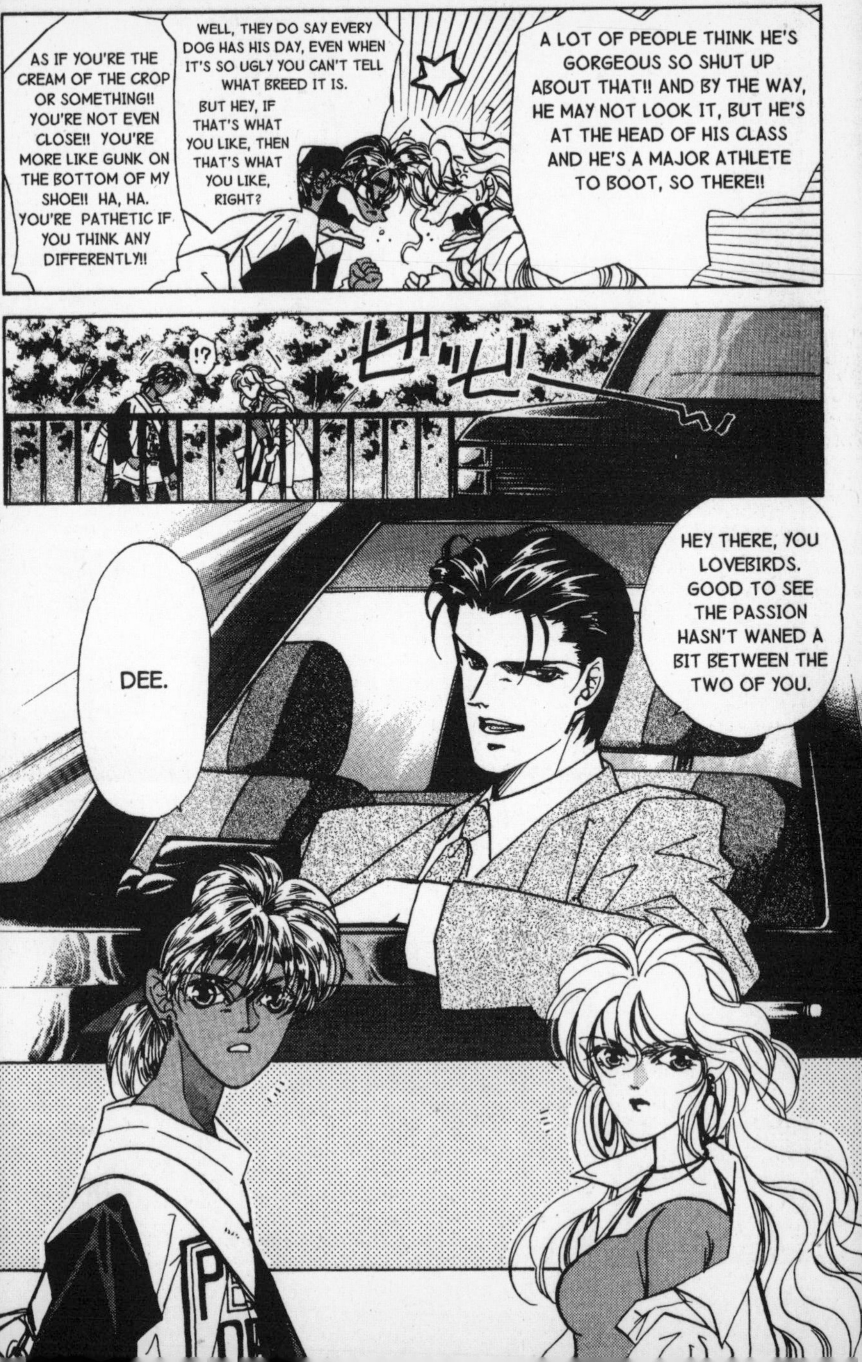
A LOT OF PEOPLE THINK HE'S GORGEOUS SO SHUT UP ABOUT THAT!! AND BY THE WAY, HE MAY NOT LOOK IT, BUT HE'S AT THE HEAD OF HIS CLASS AND HE'S A MAJOR ATHLETE TO BOOT, SO THERE!!
WELL, THEY DO SAY EVERY DOG HAS HIS DAY, EVEN WHEN IT'S SO UGLY YOU CAN'T TELL WHAT BREED IT IS.
BUT HEY, IF THAT'S WHAT YOU LIKE, THEN THAT'S WHAT YOU LIKE, RIGHT?
AS IF YOU'RE THE CREAM OF THE CROP OR SOMETHING!! YOU'RE NOT EVEN CLOSE!! YOU'RE MORE LIKE GUNK ON THE BOTTOM OF MY SHOE!! HA, HA. YOU'RE PATHETIC IF YOU THINK ANY DIFFERENTLY!!
!?
HEY THERE, YOU LOVEBIRDS. GOOD TO SEE THE PASSION HASN'T WANED A BIT BETWEEN THE TWO OF YOU.
DEE.

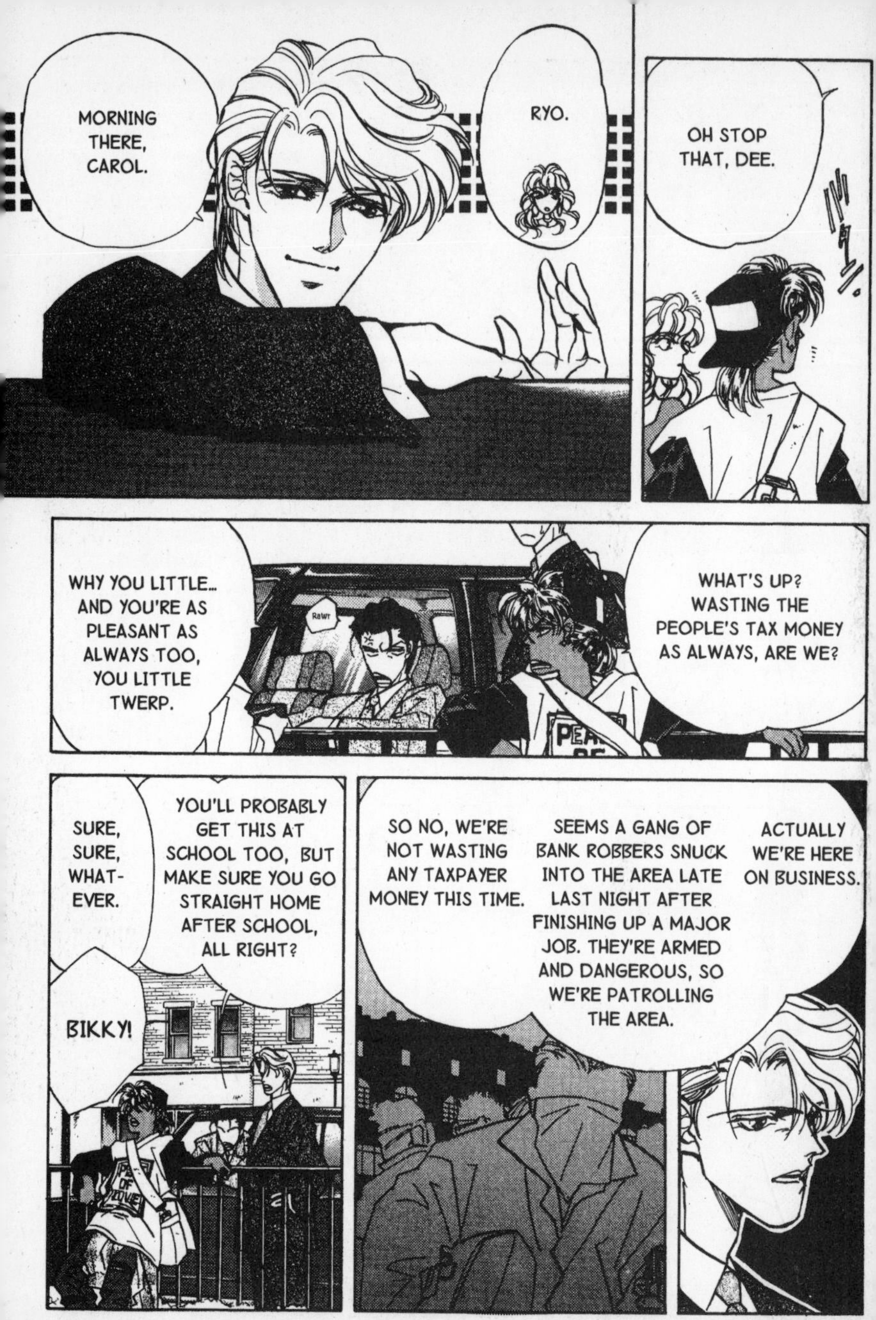
OH STOP THAT, DEE.
RYO.
MORNING THERE, CAROL.
WHAT'S UP? WASTING THE PEOPLE'S TAX MONEY AS ALWAYS, ARE WE?
RaWr
WHY YOU LITTLE... AND YOU'RE AS PLEASANT AS ALWAYS TOO, YOU LITTLE TWERP.
PEACE OF LOVE
ACTUALLY WE'RE HERE ON BUSINESS.
SEEMS A GANG OF BANK ROBBERS SNUCK INTO THE AREA LATE LAST NIGHT AFTER FINISHING UP A MAJOR JOB. THEY'RE ARMED AND DANGEROUS, SO WE'RE PATROLLING THE AREA.
SO NO, WE'RE NOT WASTING ANY TAXPAYER MONEY THIS TIME.
YOU'LL PROBABLY GET THIS AT SCHOOL TOO, BUT MAKE SURE YOU GO STRAIGHT HOME AFTER SCHOOL, ALL RIGHT?
SURE, SURE, WHAT-EVER.
BIKKY!

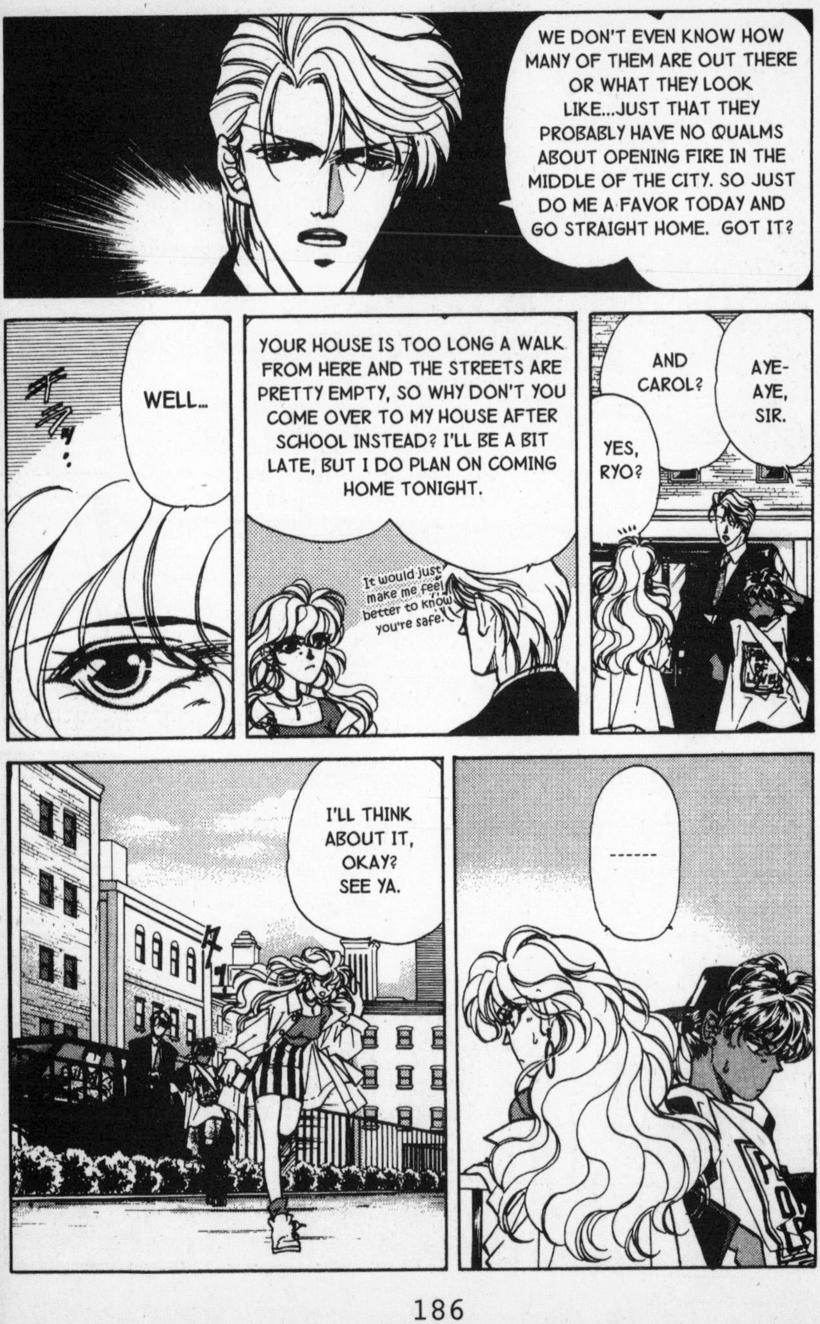
WE DON'T EVEN KNOW HOW MANY OF THEM ARE OUT THERE OR WHAT THEY LOOK LIKE...JUST THAT THEY PROBABLY HAVE NO QUALMS ABOUT OPENING FIRE IN THE MIDDLE OF THE CITY. SO JUST DO ME A FAVOR TODAY AND GO STRAIGHT HOME. GOT IT?
AYE-AYE, SIR.
AND CAROL?
YES, RYO?
YOUR HOUSE IS TOO LONG A WALK FROM HERE AND THE STREETS ARE PRETTY EMPTY, SO WHY DON'T YOU COME OVER TO MY HOUSE AFTER SCHOOL INSTEAD? I'LL BE A BIT LATE, BUT I DO PLAN ON COMING HOME TONIGHT.
It would just make me feel better to know you're safe.
WELL...

I'LL THINK ABOUT IT, OKAY? SEE YA.

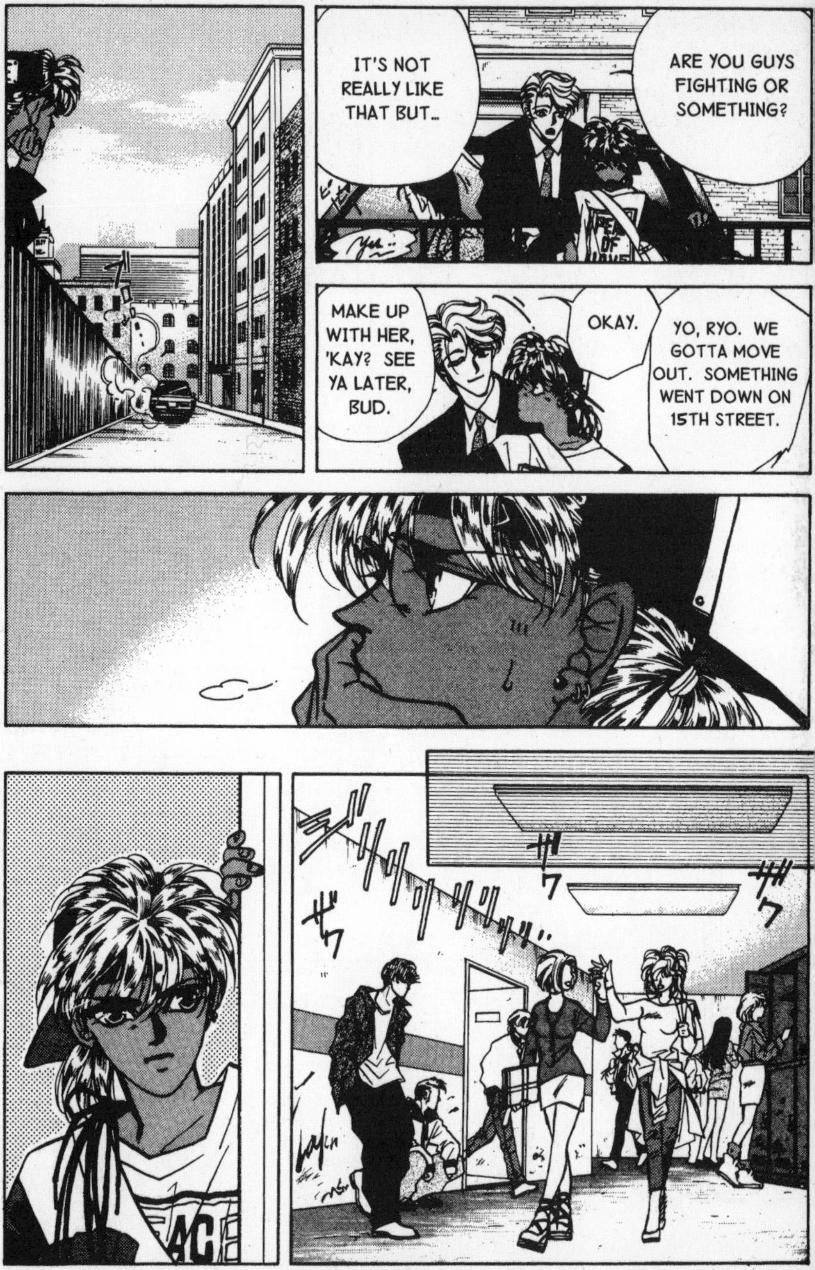
ARE YOU GUYS FIGHTING OR SOMETHING?
IT'S NOT REALLY LIKE THAT BUT...
YO, RYO. WE GOTTA MOVE OUT. SOMETHING WENT DOWN ON 15TH STREET.
OKAY.
MAKE UP WITH HER, 'KAY? SEE YA LATER, BUD.

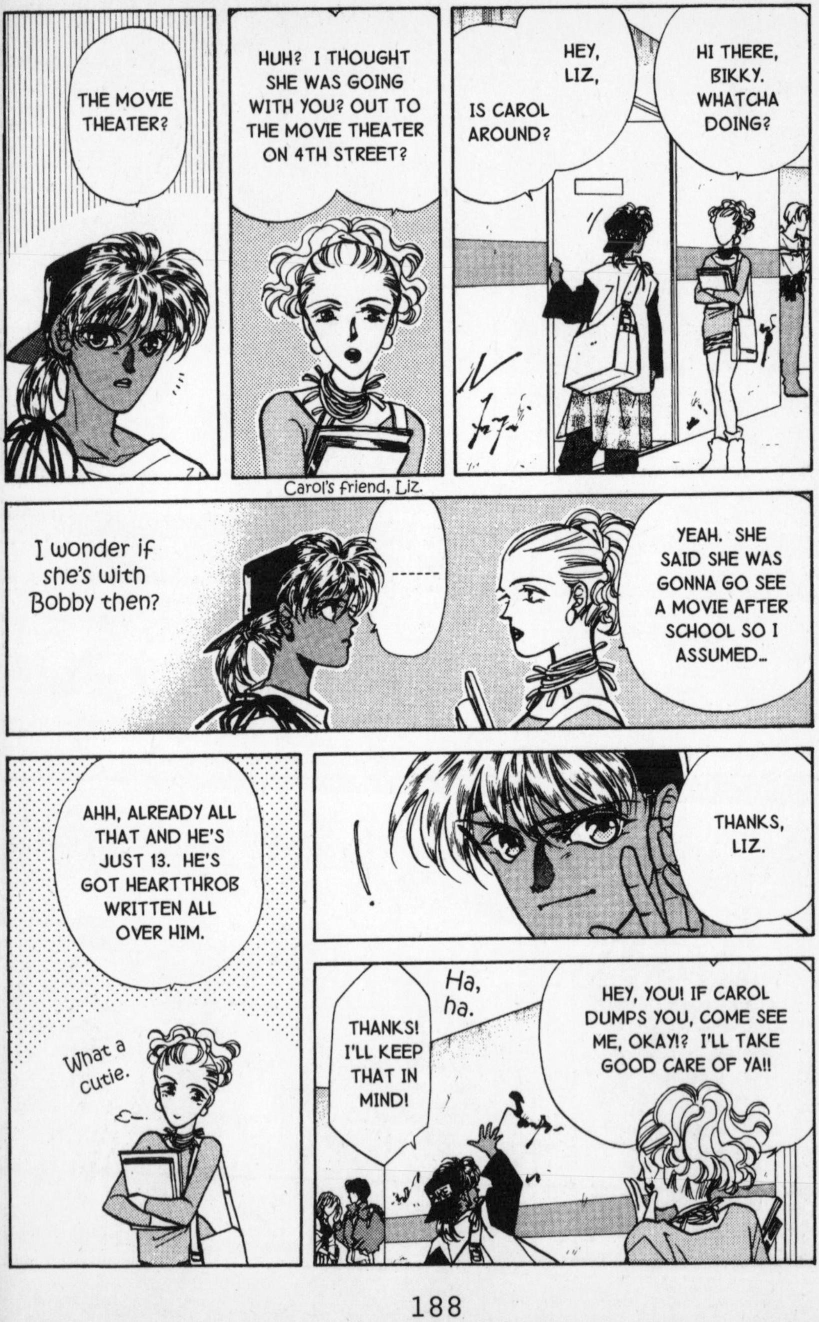
HI THERE, BIKKY. WHATCHA DOING?
HEY, LIZ, IS CAROL AROUND?
HUH? I THOUGHT SHE WAS GOING WITH YOU? OUT TO THE MOVIE THEATER ON 4TH STREET?
THE MOVIE THEATER?
Carol's friend, Liz.
YEAH. SHE SAID SHE WAS GONNA GO SEE A MOVIE AFTER SCHOOL SO I ASSUMED...

I wonder if she's with Bobby then?
THANKS, LIZ.
!
HEY, YOU! IF CAROL DUMPS YOU, COME SEE ME, OKAY!? I'LL TAKE GOOD CARE OF YA!!
Ha, ha.
THANKS! I'LL KEEP THAT IN MIND!
AHH, ALREADY ALL THAT AND HE'S JUST 13. HE'S GOT HEARTTHROB WRITTEN ALL OVER HIM.
What a cutie.

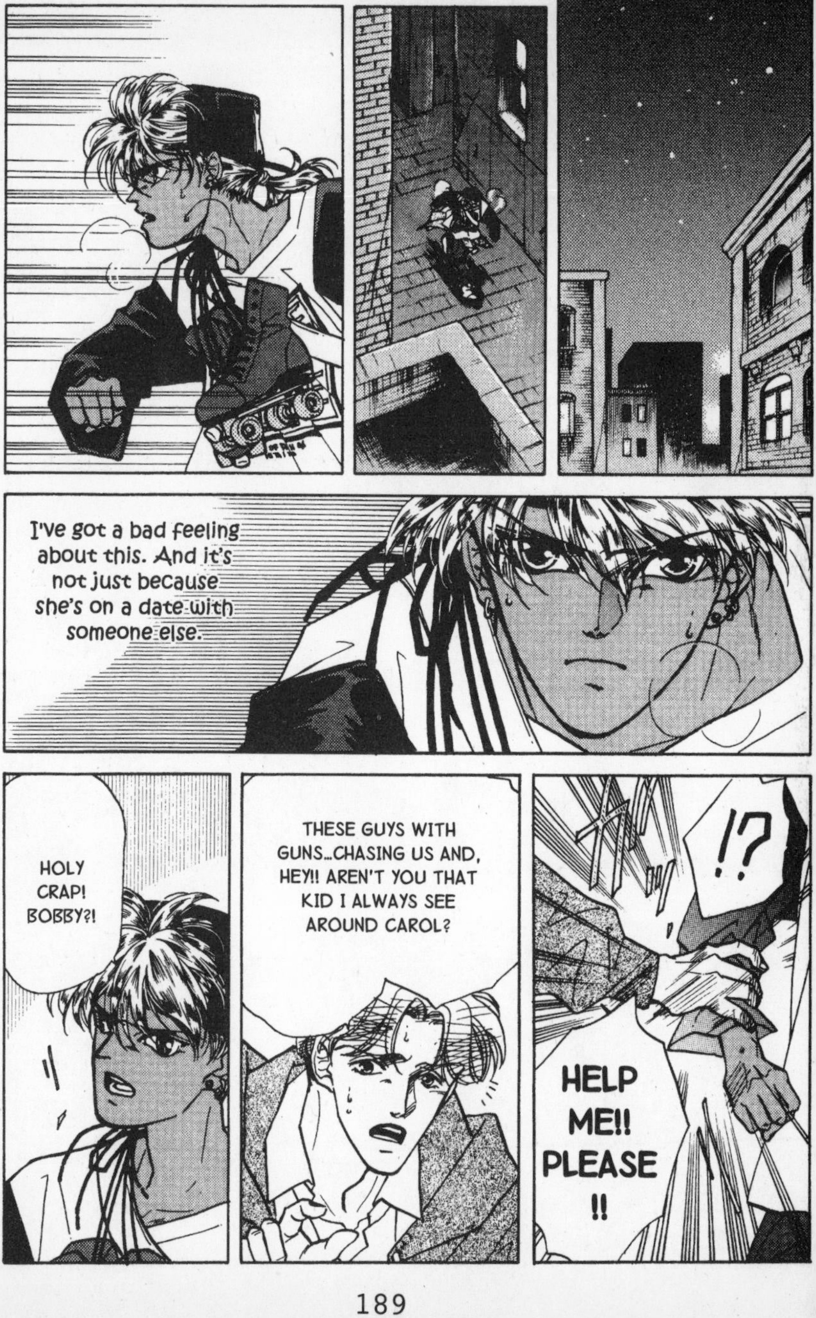
I've got a bad feeling about this. And it's not just because she's on a date with someone else.
!?
HELP ME!! PLEASE !!
THESE GUYS WITH GUNS...CHASING US AND, HEY!! AREN'T YOU THAT KID I ALWAYS SEE AROUND CAROL?
HOLY CRAP! BOBBY?!

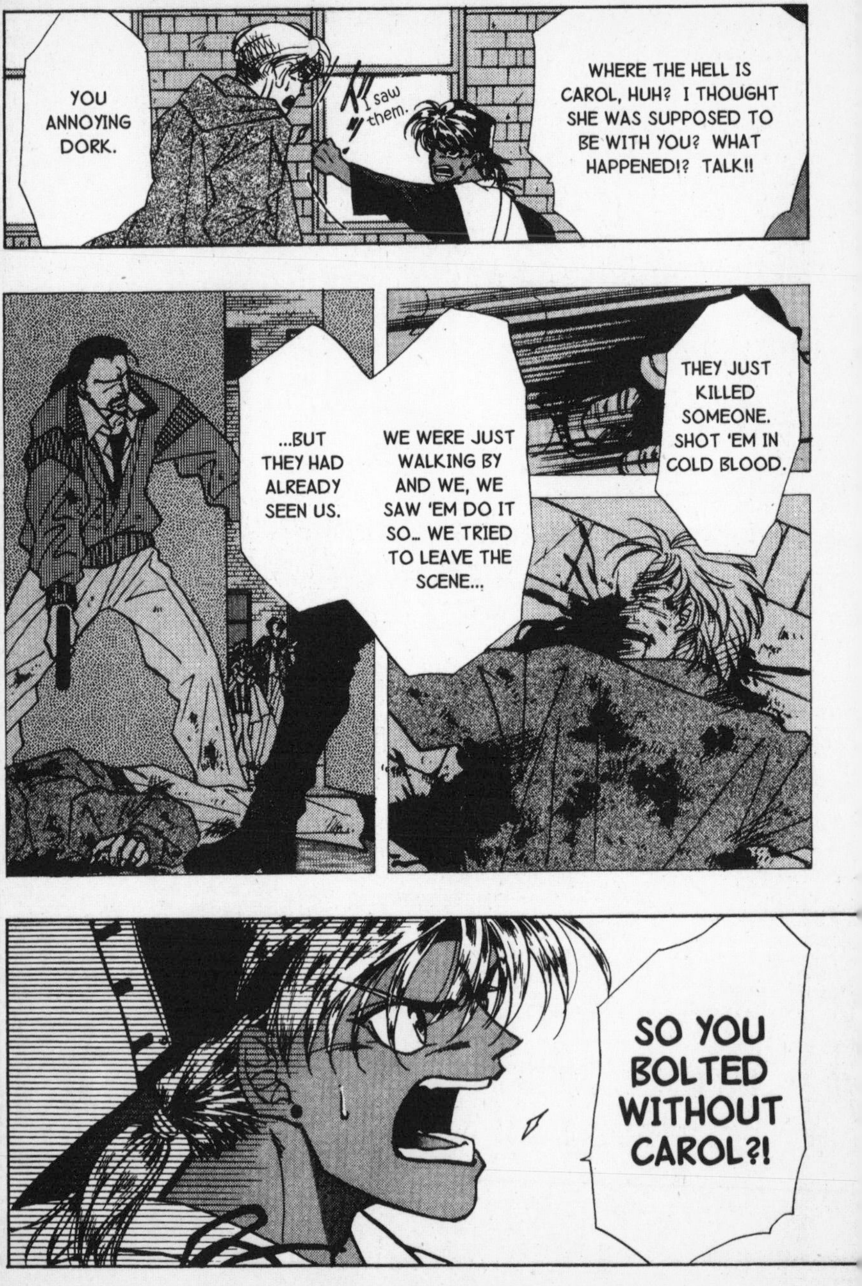
WHERE THE HELL IS CAROL, HUH? I THOUGHT SHE WAS SUPPOSED TO BE WITH YOU? WHAT HAPPENED!? TALK!!
I saw them.
YOU ANNOYING DORK.
THEY JUST KILLED SOMEONE. SHOT 'EM IN COLD BLOOD.
WE WERE JUST WALKING BY AND WE, WE SAW 'EM DO IT SO... WE TRIED TO LEAVE THE SCENE...
...BUT THEY HAD ALREADY SEEN US.
SO YOU BOLTED WITHOUT CAROL?!

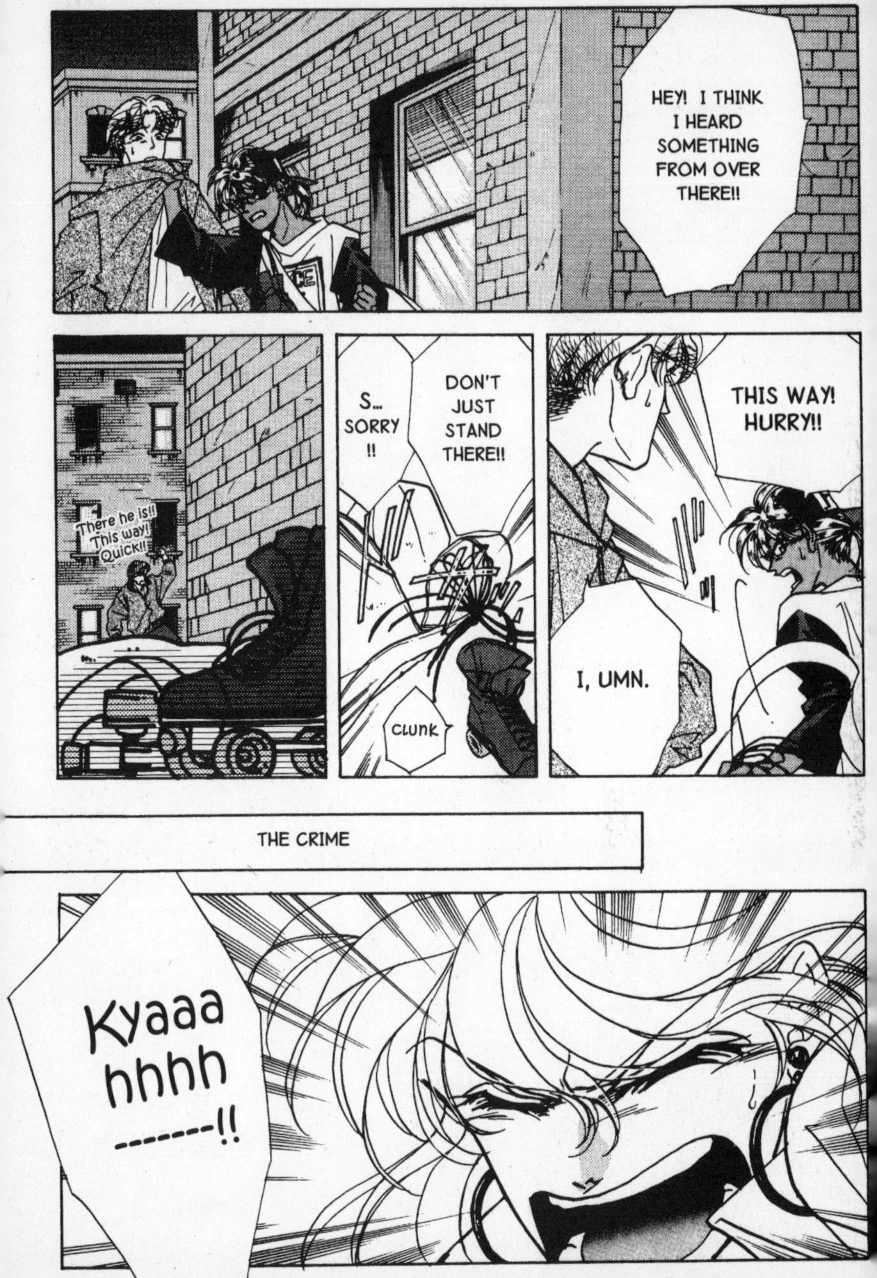
HEY! I THINK I HEARD SOMETHING FROM OVER THERE!!
THIS WAY! HURRY!!
I, UMN.
DON'T JUST STAND THERE!!
S... SORRY!!
CLUNK
There he is!! This way! Quick!!
THE CRIME
Kyaaa hhhh -------!!

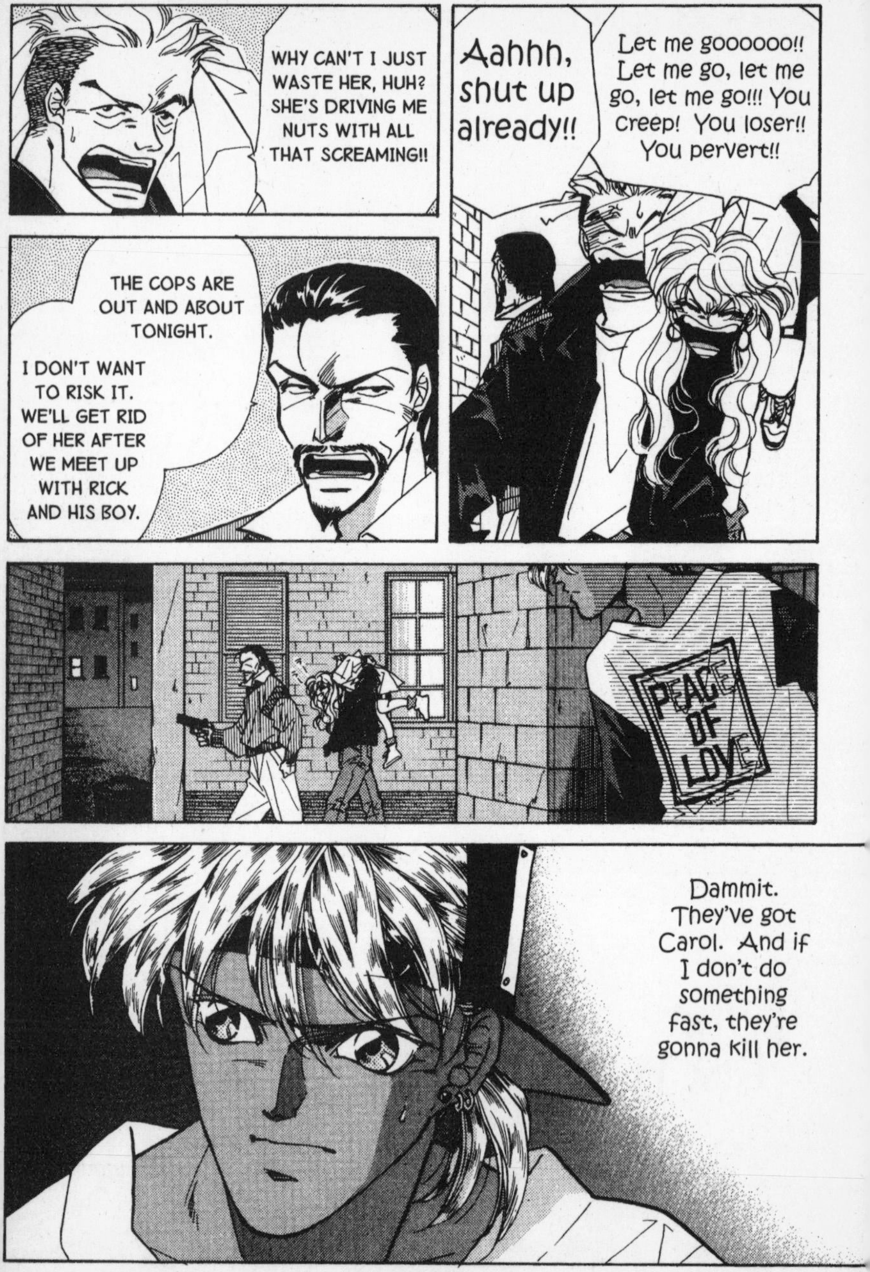
Let me goooooo!! Let me go, let me go, let me go!!! You creep! You loser!! You pervert!!
Aahhh, shut up already!!
WHY CAN'T I JUST WASTE HER, HUH? SHE'S DRIVING ME NUTS WITH ALL THAT SCREAMING!!
THE COPS ARE OUT AND ABOUT TONIGHT.
I DON'T WANT TO RISK IT. WE'LL GET RID OF HER AFTER WE MEET UP WITH RICK AND HIS BOY.
PEACE OF LOVE
Dammit. They've got Carol. And if I don't do something fast, they're gonna kill her.

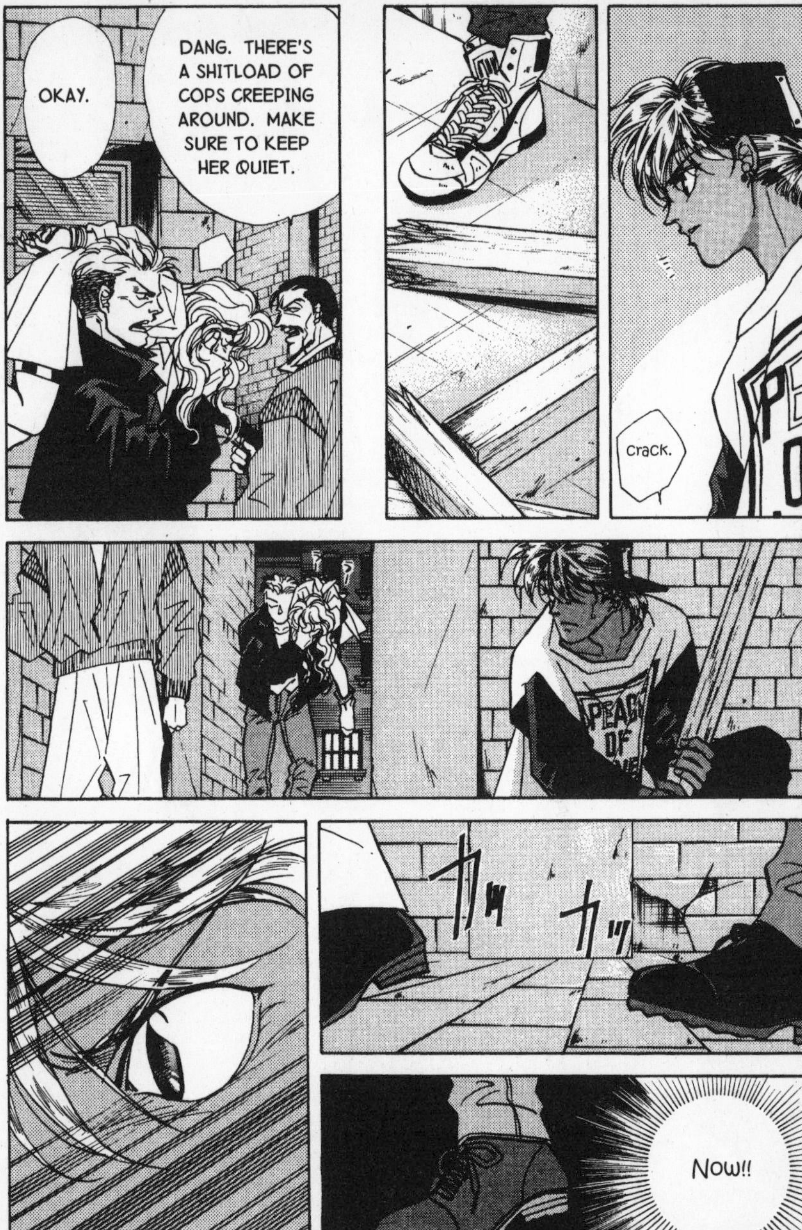
Crack.
DANG. THERE'S A SHITLOAD OF COPS CREEPING AROUND. MAKE SURE TO KEEP HER QUIET.
OKAY.
カッ
カッ
Now!!

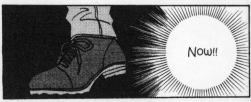

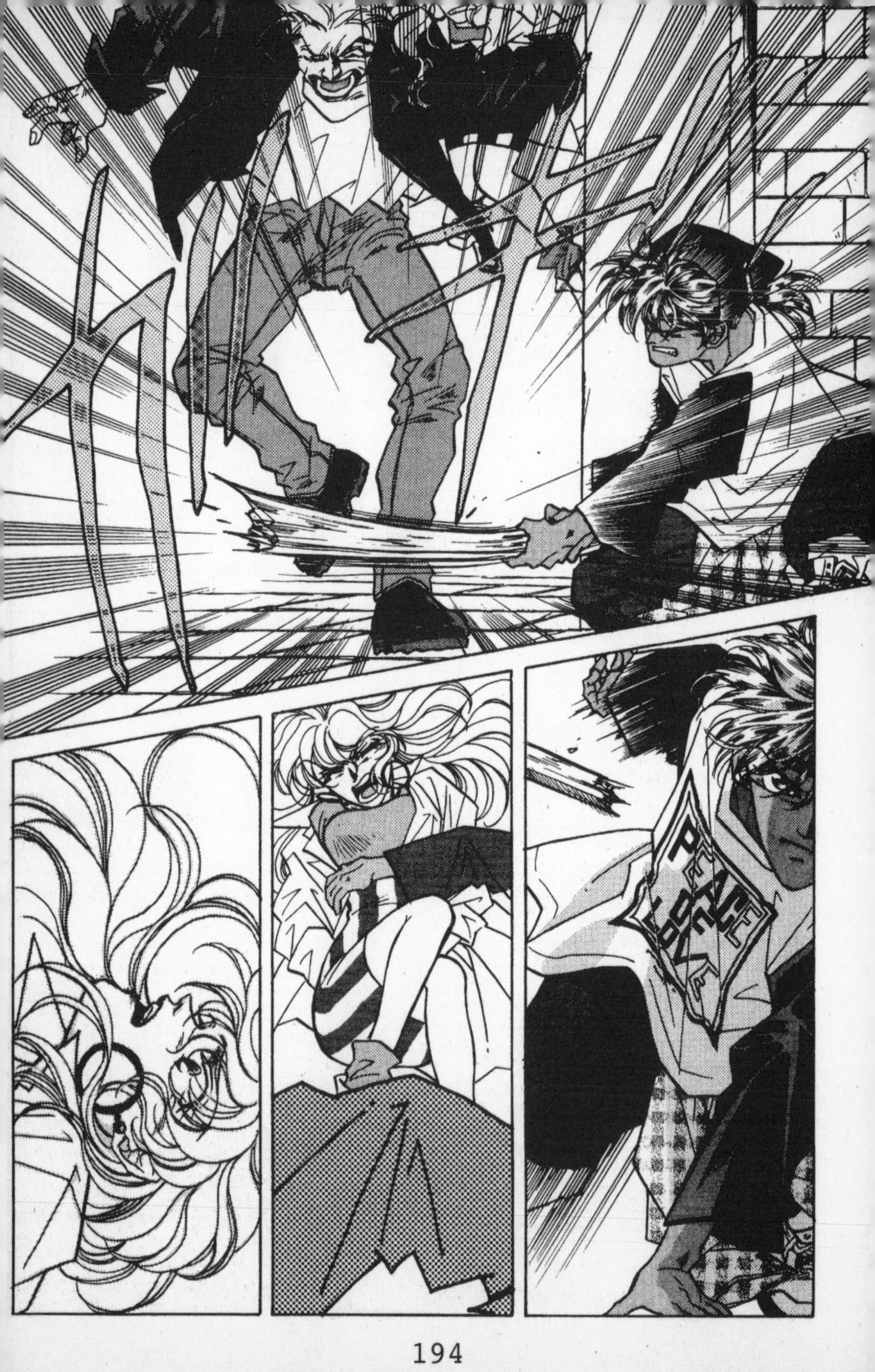

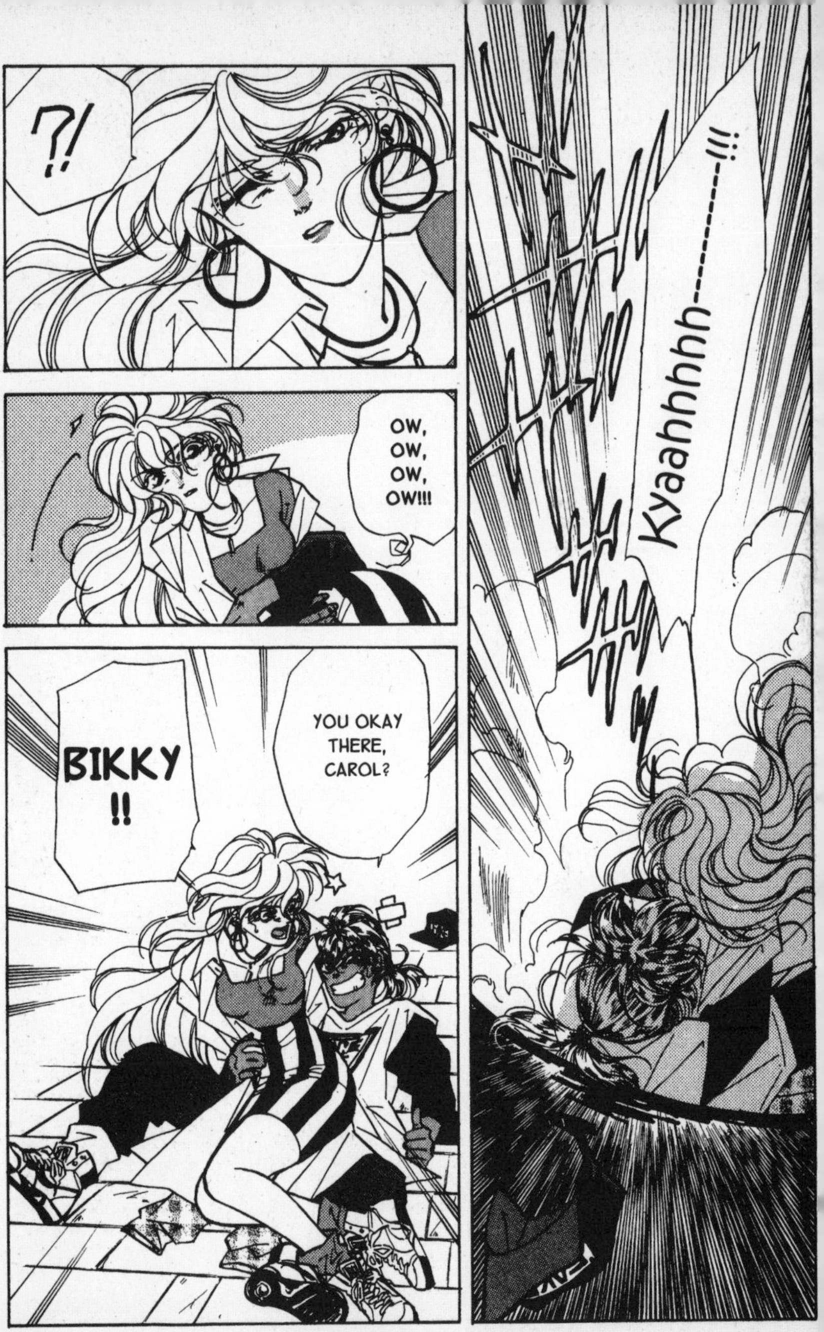
Kyaahhhh———!!!
?!
OW, OW, OW, OW!!!
YOU OKAY THERE, CAROL?
BIKKY !!

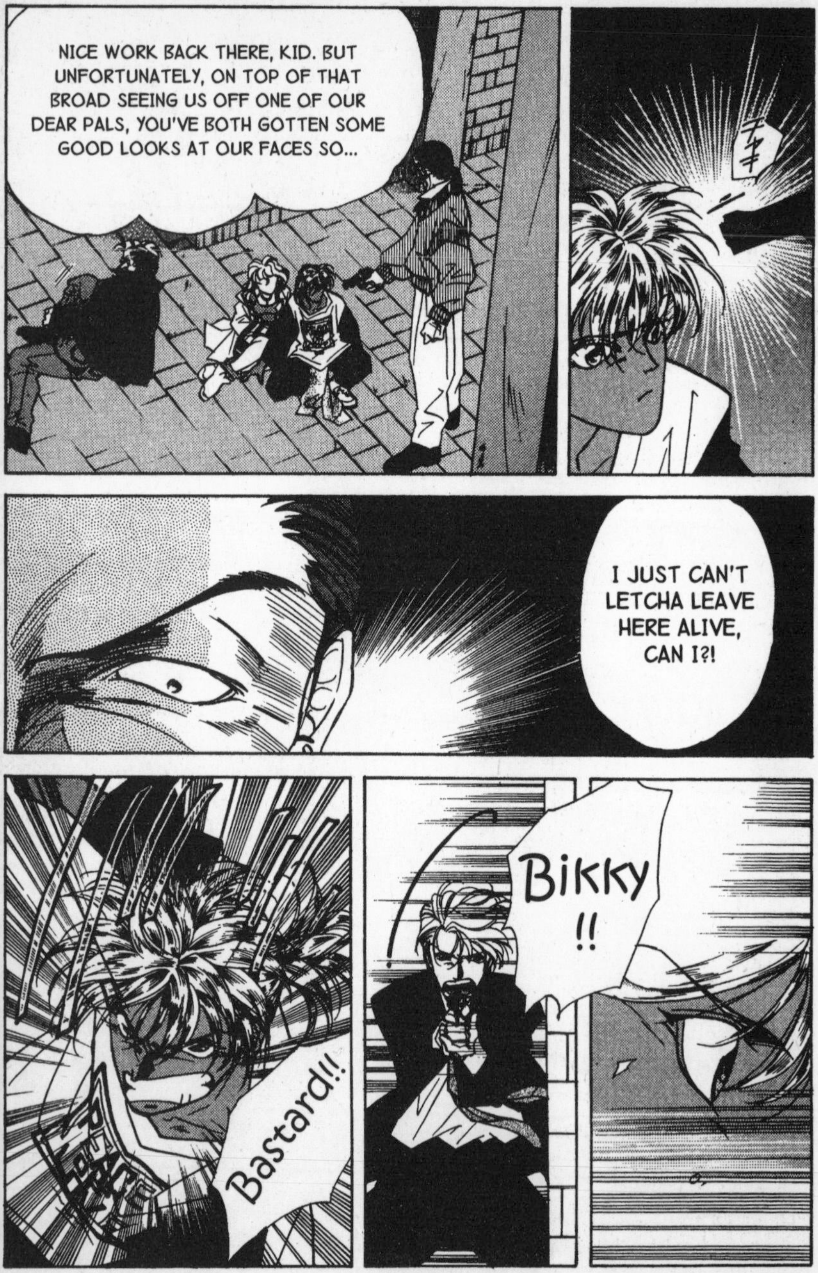
NICE WORK BACK THERE, KID. BUT UNFORTUNATELY, ON TOP OF THAT BROAD SEEING US OFF ONE OF OUR DEAR PALS, YOU'VE BOTH GOTTEN SOME GOOD LOOKS AT OUR FACES SO...
I JUST CAN'T LETCHA LEAVE HERE ALIVE, CAN I?!
Bikky !!
Bastard!!

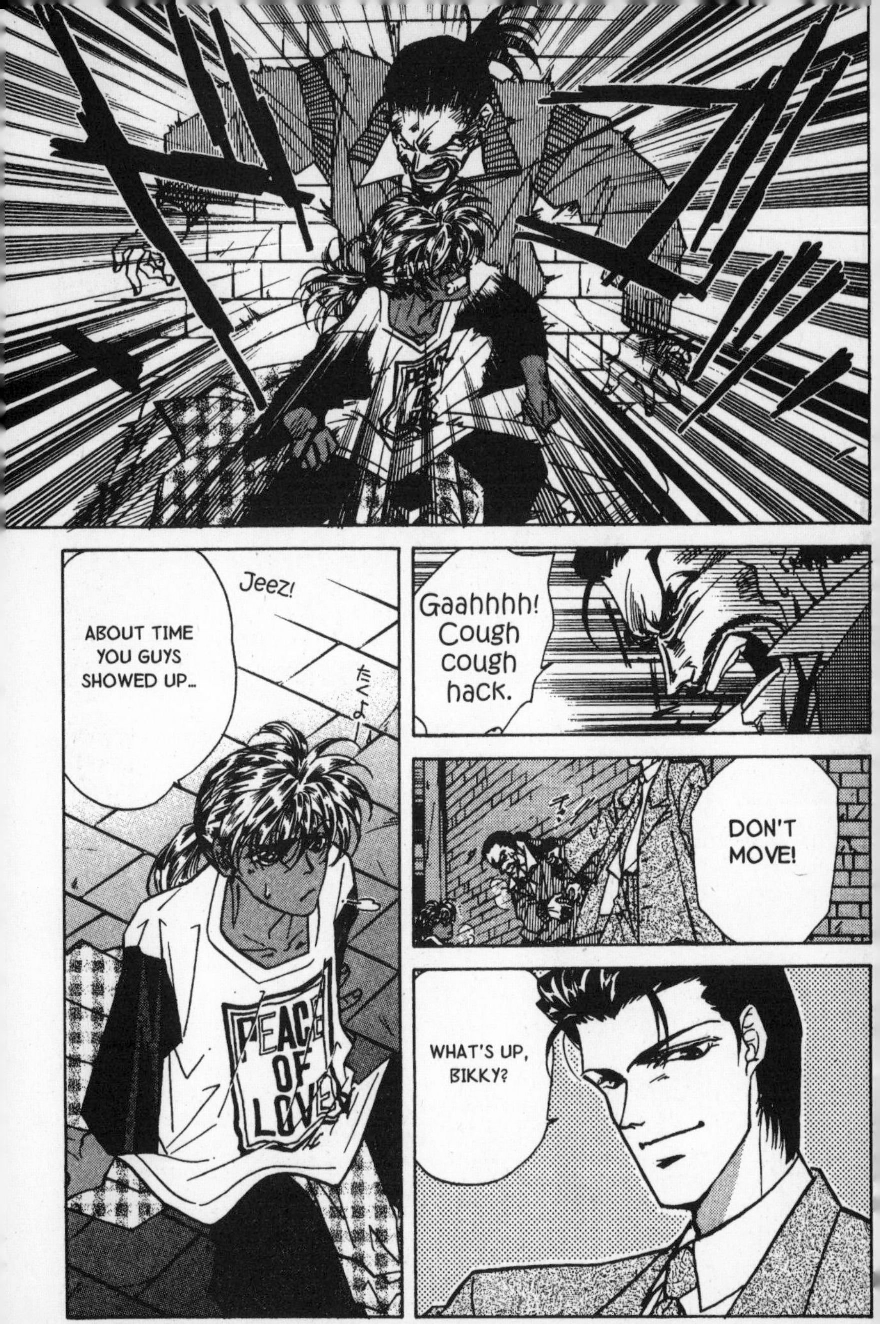
Gaahhhh! Cough cough hack.
DON'T MOVE!
WHAT'S UP, BIKKY?
Jeez!
たくよー
ABOUT TIME YOU GUYS SHOWED UP...

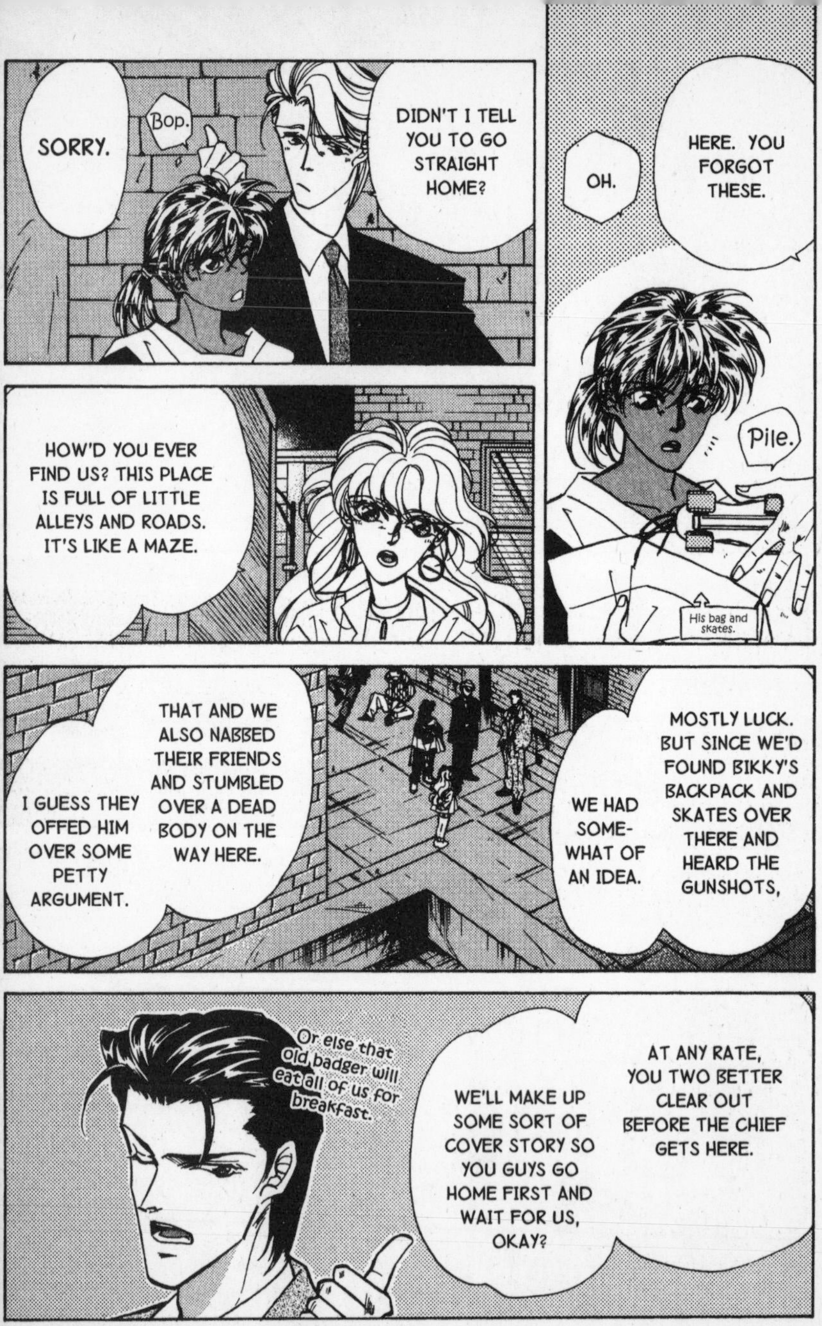
HERE. YOU FORGOT THESE.
OH.
Pile.
His bag and skates.
DIDN'T I TELL YOU TO GO STRAIGHT HOME?
Bop.
SORRY.
HOW'D YOU EVER FIND US? THIS PLACE IS FULL OF LITTLE ALLEYS AND ROADS. IT'S LIKE A MAZE.
MOSTLY LUCK. BUT SINCE WE'D FOUND BIKKY'S BACKPACK AND SKATES OVER THERE AND HEARD THE GUNSHOTS,
WE HAD SOME-WHAT OF AN IDEA.
THAT AND WE ALSO NABBED THEIR FRIENDS AND STUMBLED OVER A DEAD BODY ON THE WAY HERE.
I GUESS THEY OFFED HIM OVER SOME PETTY ARGUMENT.
AT ANY RATE, YOU TWO BETTER CLEAR OUT BEFORE THE CHIEF GETS HERE.
WE'LL MAKE UP SOME SORT OF COVER STORY SO YOU GUYS GO HOME FIRST AND WAIT FOR US, OKAY?
Or else that old badger will eat all of us for breakfast.

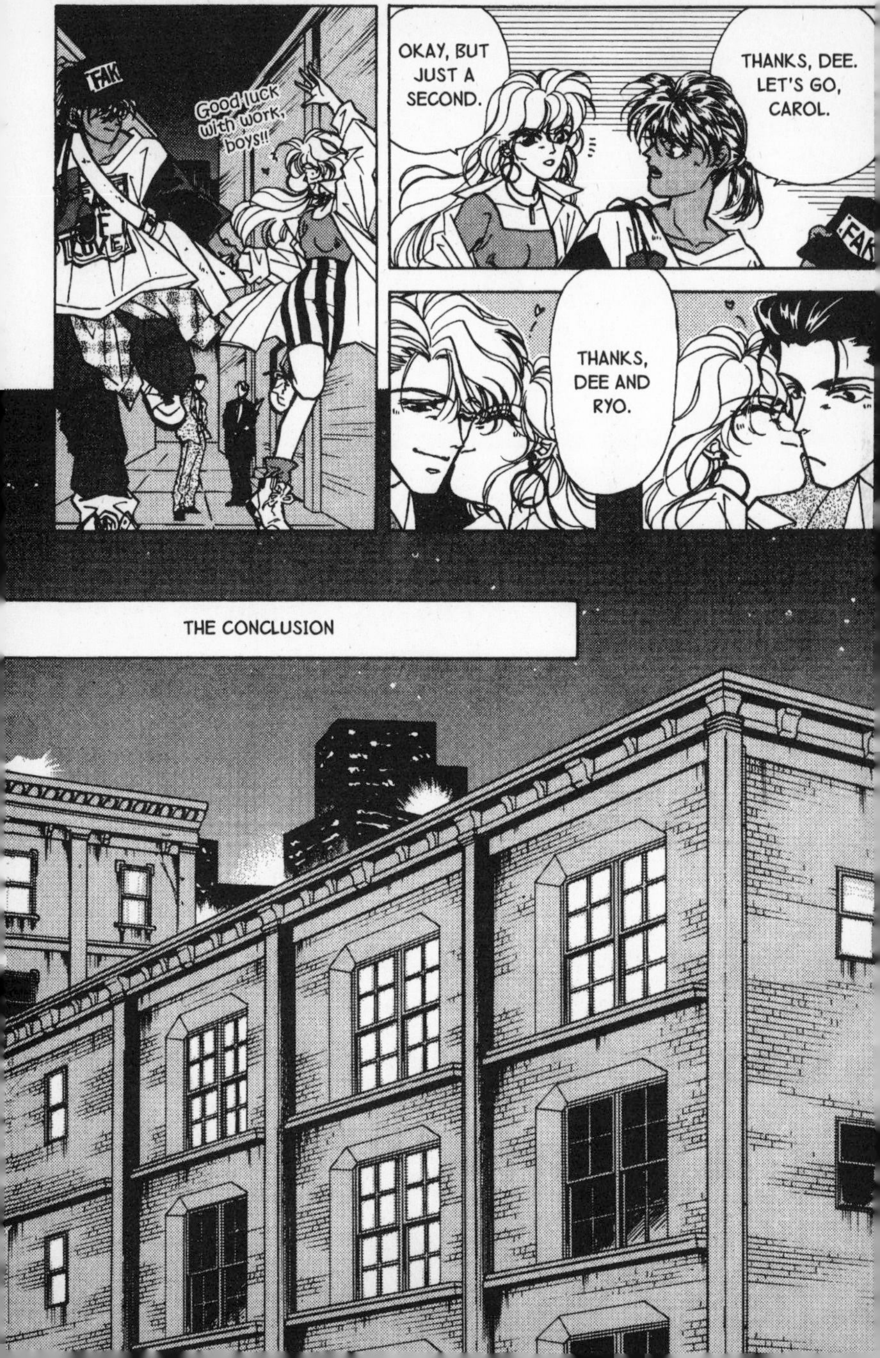
THANKS, DEE. LET'S GO, CAROL.
OKAY, BUT JUST A SECOND.
THANKS, DEE AND RYO.
Good luck with work, boys!!
THE CONCLUSION

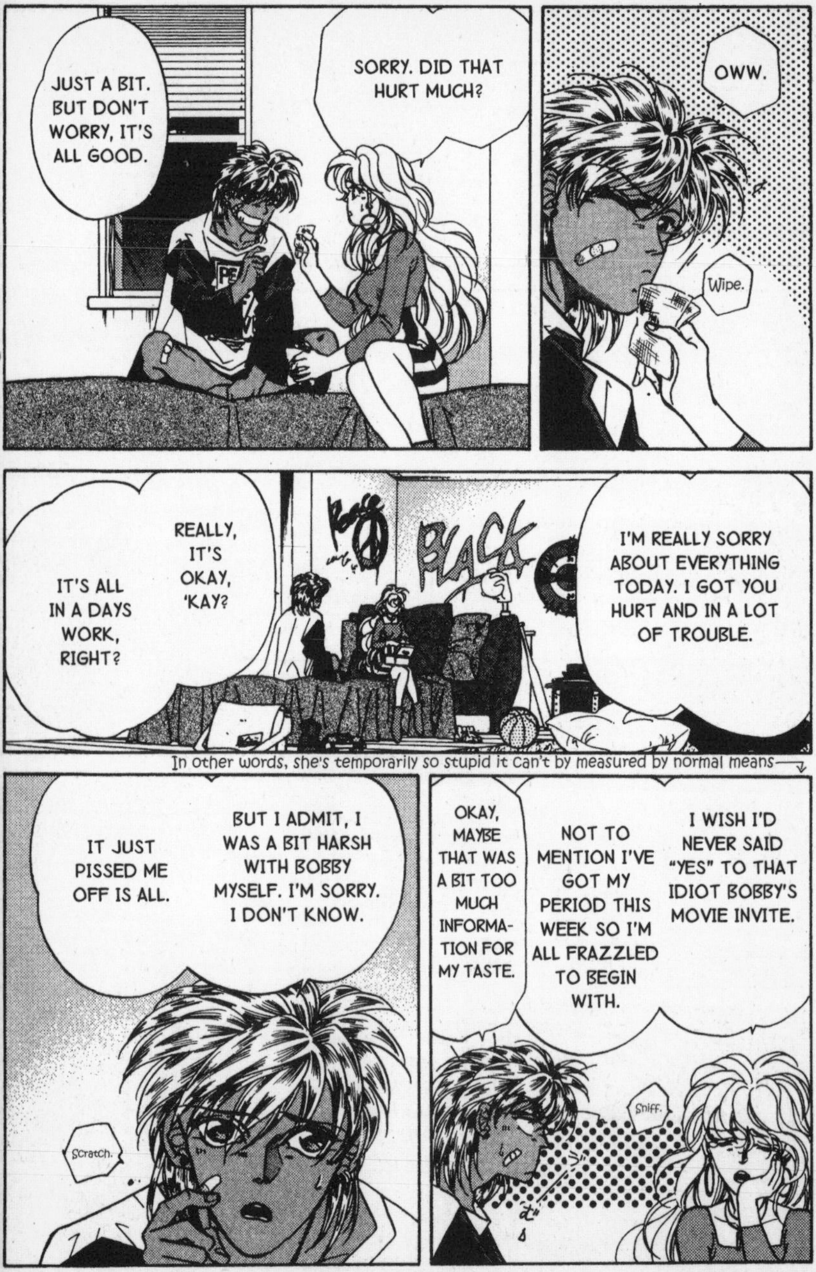
OWW.
Wipe.
SORRY. DID THAT HURT MUCH?
JUST A BIT. BUT DON'T WORRY, IT'S ALL GOOD.
I'M REALLY SORRY ABOUT EVERYTHING TODAY. I GOT YOU HURT AND IN A LOT OF TROUBLE.
BLACK
REALLY, IT'S OKAY, 'KAY?
IT'S ALL IN A DAYS WORK, RIGHT?
In other words, she's temporarily so stupid it can't by measured by normal means
I WISH I'D NEVER SAID "YES" TO THAT IDIOT BOBBY'S MOVIE INVITE.
NOT TO MENTION I'VE GOT MY PERIOD THIS WEEK SO I'M ALL FRAZZLED TO BEGIN WITH.
OKAY, MAYBE THAT WAS A BIT TOO MUCH INFORMATION FOR MY TASTE.
Sniff.
BUT I ADMIT, I WAS A BIT HARSH WITH BOBBY MYSELF. I'M SORRY. I DON'T KNOW.
IT JUST PISSED ME OFF IS ALL.
Scratch.

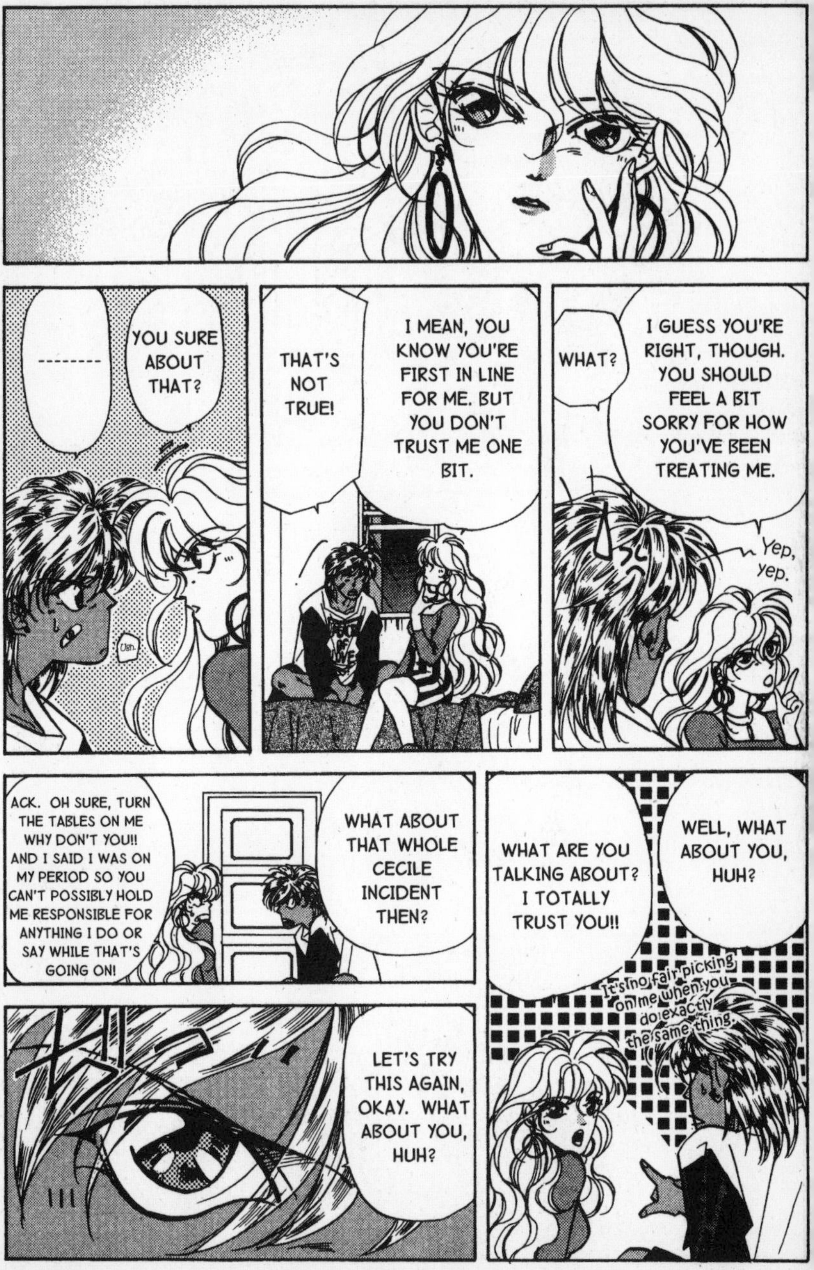
I GUESS YOU'RE RIGHT, THOUGH. YOU SHOULD FEEL A BIT SORRY FOR HOW YOU'VE BEEN TREATING ME.
WHAT?
Yep, yep.
I MEAN, YOU KNOW YOU'RE FIRST IN LINE FOR ME. BUT YOU DON'T TRUST ME ONE BIT.
THAT'S NOT TRUE!
YOU SURE ABOUT THAT?

Ugh.
WELL, WHAT ABOUT YOU, HUH?
WHAT ARE YOU TALKING ABOUT? I TOTALLY TRUST YOU!!
It's no fair picking on me when you do exactly the same thing.
WHAT ABOUT THAT WHOLE CECILE INCIDENT THEN?
ACK. OH SURE, TURN THE TABLES ON ME WHY DON'T YOU!! AND I SAID I WAS ON MY PERIOD SO YOU CAN'T POSSIBLY HOLD ME RESPONSIBLE FOR ANYTHING I DO OR SAY WHILE THAT'S GOING ON!
LET'S TRY THIS AGAIN, OKAY. WHAT ABOUT YOU, HUH?

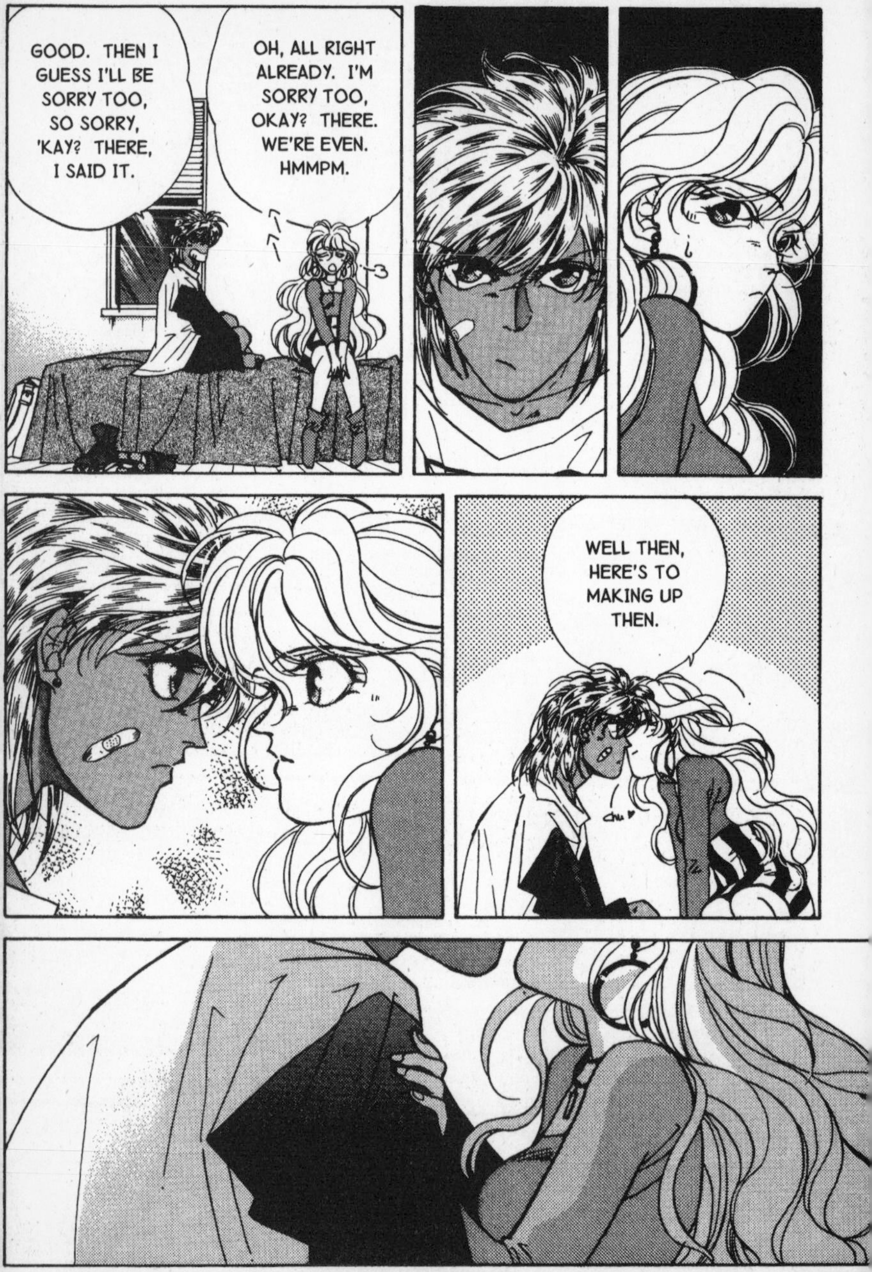
OH, ALL RIGHT ALREADY. I'M SORRY TOO, OKAY? THERE. WE'RE EVEN. HMMPM.
GOOD. THEN I GUESS I'LL BE SORRY TOO, SO SORRY, 'KAY? THERE, I SAID IT.
WELL THEN, HERE'S TO MAKING UP THEN.

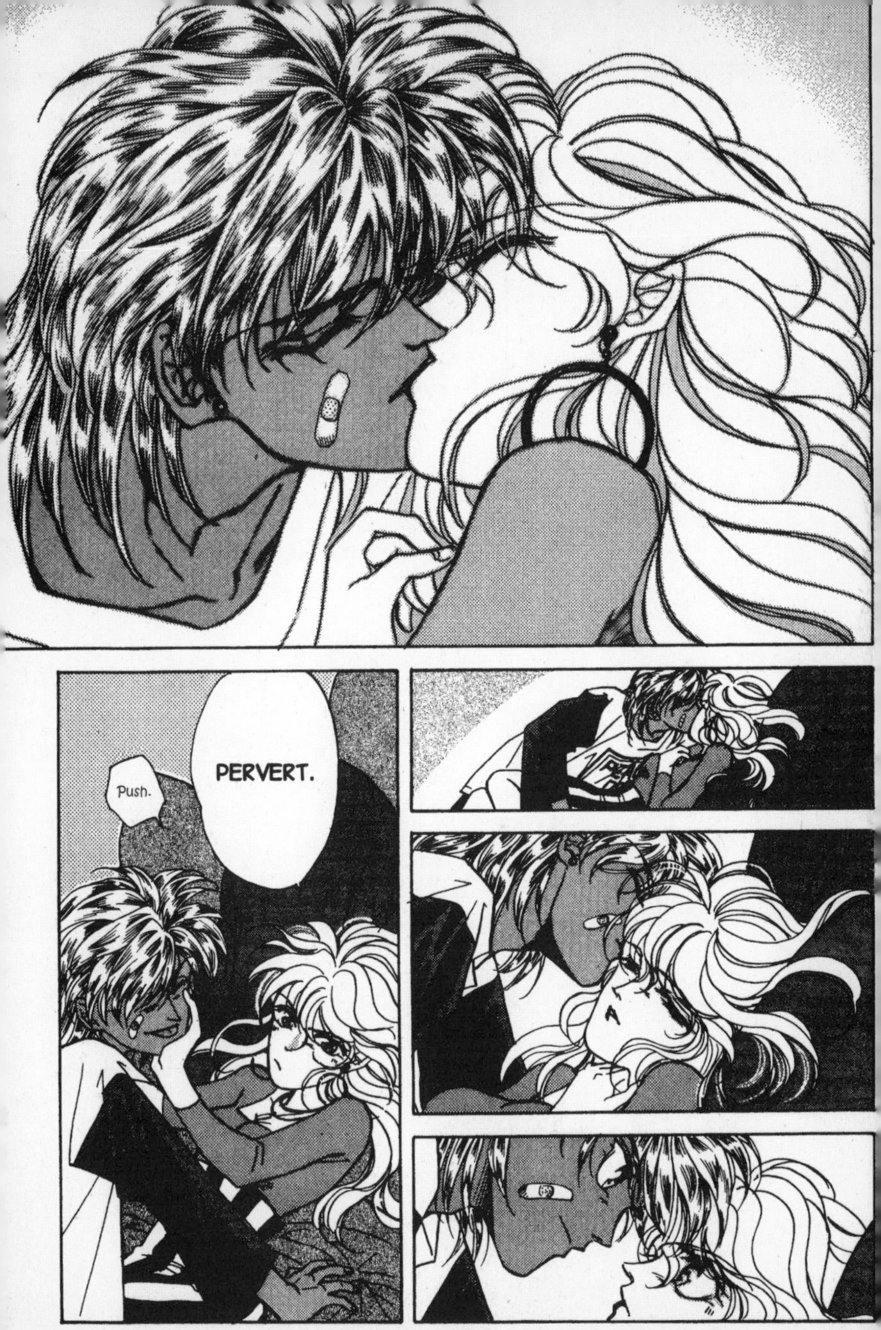
PERVERT.
Push.

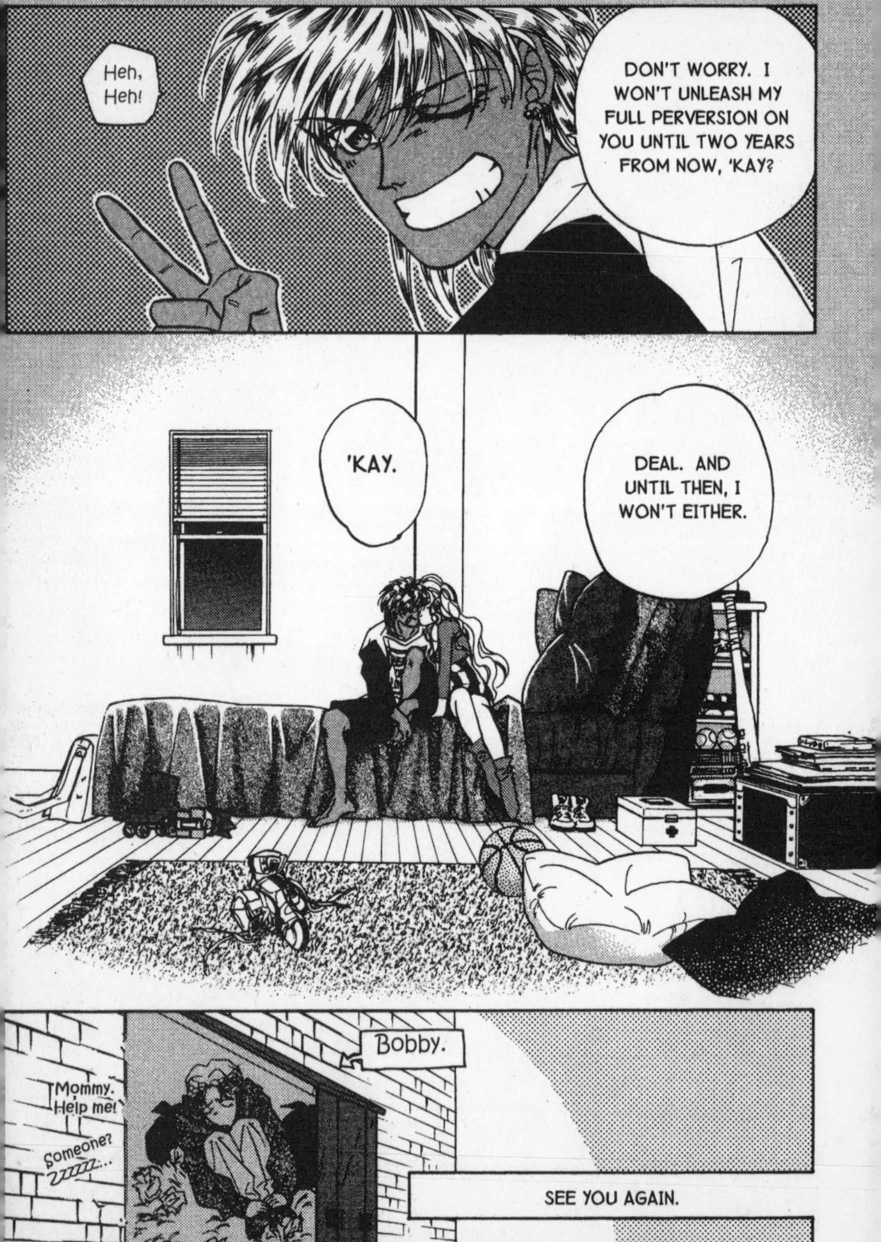
DON'T WORRY. I WON'T UNLEASH MY FULL PERVERSION ON YOU UNTIL TWO YEARS FROM NOW, 'KAY?
Heh, Heh!
DEAL. AND UNTIL THEN, I WON'T EITHER.
'KAY.
Bobby.
Mommy. Help me!
Someone? Zzzzzz...
SEE YOU AGAIN.

FAKE act.7/End.

FAKE., After Life Gym

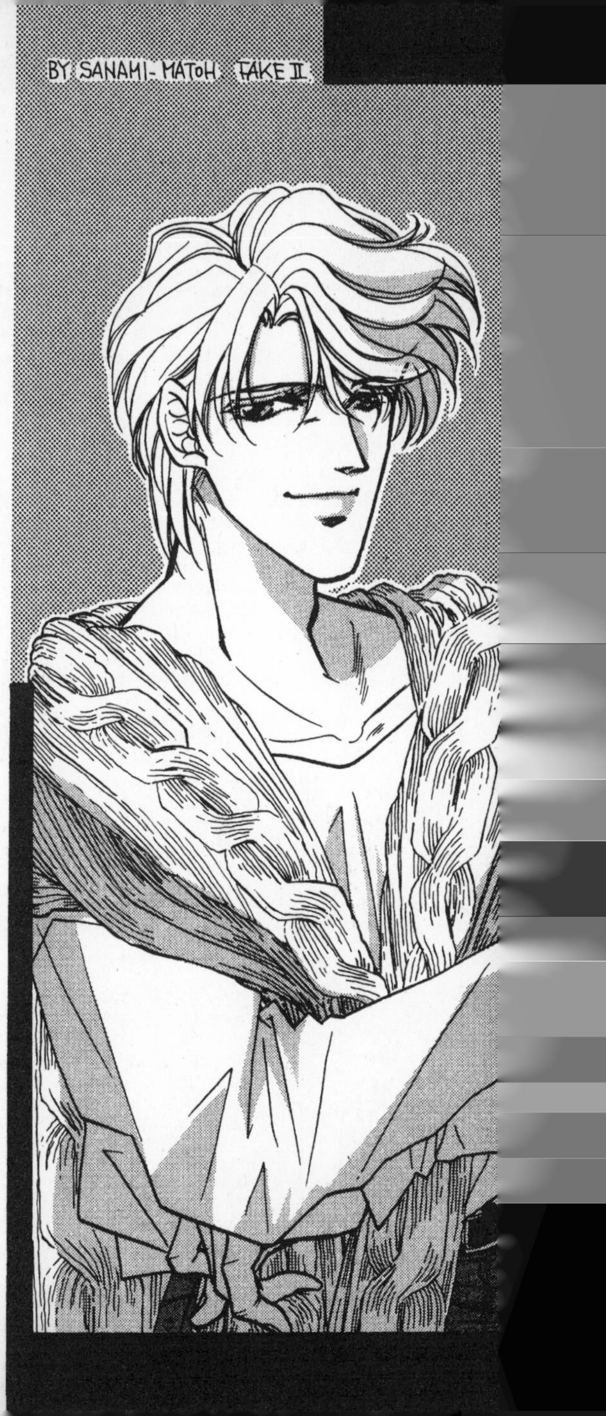
BY SANAMI-MATOH FAKE II

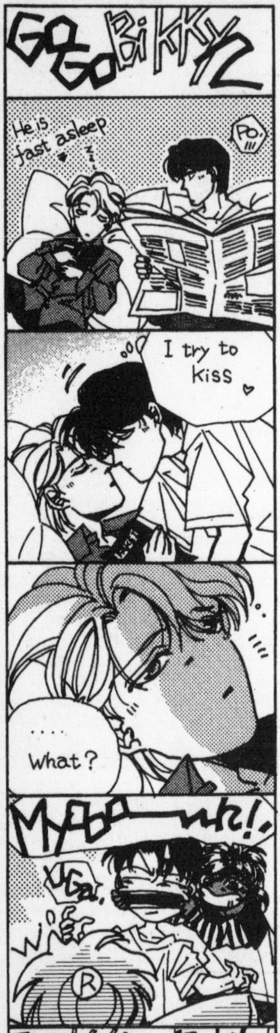
He is fast asleep
PO.
I try to kiss
....
What?
My Ba--nh!!
UGa.
Gya HaHaHa HaHaHa
Bikky!!
OH surprised..
Doki Doki Doki

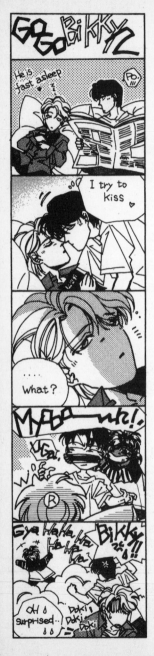

After - Talk

FIRST OFF, I'D LIKE TO SAY, "THANK YOU VERY MUCH" FOR PICKING UP "FAKE II." (WELL, HOPEFULLY YOU BOUGHT IT AND DIDN'T JUST PICK IT UP BUT, WHATEVER!!) NOW, EVEN THOUGH I'M TAKING MY TIME WITH THE FAKE STORY, WHEN IT COMES DOWN TO IT, FOR SOME REASON I JUST KEPT GETTING RUSHED AND THERE ARE ACTUALLY QUITE A FEW PAGES AND SECTIONS I HAVEN'T HAD ENOUGH TIME TO DO RIGHT SO...IT WAS QUITE A PROJECT TO GET EVERYTHING FINISHED FOR THE MANGA VERSION. AND STILL, THERE'S JUST SO MUCH THAT I WANTED TO ADD BUT COULDN'T SINCE IF I ADDED THAT, THEN I'D HAVE TO ADD SOMETHING ELSE AND SO ON AND SO FORTH. SORRY!!

- NOW, IF YOU DON'T MIND, JUST A LITTLE ADVERTISEMENT. AT THE SAME TIME THAT FAKE II HITS THE BOOKSTORE SHELVES, I'LL ALSO HAVE THREE OTHER MANGA IN STORES AT THE SAME TIME (OCTOBER 1995). THE FIRST TWO ARE "BE-ING 3" AND "BLACK X BLOOD I" FROM A DIFFERENT PUBLISHER (WHOSE NAME I WON'T MENTION HERE BUT I'M SURE IF YOU DID A BIT OF INVESTIGATING--WHICH I'D REALLY APPRECIATE--YOU'D BE EASILY ABLE TO ID WHICH ONE IT WAS), AND THE LAST ONE IS THROUGH THIS PUBLISHER, BIBLOS, CALLED "RA-I" THROUGH ZERO COMICS. (BUT NOT THROUGH BE X BOY COMICS. SORRY FOR THE CONFUSION.) IF YOU WOULD BE SO KIND AS TO PICK UP THESE OTHER ONES UP TOO, THEN I'D BE ETERNALLY GRATEFUL.
- NEXT, PLEASE, PLEASE SEND ME LETTERS ABOUT WHAT YOU THINK ABOUT THE WAY I HANDLED FAKE II.* I THINK A LOT OF YOU OUT THERE MIGHT THINK I'M BEING A BIT OF A TEASE ABOUT THIS, BUT I'M NOT GOING TO LET THEM RUSH THEIR ROMANCE. I RATHER LIKE IT THIS WAY AND THINK I'LL KEEP IT AS SUCH FOR A WHILE LONGER. AFTER ALL, IF I JUST HAD THEM PLOW ALL THE WAY TO THE END THEN, I MYSELF WOULDN'T BE ABLE TO KEEP UP WITH THE STORY ANY LONGER. SORRY, GUYS!! (IT'S NOT LIKE I'M DRAWING THE STORY SLOW TO BE MEAN TO YOU READERS. IT'S JUST THAT I NEED MORE TIME TO DRAW IT. GIVE ME TIME PLEASE!! WHATEVER!!) A...AT ANY RATE, I'LL TRY TO DO BETTER FOR THE NEXT STORYLINE SO PLEASE, PLEASE DON'T GIVE UP ON ME OR DEE & RYO YET. AND OF COURSE, BIKKY AND CAROL AS WELL!!

P.S. THANK YOU ALL SO MUCH FOR YOUR LOVELY FAN LETTERS. I'M SO SORRY I DON'T HAVE TIME TO WRITE YOU GUYS BACK. BUT REST ASSURED THAT I DEFINITELY DO READ EACH AND EVERY ONE OF THE LETTERS YOU SEND ME, SO PLEASE DON'T GET DISCOURAGED AND KEEP THEM COMING!! I'LL BE WAITING FOR THEM!!

AND ONCE AGAIN, THANK YOU SO, SO, SO VERY MUCH FOR YOUR CONTINUED SUPPORT.

* SEND LETTERS TO: TOKYOPOP, 5900 WILSHIRE BLVD., SUITE 2000, LOS ANGELES, CA 90036.

1995.

VOLUME THREE

Ryo and Dee are on the hunt for a serial killer who murders women who look like prostitutes. They're aided by FBI agent Diana Spacey, a brilliant investigator who is an old friend of Berkeley. Soon, she is caught in the serial killer's web and it's up to Berkeley and the gang to save her!

In the second act of the story, Ryo's childhood is explored, and family secrets are revealed. It's the Christmas season, and Ryo doesn't want to spend it alone. On Christmas Eve, Dee comes to wish him a "Merry Christmas" and Ryo is extremely touched by the sentiment. All of their fiery feelings finally lead to one hot scene that you'll never forget!

ALSO AVAILABLE FROM

MANGA

.HACK//LEGEND OF THE TWILIGHT
@LARGE
A.I. LOVE YOU
AI YORI AOSHI
ANGELIC LAYER
ARM OF KANNON
BABY BIRTH
BATTLE ROYALE
BATTLE VIXENS
BRAIN POWERED
BRIGADOON
B'TX
CANDIDATE FOR GODDESS, THE
CARDCAPTOR SAKURA
CARDCAPTOR SAKURA - MASTER OF THE CLOW
CHOBITS
CHRONICLES OF THE CURSED SWORD
CLAMP SCHOOL DETECTIVES
CLOVER
COMIC PARTY
CONFIDENTIAL CONFESSIONS
CORRECTOR YUI
COWBOY BEBOP
COWBOY BEBOP: SHOOTING STAR
CRESCENT MOON
CYBORG 009
D.N. ANGEL
DEMON DIARY
DEMON ORORON, THE
DEUS VITAE
DIGIMON
DIGIMON ZERO TWO
DIGIMON TAMERS
DOLL May 2004
DRAGON HUNTER
DRAGON KNIGHTS
DUKLYON: CLAMP SCHOOL DEFENDERS
ERICA SAKURAZAWA COLLECTED WORKS
EERIE QUEERIE!
FAERIES' LANDING
FAKE
FLCL
FORBIDDEN DANCE
FRUITS BASKET
G GUNDAM
GATE KEEPERS
GETBACKERS
GIRL GOT GAME
GRAVITATION
GTO
GUNDAM SEED ASTRAY
GUNDAM WING

GUNDAM WING: BATTLEFIELD OF PACIFISTS
GUNDAM WING: ENDLESS WALTZ
GUNDAM WING: THE LAST OUTPOST (G-UNIT)
HAPPY MANIA
HARLEM BEAT
I.N.V.U.
IMMORTAL RAIN
INITIAL D
ISLAND
JING: KING OF BANDITS
JULINE
JUROR 13
KARE KANO
KILL ME, KISS ME
KINDAICHI CASE FILES, THE
KING OF HELL
KODOCHA: SANA'S STAGE
LAMENT OF THE LAMB
LES BIJOUX
LOVE HINA
LUPIN III
MAGIC KNIGHT RAYEARTH I
MAGIC KNIGHT RAYEARTH II
MAHOROMATIC: AUTOMATIC MAIDEN
MAN OF MANY FACES
MARMALADE BOY
MARS
MINK
MIRACLE GIRLS
MIYUKI-CHAN IN WONDERLAND
MODEL
ONE
PARADISE KISS
PARASYTE
PEACH GIRL
PEACH GIRL: CHANGE OF HEART
PET SHOP OF HORRORS
PITA-TEN
PLANET LADDER
PLANETES
PRIEST
PRINCESS AI
PSYCHIC ACADEMY
RAGNAROK
RAVE MASTER
REALITY CHECK
REBIRTH
REBOUND
REMOTE
RISING STARS OF MANGA
SABER MARIONETTE J
SAILOR MOON
SAINT TAIL

Les Bijoux

... A GOTHIC STORY OF ... TYRANNY vs FREEDOM

Available February 2004
At Your Favorite Book & Comic Stores.

OT OLDER TEEN AGE 16+

www.TOKYOPOP.com

Many would die for a glimpse at new worlds...
Miyuki would do anything to have them go away

TOKYOPOP

100% AUTHENTIC MANGA

MIYUKI-CHAN in
WONDERLAND
By CLAMP

Available Now At Your Favorite
Book And Comic Stores!

OT
OLDER TEEN
AGE 16+

www.TOKYOPOP.com

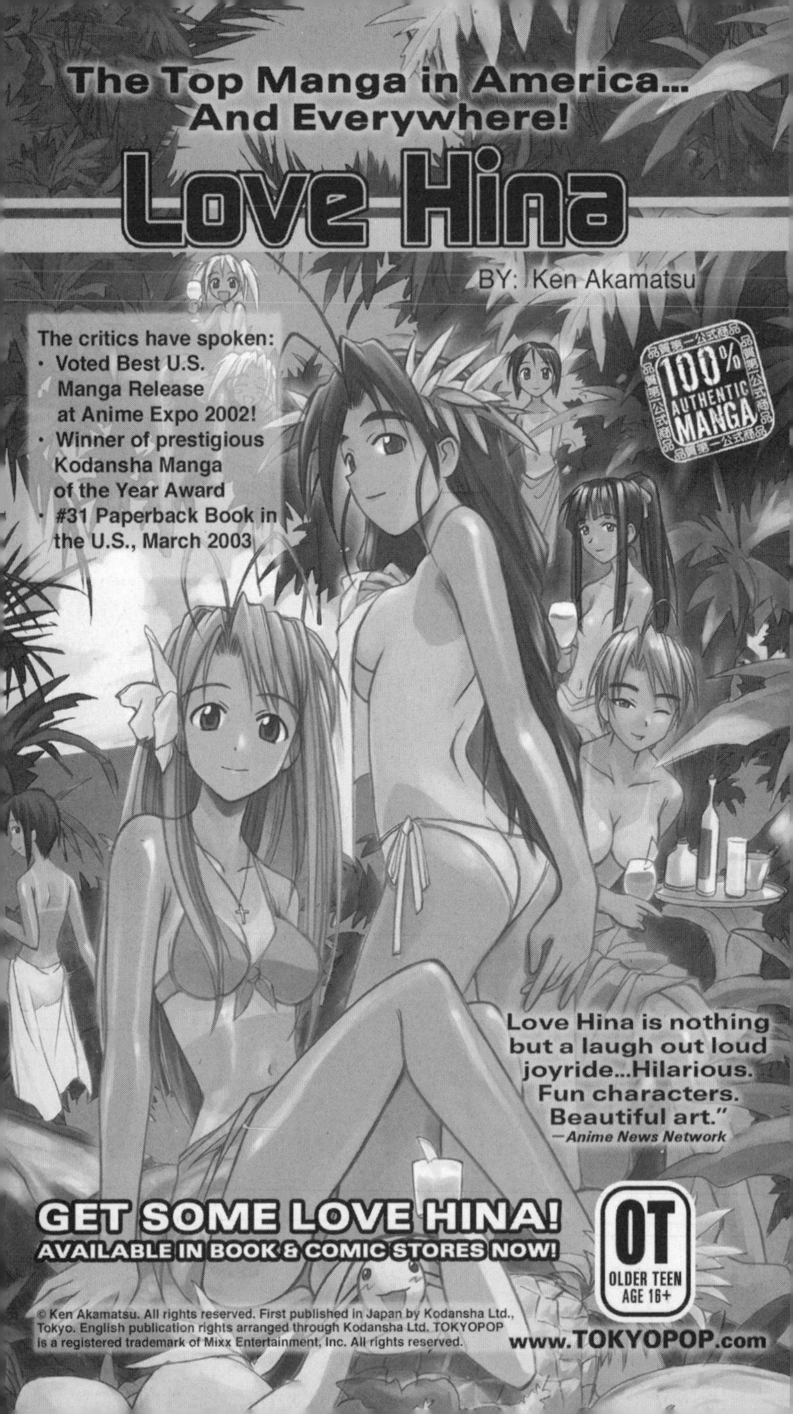
The Top Manga in America...
And Everywhere!
Love Hina
BY: Ken Akamatsu
The critics have spoken:
• Voted Best U.S. Manga Release at Anime Expo 2002!
• Winner of prestigious Kodansha Manga of the Year Award
• #31 Paperback Book in the U.S., March 2003
100% AUTHENTIC MANGA
Love Hina is nothing but a laugh out loud joyride...Hilarious. Fun characters. Beautiful art."
—Anime News Network
GET SOME LOVE HINA!
AVAILABLE IN BOOK & COMIC STORES NOW!
OT
OLDER TEEN
AGE 16+
© Ken Akamatsu. All rights reserved. First published in Japan by Kodansha Ltd., Tokyo. English publication rights arranged through Kodansha Ltd. TOKYOPOP is a registered trademark of Mixx Entertainment, Inc. All rights reserved.
www.TOKYOPOP.com